Tom Gale
311 W. 85th St.
New York, NY, 10024

Welfare Policy and Industrialization
in Europe, America, and Russia

Welfare Policy and Industrialization in Europe, America, and Russia

Gaston V. Rimlinger
Department of Economics
Rice University

John Wiley & Sons, Inc.,

New York · London · Sydney · Toronto

Library of Congress Catalog Card Number: 74-132856

ISBN 0-471-72220-0

Printed in the United States of America

10 9 8 7 6 5 4 3 2 1

Preface

This highly illuminating study by Professor Rimlinger demonstrates that the actual development of industrial societies lies somewhere between Tocqueville's diagnosis and Marx's prediction. Tocqueville had observed that the principle of equality has prodigious influence on the development of society. His stress on the tremendous advance in the equality of rights was based on the contrast between the modern era and the aristocratic nations of the past. To Marx, that equality appeared spurious, since it served to protect property and did nothing to alleviate poverty. Eventually, the mounting contrast between formal rights and real deprivations would lead to revolution and would usher in a period of true equality. In practice, welfare policies go beyond Tocqueville's diagnosis where the state provides benefits to all citizens as a matter of right. Moreover, they have helped to nullify Marx's prediction so that today workers are criticized for their acceptance of the "system."

The era of "equal rights" was initiated by the liberal repudiation of the poor man's traditional right to relief. Sooner or later this liberal position gave way, as Professor Rimlinger shows with a wealth of detail. After an interval of treating the problem of destitution from the standpoint of "our market mentality" (Polanyi), industrial societies have developed systems of social protection at a new level. As Rimlinger points out near the beginning of the book, society must find a structure that differentiates benefits in relation to what the beneficiary has paid for or how he has performed, but that also guarantees a certain minimal subsistence level below which nobody is allowed to fall. A basic minimum is the social right of all, but the protection of the level of living above that minimum is based on contractual obligations between the state and the beneficiary. To the extent that these goals are realized, modern society has gone beyond the movement from status to contract to which Sir Henry Maine referred. The welfare institutions of the nation-state combine rights to which the individual is entitled by virtue of his status as a citizen with rights to which he is entitled by virtue of contractual agreement.

In tracing this development on a comparative basis, Professor Rimlinger has made a major contribution to the several fields of poverty, the nature of political systems, the problems of manpower planning, and the social role of ideas in the changing class relations of industrial societies. He shows that the welfare system involves all citizens, not only the needy, but he also makes clear that the right of the needy to basic security depends on conformity with certain standards of behavior. By providing historical depth and a sensitive interpretation of ideologies, Professor Rimlinger has raised the discussion of these vital issues to a new level.

Reinhard Bendix

Author's Preface

This book was written because of a problem that I was confronted with a few years ago: I was to teach a course in economic and social security. It soon became obvious that although students are interested in the problem of insecurity in modern society, they have little appetite for the kind of technical detail that is unavoidable in a serious discussion of income security programs. One way to make the discussion more rewarding is to examine the programs in the relation to the interplay of the material and ideal interests that surrounded their development. This kind of approach is necessary to show the relevance of the controversies that have raged around the painful evolution of income security and health protection programs. Also this approach contributes to an understanding of the role of economic conditions and of political and social structures in the shaping of an important institution of industrial society.

My purpose here is to put the issues of economic insecurity and the means of dealing with it into a relevant context—the context of economic and social development. The result primarily is a comparative history of economic and social policy, supplemented with some theoretical considerations.

In dealing with a subject that has caused much controversy, I must acknowledge my own value judgments at the outset. I approve of the progress made during the last century in establishing income security and health protection as basic social rights of the citizen, and I accept the view that the state has a fundamental responsibility in securing these rights and in extending them as far as possible.

My approach to this subject is not accidental. It was motivated by my association during several years with Professor Reinhard Bendix, and my indebtedness to his ideas and insights is in evidence throughout the book. I owe him a special debt of gratitude for his encouragement, for his reading of the manuscript, and for his helpful suggestions on the structuring of the study. Also I am indebted to many other persons for assistance and encouragement. Professors Donald Winch, Jacques Melitz, Edgar O. Edwards, and Louis Galambos read parts of the manuscript. During a visit to Germany, Professors Elisabeth Liefman-Keil, Hans Achinger, and Wilfrid Schreiber gave their time most generously. Of the several summer research assistants, I thank especially Dr. Vincent Tarascio. For cheerful assistance in typing and retyping I thank Mrs. Vera Hite and Mrs. Florence Fulton. The most credit, for patient support, I owe to my wife, Lorraine. I alone am responsible for any shortcomings.

A major part of the study was carried out during a year's leave of absence, made possible by a Ford Foundation faculty fellowship in 1963 to 1964. A research trip to Germany was financed with a grant from the Social Science Research Council. For additional financial support I am indebted to the Center for Social Change and Economic Development of Rice University. In this field there is continuous change—especially with respect to legal provisions and operations data—but this does not create a serious problem. The basic arguments of the book have a long-run perspective.

Permission to reproduce parts of my earlier articles has been given by the *Quarterly Journal of Economics* and the *Industrial and Labor Relations Review.* Permission to quote from various publications has been granted by Praeger Publishing Company, Harvard University Press, John Wiley & Sons, Rice University, the University of Wisconsin Press, and Thames and Hudson. All translations from the French, German, or Russian are mine, except where otherwise acknowledged. The sources of material drawn from other writers are given in the footnotes. A work of this kind would be impossible without the previous research and publications of many other scholars.

Gaston V. Rimlinger

Lagos, Nigeria, 1970

Contents

PART III

Policy Objectives and Approaches

Welfare Policy and Industrialization
in Europe, America, and Russia

CHAPTER 1

Economic Development, Social Change, and Social Security

A PROBLEM OF PUBLIC POLICY

For the first time in the history of mankind, enough material goods have been produced to enable entire nations to live in comfort, even in affluence. Until recently, it was the fate of all but a small ruling minority to spend their lives in or near deprivation. This momentous change in human history is the result of the last two hundred years of economic development. It offers unprecedented opportunities for the obliteration of harsh economic and social inequalities and for the self-realization of the common man. It creates new potentialities for the rights of the individual and points to new dimensions of social justice. This situation entails a new reciprocity between members of a society, new relationships between individuals and the state, new forms of social and economic organization. The opportunities that are created by the shift from scarcity to abundance thus have their counterpart in problems of social adjustment to change. Social change destroys old and creates new vested interests in ideas, power, and material things.

The dawn of abundance has not come suddenly, nor has it as yet reached all parts of the earth, but there is, at least, the hope that some day the life of affluence will be universal. Similarly, the opportunities and the problems of the new age have evolved over a considerable period of time and will continue into the future. This book is concerned with a major aspect of this continuing interaction between economic development and social change—the development of the individual's freedom from want. More specifically, it is concerned with the evolution of social measures designed to secure this novel right for the individual. It analyzes the roads toward

1

economic security chosen by a number of countries and the implications of alternative roads for equality and freedom.

Since the end of the Middle Ages, the developing nation-states of Western Europe have been confronted with the problem of poverty. Previously, this had been a matter of only local concern. With the emergence of national states and national economies, the problem of what to do with the poor necessarily became a matter of national significance. The national governments enacted laws and issued ordinances on how those who had become dependent on society should be treated. As a rule, the execution of the laws on poor relief, vagrancy, and begging were left to the local authorities. Characteristically, the laws were much more specific on punishments to be inflicted than on relief to be granted. But, basically, they did define certain reciprocal social responsibilities, such as the individual's duty to work and the local community's duty to provide work for the able and relief for the disabled.

This manner of disposing of the problem of the poor was eventually overcome by two major sets of forces put into motion during the second half of the eighteenth century. One of these sets was the Industrial Revolution, along with the economic and social changes it engendered. The other set of forces revolved around the radical new conception of the rights of the individual that was thrust on the world by the American and French Revolutions. Approximately one hundred years after these events, the modern form of social protection from want—social insurance—was introduced in Imperial Germany. From an eighteenth century perspective, Germany was an unlikely candidate for this social innovation. Other countries followed with poor law reforms and with social insurance programs of their own. The old repressive poor laws gave way to more humane public assistance and social service programs. Today these programs have become all but universal.

A recent worldwide survey by the United States Social Security Administration shows that 120 countries have one or more social security schemes in operation.[1] The most extensive programs are in the more industrialized countries, but developing countries are eager to follow the same pattern. In many countries, social security rights have been incorporated into their constitutions.

A brief discussion of what is meant by "social security" is appropriate at this point. The term came into usage in the United States in the 1930s and has gained very wide acceptance in other countries in literal translation (*Soziale Sicherheit, Sécurité Sociale, Seguridad Social*).[2] Almost inevitably, its

---

[1] United States Department of Health, Education, and Welfare, Social Security Administration, *Social Security Programs Throughout the World 1967* (Washington, D.C.: Government Printing Office, 1967), p. vii.

[2] The Russian equivalent, *sotsial'noe obespechenie,* was officially used in 1918.

meaning varies somewhat from one national context to the other. Its common components have been summarized by the Social Security Administration:

> The term "social security program" is usually reserved, in the first place, for programs established by public law, although administration of such programs may or may not be wholly in public hands. In the second place, it is usually considered to include programs that provide some form of cash payments to individuals to make up a loss of or a deficiency in earnings occasioned by such "long-term" risks as old-age retirement, permanent disablement (or invalidity) of nonoccupational or occupational origin, and death of the family bread-winner; and by such short-term risks as temporary incapacity of non-occupational or occupational origin, maternity, and unemployment. It is also regarded as including programs that provide regular cash payments to families with children. Finally, public programs providing curative medical services to individuals (other than ordinary public health services), or that are concerned with the financing of such services, are also usually regarded as a type of social security program in countries where they exist.[3]

Social security thus includes what we usually call social insurance (compulsory programs that are usually job related and financed, at least, partly from contributions), public assistance, family allowances, and state health insurance. It does not include those aspects of modern social rights that are primarily concerned with education, training, housing, children's services, and social case-work.

The development of social security involves a number of important policy issues which each country seeks to resolve in its own fashion. Perhaps the first question is whether or not a country should adopt modern programs of social protection. In the historical context this meant whether a country should shift from a deterrent system that furnished relief based on need to a system that furnished benefits as a matter of right. The old relief system, the poor laws, applied mainly to those at the bottom of the socioeconomic ladder. It was never just relief; it started from the assumption that people were in need because of some character deficiency; relief, therefore, was provided under conditions that were intended partly as retribution for past failings and partly as a check against future failures. Social security implies an entirely different conception of social protection. Social insurance, in particular, is designed primarily for wage and salary earners, who represent a cross section of society rather than its lower layers. Its benefits are normally unrelated to the needs of the recipient; he receives them whether he needs them or not, he has no choice in the matter as participation in the

---

[3] United States Department of Health, Education, and Welfare, Social Security Administration, *Social Security Programs Throughout the World 1961* (Washington, D.C.: Government Printing Office, 1961), pp. vii–viii.

programs is almost always compulsory. This inevitably involves interference by the state with the individual's freedom to allocate his income as he sees fit. Generally, social security programs tend to redistribute income among individuals, which involves issues of equity and social justice. These matters are obviously controversial.

The adoption of a new policy of protection somehow has to be justified. The exercise of the state's power on behalf of some individuals, often at the expense of others, must have a basis of legitimacy. The question, therefore, must be answered as to what legitimizes social protection. To what extent is it the individual's responsibility to look after himself and his family, and to what extent is this a social responsibility? Clearly, the more emphasis a society puts on individual responsibility, the less room there would seem to be for social action. This, however, implies that only the interests of the individual are involved. In reality, social protection, whether it is poor laws or social security, is concerned with the interests of society as a whole as well as the ones of the individual. Even a highly individualistic society, one that stresses individual responsibility, may legitimize social protection for the common interest in social and political stability or in economic productivity.

If society recognizes the individual's right to protection, especially non-deterrent protection, this right also must be legitimized. There are two different tendencies in this legitimation. One looks on the right to benefits as something that the beneficiary has personally earned, either through payment of contributions or through performance of work. This is the contractual orientation of the right to benefits. The second kind of justification emphasizes status rather than contract. Some writers argue that the right to social security in modern society is inherent in the status of the wage or salary earner. It derives from the right to subsistence, and those who depend on their labor for subsistence have a social right to income if their working capacity fails or if no jobs are available.[4] Others consider the right to income as a perquisite of citizenship. In this case all citizens are entitled to protection regardless of how they earn their living.[5]

The manner in which social security rights are legitimized has important implications for social security policy. There are a number of crucial decisions that have to be made. The first is the decision as to who should be protected, which is another way of saying: Who has the right to protection, or who needs to be protected in the interest of the community? The protected group may be open or closed. An open program, such as the poor laws or public assistance, does not have a designated group of beneficiaries. It usually applies to all resident citizens. Social insurance programs, on the

[4]See Carlos Marti-Bufill, *Tratado Comparado de Seguridad Social* (Madrid, 1951), p. 106.
[5]*Ibid.*, pp. 142–148. See also Sir William Beveridge, *Social Insurance and Allied Services* (American edition, New York: MacMillan, 1942).

other hand, apply to closed groups. The question then is how broad the covered group should be. Should it include only wage workers in certain industries, or wage and salary earners in all industries, or should it be extended to all citizens who work, including the self-employed, regardless of their level of earnings? The question must also take into account the extent to which the dependents of beneficiaries are to be entitled to support. Obviously, the broader the conception of the right to protection, the more universal should be the coverage. Even under those circumstances, however, economic and administrative considerations may force a more narrow coverage than the country may wish to adopt.

After the decision is made about who should be protected, consideration must be given to the questions of how and against what risks. The historical trend has been to make protection more universal insofar as the coverage of persons is concerned, as well as more comprehensive with respect to the inclusion of protected risks. Different risks imply different degrees of involvement of the state in the affairs of the individual. Usually, it is easier to introduce compensation for industrial injuries. Programs that are relatively easy to administer and require only cash payments, such as old-age pensions, also can be readily accommodated. Unemployment and health insurance present more administrative difficulties and are more likely to offend strong vested interests. Wherever the medical profession is privately organized, it tends to resist the introduction of state health insurance schemes. Family allowances also involve issues on which there is division of opinion in most countries.

The question of how protection should be provided covers the whole range of issues regarding conditions of benefit payment, the level and structure of benefits, and their financing. All of these issues have implications that affect material and ideological interests. No society can afford simply to give away cash benefits or to render unlimited services. Some system of control must be established. One form of control is to pay benefits only in case of need and in an amount sufficient to meet minimum requirements. There are several types of problems associated with this procedure. One relates to the manner in which an individual's need is established; does it require a humiliating investigation of his personal and family situation, or is his need assumed from the size of his family, his age, or his income level without further investigation? The level of benefit that may be considered a necessary minimum is always open to debate. Should it prevent only physical hardship, or should it prevent "relative deprivation"? The latter takes into account what society can afford and what the poor may expect.[6] Another form of control is to pay benefits on the basis of a specified length

[6] For a very enlightening discussion of this concept, see W. G. Runciman, *Relative Deprivation and Social Justice* (London: Routledge and Kegan Paul, 1966), Chapters II to V.

of previous work or contribution. In this case it is the individual's previous record that establishes eligibility. The procedure may be liberal or restrictive, depending on prevailing attitudes toward social rights and the evaluation of economic and social or political consequences.

Whatever manner of controlling eligibility is adopted, the benefits structure may be egalitarian or differentiated. A system that pays the same benefit to all, according to an established national minimum, has great appeal to those who favor social and economic equality. A flat benefit is most consistent with the view that benefits are a social right to which all have the same claim. But if benefits are a flat amount, the level is almost necessarily low. To prevent abuse, it tends to be somewhat below what ordinarily can be earned through regular work. A low benefit level requires low taxes or contributions and, thus has the advantage of limiting the state's interference with the income allocation process. For this reason it may appeal to those who are concerned with the individual's freedom to allocate his earnings as he sees fit. Those who hold this ideological position, however, are normally also concerned with limiting income redistribution; they, therefore, tend to favor differentiated benefits, which may conflict with the desire to keep state interference with income allocation at a minimum. If the lower range of the benefit scale is to be adequate, benefits in the upper range are necessarily higher than what minimal state interference would demand. Differentiated benefits tend to require a deeper intervention in personal income allocation, but it may be a more market-consistent form of intervention insofar as it involves less interpersonal income redistribution. If benefits are related to previous earnings or contributions, they have more of a contractual than a social rights character. Although the contractual character may be found to be more suitable to a given country, its chief shortcoming tends to be social inadequacy at the lower income levels. There is always the danger that those who need protection most are able to earn it least. Society has to find the benefit structure that optimizes welfare by combining the incentive effects of differentiation with the adequacy guarantees of a stated minimum.

The question of who should pay for the benefits involves many of the same considerations as the benefit structure. The practical problem is how much of the burden should be borne by the beneficiaries themselves, their employers, or the state. The contractual approach emphasizes payments by employees and employers; in either case, the contributions may be looked on as being earned by the employees. The higher the contributions, the higher the benefits will tend to be, although in social insurance (unlike in private insurance) the relationship is hardly ever proportional. The emphasis on social rights tends to favor financing from general state revenue, which is presumably raised according to prevailing standards of distributional equity. Since social insurance programs almost always redistribute income (not merely reallocate it through time), exclusive financing via pay-roll taxes tends to put an undue burden on the low income earners.[7] The contractual ideology, by favoring commercial equity, thus exacts a price in terms of social equity. Opponents of contributions from the public treasury, however, stress the need to keep social insurance free from the dangers of government paternalism and of the politics of budget allocations.

A final problem area, which should be mentioned, is administration. The administrative issues which have relevance for this study are mainly the ones that relate to the use of social security institutions in the pursuit of ancillary social and economic goals. Since social security decisions affect the welfare of large numbers of people, the day-to-day administration of the programs may give opportunities to influence economic or political behavior. A country may choose a judicial type of bureaucratic admini-stration; or it may democratically involve the insured beneficiaries in the decision-making process; or it may exploit the system in an authoritarian fashion for the benefit of those in power.

A COMPARATIVE PERSPECTIVE

The preceding listing of problem areas is not intended to be a comprehen-sive enumeration of public policy issues.[8] Its purpose is merely to indicate broadly the kind of social and economic questions that are involved in the development of social income protection. The following chapters analyze the nature of these problems and how they were resolved over time in different countries. The analysis has a historical context—the history of industrializ-ation—since modern social security is a by-product of the shift from agrarian to industrial society. It has also a comparative context. The prob-lems of economic insecurity are similar in all industrializing countries, but the response to them differs widely. The main objective of this study is to explain the forces that have shaped modern social security systems; it is a comparative historical analysis of the responses to the challenge of insecurity in different environments. The countries compared are selected to reflect different economic, social, and political tendencies. They represent the traditions of liberalism and patriarchalism in the West and the tradition of Marxist socialism in the East. The time path of the study ranges from the preindustrial era to that of modern industrialism.

[7] For a discussion of this and related issues, see Richard A. Musgrave, "The Role of Social Insurance in an Overall Program for Social Welfare," in William G. Bowen et al. (eds.), The American System of Social Insurance (New York: McGraw-Hill, 1968), Chapter II.
[8] The best analytical treatment of public policy issues in social security is Eveline M. Burns, Social Security and Public Policy (New York: McGraw-Hill, 1956).

An outline of the main themes that underlie this study is in order. One is the changing nature of the problem of want as we move from a preindustrial society to mature industrialism. Widespread poverty is the rule in the traditional, preindustrial society. This is not looked on as a problem in itself; in fact, it may be looked on as a positive good. This was the view of the mercantilists. They spoke of the usefulness of poverty as a means of keeping the masses industrious. Poverty as such was a problem for them only to the extent that it endangered public peace. Poverty was something to be relieved but by no means to be abolished. During industrialization the problem of want changed—it had new causes and new victims. The traditional sources of hardship seemed to be God-given and immutable; people had always been poor; wars, pestilence, and bad harvests only made matters periodically worse. The industrializing society held out the promise of improved well-being but the fruits seemed unequally divided. Some quickly became rich but many more had to discover new sources of want. They had become dependent on the wage of the family breadwinner; any interruption of the ability to work or of the availability of a job spelled dire want. Having left the land, the family was no longer a production unit. The aged and the children became a greater burden. These hardships were no longer God-given: they all seemed to be man-made; they were social. The victims were no longer the traditional poor. They were now the industrial proletariat. As industrialism has matured, many of the basic hardships have been alleviated, but the tremendous wealth has created new conceptions of social rights and of freedom from want. The poor in a rich country like America suffer from "relative deprivation" because they can compare what they have with what is common in their society.

Another theme of this study is an emphasis on class relations as a determinant factor in the development of social protection. In the preindustrial Western European society the lower classes were held in what John Stuart Mill described as a position of dependence and protection. The practical meaning of this varied widely, but the sentiment that those in power should reason and decide for the common folk was rather general. Those below owed obedience and deferrence, while those above owed protection and guidance. With the rise of liberalism, this conception of social inequality came under attack. Liberty and equality demanded that all legal privileges be abolished. All citizens were to be treated equally, which meant that none had any special claim to protection on account of his (low) economic and social status. Full citizenship implied the ability to look after oneself; dependence on others was not consistent with freedom and equality. Where this liberal concept of society triumphed (in England, France, and America), social protection was slow to develop. In Germany, where liberalism and individualism struck only shallow roots, the chances for social protection were that much better. Indeed, the traditions of the Prussian patriarchal state and the paternalistic environment of the semifeudal pattern of German industrialization facilitated the pioneering efforts of Imperial Germany in social insurance. In the twentieth century, social income protection has lost much of its class attributes. The concepts of freedom and equality have changed from ideological barriers to justifications.

Closely related to class relations, as a determinant of social protection, is the nature of the political system. In the countries studied, the more democratic governments were slower to introduce social protection than the authoritarian and totalitarian governments. In democratic countries, public action depends on how various interest groups are represented and how well they are organized. There is a tendency for each group to seek legislation in its favor. Employer interest groups generally oppose the introduction of social security but labor groups favor it. This generalization, however, is a crude oversimplification. Certain labor groups, such as the American trade unions, the British friendly societies, and the German Social Democrats, were originally opponents of social insurance. German and Russian big business before World War I were generally in favor of it. The American Association of Manufacturers was an early supporter of workmen's compensation. In authoritarian and totalitarian countries the interests of the state, as seen by those in power, tend to take precedence over particular group interest. Bismarck was strongly motivated by the need to secure the loyalty of the industrial worker to the monarchy in his establishment of social insurance. Although he was acting in response to pressure from below, the system he created was guided by the interests of the existing political order. In the Soviet Union the interests of the ruling party have always been a dominant factor in the shaping of the country's social security programs, although the Bolsheviks were strongly committed to comprehensive social security even before the 1917 Revolution.

This study stresses also the role of economic factors in the development of social security. Aside from being a means to enhance welfare, social security programs also are measures that affect the quantity and quality of a country's manpower resources. The poor laws constituted a manpower policy that was fairly well suited for a time when labor was abundant and mostly unskilled. The main requirement then was the maintenance of work habits among the marginal elements of the work force. The administration of the poor laws was an attempt (not always successful) to instill discipline and industriousness. As industrialization progressed, labor became not only more scarce relative to capital, but it achieved a much higher level of skill; its spontaneous cooperation within large-scale organizations became very important. At this stage it became profitable, from the point of view of productivity, to develop and to maintain the capacity and the willingness to work. The workers' physical strength and good will had become important assets. Social insurance became one of the means of investing in human capital.[9] In the Soviet economy, social insurance has been an important means for the maintenance of industrial discipline. In market economies its explicit work-incentive role is less important, but its role as an automatic stabilizer is much more significant. This study is particularly interested in how various countries have adapted social insurance programs to their economic systems and to their national objectives.

Throughout this book, special attention is paid to the role of ideas. The changing views regarding the reciprocal rights and duties of the individual and the state are clearly important. Of particular significance are the ideas concerning the consequences of social protection. It is in this regard that prevailing economic and social theories must be taken into account. The mercantilists typically assumed that the poor had a backward sloping supply curve of labor, which meant that an increase in income entailed less labor offered. Another mercantilist idea was that wages must be kept low for a favorable balance of trade. Both of these views militated against raising the level of welfare of the common man. At a later time, the Malthusian theory of population and Social Darwinism were important intellectual weapons against poor relief. The concept of investment in human capital and the theories of aggregate demand, on the other hand, were ideas favorable to social security. Another way in which ideas were important was through studies of the extent and causes of poverty. Especially in England, at the turn of the century, surveys of poverty helped to stir the social conscience of the middle and upper classes.

The book is organized into three parts. In Part I, Chapters 2 and 3 analyse the role of the liberal tradition in England, France, and the United States from the preindustrial period to industrialization. In Part II, Chapters 4 to 7 analyze alternative paths to social security in Germany, the United States, and the Soviet Union in the context of industrialization and in that of the mature industrial society. The first two parts of the book are historical. The last, Part III, is theoretical and is a discussion of social security from the point of view of economic and social policy objectives. The concluding chapter examines the implications of the past in order to study the possible future evolution of social security.

[9] For discussions along these lines, see Gaston V. Rimlinger, "Welfare Policy and Economic Development: A Comparative Historical Perspective," *Journal of Economic History*, Vol. XXVI, No. 4 (December 1966), pp. 556–571; and Walter Galenson, "Social Security and Economic Development: A Quantitative Approach," *Industrial and Labor Relations Review*, Vol. XXI, No. 4 (July 1968), pp. 559–569.

Part I

THE LIBERAL TRADITION

F rom the closing decades of the eighteenth to the end of the nineteenth century the ideals of liberalism dominated social policy in the West. At the core of these ideals were the individualistic principles of freedom, equality, and self-help. These principles, which pervaded economic, social, and political thought, incorporated the antithesis of the concept of dependence and protection represented by the preindustrial society. A conflict between the old protectionism and the forces of liberalism was thus inevitable. But while new needs for social protection were arising, the young industrial states were busy denouncing the old protectionist system and were confidently denying that protection was either wholesome for the individual or advantageous for the nation. With advancing industrialism and the democratization of political power, the liberal principles became eroded. By the end of the nineteenth century, the setting was prepared for the modern concepts of social protection. The liberal tradition had to make room for new interpretations of the social rights of the citizen.

The task of the chapters in this section is threefold: it is (1) a discussion of the old system of social protection, (2) an analysis of the liberal break with traditional protection and (3) an analysis of the conflict between the liberal heritage and social security. Chapter 2 examines the old system as a reflection of the prevailing economic and social conditions. Poverty and inequality were not only dominant characteristics of the old society but they were considered to be unchangeable determinants of the lot of the masses. The discussion emphasizes the ideas people had about the rights of the poorer classes in such a society. We are interested in the influence of these ideas on the development of social protection.

The liberal break with traditional ideals of protection, discussed in Chapter

3, was an outright denial of the traditionalist claim that the lower classes were entitled to protection from above. Even though this shift was more dramatic in terms of ideas than in practice, it still called for elaborate ideological justifications. They were discovered in timely interpretations of the course of economic and social change, which involved new ways of looking at the rights of the poor. The break with traditionalism, of course, was strongest where liberalism was most successful—in England, France, and the United States. Each of these countries had its own variant of the progress of liberal ideals with regard to social protection and, as we shall learn, each had its own peculiar problems in overcoming these ideals. We shall examine how the persistence of liberal ideals, and of institutions based on them, became a hindrance to the development of social security. Each country had to find its own way of resolving the conflict between the liberal heritage and social security.

CHAPTER 2

Social Protection under the Old Regime

The liberal strictures against the social protection of the individual were in the main a reaction against certain ideas and policies that had evolved since the sixteenth century. The poor man, under the Old Regime, was both oppressed and pitied; he was disdained, since he had neither grace nor virtue; yet he was considered useful, even indispensable, since his labor represented the wealth of the nation. The fact that he needed protection was recognized, but mostly protection from his own vices and weaknesses. He had to be protected not so much for his own sake as for the sake of society. It was a society in which poverty was the lot of the ordinary man, a society where inequality was harsh and authority unchallenged. How were the rights and duties of the poor perceived in such a setting, and what shaped the sense of duty of those who enjoyed wealth and power? We shall try to answer these questions in an examination of mercantilistic ideas about labor and in a survey of poor law policies. Our attention will be focused on England and France, although the ideas and policies that prevailed in these two countries were widely shared in Europe.

In medieval times the care of the poor was left to private charity. The organization of relief was in the hands of the clergy, who provided assistance through the parishes and the monasteries. By the sixteenth century, which saw an alarming increase in the number of beggars and vagrants in England as well as on the Continent, the exclusive reliance on local decisions was becoming inadequate. Increasingly, the emerging national governments had to be concerned with the problems posed by the presence of large numbers of destitute individuals. Poverty, in effect, became a matter of national concern almost from the beginning of the modern nation-state. Not surprisingly, the question of how to treat the laboring poor occupied an important place in the minds of those who concerned themselves with national economic policy.

13

MERCANTILISM AND THE LABORER

There are well-known difficulties in generalizing about mercantilist policies, since they were not based on any consistent set of principles. Spengler saw in them "the centuries-old contempt of the members of the ruling and upper classes for the common man . . . transmuted into the doctrine that the common man lives only to work and breed for the state."[1] Schumpeter, on the other hand, observed that the welfare of his people "was an end in itself for many a great monarch or administrator . . . but it had to fit in with the given political pattern and with the given social system."[2] The evidence, at least for England and France, is more consistent with Spengler's emphasis. The stress of mercantilism was on nationalism, which made it the task of the laboring masses to serve the nationalistic interests of the state. In general, the mercantilists looked on labor as the source of wealth or even as wealth itself. They were thus inclined to favor populationist policies, which might benefit the welfare of the laborer. Against this, however, was the strong mercantilist belief that wages must be kept low—partly to give the country a competitive advantage in international trade, but mostly to keep the poor industrious.[3] It was taken for granted that the poor were naturally inclined to idleness, and that it was the duty of those in power to combat this evil.

What made a nation wealthy and powerful was a large number of industrious and disciplined poor who were kept fully employed. "It is manifest," wrote Mandeville, "that in a free Nation where Slaves are now allow'd of, the surest Wealth consists in a Multitude of laborious poor."[4] The poverty of the masses was by no means considered a social evil, nor were paupers a cause of concern so long as they worked and behaved themselves. On the contrary, there was a widespread belief that such poverty was not only useful but essential to the welfare of the state. The national interest demanded that "the bulk of the population be kept in a condition of poverty." This "doctrine of the utility of poverty," as Furniss has called it,[5] presents a sharp contrast to modern welfare state ideas. It had far-reaching implications for the extent to which the state should provide relief for the poor, as indicated by Mandeville's rhetorical question: "Would not a wise legislature cultivate the Breed of them with all imaginable Care, and

[1] Joseph J. Spengler, *French Predecessors of Malthus* (Durham: Duke University Press, 1942), p. 20.
[2] Joseph A. Schumpeter, *History of Economic Analysis* (New York: Oxford University Press, 1954), p. 147.
[3] For an extensive discussion of this view, see E. S. Furniss, *The Position of the Laborer in a System of Nationalism* (Boston: Houghton Mifflin, 1920), *passim.*
[4] Bernard Mandeville, "An Essay on Charity and Charity-Schools," in *The Fable of the Bees* (F. B. Kaye, ed., Oxford: Clarendon Press, 1924), Vol. I, p. 287.
[5] E. S. Furniss, *op. cit.,* Chapter VI.

provide against their Scarcity as he would prevent the Scarcity of Provision itself?"[6]

The desire for a larger population was "almost fanatical"[7] and was promoted by governments "by all means at their comand."[8] There was no lack of suggestions for various kinds of marriage incentive schemes. Reflecting the characteristic mercantilist faith in the power of legislation to solve economic and social problems, the English clergyman, Josiah Tucker (1713–1799), proposed to make marriage more "the style" through a series of measures that included restriction of posts and titles of honor or emolument to unmarried persons, freeing married persons from the Elizabethan apprenticeship requirements and allowing them to work as journeymen in any trade without payment of fees and to reside in any parish regardless of settlement.[9] The settlement requirements and other aspects of the English poor laws were repeatedly criticized for their negative effects on family life. However, the most extreme populationist measures were the ones put into effect in France by Colbert. Not only did he entice foreign workers and prohibit nationals from settling abroad, which was common mercantilist practice, but in 1666 he issued an edict aimed directly at increasing the number and the size of large families.[10] It provided exemption from payment of the *taille*[11] until age twenty-five for persons who married before age twenty and until age twenty-four for those who married in their twenty-first year. Tax exemptions were granted also to fathers with ten living children and to those with twelve children living or dead. Noblemen, who were exempt from payment of the *taille,* were granted annual pensions of one-thousand livres if they had ten living children, and two-thousand livres, if they had twelve children living or dead.

Colbert's tax exemption and pension program led to many abuses and was never successful in practice, but it presents an interesting case of an early system of "family allowances." In accordance with mercantilist objectives, it was a system designed for the benefit of the state instead of for the relief of families with especially heavy burdens. The pensions favored the rich instead of the poor. A further indication that the interest of the state

[6] Mandeville. *loc. cit.*, p. 287.

[7] E. F. Heckscher, *Mercantilism*, (trans. by M. Schapiro, London: Allen and Unwin, 1934), Vol. II, p. 158.

[8] Schumpeter, *op. cit.*, p. 251.

[9] J. Tucker, "The Elements of Commerce, and the Theory of Taxes," reprinted in R. L. Schuyler, *Josiah Tucker, A Selection from His Economic and Political Writings* (New York: Columbia University Press, 1931), pp. 68 ff. It can be observed that Tucker's views reflect also the eighteenth century swing toward freer economic activity.

[10] C. W. Cole, *Colbert and a Century of French Mercantilism* (New York: Columbia University Press, 1939), Vol. II, pp. 464 ff.

[11] A tax paid by nonprivileged classes.

was paramount was a provision that sons who had died as soldiers were to be counted as living children in order to qualify for benefits.

The doctrine that low wages were necessary to keep the poor industrious was one of the many theoretical justifications advanced throughout history to limit the comforts of the poor and the responsibilities of the rich. Stated in modern language, the workers were thought to have a backward sloping individual supply curve of labor, which meant that increases in remuneration would result in decreases of the willingness to work. It was a doctrine that made improvement of the workers' lot self-defeating and that justified harsh measures against the poor. To what extent the doctrine was based on fact or simply reflected a bias in the attitude of the upper classes toward the common man remains unknown, but the doctrine itself had many adherents both in England and in France. Cardinal de Richelieu observed disdainfully in his *Testament politique* that "all political opinions are in agreement that if the people were to live too much in ease it would be impossible to keep them within the rules of their duty."[12] Mayet, a close observer of the Lyon silk industry, wrote in his *Mémoire sur les manufactures de Lyon* that ". . . it is necessary that the worker must never enrich himself, that he has only precisely what he needs to feed and clothe himself decently. In a certain class of the people circumstances that are too easy weaken the industriousness and entail idleness and all its related vices."[13] In England this view of the worker was, if anything, even more common than in France. Although it began to lose out to the opposite view in the second half of the eighteenth century, many of the most notable pre-Smithian economic writers supported it. "Houghton, Petty, Temple, Child, and, in their earlier writings, Josiah Tucker and Arthur Young, emphatically uphold the view that high wages are equivalent to low Production."[14] In the early part of the eighteenth century, Mandeville claimed that "Every Body knows that there is a vast number of Journey-men Weavers, Tailors, Clothworkers, and twenty other handicrafts; who, if by four Days Labour in a Week they can maintain themselves, will hardly be persuaded to work the fifth."[15] With even more boldness, Arthur Young declared as late as 1771 that "Every one but an idiot knows that the lower classes must be kept poor or they will never be industrious."[16]

Underlying this interpretation of human behaviour was an estimation of

[12] Cited in H. Hauser, *La Pensée et l'action économique du cardinal de Richelieu* (Paris: Presses Universitaires, 1944), p. 145.

[13] Cited in E. Levasseur, *Histoire des classes ouvrières avant 1789* (Paris: Rousseau, 1901), Vol. II, p. 835.

[14] L. Brentano, *Hours and Wages in Relation to Production* (trans. by Arnold, London: Swan Sonnenschein Co., 1894), pp. 2–3.

[15] Mandeville, *op. cit.,* Vol. I, p. 192.

[16] Cited in Furniss, *op. cit.,* p. 118.

the personal character of the lower classes that played an important part in the treatment of poverty. Not only were the lower classes thought to be crude, ignorant, and inclined to vice and riotous behavior, they were, above all, guilty of the inclination to idleness, the mother of all vices. Although this estimation of personal character is reminiscent of the Puritan pre-occupation with the ideal of labor, the mercantilist aversion to idleness had deeper roots and was more general. As Heckscher has shown, it was as common in France as in England.[17] The fear that idleness destroys work habits and skills was voiced on both sides of the Channel. Richelieu com-pared people to mules, who are in the habit of carrying a heavy load and who consequently, are, more likely to be spoiled by a long rest than by too much work.[18] Petty went so far as to suggest that it would be "better to burn a thousand men's labours for a time, than let those thousand men by non-employment lose their faculty of labouring." [19]

Idleness had to be combated with all available means, since it was ob-served to harm both the worker and the nation. Some writers pointed out the double injury caused by idleness; it not only prevented production from taking place in the direct sense, but harmed it indirectly through the in-creased burden and demoralizing effects of begging.[20] Although the mercantilists favored punitive measures against beggars, they realized that not all unemployment could be attributed to laziness. But whether the cause of unemployment was individual or social, it was the duty of the state to intervene. "If working people are idle said Postlethwait, 'that is for want of being rightly governed.' In his opinion no blame should be laid on the idle: 'there is nothing criminal on their part'; they would work if 'sufficiently encouraged.' Other writers agreed that the persistence of idleness was proof that the state had been remiss in its duty to its subjects." [21] The economic literature of the seventeenth and eighteenth centuries is filled with schemes of how to provide employment for the poor. The applications for royal support in the development of new manufactures usually stressed the value of the undertaking with respect to providing employment, banishing idleness, and making the poor industrious. The promotion of manufactures was the mercantilists' chief social welfare measure; it was their basic remedy for dealing with the problem of unemployment and poverty. Laffemas pushed the state into the development of silk culture and manufacture in France

---

[17] Heckscher, *op. cit.*, Vol. II, p. 155.

[18] Hauser, *op. cit.*, p. 145.

[19] W. Petty, *A Treatise of Taxes and Contributions* (London, 1662), p. 60; reprinted in C. H. Hull, *The Economic Writings of Sir William Petty* (Cambridge: University Press, 1899), Vol. I.

[20] See Furniss, *op. cit.*, p. 67; E. A. J. Johnson, *Predecessors of Adam Smith* (New York: Prentice-Hall, 1937), p. 285.

[21] Johnson, *op. cit.*, p. 287.

with the argument that these were "certain remedies for the evils of idleness and poverty."[22]

In the context of nascent nationalism and the economic power struggle of the seventeenth and eighteenth centuries, the need to repress idleness and inculcate industriousness was felt very strongly. Although the methods suggested were different from the ones employed today in countries where the economic power of the state is paramount, some of the sentiments that inspired them bear a remarkable similarity. John Bellars, an enthusiastic advocate of schemes to employ the poor, prefaced one of his writings with the tag: "The Sluggard shall be cloathed in Raggs, He that will not work shall not eat."[23] It is interesting that the identical phrase "He who does not work, neither shall he eat" is also in Article 12 of the 1936 Constitution of the Soviet Union. What had been to Saint Paul mainly an exhortation against idleness, "if anyone will not work, neither let him eat,"[24] became an ominous warning in the modern state.

ENGLISH POOR RELIEF POLICY

The treatment of the unemployed able-bodied poor was always a crucial issue in relief policy. It is mostly with them that we are concerned. If they were unemployed because of unwillingness to work, two complementary approaches were open: one was to encourage work through punishment, and the other was to encourage work through character reform. To discipline and to reform the poor were natural traits of ruling class paternalism; they were part of the duty of those who ruled. Unfortunately, it was always easier to dispense punishment than to reform characters. Those who were concerned with poor relief realized, of course, that the poor were often involuntarily unemployed. Provision of work was thus an indispensable adjunct to outright relief. Work was not only desirable in the national interest, but it was viewed as a great character builder. The general insistence on work as a condition of relief, however, had one further important implication. It implied the recognition of a basic right of the poor to the means of making a living.

Sidney and Beatrice Webb characterized the relief system in existence in England from the sixteenth to the early nineteenth century as "Relief of the Poor within a Framework of Repression."[25] Much the same characterization

[22] Cole, op. cit., Vol. I, p. 35.

[23] Cited in Dorothy Marshall, The English Poor in the Eighteenth Century (London: George Routledge, 1926), p. 44.

[24] Thessalonians II, 3:10.

[25] S. and B. Webb, English Poor Law History (London: Longmans, Green, and Co., 1927), Vol. I, p. 396.

is valid for the French experience, even though in both countries there also were religiously inspired charity movements. The public authorities, with whose activities we are concerned, never had charity as a major practical objective, in spite of the assumption that rulers had a paternal concern for the welfare of their subjects. In England, France, and other European countries, governments became initially concerned with the lot of the poor not for purposes of relieving suffering, but for the maintenance of law and order. The legislation relating to the poor began with measures to punish beggars and kept its repressive character until recent times.[26]

By the sixteenth century, imprisonment, flogging, and other violent forms for the repression of begging and vagrancy were no longer regarded as adequate measures by themselves for dealing with the growing number of indigents. Not a few of them were victims of economic change. Some provision had to be made for public relief, also, maintaining a "salutary terror" against beggars. Private charity was inadequate to cope with the size of the problem. Moreover, it was recognized that indiscriminate charity often contributed to the problem of pauperism. Medieval charity had a tendency toward being indiscriminate, since its major motivation was the salvation of the giver rather than the behavior of the recipient.

National legislation always stressed the work aspects of relief. The 1601 Act for the Relief of the Poor (43 Elizabeth, c2), the keystone of the English poor laws until 1834, had as one of its objectives "to set on work all such persons, married or unmarried, who have no means to maintain themselves, and no ordinary and daily trade of life to get their living by." To reach their employment objectives the poor law authorities had four basic alternatives that they could adopt, separately or in combination: (1) they could create employment opportunities for the poor, either under public auspices or under contract with private entrepreneurs; (2) they could put pressure on the poor to find their own jobs, either by repression of begging or by making relief unattractive; (3) they could find employment opportunities for the children of the poor and have them supplement the family income; or (4) they could subsidize wages to facilitate employment of the poor. All these alternatives were used during the seventeenth and eighteenth centuries, the first being most popular at the beginning of the eighteenth century and the fourth at the end.

The Webbs emphasize that the "right of the poor" to relief and work set forth in the Elizabethan poor laws was not a right of the individual but an obligation of the parish. This distinction is of great importance for understanding the position of the worker. After the English Civil War the national government left the decision of how to carry out their obligation

[26] For a description of laws against beggars and vagabonds and of the penalties inflicted, see L. Lallemand, *Histoire de la Charité* (Paris: A. Picard, 1912), Vol. IV, pp. 149–214.

entirely at the discretion of the local authorities, the justices of the peace, and the parish wardens or overseers. This situation was conducive to a great variety of methods and experiments that incorporated generally held views about how to treat the poor. Putting the poor to work had been tried on a small scale before the Civil War in parishes as well as in Houses of Correction. These institutions served as prisons as well as places of employment, with considerable variation from place to place with respect to the stress on penal aspects and on work opportunity.

Although the idea of putting the poor to useful work was not new in the decades after the Civil War, a new stress was placed on the potential social gains to be made from this employment. Even wise and sober observers seemed to believe that the paupers were an important untapped source of national wealth. It is not surprising that we find among the chief advocates of the profitable employment of the poor an outstanding mercantilist writer like Sir Josiah Child. The Webbs have noted that "the 'profitable employment' of the poor became the common panacea of the economic writers of the last quarter of the seventeenth century, and it found a place in nearly every pamphlet on the commerce or industry of the nation."[27]

The character of this movement can best be conveyed by looking at one of these proposals and the ideas behind it in some detail. The one advanced by Child around 1670 will suit our purposes well, since he was not only a thoughtful writer but also, as chairman of the East India Company, a man with experience in practical affairs. His scheme incorporates the mercantilist views about labor as wealth and reflects a religious and paternalistic sense of responsibility for the welfare of the poor. Before developing his proposal, he lays down a set of principles, or "particulars" as he calls them, which he declares are "generally agreed by common consent."[28] Below are the ones that are relevant in the present context.

1. The poor in England "have always been in a most sad and wretched condition" and many remain "uncomfortable to themselves and unprofitable to the Kingdom."

2. "The Children of our Poor bred up in beggary and laziness . . . by their idle habits contracted in their youth, [are] rendered for ever after indisposed to labour. . . ."

3. "If all our impotent Poor were provided for, and those of both sexes and all ages that can do any work of any kind, employed, it would rebound some hundreds of thousands of pounds *per annum* to the publick advantage."

[27] Webb, *op. cit.,* Vol. I, p. 105. See also K. De Schweinitz, *England's Road to Social Security* (Philadelphia: University of Pennsylvania Press, 1943), Chapter VI, and Samuel Mencher, *Poor Law to Poverty Program* (Pittsburgh: University of Pittsburgh Press, 1967), pp. 32 ff.
[28] Quotations are from Sir Josiah Child, *A new Discourse of Trade* (fourth edition, London, n.d., c. 1677), Chapter II, pp. 86–110.

4. "It is our duty to God and Nature, so to provide for, and employ the Poor" (pp. 87–88).

The mercantilist assumptions about labor come out in his criticism of the prevailing practice in most parishes to try to get rid of paupers by sending them to some other parish. In his thinking, the poor should be attracted rather than repressed and repulsed, which was certainly a novel approach.

> The riches of a City, as of a Nation, consisting in the multitude of inhabitants; and if so, you must allow Inmates, or have a city of cottages. And if a right course be taken for the sustentation [sic] of the poor, and setting them on work, you need invent no stratagems to keep them out, but rather to bring them in. For the resort of the Poor to a City or Nation well managed, is in effect, the conflux of riches to that City or Nation and therefore the subtle Dutch, receive, and relieve, or employ, all that come to them, not inquiring what Nation, much less what parish they are of (p. 95).

To mobilize this source of riches, he proposed that adjacent parishes combine for this purpose and establish an "assembly of men" of substance. This organization would be incorporated by Act of Parliament under "the name of Fathers of the Poor, or some other honourable and significant title" (p. 97). This paternal corporate body was to be given the authority and the resources for the management of poor relief. Child counted on religiously minded and public spirited citizens to undertake the task of organization.

> The Fathers of the Poor may have Liberty to admit into their society . . . any persons that are willing to serve God, their King, and Country, in this pious and publick work, the persons desiring so to be admitted, paying at their admission 100 £ or more into the poor's treasury, as a demonstration of the sincerity of their intentions to labour in and cultivate this most religious vineyard (p. 100).

That such noble sentiments were not too common may be inferred from Child's remark that there may not be enough citizens available to undertake the task.

Child's proposal reflected a rather optimistic and, perhaps, naive view of the problem of poor relief. He seemed to think that, in general, the idle poor would accept the opportunity for employment in a workhouse and that no harsh measures were necessary to make them work. There were other prominent individuals who shared his optimism. Sir Matthew Hale, the Lord Chief Justice of England, proposed the profitable employment of the poor in his *Discourse Touching Provision for the Poor* which appeared in 1683. Andrew Yarranton, a successful businessman, stressed the employment and training of pauper children in his *England's Improvement by Sea and Land* (1677); another prominent merchant, Thomas Firmin, not only published a proposal but actually erected a building and put it into operation in the 1690s.

Another Promoter, John Bellers, projected a somewhat utopian "College of Industry" that would, through wise and humane treatment of the poor, yield "all sorts of useful production" and turn "useless and chargeable individuals into productive members of society."[29]

Many who took a harsher position toward the poor also were opposed to finding jobs for them. Prominent among them was John Locke, who felt that vigorous measures to correct the vices and indolence of the poor were more appropriate than creating jobs for them in public institutions. His approach was based on the premise that there was a growing burden of idle paupers that "proceeded neither from scarcity of provisions nor from want of employment for the poor."[30] Locke attributed the presence of idleness to "a relaxation of discipline and corruption of manners" and proposed, as a first step toward its elimination, the closing of brandy shops and ale houses. Having thus deprived the poor of one of their few sources of diversion, he intended to subject all able-bodied persons found begging to diverse kinds of disciplinary action, including hard labor on His Majesty's ships and in Houses of Correction. In this manner he hoped the poor would be induced to find jobs. For those who could not find jobs in their parish at going rates, Locke proposed a system under which they would be forced to work at less than the going rate for any one who wished to employ them. And, if that failed, he would assign the paupers to rate payers for maintenance and employment. Only for the physically handicapped and for children was he prepared to provide public employment in special "working schools" that were to be erected in each parish.[31] Although his recommendations were not passed into law, they were in line with popular sentiment at the time.

The intellectual debate of the late seventeenth and early eighteenth centuries over the need to provide work and the expediency of compelling the poor to find jobs was bound sooner or later to yield to practical experiments. The hope of making a profit and the vision of great benefits to the nation gave way to the more modest aim of making the poor earn, at least, the cost of their maintenance. But the various workhouses that came into existence, whether under the immediate jurisdiction of the parish or under incorporated "Guardians of the Poor," were forced to realize that even this limited objective was not attainable as a rule. The paupers who were unable to earn a subsistence on their own generally also failed to earn their

[29] Webb, *op. cit.*, p. 108. See also T. E. Gregory, "The Economics of Employment in England, 1660–1713," *Economica,* Vol. I (1921), pp. 37–51.

[30] J. Locke, *A Report of the Board of Trade to the Lords Justices Respecting the Relief and Employment of the Poor* (1697), cited in Webb, *op. cit.,* Vol. I, p. 110. Locke was a member of the Board of Trade.

[31] Webb, *op. cit.,* Vol. I, pp. 109–112.

keep when put to work in the workhouse. Another and very old system of providing public employment continued in existence alongside the workhouse. This was the "Roundsman" system. "It was, in fact, a sort of billeting of the unemployed labour upon the parishioners in rotation, each in turn having to provide maintenance and being free to exact service."[32] The poor laws were thus a social system for maintaining employment as much as a system of relief.[33]

One of the most significant outgrowths of the eighteenth century poor law practices was the Speenhamland system that was started informally in Berkshire in 1785. It had a profound significance for the development of the worker's right to social protection during the following century, because it helped to call forth a severe reaction against the right to relief in a period of widespread economic distress. The Speenhamland system combined the roundsman system with allowances in aid of wages. The poor law authorities subsidized the wages of every laborer below a certain level according to a scale tied to the price of bread and the size of his family. This system spread to other parts of the country after 1795 and became most prevalent in the southern agricultural counties. The fact that it would eventually undermine the incentive to work and would demoralize the laborer was not foreseen by its authors. It was the answer of "traditional" society to the disruptive forces unleashed by the Industrial Revolution at home and the political revolution abroad. It pitted the old principle of regulation of the worker's lot by society against the new principle of subjecting his welfare to the vagaries of the free labor market. By trying to establish a living family wage, it was in direct conflict with the development of the free labor market required by the emerging industrial system.[34]

How much the poor laws contributed toward improving either the behavior or the character of the poor is hard to evaluate. The numerous criticisms that the system, instead of encouraging willingness to work, actually encouraged idleness probably have some foundation. A law passed in 1723 authorized parish overseers to refuse outdoor relief and send applicants to the workhouse. This "offer," which a century later became a cardinal principle of poor law practice, made the workhouse into a relief deterrent. Most of the workhouses and almshouses, even when they were started in a burst of philanthropic fervor, usually ended up as "houses of terror." They were dreaded by the poor and denounced by thoughtful people as filthy breeding places of disease, vice, and corruption. There were

[32]*Ibid.*, p. 190.

[33]J. L. and B. Hammond, *The Village Labourer 1760–1832* (fourth edition, London: Longmans, Green, and Co., 1927), p. 127.

[34]For an interpretation of the Speenhamland system along these lines, see K. Polanyi, *The Great Transformation* (Boston: Beacon Press, 1957), Chapter VIII.

other forms of deterrence, for instance, the publication of the names of the poor and the compulsory wearing of badges identifying relief recipients, but they do not seem to have played an important role. Probably the most effective deterrent was the fact that relief was handled at the local level, which meant that local citizens had to bear the cost and the applicants often were personally known to the overseers.

The repressive features of the poor laws and the attempts to regulate the lives of the poor weakened considerably during the second half of the eighteenth century. Mercantilism was on the wane, and more humanistic ideas were gaining prominence. The social rights of the worker were beginning to be shaped by the ideological forces associated with emerging liberalism and industrialism.

EVOLUTION OF POOR RELIEF IN FRANCE

The French pattern of poor relief prior to the nineteenth century had the same general objectives as the English one, but there were important differences in practice. There was no law comparable to the 43rd of Elizabeth that established a system of poor relief. Relief remained a local responsibility, even though the central government intervened more frequently with local authorities during the seventeenth and eighteenth centuries than it did in England. France never recognized a legal right to support of the poor, not even in the indirect sense of recognizing and enforcing a legal obligation of the parish to provide relief. The Church played a more important administrative role, and men of the nobility, rather than merchants, were likely to take the initiative in founding a poorhouse. France had a more effective police system and, as a consequence, the repression of vagrancy was often carried out more vigorously than in England. A reflection of the growing *étatism* in France during the seventeenth and eighteenth centuries was an increasing attention paid by the national government to the problem of pauperism. It is very interesting that in France, also, there was a declaration of every man's right to subsistence at the end of the eighteenth century. As in England, this declaration was inspired by the humanistic social currents of the second half of that century. But, in other respects, it was quite different, since, as we shall see, it was sponsored by the most radical of the revolutionaries instead of by the defenders of traditionalism.

The French decrees relating to the poor in the sixteenth century were similar to the English in that they combined provisions for the relief of invalids with threats of repression and the obligation to work for able-bodied paupers. In the larger towns, attempts were made to employ beggars on public works. The *Parlement* of Paris, for instance, issued a regulation in 1532 ordering that all beggars be seized and made to clean streets and work on fortifications and bridges.[35] Severe punishments were stipulated against begging but, as usual, to no avail.

More determined attempts to set the poor to work were made during the seventeenth century. These attempts differed from the English proposals at the end of the century in that they were often promoted at the insistence of the central government, which enrolled the aid of the clergy to start local organizations and to raise funds from private individuals. These schemes were less concerned with making a profit from pauper labor than with clearing the beggars from the street and shutting them into workhouses.[36] The use of workhouses as a means for creating national wealth and as "schools of industry" was not ignored. Laffemas and La Gomberdière, both ardent mercantilists, suggested establishments for these purposes in the early seventeenth century.[37] Meanwhile, the movement to "lock-up the poor," as the French call it, was spreading slowly to the major cities in France.[38] The attitude was that the poor had to be taken in hand and brought up properly, "en la crainte de Dieu et au travail." One of the more successful experiments, which became a model for other cities, was the *Hôpital Général* (general poor and workhouse) of Lyon, which had 1500 inmates by 1650.[39] Whether the success of this enterprise lasted longer than that of some of the more promising English workhouses remains unclear.

During the second half of the seventeenth century, the drive to lock up the poor increased its momentum. Following the Lyon model, a *Hôpital Général* was established in Paris by royal decree in 1656. The king, Louis XIV, stated in a letter to the directors of the *Hôpital* that the poor were scandalizing the good folk through their begging and laziness and that locking them up had become "absolutely necessary for the glory of God and the Catholic religion."[40] The *Hôpital* stressed discipline and work as well as religious education and industrial training. The directors were given the right to flog the poor and to have them sent to the galleys for insolence and disobedience. To feed the inmates, whose number exceeded four thousand after six months, they were allowed to collect remnants from the tables of the rich, an idea that Mazarin had advanced a few years earlier in an anonymous *mémoire* on how to care for the poor.[41]

[35] Camille Bloch, *L'assistance et l'état en France à la veille de la Révolution* (Paris: A. Picard, 1908), p. 44. See also E. C. Balch, "Public Assistance of the Poor in France," *Publications of the American Economic Association,* Vol. VIII (1893), Nos. 4 to 5, pp. 21 ff.

[36] Cole, *op. cit.,* Vol. I, p. 134.

[37] Hauser, *op. cit.,* p. 158.

[38] L. Lallemand, *op. cit.,* Vol. IV, pp. 250 ff.

[39] Cole, *op. cit.,* Vol. I, p. 265.

[40] *Ibid.,* p. 268.

[41] *Ibid.,* pp. 234, 266 ff.

Similar institutions were springing up with royal encouragement in a number of provincial towns. Not surprisingly, Mazarin's successor as chief minister, the indefatigable Colbert, showed a great interest in the creation of workhouses and in the repression of all kinds of idleness. Shortly after his rise to power, and most likely on his advice, the king issued a declaration (June 12, 1662) prescribing the founding of *hôpitaux généraux* in all towns and cities of the kingdom.[42] Other royal edicts and ordinances followed. Colbert, who was moved as much by the need to maintain public order as by the desire to keep the poor industrious, favored extremely harsh measures. He used able-bodied beggars to man his galleys, dig his canals, and to perform other arduous tasks. He wanted persons who were repeatedly caught begging to be locked up permanently and compelled to do hard labor. His idea of the workhouse was a penal institution to frighten the idle and force them to be useful to society. In keeping with Colbert's spirit were the regulations, issued for Paris in 1680, that provided that the children of artisans and poor inhabitants who treated their parents badly, or who were too lazy to work, and girls who were debauched, or in danger of becoming debauched, were to be shut up in workhouses. This action could be taken on the complaint of parents, or relatives if the parents were dead, or the parish priest.[43] Nothing could be more indicative of the paternalistic element in the system than the state's readiness to step in and take over the parental duty of properly rearing the children of the poor.

The relief system that developed in the seventeenth century kept its leading features until the second half of the eighteenth century. By then, the steady growth in the number of beggars, the humanistic spirit of the Enlightenment, and many critical voices demanded a new approach. Two main avenues of development presented themselves: one was the traditional approach, which meant further intensification of the system of repression coupled with religious admonitions and compulsory labor; the other was a new approach which consisted in lessening indiscriminate repression, more careful distinction between deserving and shiftless poor, and the provision of voluntary employment opportunities free from the penal conditions of the workhouse.

The traditional approach was incorporated in a law of August 3, 1764, which Bloch calls the "last solemn expression of the ideas of the old monarchy."[44] But even this law showed signs of progress in that it recognized that not all unemployed individuals were vagrants. It was a response to widespread abuse in the form of indiscriminate arrests, which was caused, in part, by a system of bonus payments for the arrest of vagrants. The law

[42] Lallemand, *op. cit.,* Vol. IV: 1, p. 262.
[43] Cole, *op. cit.,* Vol. II, p. 480.
[44] Bloch, *op. cit.,* p. 160.

of 1764 treated as vagrants all those who had no visible means of support, had not been employed for six months, and had no trustworthy person testifying to their good character. For the able-bodied vagrants the penalty was again the galleys, three years for a first offense, and life for a third. The aged and the sick and women and children were to be locked up in the *hôpitaux*. It was soon evident that not all those eligible for the galleys could be sent there, the cost alone of such an operation would have been prohibitive. To help out in this situation, a new institution, the *dépôt de mendicité* was created by administrative order in 1767. These *dépôts* were intended as penal labor institutions "half-way between a prison and a garrison. But only the frightful prisons of ancient France could rival them as a place of horror."[45] Unlike the *hôpitaux,* they were directly under the jurisdiction of the national government and were to serve primarily as temporary places of detention. How long individuals were actually detained in them is not clear, but it is evident that they collected all kinds of people, men and women, old and young, the honest worker without a job as well as the criminal vagrant, the healthy and the sick, the innocent as well as the debauched, in other words, the content of the English general workhouse.

The alternative approach of more humane treatment and voluntary employment opportunities, combined with an expansion of outdoor relief, was widely debated by the advocates of human rights of the Age of Reason. In government, it was associated with Turgot and Necker, ministers of Finance to Louis XVI, and with the thinking of the national administration during the Revolution, especially that of the *Comité de Mendicité* established by Constituent Assembly in 1790. Turgot developed some of his basic ideas on the problem of poor relief in his article on foundations that he wrote for the *Encyclopédie.* This article is remarkable in that it declares both the right of the poor to support and the desirability of governmental laissez-faire. Turgot declares categorically for the rights of the poor against the wealth of the rich: "Le pauvre à des droits incontestables sur l'abondance du riche. L'humanité, la religion, nous font également un devoir de soulager nos semblables dans le malheur."[46] The concept of the rights of the poor and the duties of the rich had always been present in the idea of Christian charity, but to Turgot and the Humanists of the eighteenth century it meant more than that. It implied a duty of the state to take action for the benefit of the poor. As a government official, Turgot advocated public works to employ the poor, but he did not want the state or private organizations to support the poor. One of his main criticisms of private foundations, including the *hôpitaux,* was that they often tried to provide services each individual should provide for himself. He insisted on every man's duty to work.

[45]*Ibid.*, p. 178.
[46]*Oeuvres* (Schelle edition, Paris: Felix Alkan, 1919), Vol. I, p. 585.

Every healthy man has to secure his subsistence through work, for if he is fed without working, it is at the expense of those who work. What the state owes to each of its members, is the destruction of the obstacles that hinder his enterprise [*industrie*] or disturb the enjoyment of the goods that are its rewards. If these obstacles persist, specific acts of kindness will not reduce the general poverty, since its cause remains untouched.[47]

Turgot's ideological position is of interest because he stood halfway between the old paternalistic system and the new liberal conceptions. To understand his advocacy of laissez-faire, which he called "le grand, l'unique principe," and his willingness to develop a system of public employment for the poor, one must distinguish between what he believed to be desirable objectives and current necessities. Ideally, he was in favor of voluntary associations for mutual self-help to meet the contingencies of old-age, sickness, and accidents, which he knew would exist even if there were no general unemployment.[48] Under the existing circumstances of widespread unemployment and poverty which, as a liberal economist, he attributed to bad legislation and an oppressive fiscal system, he favored nonrepressive governmental relief. In other words, it was the economic and social system that was in need of reform rather than the individual. Until the system was reformed, there was a need to provide public employment opportunities. He was a practical administrator as well as an economist. He began his scheme to employ the poor when he was *intendant* of the Limousin. During the famine of 1769, which was obviously aggravated by poor transportation facilities and restrictions on the grain trade, he saw no way out but to appeal to the national government. In a letter to the *Controlleur Général,* he explained that "the king is the father of all his subjects, and it is from him that they expect the help that none other can provide."[49] His general attitude toward the indigent is well reflected in the instructions he issued with regard to locking up beggars in the *dépôts.* "This should not be resorted to except with the moderation necessary to avoid the risk of confusing two things as different as genuine poverty and voluntary mendicacy arising from licentiousness and sloth. The former should not merely be relieved but also respected; only the latter deserves to be punished."[50] When he became minister, he closed the *dépôts de mendicité,* which he considered unnecessary and even dangerous.[51]

After Turgot's short incumbency as minister (1774 to 1776), there was some tendency to revert to more repressive measures. But this was a temporary expedient, for the time was passed when repression, forced labor, and

[47] *Ibid.*, p. 590.
[48] He was well aware of the problems involved in creating such associations and discussed them with considerable insight in a private letter written in 1762. See *ibid.,* Vol. II, p. 234.
[49] *Ibid.,* Vol. III, p. 126
[50] *Ibid.*, p. 250.
[51] Bloch, *op. cit.*, pp. 190 ff.

religious admonition were considered to be the answer to the problem of poverty. This was no longer likely in a time when learned academies were widely organizing public discussion of topics such as "How to render the poor useful to the state without making them unhappy." The *Philosophes* had rejected the mercantilist disdain for the poor man and had spoken for his right to happiness. Voltaire had declared that "the principal point is not to have a superfluity of men, but to render those of them that we have as little unhappy as possible," and D'Holbach and Helvetius "viewed life and happiness as the proper end of all human activity." [52] Montesquieu thought that "the state owes all citizens an assured subsistence," and Rousseau remarked that "when the poor were good enough to let some become rich, the rich promised to feed all those who had nothing to live on." [53]

Necker, Turgot's successor, accepted neither Turgot's economic liberalism nor the view of society advanced by the *Philosophes*. He shared with the latter the idea that poverty was inherent in the existing social order. Yet, although he granted that existing inequality of wealth and advantages was the cause of poverty, he argued that this inequality, and consequently poverty, were inevitable in an organized society. "La pauvreté est malheureusement une des conditions inséparables de l'état de société : il y aura toujours des hommes exposés à l'indigence . . ." [54] This fatalistic view did not lead him to argue for a governmental policy of nonintervention. On the contrary, it was the basis for intervention, since the state, which had laws to protect the property of the rich, had to have laws to alleviate the suffering of the poor.

> It is up to the government, as interpreter and guardian of social harmony, to do for this large and disinherited class all that order and justice will allow; it must make thoughtful use of all the means at its disposal to soften the harshness of old conventions and to lend a helpful hand to those who need protection against the laws themselves; then, among the statutes which determine the rights of citizens against each other, it will discover the duties of society as a whole toward the unfortunate. [55]

Not in laissez-faire, but in wise legislation and in the practice tempered by religious sentiment were the seeds of social harmony. Without religion, Necker believed, the disinherited masses could not be resigned to their lot; individual self-interest cannot serve as a guide to the role of the state in social matters. [56] His poor relief policy while he was in office was more

[52] See J. J. Spengler, *op. cit.*, pp. 227–249.
[53] Cited in E. Levasseur, *Histoire des classes ouvrières et de l'industrie en France de 1789 à 1870* (second edition, Paris, 1903), Vol. I, p. 63.
[54] Necker, *De l'administration des finances de la France* (Paris, 1785), Vol. III, p. 139.
[55] *Ibid.*, pp. 141–143.
[56] For an extensive discussion of these views, see his *De l'importance des opinions religieuses* (London, 1788), pp. 39 ff and *passim*.

repressive than Turgot's, but he continued the creation of public employment. Although his work programs put less emphasis on voluntary employment, he did lessen the repressive and disciplinary features of the newly reopened *dépôts*.

The ideas that had been discussed for a generation and the experiments that had been undertaken saw their ultimate fruition in the poor relief doctrines and policies of the Revolution. Before the Revolution was three weeks old, a complete reorganization of poor relief was demanded in order to assure work for the able-bodied and support for those who could not work. This was demanded in the name of human rights, because "where there exists a class of men without subsistence, there exists a violation of the rights of humanity."[57] These propositions were accepted by the majority of the Constituent Assembly that set up the *Comité de Mendicité* in 1790. La Rochefoucauld-Liancourt, the leading member of the committee, was enthusiastically applauded by the Assembly, when he declared that:

> Every man has a right to subsistence. This fundamental truth of any society which has an imperious claim to a place in the Declaration of the Rights of Man, should be the basis for any law and for any political institution which proposes to extinguish mendicancy. The duty of society is therefore to seek to prevent misfortune, to relieve it, to offer work to those who need it in order to live, to force them if they refuse to work, and finally, to assist without work those whose age or infirmity deprive them of the ability to work.[58]

However, neither his committee nor the Constituent Assembly, accepted the concept of every man's right to a living income. One of the fundamental articles of the "Declaration des droits de l'homme et du citoyen" of September 3, 1791, made poor relief a national responsibility but did not speak of any right to subsistence or work. This right was proclaimed after the Revolution had veered to the left and more radical spirits were in power. The Republican Constitution adopted by the Convention in 1793 declared solemnly: "Public relief is a sacred debt. Society owes subsistence to citizens in misfortune, either by providing work, or by providing the means of existence to those who are unable to work."[59] At this time, the *étatiste* tendencies long latent in France had reached a peak. This contrasts sharply with England where the right to a living wage had grown out of a scheme that had been introduced locally by Justices of the Peace, who were one of the pillars of traditional society. In both countries this right was introduced in an environment of social crisis.

[57] Cited in Levasseur, *Histoire . . . de 1789 à 1870*, Vol. I, p. 64.
[58] *Ibid.*, pp. 63–64.
[59] *Ibid.*, p. 106.

On the practical side, the poor relief achievements of the Revolution were less glorious than in the realm of principle. In spite of all the pronouncements on the individual's right to support, he was never given an effective legal claim to this support.[60] The *Comité de Mendicité* of the Constituent Assembly and the *"Comité de Secours Publics"* of the Legislative Assembly made investigations, issued critical reports, and submitted projects, but nothing fundamental was done to change the pattern of public relief. The government proceeded to remove the church from its dominant position in this area and made funds available to expand the public workshops in Paris and in the provinces. Often "tumultuously organized," to use Levasseur's description, these workshops became at their worst dangerous centers of popular unrest and at their best failed to provide useful work on a meaningful scale. The Convention went a step further and passed two laws in 1793, one (March 13) to reorganize poor relief along the lines suggested by the committees of the previous two governments, and the other (October 15) to establish *dépôts de répression* for inveterate vagrants. Neither of them was put into effect, nor was the wild universal pension scheme that was decreed in 1794.[61] After the Revolution had run through a series of more or less inconsistent and unrealizable projects, poor relief returned to more traditional patterns. The reorganization was begun under the Directory and further rationalized under Napoleon. The new system, soon to be influenced by the Malthusian ideas of poor relief, was based on communal boards for the distribution of outdoor relief and on workhouses for institutional relief.[62]

TRADITIONAL SUBORDINATION ON THE WANE

The fact that the new rights of the worker had been proclaimed in the last decade of the eighteenth century was an indication that his traditional social subordination was on the wane, in both England and France, and that a new era in social relations was about to begin. The tradition of subordination had been a legacy of the medieval social order, but its meaning changed with the rise of the national state and, later, with the rise of industrialism. It took on particularly harsh hues during the heyday of mercantilism but softened considerably during the second half of the eighteenth century which, especially in France, was because of the humanistic

---

[60] The Constitution of 1793 was suspended shortly after its adoption.

[61] For a brief description of this scheme, see *ibid.*, pp. 106–108. An illustration of the spirit of the scheme is the requirement that the names of the pensioners were to be read periodically, "accompanied by patriotic songs in honor of work."

[62] See Balch, *op. cit.*, pp. 71 ff.

influence of the Enlightenment. In England similar changes occurred. Dorothy Marshall observes that "by the end of the century a complete revolution had taken place in men's thoughts with regard to the Poor. The danger was no longer that those in authority might be too severe, but that they might be too lenient."[63] These changes were signs of the waning old order. They came at a time when new ideas about the individual and the state were challenging the feudal legacy of a paternalistic social order. What the triumph of the new ideas would mean for the social rights of the worker as yet could be only dimly perceived.

In France the impact was swift. The Revolution destroyed the old order. After briefly holding out utopian promises of universal protection, it ended with a complete break in the movement toward greater state protection for those in need. It must be observed that the state had been at the center of this movement, first the absolutist state and then the radical republican state. But the liberal forces that inherited the state after the Revolution disavowed these efforts. They declared the worker free and independent, that is, without any claim to the protective arm of the state.

In England the passing of the traditional order was not so abrupt. The forces of liberalism grew with the transformation of the social structure under the impact of industrialization. They were not enthroned by political revolution. Moreover, the target of the liberal forces was not an absolutist regime that had no worthy defenders left, but an aristocratic social and political order that still had great vitality. Against the liberal theory of society in which each individual was free and self-dependent, the defenders of traditionalism advanced an alternative theory which was not without appeal. John Stuart Mill called it the theory of dependence and protection, according to which

> ... the lot of the poor, in all things which affect them collectively, should be regulated *for* them, not *by* them. They should not be required or encouraged to think for themselves, or give to their own reflection or forecast an influential voice in the determination of their destiny. It is supposed to be the duty of the higher classes to think for them, and to take the responsibility of their lot, as the commander and officers of an army take that of the soldiers composing it. ... The relation between rich and poor, according to this theory (a theory also applied to the relation between men and women) should be only partly authoritative: It should be amiable, moral, and sentimental: affectionate tutelage on the one side, respectful and grateful deference on the other. The rich should be *in loco parentis* to the poor, guiding and restraining them like children.[64]

[63] *Op. cit.,* p. 55.

[64] J. S. Mill, *Principles of Political Economy* (revised edition, New York: Colonial Press, 1900), Vol. II, p. 266. See also R. Bendix, *Work and Authority in Industry* (New York: Wiley, 1956), pp. 47 ff where this theory is discussed in relation to traditionalism in the management of labor.

Mill wrote about an idealized image of the past held by some of his contemporaries instead of about historical reality. Nevertheless, as he points out, the attitudes and feelings depicted do have historical validity. They were part of the intellectual and emotional framework of the waning traditional setting and, therefore, were motivating forces in history. In fact, it was this paternalistic attitude that liberalism had to overcome in order to legitimate the denial of the poor man's claim to social protection.

CHAPTER 3

The Liberal Break and Its Legacies

The liberal capitalist civilization that emerged in the late eighteenth century rejected the traditional protectionism of the old social order. It denied the poor man's claim to a right to protection by society; it discarded the concept of paternal responsibility of the rich for the poor. In the liberal industry state, every man was to be free to pursue his fortune and was to be responsible for his success and failure. Needless to say, in practice the break with traditionalism was neither so radical nor so complete as these statements might imply. Elements of traditionalism always survived and blended with new ideas and policies. However, for the development of social security in the West, the liberal break was of fundamental importance. This importance lies less in the break itself as in its legacies, since the ideas and institutions that were forged in the course of combating traditional protectionism, in turn, acquired deep roots in the national consciousness. We are particularly concerned with the persistence of these ideas and institutions in the face of changing economic, social, and political conditions. At one stage the liberal legacies acted as barriers to the emergence of modern social security rights; at the next stage they shaped the nature of these rights.

The task of this chapter is twofold: (1) to examine the break with the tradition of repressive paternalism, and (2) to analyze the legacy of liberalism in different national settings. The attack on the old system was not simply the result of liberal ideas. The fact was that the social relations represented by the old system were in conflict with the economic and social requirements of industrialization. We shall examine this conflict in the English case. Next, we shall look at the forms taken by the intellectual attack on traditional protectionism in England, France, and the United States. Finally, we shall study the policies established under the aegis of liberalism and the shift from these policies to welfare state policies. As one should expect, the persistence

35

of liberal policies varied from country to country with the strength of the liberal tradition. Particular attention in this regard will be paid to the United States, since it was in this country that liberalism was most deeply rooted and social protection was most stubbornly resisted. Here, the influence of liberal ideals was strongest in the shaping of modern social rights.

SOCIAL PROTECTION AND THE IMPERATIVES OF INDUSTRIALIZATION

The old poor laws had developed in an agrarian economy, where market forces played only a secondary role in the allocation and remuneration of labor. One characteristic of the old order was that in spite of the subordination of the lower classes, the common man "was conscious more of freedom from personal authority than of subjection."[1] In this context, the regulation of work and wages and the discipline of the poor laws were considered necessary to keep the workers from abusing their freedom, either by taking advantage of local circumstances to extort higher wages or by leading a life of indolence. With advancing industrialization and more dynamic markets, these legal safeguards became unnecessary and impractical. The discipline of the competitive labor market and the authority of the factory owner provided more automatic means to control the behavior of the work force. What the industrial economy required was an environment that would promote a mobile work force that was responsive to wage incentives.

The old poor laws were a hindrance to labor mobility and to the workers' commitment to an urban, industrial life. How significant their effect was in this regard is difficult to establish. Many contemporary observers believed the problem to be serious. Adam Smith had already denounced the poor relief system for its hindrance of the "free circulation of labor."[2] He considered it a violation of natural liberty and a cause of the persistence of very unequal wages in places only a short distance from one another. That the poor laws had been designed for a society in which it was thought more desirable to keep a man tied to his village than to encourage him to move about was implicit in the Law of Settlement of 1662. Under this law new arrivals in a parish could be removed against their will to their "settlement parish" if they were thought likely to become chargeable. The effects

[1] S. and B. Webb, *English Poor Law History* (London: Longmans, Green, and Co., 1927), Vol. I, p. 420.
[2] A. Smith, *The Wealth of Nations* (Cannan edition, New York: Modern Library, 1937), pp. 135 ff. A recent revaluation of M. Blaug pays little attention to the question of labor mobility; see "The Myth of the Old Poor Law and the Making of the New," *Journal of Economic History*, Vol. XXIII (June 1963), pp. 151–184.

of this law were not nearly so restrictive as Adam Smith thought them to be, and they were made less so by the Poor Removal Act of 1795. Nevertheless, even if, in fact, they did not make it legally difficult for workers to leave their parish, they very likely added to the risk of leaving and to the psychological barriers of labor mobility.

Complaints about the impact of the poor laws on labor mobility were most numerous in the southern agricultural counties of England, after the return to peace in 1815. For a number of reasons, including agricultural changes, natural population growth, and the return of discharged soldiers, the area suffered from a serious labor surplus. It was also in this area that the Speenhamland system was most widespread, and heavy underemployment and unemployment sharply increased the burden of relief on the taxpayers. Redford notes that:

> The landowners and ratepayers of the southern agricultural counties complained that their surplus labourers refused to make a long and hazardous journey to the manufacturing districts in the north of England; this, they maintained, was due to fear of poor removal, which made the labourers unwilling to leave a secure settlement for the prospect of high but uncertain wages in industry.[3]

Another fundamental defect of the Speenhamland system of relief was its adverse incentive effects. Created in the spirit of the old order, its aim was simply a living family wage, but this brought it into conflict with the economic rationality of modern industry. By tying the income of the laborer to the price of bread and the size of his family, it severed the economic link between labor and its reward. The man able to earn an amount equal to that set by the "scale" of the Justices of the Peace was no better off than the man who managed to earn only half that amount. The second man received a subsidy while the first one took care of himself. The man who was either inefficient or lazy, or who worked for an inefficient employer, was singled out for public support. The Webbs, who were certainly not unsympathetic to the cause of the poor, have pointed out the irrationality of this system: "To single out the dull-witted employer and the lazy workman for special grants out of public funds, to the detriment of the keen organizer and zealous worker, was obviously bad psychology as well as bad economics."[4] These circumstances made it possible for uneconomic activities to exist alongside and to the detriment of the more economic employment of labor and capital.

Undoubtedly, the most severe conflict between the imperatives of industrialization and the poor law was the rapidly growing burden of relief in the late eighteenth and early nineteenth centuries. The increased burden

[3]A. Redford, *Labour Migration in England, 1800–1850* (Manchester: University Press, 1926), p. 77.
[4]*Op. cit.,* Vol. II, p. 15.

was related to rapid increase in population, for which contemporaries held the poor laws, at least, partly responsible. The correctness of this view has been subject to considerable debate, since the question is of basic importance.

One of the crucial problems a society faces in the shift from an agrarian to an industrial economy is the so-called demographic transition.[5] The behavior of birth and death rates during the early phase of the transition leads to a rapid increase in population. This is what happened during the Industrial Revolution in England. Although the birth rate was not as high as we find it in some underdeveloped countries today, the death rate was lower than the birth rate and was decreasing while the birth rate held its own.[6] Between 1781 and 1831 the population of Great Britain rose from 9,250,000 to 16,539,000.[7] The key to this increase was the failure of the birth rate to come down as the death rate dropped and, in that sense, Marshall argues, contemporaries were right in looking to the high birth rate as the cause of population growth. The momentous increase in population was bound to have a profoundly disturbing effect, especially since between 1811 and 1831 a series of exceptionally bad harvests conspired with the "population explosion" to intensify the problem of relief. After three centuries of populationist thinking and efforts to increase population, the country was confronted with the specter of a "redundant population," the majority of whom seemed destined to live in poverty.

It was left to the Reverend Thomas Robert Malthus to formulate his inexorable theory of population growth and to dramatize the poor laws as a cause of population growth. His arguments furnished the mainstay of the intellectual attack on the right to poor relief in England and, to a lesser extent, in France.

THE INTELLECTUAL ASSAULT ON THE RIGHT TO RELIEF IN ENGLAND

Malthus' *Essay on the Principle of Population* must be ranked as one of the most influential works in the history of economic literature. Already in the

[5] For a discussion of this problem, see A. J. Coale and E. M. Hoover, *Population Growth and Economic Development in Low-Income Countries* (Princeton: Princeton University Press, 1958), pp. 13 ff.
[6] For an analysis of the behavior of birth and death rates and their relation to population growth during this period, see T. H. Marshall, "The Population Problem during the Industrial Revolution," *Economic History*, 1929, reprinted in E. M. Carus-Wilson, *Essays in Economic History* (London: Edward Arnold, 1954), pp. 306-330.
[7] J. H. Clapham, *An Economic History of Modern Britain: The Early Railway Age 1820–1850* (Cambridge: University Press, 1926), pp. 53–54.

first edition (1798), Malthus argued forcefully that the poor laws not only increased population but lowered the general standard of living and raised the number of paupers. Their effects were thus the opposite from what had been intended.

> The poor-laws of England tend to depress the general condition of the poor in these two ways. Their first obvious tendency is to increase population without increasing the food for its support. A poor man may marry with little or no prospect of being able to support a family in independence. They may be said, therefore, in some measure to create the poor which they maintain; and as the provision of the country must, in consequence of the increased population, be distributed to every man in smaller proportions, it is evident that the labor of those who are not supported by parish assistance, will purchase a smaller quantity of provisions than before, and consequently, more of them must be driven to ask for support.
>
> Secondly, the quantity of provisions consumed in workhouses upon a part of the society, that cannot in general be considered as the most valuable part, diminishes the shares that would otherwise belong to the more industrious, and more worthy members; and thus in the same manner forces more to become dependent. If the poor in the workhouses were to live better than they now do, this new distribution of the money of the society would tend more conspicuously to depress the condition of those out of the workhouses, by occasioning a rise in the price of provisions.[8]

Aside from these devastating economic consequences, Malthus stressed harmful social effects. He argued that poor relief undermined the individual's spirit of independence and destroyed his industriousness. These arguments, of course, echoed much older views, but they were undergoing subtle changes. Liberalism related industriousness to freedom and independence instead of to obedience and fear of starvation.

In later editions of the *Essay* the poor laws were treated at much greater length than in the first.[9] This was assured by the heated controversy that Malthus helped to generate, as well as by the constantly rising poor rates and a widespread dissatisfaction with the administration of poor relief. The theme that reliance on government relief was destructive of the liberty of the people (which later became a frequent argument against social security) was later developed more fully by Malthus than his mere hint in the first edition. He denounced the lower classes for "their habit of attributing" their distress to their rulers. To him this habit was "the rock of defense, the

[8] *First Essay on Population (1798)*, reprinted for the Royal Economic Society (London: MacMillan and Co., 1926), pp. 83–84.
[9] In the first edition the poor laws are discussed at length in only one chapter. In the sixth edition (1826) there are three chapters dealing with the poor laws in addition to one chapter entitled "A Plan for the Gradual Abolition of the Poor-Laws proposed."

castle, the guardian spirit of despotism." It "affords to the tyrant the fatal and unanswerable plea of necessity. It is the reason why every free government tends constantly to destruction."[10] This was the line of reasoning that rejected the dependence and protection of traditional society and offered in its stead self-dependence and freedom. The consensus of liberalism was that man had a natural right to liberty, but not to protection. For Malthus the denial of protection was based on the laws of nature.

> ... there is one right which man has generally been thought to possess, which I am confident he neither does nor can possess—a right to subsistence when his labour will not fairly purchase it. Our laws indeed say that he has this right, and bind the society to furnish employment and food to those who cannot get them in the regular market, but in doing so they reverse the laws of nature; and it is in consequence to be expected, not only that they should fail in their object, but that the poor, who were intended to be benefited, should suffer most cruelly from the inhuman deceit thus practised upon them.[11]

Having established that the poor had no right to support, that they had no claim against the government or the rich, that they were responsible for their own misfortune, that their woes were the result of their own lack of prudence and forethought, and that relief was against the laws of nature and conducive to loss of liberty and to greater misfortunes, Malthus saw no alternative but to abolish the poor laws. All other remedies, such as emigration or less luxurious living by the rich, were mere palliatives that had at best only short-run favorable effects. The abolition of the poor laws would restore certain checks to population growth, would stop the decaying of the spirit of liberty and self-dependence, and would improve society both morally and materially. He was not unaware of the hardships that an immediate cessation of the poor laws would cause and, therefore, advocated a gradual approach, which included educating the poor in the rules of proper conduct.

In spite of his rejection of traditional protection, Malthus still harbored strong paternalistic sentiments. If the upper classes no longer had the duty to support the poor, they still were expected to provide moral guidance. While the relief payments were being contracted, he suggested, vigorous educational steps should be taken. It was to be the responsibility of clergymen to inculcate among the lower classes the idea that they must be self-dependent. In each church, after the publication of marriage bans, the minister was to give a stern sermon on the obligation of every man to support his children and on the immorality of marrying without being capable of support. In charging the clergy with this educational role, Malthus was in strong agreement with other poor law reformers who looked to religion

[10]*Essay on the Principle of Population* (sixth edition, London: 1826), Vol. II, pp. 311–312.
[11]*Ibid.*, pp. 319–320.

as a means for instilling the new concept of civic responsibility. Religion was, after all, a language that the poor man could understand, and its system of rewards and punishment could readily be adopted to the situation. Anyone who was irresponsible enough to marry without a clear prospect of being able to support a family was simply to be doomed for his immorality.

> When nature will govern and punish for us, it is a very miserable ambition to wish to snatch the rod from her hands, and draw upon ourselves the odium of executioner. To the punishment therefore of nature he should be left, the punishment of want. He has erred in the face of a most clear and precise warning, and can have no just reason to complain of any person but himself when he feels the consequences of his error. All parish assistance should be denied him; and he should be left to the uncertain support of private charity. He should be taught to know, that the laws of nature, which are the laws of God, had doomed him and his family to suffer for disobeying their repeated admonitions. . . .[12]

The reason for dwelling at length on Malthus is partly because he was the most outstanding political economist among the poor law reformers and partly because his views were widely accepted and highly influential.[13] The primary cause for the success of his arguments was not their scientific validity, which is open to question, but the fact that economic and social circumstances made his age receptive to his reasoning. On a very pressing problem he was able to offer a solution that was not only convenient but even flattering to those gaining most in wealth and power by industrialization; their own good fortune could, after all, be justified by the same kind of reasoning that justified the misfortune of the poor. Success was the proof of prudence and forethought just as misery was the evidence of the lack of these qualities.

Attacks on the poor laws, of course, were not new but, in the face of staggering increases in the cost of maintaining the poor and under the new climate of opinion, they had an unprecedented impact. The Reverend Joseph Townsend had suggested before Malthus that the poor laws interfered harmfully with the natural play of social forces. But Townsend was still an adherent of the old idea, associated with DeFoe, Mandeville, and Locke, that poverty was necessary to keep the poor well-behaved. "Unless the degree of pressure be increased," he wrote, "the labouring poor will never acquire habits of diligent application and severe frugality. To increase this pressure, the poor's tax must be gradually reduced. . . ."[14] The Malthusians had left behind the negative stress on the "usefulness of

[12]*Ibid.*, p. 339.
[13] Of course, his views were also widely attacked, but the opponents had much less influence on poor law policy.
[14]Quoted in Webb, *op. cit.*, Vol. II, pp. 11–12.

poverty."[15] They emphasized the need for prudence and forethought, which would overcome poverty. In this sense, the Malthusian attitude toward the poor was less somber and less fatalistic than the Lockian. It contained, at least, the implicit hope that the poor might reform, that they might acquire those middle class habits of frugality and sobriety that would make them prosperous. Attempts at reforming the poor were not new in the early nineteenth century, but where the mercantilists expected, at most, to change the behavior of the poor—to give them better work habits—the Malthusians wanted to change their character, to give them the new aspirations and virtues needed to improve their lot. It is in this perspective that we must evaluate the new emphasis put on religion and education for the poor, which contrasts with the more generally held view in earlier centuries that the lower classes would have to stay ignorant as well as poor.

The Malthusian attack on the right to relief combined the theory that population tended to increase faster than provisions with the liberal principles of individual freedom and self-dependence. There was no logical reason why these two sets of principles should be combined and, as observed earlier, Malthus was by no means an all-out liberal. The liberal attack did not stand or fall with the Malthusian theory of population; Malthusianism was only one string on the liberal bow. One of the leading classical economists, Nassau Senior, who also was a member of the commission to reform the poor laws, stated the straight liberal case against the poor laws, without recourse to Malthus.[16]

Senior had a historic vision of the significance of poor law reform in relation to social and economic progress. Although the reforms he supported were later denounced as cruel and heartless, in his perspective they were an instrument of emancipation for the working class. His interpretation of poor law history stressed the limitations on the freedom of the worker. The poor laws conflicted with his utilitarian tenet that the realization of the greatest social happiness, hence, social progress, was dependent on leaving each individual free to pursue his self-interest. Historically, therefore, the poor laws had hindered progress.[17] He pointed to their illiberal origin and noted that it "was an attempt substantially to restore the expiring system of slavery."[18] The laws were enacted for the convenience of the masters. In a

[15] Malthus personally still seemed to think that poverty was morally useful in the sense, shared by many theologians, that poverty instilled virtues.

[16] For a full discussion of his views, see Marian Bowley, *Nassau Senior and Classical Economics* (London: George Allen and Unwin, 1937).

[17] These views are developed in his article on the English poor laws which appeared in the *Edinburgh Review* in October 1841 and was reprinted in *Historical and Political Essays* (London, 1865), Vol. II, pp. 45–115. Although the article was written several years after the poor law reform, Bowley shows that he held the same basic views in 1832.

[18] *Historical and Political Essays*, p. 47.

review of the amendments between the fourteenth and sixteenth centuries, he showed how the poor laws were consistently designed to restrict the freedom of the workman. The 43rd of Elizabeth (1601), that was now honored for the right of support it gave the poor, was only "part of a scheme prosecuted for centuries, in defiance of reason, justice, and humanity, to reduce the labouring classes to serfs, to imprison them in their parishes, and to dictate to them their employment and their wages."[19] Having deprived the poor of their freedom, the ruling classes, of course, were forced to contribute to their support. In time, this support not only came to be looked on as a right, but by the second half of the eighteenth century, the even more "dangerous opinion" began to prevail that the poor had a right to comfortable subsistence regardless of the value of their labor. This was an attempt "to give the labourer a security incompatible with his freedom," and the inevitable result was to place him "in the condition, physically and morally, of a slave."[20]

Senior wanted to free the poor from the shackles of this servitude, which many were apparently either too ignorant or too degraded to perceive and resent. He wanted to free the industrious from having to help support the indolent. He wanted to make the poor self-dependent individuals in a society based on contractual instead of status relationships. In a letter to Lord Althorp in March 1833, he wrote: "We deplore the misconception of the poor in thinking that wages are not a matter of contract but of right."[21] The poor man was shortsighted and deluded partly because under the system prevailing before reform he had "all a slave's security for subsistence without his liability for punishment."[22] From this fate, the worker had to be rescued not only because slavery is uneconomical but because "it destroys all the nobler virtues, both moral and intellectual . . . it leaves the slave without energy, without truth, without industry, without providence."[23] The movement of history was away from the degradation of slavery and serfdom and toward the ennoblement of freedom and responsibility.

The theory of human behavior that underlies this interpretation of social progress does not necessarily conflict with public provision for the aged and the impotent. Neither Senior nor the other members of the Poor Law Commission demanded the abolition of this kind of relief, although

[19]*Ibid.*, p. 57.
[20]*Ibid.*, p. 115.
[21]Quoted in Bowley, *op. cit.*, p. 291.
[22]Quoted in Bowley, *op. cit.*, p. 292.
[23]*Historical and Political Essays*, p. 47. It is interesting that the Hammonds, who were of a quite different political and economic persuasion than Senior, also drew parallels between slavery and the old poor law. However, they stressed the fate of pauper children in the workhouses instead of the effects of able-bodied relief. See J. L. and B. Hammond, *The Rise of Modern Industry* (eighth edition, London: Methuen and Company, 1951), pp. 197 ff.

they thought that it should preferably be given in the workhouse instead of in the home. Inconsistent with the theory was the legal right to support for anyone physically able to help himself. Even in this respect, however, Senior did not go so far as Malthus in demanding complete abolition. He was willing to go along with relief for the able-bodied if this relief did not leave the poor better off than ordinary workers who were employed. In other words, the limits of the right of support were dictated by its impact on the freedom of the market.

THE CONDEMNATION OF THE RIGHT TO RELIEF IN FRANCE

Although France had never created a legal right to relief, the French liberal economists spared no effort in denouncing the concept. Their arguments were quite similar to those advanced in England and were supported by reference to English experience. This was a shift away from the humanitarian trend of the second half of the eighteenth century. Before the Revolution even ardent advocates of laissez-faire like Turgot acted on the assumption that the state had a definite obligation toward the poor. But, it will be recalled, he did so because he considered poverty a result of bad, illiberal institutions. Now that the institutions of the Old Regime had been replaced by a laissez-faire system, the causes of poverty could no longer be institutional and, therefore, had to be personal. The advocates of French liberalism, like their English counterparts, used Malthus to support this view. "Virtually every French defender of Malthus belonged to the liberal school" writes Spengler. "In substance the liberals believed that, given free competition, individual responsibility, and the diffusion of prudence and forethought, capital per head would accumulate, wage levels would rise, and the lot of the masses would steadily improve."[24] Consistent with these views, the liberals, and the rising class of industrialists attracted to their ideas, were opposed to the right of public relief. Jean-Baptiste Say, a Malthusian before he read Malthus, according to Spengler, argued against the right to relief in a freely competitive society. "It has often been much debated, whether individual distress has any title to public relief. I should say none, except inasmuch as it is an unavoidable consequence of existing social institutions. If infirmity and want be the effect of the social system, they have title to public relief: provided always, that it be shown, that the same system affords no means of prevention or cure."[25] The successors to Say's chair at

[24]J. J. Spengler, "French Population Theory since 1800, I," *Journal of Political Economy,* Vol. XLIV (October 1936), p. 585.
[25]J.-B. Say, *A Treatise on Political Economy* (trans. from the fourth edition, Philadelphia: Grigg and Elliot, 1836), pp. 438–439.

the College de France, P. Rossi and M. Chevalier, held similar views regarding individual responsibility and the right to relief. The most active French exponent of Malthus was Joseph Garnier, the editor of the *Journal des Économistes*. He argued that not only have the poor no legitimate claim to assistance but that the granting of any right to assistance would be "logically equivalent to establishing communism."[26] There was a genuine fear among French liberals about any measure that might expand the scope of the governmental bureaucracy, quite aside from the assumed economic consequences of relief.

Not all the French opponents of public relief were strict Malthusians. For instance, Frédéric Bastiat, a believer in human perfectibility, who accepted only a highly modified version of the Malthusian population theory, rejected even private charity because, he thought, it tended to paralyze foresight, "the virtue most proper for the elevation of the laboring class."[27] Public relief he considered even more harmful because it meant centralization of authority and responsibility, and "the more the State centralizes, the more it transforms natural responsibility into artificial solidarity, the more it removes the providential character of justice, punishment, and preventive check...."[28] Bastiat had a lot more faith than Malthus in the strength of the preventive check, and in the human capacity for self-restraint, but he was not willing to run the risk to undermine these noble character traits by the right to claim public assistance. A similar position was taken by another economist, Charles Duchatel, who declared flatly that "To guarantee assistance is to encourage vice, dissipation, disorder..."[29] Official acceptance of the reasoning of the liberal economists is indicated in a circular letter entitled *Du paupérisme et de la charité légale,* which was sent by the Minister of the Interior to all the *Préfets* of the kingdom in 1840. He admonished his representatives in the *Départements* that they "must not ignore the objections which the most enlightened economists have advanced against legal charity."[30] He thought it very dangerous to let the poorer classes get the impression that they had some sort of legitimate claim against the wealth of the country. That would soon mean no more foresight and no more economizing and, then, no more work. The advantage of private charity, the Minister thought, was that "the poor man never gets the idea that he can claim it as a right."[31] The argument was advanced also that

---

[26] Spengler, *loc. cit.*, p. 588.
[27] See his *Harmonies Économiques* in *Oeuvres Complètes* (Paris: Guillaumin and Cie, 1870), Vol. VI, p. 530.
[28] *Ibid.*, pp. 615-616.
[29] *De la Charité dans ses rapports avec l'état moral et le bien-être des classes de la société* (1829), cited in F. Schaller, *Un aspect du nouveau courant social* (Neuchatel: Editions de la Baconnière, 1950), p. 41.
[30] Schaller, *op. cit.*, p. 49.   [31] *Ibid.*

the right to public assistance led to deprivation of freedom because it often involved the obligation to work, and this, one writer argued, was contrary to the will of Divine Providence.[32] This was not a liberal but a conservative voice of opposition. Many conservatives agreed with the liberals that private charity and voluntary public assistance were preferable by far to a formal right to relief primarily because the poor could not count on such uncertain sources of support. In many ways this principle of uncertainty expresses a lower social opinion of the poor man than the principle of less eligibility. In France, the feeling was still that the poor had to be threatened with the possibility of starvation to be kept industrious. And this feeling was not limited to people who only casually had thought about the problem. A widely recognized authority on the economics of poverty and relief, Antoine-Elisée Cherbuliez, found only irregular charity tolerable and condemned the idea of a right to assistance as being both harmful and unjust.[33] A rather thoughtful examination of the issue of legal versus voluntary assistance was presented in Batbie's economics lectures at the University of Paris from 1864 to 1865. Batbie stressed the fact that much poverty was due to causes completely beyond the control of the individual and listed a number of important advantages offered by a system based on the legal right to relief. But he still came out against it: "I would consider it a very great evil if the right to assistance were established in our country."[34] Overwhelming all other considerations in his mind was the simple idea that uncertainty of relief was necessary in order to preserve foresight. The obstinacy with which French writers held to this unproved assumption about the motivation of the lower classes was remarkable.

THE CASE AGAINST RELIEF IN AMERICA

The American colonies had taken over the English concept of the right to relief, although they never faced the problem of pauperism on a scale comparable to that of the mother country. Later, the young United States shared in the revulsion against this right. The liberal condemnation of relief was the same as in the old countries, except for the absence of the Malthusian emphasis.[35] The first American economist of note, Henry C. Carey, was both

[32] F. Naville in a lecture to the Académie Française in 1829, cited in Schaller, op. cit., pp. 43-46.
[33] He wrote a number of items on the subject, including an Étude sur les causes de la misère (1853) and the article on "Bien-faisance Publique" in Dictionaire de l'économie politique (1864).
[34] A. Batbie, Nouveau cours d'économie politique (Paris: Cotillon, 1866), Vol. II, p. 207.
[35] See Edward T. Devine, Principles of Relief (New York: MacMillan, 1914), pp. 291 ff; also John Cummings, Poor-Laws of Massachusetts and New York, Publications of the American Economic Association, Vol. X, no. 4 (1895), pp. 45 ff.

a leading adversary of Malthus and a confirmed opponent of poor laws.[36] Because the paupers were often recent immigrants, sometimes straight from British poorhouses, it early became part of the American view that pauperism was an alien, imported disease.[37] It was associated with the failure to adapt to the new country and to take advantage of its bountiful opportunities.

This concept of personal failure, of weakness in the face of challenge, was to reappear later in more elaborate form. It was in the decades following the Civil War, when massive immigration and rapid urbanization created new social problems, that the American case against poor relief was forged. It was probably no sheer coincidence that in the period of rapid industrialization America discovered in Social Darwinism a doctrine that condemned the poor just as effectly as Malthusianism had condemned them during industrialization in England. In both instances, it could be demonstrated, theoretically, that attempts to help the poor could lead only to greater distress in the long run.

Within less than a decade after the Civil War the Darwinian theories of evolution and natural selection had gained a solid foothold among American scientists.[38] The application of these theories to social life and their use as a defense of ruthless laissez-faire owes most to Herbert Spencer and to his American disciple, William Graham Sumner. Spencer looked on progress as the result of a constant struggle by which organisms "purify" themselves; the weak, the sickly, and the malformed are weeded out and kept from reproducing their own kind. The discipline that this natural selection imposes bears a striking resemblance to the discipline Malthus saw in the effects of the principle of population. In both instances, human distress is explained by natural, biological forces, which cannot be altered by any kind of legislation. However, as we shall learn, Spencer associated the human suffering with social progress, but Malthus regarded it as evidence of insufficient progress. Spencer looked on civilization and well-being as the ultimate outcome of the struggle for existence:

> . . . the well-being of existing humanity, and the unfolding of it into this ultimate perfection, are both secured by the same beneficent, though severe discipline, to which animate creation at large is subject: a discipline which is pitiless in

---

[36] See his *Principles of Political Economy* (Philadelphia: Carey, Lea, and Blanchard, 1838), Part II, pp. 228 ff.

[37] See, for instance, *New Moral World* (London, 1844), in John R. Commons (ed.), *A Documentary History of American Industrial Society* (New York: Russell and Russell, 1958), Vol. II, pp. 59–60; also John B. McMaster, *A History of the People of the United States* (New York: Appleton and Co., 1923–1924), Vol. VI, p. 82.

[38] See Richard Hofstadter, *Social Darwinism in American Thought 1860–1915* (Philadelphia: University of Pennsylvania Press, 1945), Chapter I.

working out of good: a felicity-pursuing law which never swerves for the avoidance of partial and temporary suffering. The poverty of the incapable, the distresses that come upon the imprudent, the starvation of the idle, and those shoulderings aside of the weak by the strong, which leave so many "in shallows and in miseries," are the decrees of a large, far-seeing benevolence. It seems hard that an unskilfulness which with all his efforts he cannot overcome, should entail hunger upon the artisan. It seems hard that a laborer incapacitated by sickness from competing with his stronger fellows, should have to bear the resulting privations. It seems hard that widows and orphans should be left to struggle for life or death. Nevertheless, when regarded not separately, but in connection with the interests of universal humanity, these harsh fatalities are seen to be full of the highest beneficence—the same beneficence which brings to early graves the children of diseased parents, and singles out the low-spirited, the intemperate, and the debilitated as the victims of an epidemic.[39]

Defenders of poor laws were simply misguided sentimentalists, who, in the end, would impose far greater hardship on society than that which they sought to relieve. Here is what Spencer said of the false friends of the poor:

That rigorous necessity which, when allowed to act on them, becomes so sharp a spur to the lazy, and so strong a bridle to the random, these paupers friends would repeal, because of the wailings it here and there produces. Blind to the fact that under the natural order of things society is constantly excreting its unhealthy, imbecile, slow, vacillating, faithless members, those unthinking, though well-meaning, men advocate an interference which not only stops the purifying process, but even increases the vitiation—absolutely encourages the multiplication of the reckless and incompetent by offering them an unfailing provision, and discourages the multiplication of the competent and provident by heightening the perspective difficulty of maintaining a family.[40]

For Malthus, the evil consequences of the poor laws worked through the quantity of the population; for Spencer, the evil effects were mainly on the quality of the population.

Spencer applied this genetic argument also to "injudicious" private charity. Both public and careless private charity hindered the process of social adaptation, by which the individual acquired "the capacities needful for civilized life."[41] There is a close relationship between these "capacities" and the basic economic virtues of prudence, industriousness, and forethought which make for economic success. A type of charity that would promote these virtues would therefore help in the process of social adaptation. Spencer clarified that his arguments against charity do not apply to "that charity which may be described as helping men to help themselves."[42] He

---

[39] Herbert Spencer, *Social Statics* (London: Williams and Norgate, 1868), pp. 353–354.
[40] *Ibid.*, pp. 354–355.
[41] *Ibid.*, p. 355.   [42] *Ibid.*, p. 357.

was convinced that only private voluntary efforts could achieve this aim and that legal measures always had the opposite effect.[43] Voluntary benefactors, he argued, "will not carry such efforts so far as to impede their own multiplication, they will carry them far enough to mitigate the ill-fortunes of the workers without helping them to multiply."[44]

Spencer had a much greater impact on intellectual life in America than in England, his own country. Although many of his ideas have not withstood the test of time, they were powerfully attractive in the post-Civil War decades, since they offered a scientific rationale for policies already in practice.[45] His most forceful American disciple was William Graham Sumner, a Yale Professor of Political and Social Science, who combined the ideas of natural selectivity and struggle for survival of the fittest with classical economics and a mixture of Puritanism and American individualism. For Sumner, the social order was "fixed by laws of nature precisely analogous to those of the physical order. The most that men can do is by ignorance and self-conceit to mar the operation of social laws."[46] The impact of these laws varied with the state of society; the nature of man's struggle for existence can change, but the struggle itself was inescapable. With a sternness befitting a Puritan's view of the fallen angels, Sumner grimly observed that "Man is born under the necessity of sustaining the existence he has received by an onerous struggle against nature, both to win what is essential to his life and to ward off what is prejudicial to it."[47]

The mechanism of natural selection enabled those best adapted for survival to come out on top and left the unfit to succumb eventually in the struggle. Thus, declared Sumner, "The millionaires are a product of natural selection, acting on the whole body of men to pick out those who can meet the requirement of certain work to be done."[48] The "poor and the weak," on the other hand, included "the negligent, shiftless, inefficient, silly, and imprudent," as well as the "idle, intemperate, and vicious."[49] The process of natural selection was not something impersonal. Success and failure were

[43] For his views on the English poor laws, see his *The Man Versus the State* (1892) (Caldwell, Idaho: Caxton Printers, 1946), pp. 24 ff.

[44] *Political Institutions* (London: Williams and Norgate, 1885), pp. 610–611.

[45] Henry Ward Beecher wrote to Spencer in 1866: "The peculiar condition of American society has made your writing far more fruitful here than in Europe." Quoted in Hofstadter, *op. cit.,* p. 18.

[46] "The Challenge of Facts" in A. G. Keller and M. R. Davie, *Essays of William Graham Sumner* (New Haven: Yale University Press, 1934), Vol. II, p. 107.

[47] *Ibid.,* p. 87.

[48] "The Concentration of Wealth: Its Economic Justification" in *Essays of William Graham Sumner,* Vol. II, p. 172.

[49] *What Social Classes Owe to Each Other* (New York: Harper and Brothers, 1883), p. 21.

dependent on personal virtues which had to be cultivated by the individual.[50] In this regard he was very close to Malthus and, in fact, called Malthusianism the necessary condition for economic success.[51]

Nevertheless there was an important difference between Malthus and Sumner. Malthus, it will be recalled, was willing to let nature punish those who lacked self-control, but he also emphasized the need to educate the lower classes in self-dependence. He looked to the clergy and to religious sentiment as instruments in raising the sense of duty among the poor. With regard to teaching the lower classes standards of conduct, Malthus still subscribed to the old order of dependence and protection, as did most of the classical economists, even though they strongly believed in individual freedom. Sumner, on the other hand, rejected even this limited responsibility of the ruling toward the lower classes.

> In our modern state, and in the United States more than anywhere else, the social structure is based on contract. . . . In a state based on contract sentiment is out of place in any public or common affairs. It is relegated to the sphere of private and personal relations, where it depends not at all on class types, but on personal acquaintance and personal estimates. . . . A society based on contract is a society of free and independent men, who form ties without favor or obligation, and cooperate without cringing and intrigue. . . . It follows . . . that one man, in a free state, cannot claim help from, and cannot be charged to give help to, another.[52]

Even among economists who did not share the Social Darwinism of Spencer and Sumner, the dominance of laissez-faire views and an almost fundamentalist aversion to state interference precluded the acceptance of anything but the most minimal protective role of the state. Orthodox economic thinking in the post-Civil War decades considered as axiomatic the idea that poor laws were harmful and unacceptable unless they were of the most rigorous kind. In fact, this view was accepted by many who questioned the tenets of laissez-faire economics. Francis Amasa Walker, a leading economist, looked favorably on all kinds of protective legislation, including the regulation of the working hours of women and children, health legislation, and factory inspection but, on poor laws, he was orthodox: "The workhouse test for all the able-bodied poor, and genuine hard work, up to the limit of strength, are imperatively demanded by the interests of productive labor. Wherever there is a possible choice between self-support and public sup-

---

[50] It is not clear to what extent Sumner thought heredity and environment influenced individual behavior. In his "Parable" in *Essays of William Graham Sumner*, Vol. I, pp. 497–499, he depicts three brothers with equal life chances achieving greatly different degrees of success.

[51] *What Social Classes Owe to Each Other*, p. 74.

[52] *Ibid.*, pp. 24–27.

port, the inclination to labor for one's own subsistence should be quickened by something of a penalty upon the pauper condition . . ."[53] The experience of the English poor laws was usually referred to as the proof of the correctness of this harsh conclusion.

THE NEW POOR LAW AND ITS AFTERMATH IN ENGLAND

In England the debate over the right to relief marked not merely an ideological break with the past but culminated in a new legislation that governed the country's poor relief for the next three quarters of a century. During this period, the country became a mature industrial state, and forces were set in motion to reverse the narrow conception of the individual's right to social income protection. The principles of the Poor Law of 1834, however, had a remarkable staying power. Even after they were defeated, in the social security legislation of the turn of the century, their influence lingered on.

Although the major pressure for reform came from those who wanted relief from the higher poor rates, the task of reform as envisaged by the Poor Law Commission that was set up in 1832 was much broader. In effect, this task was to make the poor-relief system consistent with the economic and social principles of the emerging industrial society. This society emphasized contract instead of hereditary status, and its economic rewards were governed by a changeable market rather than by traditions and customs. That the Commission could conceive of its task in such broad terms was in no small part the result of the preceding years of public debate concerning the problem of provision for the poor. Select Committees of the House of Commons in 1817 and in 1824 had looked into the operations of the poor laws. They had been critical of the prevailing situation, but had failed to produce reforms that the government would support. The time, then, was not yet ripe for radical change, but public sentiment was moving in that direction. Malthus, who has been called the "father of the new poor law,"[54] did perhaps more than anyone else to prepare public opinion for a major readjustment such as the abolition of outdoor relief to the able-bodied poor. "Without the discussions raised by the *Essay on Population*," says Bonar, "it is very doubtful if public opinion would have been so far advanced in 1834 as to make a bill, drawn on such lines, at all likely to pass into law."[55] Thus, regardless of the scientific merits of his analysis, Malthus forged some of the most powerful intellectual weapons for changing the place of the poor in the social fabric. One of the men directly responsible for

[53] Francis A. Walker, *Political Economy* (New York: Henry Holt and Company, 1888), p. 363.
[54] James Bonar, *Malthus and His Work* (London: MacMillan and Co., 1885), p. 304.
[55] *Ibid.*, p. 317.

bringing the logic of political economy to bear on the formulation of the new poor law was Nassau Senior, a member of the Poor Law Commission. He was, according to his biographer, "the chief analytical force of the Commission, and he carried it beyond a mere government inquiry into administration into the sphere of social economics."[56] Another political economist who became an influential member of the Commission was Edwin Chadwick, a disciple of Bentham.

Chadwick's major role in the preparation of the new poor law was in the formulation of its central principle—the principle of "less eligibility."[57] This famous principle, as the Poor Law Commission explained it, was that an individual should be given relief only on condition "that his situation on the whole shall not be made really or apparently so eligible as the situation of the independent labourer of the lowest class."[58] The significance of this principle, as Finer points out,[59] was that it made it theoretically possible to reconcile relief to able-bodied workers with the development of a free labor market and a spirit of industriousness, foresight, and independence among the workers. It was a new approach to manpower policy which, if "adequately enforced," made relief not only "safe" but "even beneficial."[60] Above all, it reflected the commercial values of the new market civilization.

With the aid of a staff, and mainly in the second half of 1832, the Commissioners rather hastily gathered an enormous amount of detailed data on the operations of the poor laws in various parts of the country. The preliminary digest of their findings[61] (published in 1833) is remarkable for its skilful mingling of facts and conclusions, which was designed to show that the system was wholly bad. If there was a single situation in which the poor laws had a beneficial effect, it cannot be easily found in the *Extract*. But the evils, together with cause and effect, can be readily spotted. This can be illustrated by looking under the heading "Allowance," where we find, with numerous page references, such typical index entries as: "Invariably demoralizes the labourers," "Destroys the ratio between wages and work," "Increase of, has diminished inclination to emigrate," "Induces the labourer to refuse allotments of land," "Induces extravagant habits on the part of labourers, mechanics, and weavers," "Has destroyed the veracity, industry, frugality, and domestic virtues of the labourer," "Makes labourers

[56] Bowley, *op. cit.*, p. 286.
[57] S. E. Finer, *The Life and Times of Sir Edwin Chadwick* (London: Methuen and Company, (1952), p. 74.
[58] *Report from His Majesty's Commissioners for Inquiring into the Administration and Practical Operation of the Poor Laws* (London, 1834), p. 228.
[59] Finer, *op. cit.*, p. 45.
[60] *Report . . . of the Poor Laws*, p. 227.
[61] Entitled *Extract from the Information Received by His Majesty's Commissioners as to the Administration and operation of the Poor-Laws* (1833).

possessing small property desirous of dissipating it," "Induces men to desert wives and children," "After ruining capitalist, re-acts upon labourer, in leaving him destitute."[62] This revealing catalogue of the contents of the preliminary report could be duplicated for other aspects of the relief system. It indicates, for instance, that there have been a number of instances where the allowance was discontinued, which did not cause distress, but actually improved the moral character of the laborers.[63]

The famous 1834 *Report* of the Poor Law Commissioners contains essentially the same diagnosis and suggests the same remedies as the ones presented in the *Extract,* with perhaps an even more concentrated emphasis on the allowance system as the chief culprit. The emphasis on the allowance system and its disastrous consequences helped to establish the conclusion that the fundamental problem was pauperism, not poverty. The immediate cause of economic distress was simply the lack of prudence, forethought, and industry among the pauperized sections of the laboring class. But these character deficiencies were not necessarily inherent in the working class, nor were they the result of the existing economic and social system; they were caused by the poor laws and, especially, by the allowance system. To blame bad laws and bad administration for such a profound impact on human behavior is reminiscent of the mercantilist attitude toward the role of legislation, but now, of course, the belief in the potentialities of legislative action was inspired by Bentham. Although they believed that bad laws created this kind of mischief, the poor law reformers also were convinced that proper laws created immense benefits. Their recommendations for remedial measures were as uncomplicated as their diagnosis of the problem.

The section of the 1834 *Report* that deals with remedial measures begins with an important statement regarding the purpose of public relief: it should be concerned only with relief of *indigence,* "the state of a person unable to labour, or unable to obtain, in return for his labour, the means of subsistence." Public provision "should not extend to the relief of poverty; that is, the state of one, who in order to obtain a mere subsistence, is forced to have recourse to labour."[64] In the minds of men like Senior and Chadwick, this was a clear-cut statement of the state's responsibility for the individual; the state was not going to let an able-bodied man die for lack of food or shelter *if* he tried to help himself, but as long as he was able to eke out a mere subsistence, he was not entitled to relief. Although this may sound like a harsh formulation of the rights of the poor, it was more generous than the position taken by Malthus which, it will be recalled, was that the poor man had no right whatsoever to public relief. It should be emphasized, however,

---

[62]*Ibid.,* pp. viii–ix.
[63]Where evidence is introduced to support this claim, it is usually of a very flimsy kind.
[64]Poor Law *Report,* p. 227.

that the limited economic "right" of the destitute, which is implicit in the *Report,* was not based on any abstract rights of the individual or the citizen but was conceived in strictly utilitarian terms. The poor were entitled to this support simply because it was thought to be conducive to the greatest happiness for the greatest number. The basic difference between Malthus, on the one hand, and Senior and Chadwick, on the other hand, was in their interpretation of human behavior and in the possibility of reforming it. Although he wrote about moral restraint and preached the virtues of fore-sight Malthus, in the end, had little hope that the majority of the poor would manage to control the drive between the sexes which condemned them to destitution. For Senior and Chadwick and the Poor Law Commission, reform of the character of the poor was a relatively simple, almost mechanical, matter. It was primarily a matter of enacting two basic principles that would eliminate most evils and would make the poor laws consistent with the requirements of the rising industrial order.

The all-important principle of less eligibility was expected to define automatically an amount of relief that would be no more than mere sub-sistence. This was consistent with the objective of relief and avoided the drawback of making it attractive. The companion principle of the workhouse test was to make sure, also quite automatically, that even this minimal relief would go only to those who needed it and were willing to earn it. The Commission wanted to declare unlawful, with minor exceptions, "all relief whatever to able-bodied persons or their families, otherwise than in well-regulated workhouses." [65] It argued that this principle "would be a self-acting test of the claim of the applicant. . . . If the claimant does not comply with the terms on which relief is given to the destitute, he gets nothing; and if he does comply, the compliance proves the truth of his claim—namely, his destitution." [66] Thus, at least in theory, every man was free to work or not to work; there was no legal duty to work, but no able-bodied man was sup-ported without work. For the "redundant" agricultural laborer or the technologically displaced handloom weaver who did not want to starve to death, the choice was essentially one between the discipline of the factory or that of the workhouse. The Commission's recommendations, therefore, tended to reinforce the free labor market. The insistence that relief to able-bodied individuals be given only in a "well-regulated workhouse" also tended to strengthen the industrial system of authority. It did this in a direct way by cutting off the retreat of the worker to the village relief roll, and in an indirect way, as Bendix argues, by giving "added justification to the manu-facturers' exercise of iron discipline in their enterprises." [67]

[65]*Ibid.,* p. 262.
[66]*Ibid.,* p. 264.
[67] *Work and Authority in Industry,* p. 99.

The Poor Law Amendment Act of 1834 put the principle of "less eligibility" into effect and created a new administrative structure. From the beginning, there were problems with the enforcement of this principle, especially in the industrial north. As time went on, its shortcomings became more obvious. The fundamental source of difficulty stemmed from the ideas about poor people and about the causes of poverty that were held by the poor law authors. Only if pauperism, in fact, had been primarily the result of the defects of the old poor law could the removal of these defects have the far-reaching effects on the workers that were anticipated. But the problem of pauperism was closely interrelated with the economic and social dislocations that accompanied the rapid transformation from an agrarian to an industrial society. The structural underemployment in agriculture, the technological unemployment among the handloom weavers, the cyclical fluctuations in income that hit with unaccustomed severity, the uncertainties of the changing environment, these matters were not ones that could be swept away by less eligibility and the workhouse test. But they were sources of individual discouragement, of family hardship, of social alienation and, therefore, of pauperism. Other important sources of destitution that were systematically ignored through the reformers' stress on character deficiency induced by the allowance system were disease, crowded and squalid living quarters, unsanitary working conditions, dangerous working conditions (especially in the ever-deepening coal mines), unduly long working hours, and the lack of adequate educational and recreational facilities. The "low and grovelling mode of living"[68] that the population of the new towns was enduring day after day was not propitious for the development of the virtues of forethought, industriousness, and sobriety that the authors of the poor law *Report* were hoping for.

To be sure, the poor law authorities were not unaware of these conditions and of their effects on the working population.[69] Yet, the reformers of 1834 were not about to let these complexities stand in the way of a clear-cut break with the past, hard as that might be on the poor. The awareness of the environmental causes of pauperism and of the potentials of education seemed to have strengthened rather than weakened the Commissioners' conviction that the principles of 1834 were an essential first step. Chadwick was not only the main champion of these principles but also was ardently interested in education, sanitation, and accident prevention as a means to prevent pauperism. He played a leading role in promoting investigations to show the links between squalid living conditions and disease and between disease and poverty. In an 1838 memorandum entitled *Instructions for Entering the Causes of Pauperism,* he lists among the possible causes of pauperism the

[68] See J. L. and B. Hammond, *The Bleak Age* (Penguin Books, 1947), p. 52.
[69] See *Report* (1834), p. 363.

defective upbringing of orphans in mixed workhouses, disease, accidents, lunacy, idiocy, drunkenness, and crime.[70] The annual reports of the Poor Law Commissioners set up under the act of 1834, also helped to indicate these relationships.[71] Other public investigations into working conditions in factories and mines and Chadwick's own famous *Report on the Sanitary Conditions of the Labouring Population* revealed that the situation in which the masses of workers found themselves was conducive to neither health nor sobriety. But these revelations did not lead to the rejection of the principles of 1834, even though these principles had gained their authority, at least in part, by attributing pauperism to character deficiency. However, the revelations did spur measures for the protection of the helpless, of children and women, and for sanitation and accident prevention.

Measures of this kind, even when prescribed by law, were not inevitably in conflict with the free market; they were viewed by many as necessary for the proper functioning of a free market system. The basic attitude of the nineteenth century was that, in the long run, pauperism as a social problem would disappear, but for that to happen the principles of the new poor law had to be enforced. This assumption explains, in part, the longevity of these principles and the willingness to enforce them in spite of obvious hardships. As long as individualism and faith in the free market were dominant social values, the stress remained on character deficiency as the main source of poverty, and the remedy for this deficiency continued to be less eligibility and the workhouse test.

When the first steps were taken toward modern social protection in the 1890s, the liberal critics raised their voice. A case in point was compulsory insurance against industrial accidents. Although the amount of protection provided was very limited, liberal critics denounced it as a violation of individual freedom and responsibility.

English courts held that the employer was not liable where accidents involved the negligence of fellow workmen. Under this doctrine of common employment, it was very difficult for an injured worker to collect damages; it was argued that he was aware, or ought to be, of the risks connected with the job and that he assumed these risks voluntarily on accepting employment. He was free, in theory, to bargain with the employer for higher wages as compensation for the hazards to which he was exposed. The Workmen's Compensation Act of 1897 restricted this contractual freedom and imposed compulsory protection in the form of insurance. In a lecture delivered at Harvard the following year the noted English jurist, Albert V. Dicey, pronounced the liberal verdict against the Act. "This legislation,"

---

[70] Cited in Finer, *op. cit.*, pp. 147–148.
[71] See, for instance, the discussion on sanitation in the *Fourth Annual Report of the Poor Law Commissioners for England and Wales* (London, 1838), pp. 103–150.

he said, "bears all the marked characteristics of collectivism. Workmen are protected against the risks of their employment, not by their own care or foresight, or by contracts made with their employers, but by a system of insurance imposed by law upon employers of labour. The contractual capacity both of workmen and masters is cut down. The rights of the workmen in regard to compensation for accidents have become a matter not of contract, but of status."[72]

By then, however, these rigid liberal views were strongly on the defensive. Several factors were involved in the mounting criticism of the existing order. One was the growing strength of organized labor, especially through the organization, from the 1880s onward, of the less privileged, unskilled laborers. The 1880s were a turning point in labor history, marked by the beginning of a new working class militancy. The working class was gaining significantly in political power, both through the extension of the franchise in 1885 and through the organization of the Labor party in the 1890s. This democratization of power inevitably challenged the commercial conception of the rights of the poor embodied in the 1834 law and influenced the debate concerning social protection that again was coming into the forefront at the end of the century.

Another factor that should be pointed out was the change in attitude among certain segments of the middle and upper classes. In England, Dicey observed, "The rich have but feebly resisted, even if they have not furthered, collectivist legislation."[73] Pareto made similar but more sweeping observations on the political behavior of the upper classes. "The weakening of all spirit of resistance among the upper classes, and even more, the persistent efforts they make to accelerate their own ruin without being aware of it, is one of the most interesting phenomena of our time."[74] His somewhat questionable interpretation of this behavior was that democracy and increasing wealth had given rise to a general sense of morbid pity for the less fortunate, and that the *bourgeoisie* had become degenerate and, consequently had lost the courage to defend itself.[75] A different interpretation was given by Beatrice Webb, who observed that among Englishmen of intellect and property there was a growing "collective consciousness of sin."[76] Men and women who had been reared in riches had become disenchanted with an industrial society that had provided great wealth for a few but had disinherited the masses. They found grave social dangers in such an inequitable situation.

---

[72]A. V. Dicey, *Law and Public Opinion in England* (second edition reprinted, London; MacMillan and Co., 1952), pp. 283–284.

[73]*Op. cit.*, p. 219.

[74]Vilfredo Pareto, *Les systèmes socialistes* (Paris: Giard et Brière, 1902), Vol. I, p. 73.

[75]See his *Manuel d'économie politique* (Paris: Giard et Brière, 1909), pp. 102, 496.

[76]Beatrice Webb, *My Apprenticeship* (London: Longmans, Green, and Co., 1926), pp. 154 ff.

Obviously this kind of attitude among the ruling groups of a society could be of enormous importance for the development of social protection.

A factor that powerfully helped to promote the change in attitudes was the shocking revelation of widespread destitution in the midst of unprecedented national wealth. A sensational pamphlet, *The Bitter Cry of Outcast London,* which appeared in 1883, was a jolt to the Victorian conscience.[77] It accelerated a growing agitation over the problem of poverty. Some middle class reformers sought to alleviate the plight of the poor through personal involvement in the settlement house movement, founded by Canon Samuel A. Barnett; others saw the solution in the fundamental economic and social reforms proposed by the Fabian Society. But until almost the end of the century, as Professor Gilbert points out, the Charity Organization Society was the most influential determinant of middle class opinion about the poor.[78] The C.O.S. represented the main effort of the free market society to solve the problem of poverty without government intervention. Through the systematic coordination of all private charities, it attempted to make the most of private voluntary efforts. But the poor "who were beyond the societies' resources to help, however worthy they might be, or however piteous their case, were consigned to the poor law relief, which the society hoped to see again as unbendingly austere as the 1834 Poor Law Commission intended it should be."[79]

The methodical approach to the problems of the poor represented by the work of the C.O.S. was bound to reveal one point that the sensationalism of *The Bitter Cry* had obscured: the fact that the size of the problem of destitution was of a magnitude that private efforts could not hope to cope with. If there was any doubt left in this regard, it was dispelled by the massively documented studies of Charles Booth and Seebohm Rowntree.[80] It had to be recognized that the old poor law and private efforts were inadequate. After three quarters of a century of widespread acceptance of the idea that poverty as a social problem was bound to disappear as the country's wealth increased, the Poor Law Commission of 1905 to 1909 had to concede the opposite. "It is very unpleasant to record that, notwithstanding our assumed moral and material progress, and notwithstanding the enormous annual expenditure, amounting to nearly sixty millions a year, upon poor relief, education, and health, we still have a vast army of persons

[77] For a discussion of its impact, see Bentley B. Gilbert, *The Evolution of National Insurance in Great Britain* (London: Michael Joseph, 1966), pp. 28 ff.

[78] *Ibid.,* p. 51.

[79] *Ibid.,* p. 51.

[80] Charles Booth's *Life and Labour of the People of London* took seventeen years to complete and ran seventeen volumes. For a brief discussion of Booth and Rowntree, see M. Bruce, *The Coming of the Welfare State* (London: B. T. Batsfor, 1961), pp. 143–146.

quartered upon us unable to support themselves and an army which in numbers has recently shown signs of increase rather than decrease."[81] It had become evident also that the problem was not simply one of character defect. The findings of the Commission left no doubt that there were many causes of poverty and that often they were closely interrelated with various structural and operational features of the industrial system.[82] Nevertheless, the majority of the Commissioners, although recommending the transformation of poor relief into more modern public assistance and supporting the concept of state unemployment insurance, still looked to charity and private voluntary action as the first line of defense against poverty.

In spite of the lingering resistance to social protection, the time was past when the social rights of the British citizen could be measured by the workhouse test. There was a widespread revulsion against the principles of 1834. The old-fashioned liberalism was giving way to the New Liberalism of David Lloyd-George and Winston Churchill. For Churchill, "the cause of Liberalism . . . [was] the cause of the left-out millions."[83] Among the Conservatives also, there was support for old-age pensions. The Unionist leader Joseph Chamberlain, was one of the early advocates of old-age pensions. Paradoxically, the largest organized opposition to pensions came from the friendly societies, that symbol of working class self-help and self-respect.[84] Part of their concern was a fear of government competition for the pennies of the workingman.

The first major break with the principles of 1834 was the Old Age Pension Act of 1908. It provided for pensions to be paid on the simple conditions that the person was old and in reduced circumstances, without any previous contribution required of the beneficiacy. "Non-contributory pensions", writes Gilbert, "were regarded as a wildly extravagant piece of class law making."[85] The crucial point, of course, was that the pensions were paid as a matter of social right, without subjecting the recipient to the hated means test and without lecturing him on how to behave in order to be worthy of support. By making the pensions noncontributory, it was possible to rescue many aged from the threat of the poor law treatment. The central idea was to provide a basic income that was free from the taint of the despised poor law. In this sense, revulsion against the old poor laws helped to shape the new social rights of the British citizen.[86] British social protection

[81]*Report of the Royal Commission on the Poor Laws* (London: H.M. Stationery Office, 1909), Vol. I, p. 78.
[82]*Ibid.*, Vol. I, Part IV, Chapter X and Part VI, Chapters I and II.
[83]Bruce, *op. cit.*, p. 148.
[84]See Gilbert, *op. cit.*, pp. 165 ff.
[85]*Ibid.*, p. 159.
[86]See E. M. Burns in W. G. Bowen *et. al.*, *The American System of Social Insurance* (New York: McGraw-Hill, 1968), p. 233.

was inaugurated on the basis of minimal but equal benefits for all, a characteristic that it kept until recent times.

In the sense that it was trying to remedy the shortcomings of poor relief, the 1908 Act was still looking backward. It was concerned with a group that was mostly poor and unable to work. The National Insurance Act of 1911, on the other hand, was cast in a rather different mold. It provided health and unemployment insurance mainly for those who were still actively in the work force and who normally were self-supporting. The motivation behind this form of protection had much less to do with philanthropy than the motivation behind old-age protection. One of its chief concerns was national efficiency. The leaders of the New Liberalism understood the relationships between ill health, unemployment, national economic strength, and national defense. Recruitment for the Boer War had revealed a shockingly large number of young men unfit for military service. David Lloyd-George went to Germany to observe firsthand the effects of health protection on national vitality and efficiency. It became increasingly clear that a national minimum of protection was not merely essential as a basic social right but also was a factor in the conservation of the scarce human resources demanded by modern industry.

In the decade preceding World War I, the principles and policies of the old poor laws were thus finally overcome. Some of the liberal ideals nevertheless persisted in the organization of health and unemployment insurance. Both programs were made contributory, on the argument that this provision would help preserve a sense of individual responsibility among the workers. The Socialists wanted all programs to be noncontributory—financed entirely by the state and the employers. In both programs, cash benefits and contributions were set at a flat amount, consistent with the idea of a national minimum and the country's egalitarian conception of social rights.

LIBERALISM AND PROTECTIONISM IN FRANCE

In France the struggle for the establishment of social security rights followed a different course, reflecting the country's own historical peculiarities. The liberal policy of nonprotection was seriously challenged by the social policies of the Second Republic and the Second Empire.[87] In fact, the views of Napoleon III anticipated the arguments of Bismarck for the establishment of a system of social protection. Both strongly favored the protection of the

---

[87] See E. Labrousse, *Le mouvement ouvrier et les idées sociales en France* (Paris: Tournier et Constans, 1949); G. Duveau, *La vie ouvrière en France sous le Second Empire* (Paris: Gallimard, 1946); also E. Levasseur, *Histoire des classes ouvrières et de l'industrie en France de 1789 à 1870* (second edition, Paris, 1904), Vol. II.

working masses for the purpose of securing their loyalty to the state. Yet, in-steady of setting precedents, France lagged behind other industrial countries in the development of social rights.

The reasons for this paradoxical situation are deeply embedded in the socio economic and political system of the Third Republic.[88] A relatively slow rate of industrial transformation during the nineteenth century had produced, by the end of the century, an in-between economy in which neither the industrial nor the agrarian sector was dominant or rapidly be-coming so. Society was divided into interest groups that disagreed funda-mentally in many areas but tended to balance each other. The political struc-ture was equally fragmented and revealed a great ideological heterogeneity, even among those who considered themselves socialists of one kind or another. This situation was compatible with the preservation of the status quo amid fierce ideological struggles. None of the interest groups were able to gain effective control of the state and all benefited from limiting its power, which was to a significant extent in the hands of an efficient bureau-cracy. In this political system the responsiveness of the government to the wishes of the electorate was bound to be weak and to yield often a higher ideological than legislative output. Ideological conflicts sometimes made it difficult to achieve practical solutions even in matters where there was sub-stantial agreement in principle.

By the end of the nineteenth century there was general agreement among the political groups that the state had to protect the individual against economic insecurity. This general agreement on an objective, however, was not easily translated into an agreement on the means to achieve it. It found its expression in a wild political competition of alternative proposals within the legislature. Between 1889 and 1906 no less than 46 old-age pension proposals were advanced in the *Chambre des Députés*.[89] In 1903 the Chamber finally adopted a limited contributory old-age social insurance scheme by an overwhelming vote of 501 to 5,[90] but a law embodying such a scheme for workers and peasants was not enacted until 1910. In the mean-time, however, pension laws had been enacted for railroad workers (1890) and coal miners (1894); in both instances, the pensions applied to industries that had a tradition of state intervention. The first workmen's compen-sation act was passed in 1898, after a twenty year debate, and in 1905 an old-age assistance (noncontributory) law was enacted.

France, of course, was not unique with respect to the controversial issues

[88] See the suggestive interpretation in S. Hoffmann, *In Search of France* (Cambridge: Harvard University Press, 1963), pp. 3 ff.
[89] E. Levasseur, *Histoires des classes ouvrières et industrielles en France sous la Troisième République* (Paris: Arthur Rousseau, 1907), p. 507.
[90] *Ibid.*, p. 508.

raised by social security legislation, but it was more difficult in France than elsewhere to achieve a consensus on practical solutions. The consequences of this are indicated in the Pension Law of 1910 and in the debate preceding it. The debate involved the usual issues of the responsibilities of the state versus those of the individual. The liberals in the legislature wanted minimum benefit levels financed in part by the individual, whereas the socialists insisted on very generous benefits to be paid for entirely by the state and the employer. In their speeches the socialists argued in terms of the fundamental right of the individual to a guarantee of subsistence by the State and reminded their listeners that this was one of the rights of the citizen proclaimed in 1793. Their arguments were strikingly close to the ones advanced in the late eighteenth century for the same purpose. The trade unions took the same attitude. The *Confédération Générale du Travail* violently denounced the idea of a contribution by the worker and declared that pensions were solely the responsibility of the employers and the state. Business interests, on the other hand, rejected social insurance altogether because it was compulsory. Their objection to compulsion was supported with the argument that foresight was a moral issue and, therefore, must remain in the realm of individual freedom.[91] The Pension Law of 1910, which was the outcome of this prolonged debate, was typically enough a self-defeating compromise. The socialists went along with the contributory provision, considering the law as merely a first step toward their objective. The liberals probably accepted compulsion because they realized that there were no teeth in the law. Indeed, it soon developed that this law could not be enforced because the courts found that neither the worker nor the employer could be forced to pay the contribution.[92] Consequently, French social insurance, had to wait until a new law was enacted in 1928, and it did not gain major significance until 1945.

THE STRUGGLE WITH THE LIBERAL LEGACY IN THE UNITED STATES

In the United States the commitment to individualism—to individual achievement and self-help—was much stronger than either in England or in France. The survival of the liberal tradition, therefore, was found to be stronger and the resistance to social protection more tenacious. The vogue of Spencer and Sumner was an obstacle to an intellectual shift in favor of the poor man. By the end of the nineteenth century, the social workers gathering at the annual Conference of Charities and Corrections still

[91] E. Levasseur, p. 508.
[92] See A. Rouast and P. Durand, *Sécurité Sociale* (Paris: Dalloz, 1960), p. 10.

generally shared the attitude that the able-bodied pauper should be offered relief only "under strict rules inside an institution."[93] As far as public policy was concerned, the almshouse was still the "fundamental institution in American poor relief."[94] In the area of voluntary efforts, the charity-organization-society approach had been imported from England, with the same objective of helping the "worthy" poor and bringing the "unworthy" to their deserved punishment.[95] Although a few critical voices were heard on behalf of the rights of the poor,[96] the accepted view was still that poverty was primarily a matter of character deficiency and had to be dealt with on a strictly individual basis.[97] The social plague of the slums had been exposed,[98] but it neither shocked the national conscience nor did it establish the role of the environment as a fundamental cause of pauperism.

By the turn of the century, the idea that the poor man had a claim to a share in the national income other than the market value of his labor was still utterly foreign. There was neither a strong socialist movement nor a tradition of Tory democracy to give stature to such an idea. If the American citizen was to gain the social rights that were being granted in Europe, a means had to be found to legitimize these rights within the context of an individualistic society. Forces working in this direction were gathering, but success was slow to come.

The deep transformation of American society under the impact of rapid industrialization in the late nineteenth and early twentieth centuries created the necessity for major readjustments in the relationship between the individual and the state. The emergence of a national market, brought forth by a national system of transportation, the development of large-scale industry, and a technology of mass production, gave rise to concentrations of economic power and control that were singularly incongruous with the spirit of frontier individualism. Big business and financial manipulators became convenient but misleading targets for those who suffered from the strains of rapid economic change. Those at the bottom of the economic ladder remained voiceless for all practical purposes, but there were other, more vocal, groups who managed to create an atmosphere of reform.

It was in the presidential campaign of 1912 that the "Quest for Social

[93] Frank J. Bruno, *Trends in Social Work 1874–1956* (New York: Columbia University Press, 1957), p. 27.

[94] *Ibid.*, p. 74.

[95] See Frank D. Watson, *The Charity Organization Movement in the United States* (New York: MacMillan, 1922), *passim.*

[96] See, for instance, R. H. Bremner, *From the Depths* (New York: New York University Press, 1956), Chapters IV and V.

[97] Kathleen Woodroofe, *From Charity to Social Work* (London: Routledge and Kegan Paul, 1962), pp. 90 ff.

[98] See, for instance, Jacob A. Riis, *How the Other Half Lives* (New York: Charles Scribner, 1900).

Justice," to use professor Faulkner's term,[99] reached a national climax, at least, in terms of alternative formulations of individual social rights. All political parties sensed the need for a reformulation of the relationship between the individual and the state. American socialists followed their European comrades in insisting on the duty of the state to guarantee the economic security of the individual at social expense, but they had similar mixed feelings about remedial legislation short of fundamental social change.[100] Of greater significance was the "New Nationalism" of Theodore Roosevelt and his Progressive party; their platform called not merely for workmen's compensation but for the "protection of home life against the hazards of sickness, irregular employment and old age through adoption of a system of social insurance adapted to American use."[101] Inspired by the writings of Herbert Croly, Roosevelt formulated a nationalistic rationale for the protection of the individual that paralleled the one of Lloyd-George and Winston Churchill.[102] As early as 1901, Roosevelt had written in McClure's Magazine: "It is impossible to have a high standard of political life in a community sunk in sodden misery and ignorance."[103] This theme was prominent in his 1912 campaign.[104] His 1912 platform echoed the conservation theme of the Progressive Movement by calling for "the conservation of human resources through an enlightened measure of social and industrial justice."[105]

The country, in 1912, was not yet prepared to follow Roosevelt's lead. It preferred instead Woodrow Wilson's concept of the "New Freedom," which was based on faith in the competitive system but not on laissez-faire. In his campaign speeches Wilson never failed to stress the difference between his and Roosevelt's conceptions of how to protect the economic welfare of the citizen. He attacked Roosevelt's social program as an attempt to "set up guardians" over the people in order "to take care of them by a process of tutelage and supervision in which they play no active part."[106] This approach, he warned, would leave the individual at the mercy of

[99] Harold U. Faulkner, *The Quest for Social Justice 1898–1914* (New York: MacMillan, 1931).
[100] See their 1904 and 1912 platforms in Kirk H. Porter and Donald B. Johnson (eds.), *National Party Platforms* (Urbana: University of Illinois, 1956), pp. 189–190.
[101] *Ibid.*, p. 177.
[102] Croly's basic argument was that the masses had lost out in the race for America's promise and that this threatened the realization of America's dream. See his *The Promise of American Life* (Cambridge: Belknap Press of Harvard Press 1965). For an interpretation of Croly's influence on Roosevelt, see George E. Mowry, *Theodore Roosevelt and the Progressive Movement* (Madison: University of Wisconsin Press, 1946), pp. 146–147.
[103] See *The Works of Theodore Roosevelt* (National edition, New York: Charles Scribner, 1926), Vol. XIII, p. 262.
[104] See, for instance, *ibid.*, p. 17.
[105] Porter and Johnson, *op. cit.*, p. 177.
[106] *A Crossroads of Freedom* (J. W. Davidson (ed.), New Haven: Yale University Press, 1956), p. 237.

government: "The minute you are taken care of by the government you are wards, not independent men."[107] To this he added the strictly partisan argument that the very same people who wished to bestow this false benevolence upon the worker were also seeking to legalize monopolies instead of abolishing them. And "once the government regulates monopoly, then monopoly will have to see that it regulates the government."[108] The worker would consequently be left dependent on those who had previously robbed him of his capacity for self-help. "After all this is done, who is to guarantee to us that the government is to be pitiful, that the government is to be righteous, that the government is to be just?"[109]

This line of reasoning left little room for alternative solutions to the problem of protection. "I don't want a smug lot of experts to sit down behind closed doors in Washington and play Providence to me," said Wilson.[110] "I am one of those who absolutely reject the trustee theory, the guardianship theory. I have never found a man who knew how to take care of me."[111] This kind of partisan distortion of the crucial question of social protection relied for its success on the deeply embedded values of self-help and individual achievement. Wilson, no doubt, was correct in his instinct that most Americans favored his "program of liberty" over Roosevelt's "program of regulation." He told his audiences that they wanted justice, not benevolence; that workers did not want any special privilege, except liberty, which knew no privilege. "America stands for opportunity. America stands for a free field and no favor."[112] Opportunity is the wellspring of American prosperity, whereas "benevolence never developed a man or a nation."[113]

The 1912 political campaign has been used here as a convenient benchmark for gauging the movement toward social protection in the United States. There is no question that by then the ideology of laissez-faire had lost out and some aspects of the welfare state were accepted by all political parties.[114] The victory of Wilson over Roosevelt, however, indicated that the country was not yet prepared to go beyond a compromise with the liberal tradition. The acceptable level of protection was still far from a guarantee of a basic minimum of existence, or even a systematic alleviation of economic

---

[107] *Ibid.*, p. 78.

[108] *Ibid.*, p. 77.

[109] *Ibid.*, p. 78.

[110] W. Wilson, *The New Freedom* (Garden City and New York: Doubleday Page, 1916), p. 60.

[111] *Ibid.*, p. 61.

[112] *Ibid.*, p. 221.

[113] *A Crossroads of Freedom*, p. 294.

[114] The Republican party platform called for public health legislation, the legal limitation of the labor of women and children, and "generous and comprehensive workman's compensation laws." See Porter and Johnson, *op. cit.*, p. 183.

hardship. Its principle aim was the restoration and maintenance of conditions that were compatible with individual self-help. The doctrine that every individual could look out for himself was only partly altered—to the extent that it was made contingent on the maintenance of the freedom and capacity to compete. In the long run this proved to be an important and elastic concession but, for the time being, it received a fairly narrow interpretation.

Although laissez-faire was on the defensive, the social insurance movement could not get ahead without an intellectualization of its means and ends. The connection between social insurance and the broader aims of society had to be worked out. It became necessary, in other words, to formulate a social insurance ideology relevant for American conditions. One of the early contributors to this intellectual reformulation was Professor Henry Seager of Columbia University.[115] Seager tried to show that the need for social insurance is inherent in industrial society, regardless of a country's political organization. He did not limit himself to noting the empirical facts about the workers' need for protection but developed a sociological argument to show that this need was a consequence of industrialization, and that reliance on individualistic self-help was no longer a realistic solution. His argument rested on the transformation of the habits of thrift of the farmer and craftsman as they become permanent industrial wage-workers. Seager's conclusion was inescapable; the spirit of individualistic self-help was appropriate for an agrarian society, but an industrial society needed cooperative action "impelled when necessary by the compulsory authority of the state."[116] He called for a "program of social reform," the purpose of which was to "raise the whole mass of wage earners to higher standards of efficiency and earnings and to more intelligent appreciation of all of life's possibilities."[117] This statement embraced the central themes of the rising social insurance movement, which sought to combine the aspirations for social betterment of the Progressive era with the contemporary drives for conservation, efficiency, and cooperation. It should be recalled that during this era the idea of cooperation, instead of unrestricted competition, gained wide acceptance in American industry while, also, scientific management promised a new age of industrial efficiency.

It is only in recent years that the significance of investment in human capital during industrialization has been fully recognized. For the early advocates of social insurance in America, however, social insurance was a major step toward the conservation and increased efficiency of human resources. By stressing these aspects of social insurance, its advocates de-

---

[115] Henry R. Seager, *Social Insurance* (New York: MacMillan, 1910).
[116] *Ibid.*, p. 150.
[117] *Ibid.*, p. 150.

veloped a justification for a social protection that appealed to American values and was free from the close association of protection with dependence.

Thus it is not surprising to find the efficiency theme and the appeal to enlightened employer self-interest to be major features of the emerging ideology of American social insurance. Nor is it surprising that social insurance made most rapid progress where employer gains were most readily demonstrated. This was in the area of workmen's compensation. John R. Commons, one of the leaders in the workmen's compensation movement, was a master in the appeal to employer self-interest for the sake of social causes. Referring to his Wisconsin experience, he explained that employers were shown that they could make more profit by coming under the state's industrial accidents law. "It was shown that, by preventing accidents, nobody, not even the consumers by higher prices, would bear any burden in paying the benefits to workmen stipulated in the compensation laws. In other words, appeal was made to a new kind of 'efficiency,' efficiency in preventing accidents, by which costs of production could be reduced, with the result that prices need not be increased." [118] The appeal was to self-interest, not to paternalism or social solidarity.

Behind the movement for industrial safety was the momentum of the conservation movement, which got under way after the turn of the century. This was an important indication of maturing industrialism in America, especially since conservation was extended to include human resources. The growing awareness of the significance of the conservation of human resources naturally worked in favor not only of workmen's compensation but social insurance generally and health insurance in particular. Although the economic significance of health has only recently attracted serious attention from economists, a keen student, Irving Fisher, was already concerned with the problem at the turn of the century. His findings became part of the Report of the National Conservation Commission. [119] In this report, Fisher linked the promotion of health, or what he called national vitality, to the productive efficiency of the country. In his view, the preventable economic waste due to premature death and preventable illness was enormous. He estimated that the annual preventable loss from death and illness was at least $1.5 billion, [120] which represented approximately five percent of national income in 1910.

It was not long before it was realized that widespread health insurance could become an important means for the improvement of the nation's

[118]John R. Commons, *Institutional Economics* (Madison: University of Wisconsin Press, 1959), Vol. II, p. 857.
[119]Fisher's contribution was also published separately. See Irving Fisher, *National Vitality, Its Wastes and Conservation* (Washington, D.C.: Government Printing Office, 1910).
[120]*Ibid.*, p. 634.

health, just as workmen's compensation laws became an inducement to improve industrial safety. The leadership of the social insurance movement was taken over by the American Association for Labor Legislation, an organization made up of academicians, prominent social workers, and labor and civic leaders.[121] In 1913 the association organized the first American conference on social insurance. One of the basic themes of this conference was the conservation of human resources. The case for sickness insurance under social security was presented by I. M. Rubinow.

Rubinow made a strong case for compulsory health insurance on the basis of the economic waste of ill-health to the nation, the inability of workers to pay for adequate care or insurance on their own, and the lag of America behind Europe in this area of social action.[122] He reminded his listeners that a committee of experts had estimated that the annual loss to American producers through disease was "equal to nearly eight hundred millions of dollars."[123] His own computations, using European rates of sickness incidence, showed that America lost annually 200 million man-days of productive work on account of illness. Rubinow discarded voluntary efforts and commercial insurance as being inadequate for the task and unsuitable for an objective of overriding national significance. For it was not merely the interest and welfare of the individual that was at stake but the collective interest and public welfare of the entire nation. This required a collective rather than an individualistic solution. Although the cost of the proposed insurance scheme was high, Rubinow, the chief statistician for an insurance company, informed his audience that "it is an investment that will pay handsome dividends in the increase of national health, happiness and efficiency."[124]

Similar arguments were advanced by the Commission on Industrial Relations, which was created by Congress in August 1912 to investigate the rising tide of industrial unrest. In its final report the commission noted that investigations made on its behalf indicated that the wage loss due to sickness was equal to 500 million dollars a year, in addition to which wage earners spent at least another 180 million dollars on medical expenses. "Much attention is now given to accident prevention," the report continues, "yet accidents cause only one-seventh as much destitution as does sickness, and one-fifteenth as much as does unemployment. A great deal of unemployment is directly due to sickness, and sickness in turn follows unemployment."[125] This last link of the causal interaction is explained in the report by the argu-

---

[121]Among the academicians were J. R. Commons and R. T. Ely from the University of Wisconsin, H. W. Farnam and I. Fisher from Yale, and H. R. Seager from Columbia.
[122]I. R. Rubinow, "Sickness Insurance," *American Labor Legislation Review*, Vol. III No. 2 (June 1913), pp. 162–171.   [123]*Ibid.*, p. 163.   [124]*Ibid.*, p. 170.
[125]*Final Report of the Commission on Industrial Relations* (Washington: Government Printing Office, 1916), pp. 124–125.

ment that "sickness among wage earners is primarily the direct result of poverty."[126] By stressing the causal interactions between disease, unemployment, and poverty, the commissioners highlighted the social nature of the problem of ill-health and, hence, the need for social action. American society, in the view of the commissioners, had left more responsibility to the individual than he could handle. "The greatest share of responsibility rests upon the individual, and under present conditions he is unable to meet it. This inability exists by reason of the fact that the majority of the wage earners do not receive sufficient wages. . . ."[127] Given this situation, the commissioners concluded "that new methods of dealing with the existing evils must be adopted. . . . A system of sickness insurance is the most feasible single method."[128] They recommended a compulsory system which shared the cost among employees, employers, and the community, since all shared in the benefits of better health. Among the more important benefits expected was a strong inducement to the spreading of preventive health measures. This particular stress is not surprising, since John R. Commons was a member of the commission.

The social benefits of health insurance figures prominently also in the inaugural address of Irving Fisher, in 1916, when he became president of the American Association for Labor Legislation. Addressing an audience of the joint meeting of the national associations of economists, sociologists, and statisticians, as well as his own organization, Fisher declared that "After some fifteen years' study of the preventability of sickness, I am convinced that the great virtue of health insurance, for decades, perhaps centuries to come, will lie in the prevention of illness."[129] Because of this strong belief in the social advantages of health insurance, and his awareness that many workers could not afford it on their own, he came out strongly in favor of a universal and compulsory public scheme. "Workmen's health insurance," he argued, "is like elementary education. In order that it shall function properly it must be universal, and in order to be universal, it must be obligatory."[130] Aside from the benefits directly derived by the worker through better medical care, Fisher perceived additional gains. Among these he included the prolongation of the years of earning capacity, more complete and more prompt recovery from illness, a lessening of industrial discontent, a reduction of poverty caused by disease, and a slight raise in the general level of wages through increased labor productivity. The challenging conclusion from one of the country's most prominent economists was that "there is no other measure now before the public which equals the power of health insurance toward social regeneration."[131]

[126]*Ibid.*, p. 125.   [127]*Ibid.*, p. 125.   [128]*Ibid.*, p. 125.
[129]Irving Fisher, "The Need for Health Insurance," *American Labor Legislation Review,* Vol. VII, No. 1 (March 1917), p. 17.   [130]*Ibid.*, p. 14.   [131]*Ibid.*, p. 23.

Although efficiency was the central theme of the emerging social insurance ideology, there were, of course, a number of subsidiary themes. The idea that social insurance was a consequence of industrialization and, hence, a necessary feature of any industrial society, regardless of its economic or political system, was taken for granted by the adherents of the social insurance movement. There were opponents who argued that social insurance was an invention of authoritarian and paternalistic Germany for the purpose of keeping the working class weak and submissive. In response to this argument it was easy to point out that the German working class had not become weak and submissive, and that social insurance also was greatly appreciated in a democratic country like England, the home of liberal economic thought. Similarly, it was necessary to demonstrate that in spite of the fact that America was the land of opportunity, and that on the average workers were much better off here than abroad, there was still an urgent need for social insurance. Those who were in the social insurance movement knew very well that it is not the average income but the deviations from the average that matter most with regard to income security. The need for social insurance both in terms of worker income and in terms of the failure of voluntary insurance efforts, was a recurring theme of the debate.[132] There was some disagreement as to whether this need of a given class made social insurance laws class legislation but not too much attention was paid to this issue.

There was general, if often only implicit, agreement about the concept of social insurance as a necessary, corrective adjunct to the free market mechanism. In other words, it was not viewed as a tool of basic economic and social reform. A participant in the 1913 Social Insurance Conference stated bluntly: ". . . regardless of how one may feel about the unfair distribution of wealth at present, a discussion of social insurance is not a place for airing such opinions and the problem of social insurance can be tackled in a thoroughly democratic American way so that class feelings are lessened, not strengthened."[133] Social insurance was not to hinder economic incentives; it was to work through rather than to interfere with the market mechanism. Benefits were to be clearly differentiated from charity and relief; they were not to be a dole but an encouragement to thrift. As Devine explained to the 1913 conference, American social insurance was to be a mechanism by which the competitive market could distribute an industry's

---

[132] See, for instance, I. M. Rubinow, *Social Insurance* (New York: Henry Holt and Company, 1916), Chapter III; F. Spencer Baldwin, "Old Age Insurance," *American Labor Legislation Review*, Vol. III, No. 2 (June 1913) pp. 202–212; Joseph P. Chamberlain, "The Practicability of Compulsory Sickness Insurance in America," *American Labor Legislation Review*, Vol. IV, No. 1 (March 1914), pp. 49–72.

[133] From the general discussion of the conference, *American Labor Legislation Review*, Vol. III, No. 2 (June 1913), pp. 185–186.

"full cost of its produce in human lives and physical vigor."[134] He argued that industry eventually and "in accordance with the well-known principles of competition, will adjust the price of commodities and of labor in such a way as to fairly distribute the burden."[135] Speaking of the incentive effects of compulsory health insurance, Commons suggested that to the extent that disease is preventable "the proper American way is to offer to our business-men a chance to make a big profit by preventing it."[136] He became an ardent advocate of the extension of the prevention principle to unemployment insurance. He explained later: "I was trying to save Capitalism by making it good."[137] This sentiment was no doubt shared by the majority of the early social insurance advocates.

The American advocates of social insurance did not conceive it as a tool for political action. In this regard their outlook differed radically from Bismarck's. Most of their arguments had an academic, analytical flavor. Their appeal was to intellectuals, enlightened employers, and government and civic leaders; they did not seek to mobilize mass support for their cause. Indeed, the lack of strong, organized political backing was the major weakness of the nascent American social security movement. Rubinow lamented the fact that the large majority of Americans, including professional economists, businessmen, and even wage-workers still believed that conditions in the United States were so different from Europe "as to make the organization of social insurance both superfluous and impossible."[138] The promoters of American social insurance at this time were primarily college professors, social workers, and isolated government officials and civic leaders. Organizations such as the National Conference of Charities and Correction and the American Medical Association established committees on social insurance, and a number of states appointed social insurance commissions. However, the main organizational backing of the movement came from the American Association for Labor Legislation, which was more a professional than a political organization. Nevertheless, the association carried out excellent educational campaigns. It drafted model bills, provided a forum for the discussion of basic issues as well as detailed provisions, and offered expert assistance to interested legislative authorities. But without broad support from the major political parties, or from business and trade unions, the movement was doomed to a stunted growth.

[134] Edward T. Devine, "Pensions for Mothers," *American Labor Legislation Review,* Vol. III, No. 2 (June 1913), p. 192.
[135] *Ibid.,* p. 192.
[136] John R. Commons, "A Reconstruction Health Program," *The Survey* (September 6, 1919), p. 798.
[137] John R. Commons, *Myself* (Madison: University of Wisconsin Press, 1963), p. 143.
[138] *Social Insurance,* p. 28.

An exploration of the attitude of the business community in this early struggle to establish new social rights for the American citizen, is instructive. Let us keep in mind that this was a period during which industry was confronted with the labor and managerial problems of a maturing industrial society. Although the prevailing business ideology continued to stress individualistic values and to glorify individual achievement and self-help, the realities of the industrial environment were increasingly at odds with the individualistic slogans. The rise of giant corporations and large-scale enterprises meant that, with mounting frequency, the man in authority in industry was a hired manager who had worked his way up in the industrial bureaucracy, instead of a self-made rugged capitalist. With the expanding scale of firms and mass production methods, managerial problems inevitably became more complex.

One of the important discoveries by management in the early part of the century was the complex nature of the so-called labor problem. The tremendous surge of trade unionism, from 447,000 members in 1897 to 2,140,500 in 1910, and 5,047,800 in 1920, presented an unprecedented challenge to managerial authority.[139] But quite aside from this challenge and the disturbing growth of industrial unrest, the nature of modern production methods had outmoded labor management based on the notion that it was simply a matter of eliminating misfits and malcontents. The costs of hiring and firing had become a matter for serious consideration.[140] Moreover, efficiency in large-scale and complex production units is highly sensitive to the spontaneous cooperation of the work force. The problem of labor management gradually was viewed in the light of the need to create an environment and conditions that would affect individual behaviour in a manner consistent with the promotion of efficiency. The safety, health, and security of the worker thus became necessarily a matter of concern to the manager. Neither could the employer remain indifferent to how the worker felt about his job.

These considerations of profit and loss, rather than a burst of philanthropy or a gnawing conscience over social rights, were the determining factor in the support the business community gave to the enactment of workmen's compensation laws in the years preceding World War I.[141] This was the only form of social insurance that had widespread business support before

[139] Leo Wollman, *Ebb and Flow in Trade Unionism* (New York: National Bureau of Economic Research, 1936), p. 16.

[140] See, for instance, Magnus W. Alexander, "Hiring and Firing: Its Economic Waste and How to Avoid it," *Annals of the American Academy of Political and Social Science,* Vol. LXV (May 1916), pp. 128–144.

[141] For an excellent discussion of the struggle over workmen's compensation, see Roy Lubove, *The Struggle for Social Security 1900–1935* (Cambridge, Mass.: Harvard University Press, 1968), Chapter III.

the 1930s. It must be remembered that indemnification for industrial accidents was subject to social control before workmen's compensation. Business support of workmen's compensation must be regarded in the light of the combined effects of rapidly rising industrial accident rates[142] and the spreading of employer liability laws, which increased the legal risks facing employers. Aware of these problems, and dreading that unions might push for unfavorable legislation, the National Association of Manufacturers undertook extensive investigations at home and abroad. At its annual convention in 1910, the NAM revealed that 90 percent of its members were dissatisfied with existing arrangements, which were described as costly to the employer, of little benefit to the worker, and a source of industrial unrest.[143] On presentation of a report, based on 10,000 replies, the convention adopted the following resolutions:

> Whereas, the National Association of Manufacturers occupies a leading position in all constructive work for industrial betterment and particularly for harmonious relations between American employers and wage-workers, and

> Whereas, the United States is less advanced than progressive European nations in respect to employers' liability and industrial accident indemnity to the detriment of the nation, its institutions and its people;

> Be It Resolved, that the present system of determining employers' liability is unsatisfactory, wasteful, slow in operation, and antagonistic to harmonious relations between employers and wage-workers; that an equitable mutually contributory indemnity system, automatically providing relief for victims of industrial accidents and their dependents, is required to reduce waste, litigation and friction, and to meet the demands of an enlightened nation;

> Be It Further Resolved, that prevention of accidents is of even greater importance than equitable compensation to injured workers.[144]

The basic themes of industrial betterment, harmonious relations, and prevention of waste clearly are in evidence in the resolutions. Notice should be taken also of the fact that the NAM was expecting workers to contribute to the scheme.

---

[142]During the years 1906 to 1907 accident rates reached a peak; U.S. Bureau of Labor Statistics, "The Safety Movement in the Iron and Steel Industry," *Bulletin*, No. 234 (Washington, D.C.: Government Printing Office, 1918), p. 45. One of the most influential studies was a survey of Pittsburgh industries, sponsored by the Russel Sage Foundation. It was filled with gruesome statistics of deaths and injuries. Published in popularized form, it became a best seller, C. Eastman. *Work-Accidents and the Law* (New York: Charities Publication Commission, 1910).

[143]Albert K. Steigerwalt, *The National Association of Manufacturers, 1895–1914,* Michigan Business Studies, Vol. XVI, No. 2 (1964).

[144]Cited in F. C. Schwedtman and J. A. Emery, *Accident Prevention and Relief* (New York: National Association of Manufacturers, 1911), p. xiv.

Employer activity in favor of workmen's compensation was not restricted to the NAM. The National Founders' Association collaborated with
the National Metal Trades Association in the preparation of proposals for a
workmen's compensation act. The iron and steel industries had reason to be
concerned with the problem, since they had some of the highest accident
rates in the country. But what seems to have prodded them into action was
an avowed desire to prevent union leaders from securing "oppressive and
unjust laws of far-reaching consequence."[145] Of course, employers in these
industries also were genuinely concerned with accident prevention, for
reasons of efficiency and industrial betterment, as well as for the purpose of
removing the grounds of the agitator for an appeal to sympathy and
support.[146] Another employer association, the United Typothetae of
America, supported workmen's compensation laws as early as 1909.[147] The
National Civic Federation, a unique organization that included among its
members large employers and labor and civic leaders, also was strongly in
favor of compensation legislation. Since its declared objectives were the
"prevention of industrial revolution threatened by extremists and the promotion of industrial peace," it was understandable, as Bonnett reported,
that its greatest legislative efforts were "exerted in studying and discussing
workmen's compensation and accident prevention, in formulating model
bills, and in attempting to secure their enactment by legislative bodies."[148]
Another important organization, the National Industrial Conference Board,
a body composed of national and state industrial association, concluded that
the "compensation principle is in line with the best conceptions of equitable
industrial relationships."[149] By the middle of the second decade of the
century, the fundamental principle of workmen's compensation, namely,
the substitution of definite and speedy compensation in the place of uncertain relief through litigation, was generally accepted by American
industry.

Nevertheless, there were still many businessmen, especially small
employers and those in less industrialized states, who remained in opposition. Some objected to any kind of safety or compensation legislation
"because they thought it was simply a step toward Socialism."[150] Others, like

[145] Clarence E. Bonnett, *Employers' Associations in the United States* (New York: Macmillan,
1922), p. 120.
[146] *Ibid.*, p. 125.
[147] *Ibid.*, p. 253.
[148] *Ibid.*, p. 414.
[149] National Industrial Conference Board, *Workmen's Compensation Acts in the United States,
Research Report No. 1.* April 1917 (Boston: N.I.C.B., 1919), p. 56.
[150] Comment by A. P. Webster of the John Deere Plow Company at the Second National
Conference of Health Insurance Commissioners, *American Labor Legislation Review,* Vol.
VIII, No. 2 (June 1918), p. 179.

the Philadelphia Board of Trade, argued that workmen's compensation laws made employers responsible for the workers' "reckless indifference to danger."[151] This is a reminder that denunciations of the worker's character had not disappeared with the growing concern with "harmonious relations." The manufacturer associations in the Southern states often disagreed with the NAM on the compensation issue. For instance, the Secretary of the Tennessee Manufacturers' Association reported with obvious satisfaction that "it was largely due to the activities of the employer class that a Work-men's Compensation Law was not enacted in Tennessee during either the 1913, 1915, or 1917 sessions of the Legislature."[152]

Although the idea of compensation was widely accepted, American individualism reasserted itself in an ideological struggle over the organization of workmen's compensation. The question was whether the system should be organized on the basis of state insurance plans or through private insurance companies. A vociferous campaign against state insurance funds was led by an alarmed insurance industry. Speeches, pamphlets, and bulletins warned of the contagious evils of this invasion of private enterprise. E. S. Lott, the president of the United States Casualty Company, was one of the outspoken prophets of doom: "State-fund insurance in our country has made a little hole in the dyke—that great dyke which for long years has pro-tected American individualism. If we permit the hole to grow larger, it will grow large enough to let through sufficient water to inundate *all* private enterprise." He called for help to preserve the dyke, "that dyke builded and preserved by the hands and lives of staunch Americans since the Declaration of Independence; that dyke which protects individual freedom, individual initiative and individual responsibility from the mad waters of socialism."[153] Although the self-serving nature of these comments is obvious, they are significant as an indication of the obstacles to social protection even when the idea of protection itself was not at issue.

The insurance interests were reportedly in favor of the compensation principle,[154] but they saw the threat of bolshevism in state insurance funds. The Red Scare and attacks on state socialism, which were mingled with anti-German sentiments, were exploited especially after the war. Frederick L. Hoffman, a vice-president of the Prudential Insurance Company, told an

[151] Cited in Robert H. Wiebe, *Businessmen and Reform: A Study of the Progressive Movement* (Cambridge, Mass.: Harvard University Press, 1962), p. 197. Wiebe underrates the employers' interest in workmen's compensation and overemphasizes their opposition.

[152] C. C. Gilbert, *Why the Employers of Tennessee Rejected Monopolistic State Insurance* (New York: Workmen's Compensation Publicity Bureau, 1920), p. 6.

[153] E. S. Lott, *The Hole in the Dyke* (pamphlet, no publisher, no date), pp. 13–14.

[154] Edwin W. DeLeon, "Casualty Insurance Companies and Employers' Liability Legislation," *Annals of the American Academy of Political and Social Science*, Vol. XXXVIII, No. 1 (July 1911), p. 21. DeLeon was president, Casualty Company of America.

insurance conference in 1918 that "extreme vigilance is necessary if the interests of the people are to be safeguarded against the danger of paternalism and autocracy inherent in every theory of state socialism."[155] He was persuaded that the insurance industry was peculiarly sensitive to the inherent evils of socialism. "Insurance, on account of its intimate relation to individual needs and personal welfare, is peculiarly one of the functions which should not be brought within the control of an always more or less autocratic and arbitrary bureaucracy."[156] Sample expressions of this kind could be multiplied many times. One of the agencies that conducted the campaign on behalf of the industry was the Workmen's Compensation Publicity Bureau. During the 1920s, it published the Workmen's Compensation Bulletin, which listed the following as one of its aims: "to answer the active propaganda for monopolistic state-fund insurance carried on by a number of radical organizations." The label of radical organization was used liberally. The very first number of the bulletin accused the American Association for Labor Legislation of having abandoned American principles of government and of advocating state socialism.[157]

If workmen's compensation remained controversial, the prospects for businessmen's acceptance of other forms of social insurance were slim indeed. At its 1910 convention, where the NAM endorsed workmen's compensation, it denounced compulsory sickness and old-age insurance as "a departure from accepted doctrines, contrary to American ideas and detrimental to thrift and economy."[158] Ten years later, at the 1920 convention, the NAM's Committee on Industrial Betterment, Health, and Safety referred to state insurance as "one of the vicious German ideas yet existent in this country."[159] In 1922 the same committee issued a final report condemning public sickness and old-age insurance as "unnecessary and unwise" and "unsound economically, placing an unknown burden upon the healthy."[160]

The National Civic Federation also expressed strong disapproval of compulsory sickness insurance.[161] A spokesman for the NCF linked the demand for this insurance to disloyalty to the country's institutions. "Do we realize that the proponents of social insurance are the very persons who would undermine our institutions. Is it necessary to bring compulsion here,

---

[155] Frederick L. Hoffman, Autocracy and Paternalism vs. Democracy and Liberty (New York: International Association of Casualty and Surety Underwriters, 1918), p. 21.
[156] Ibid., p. 22.
[157] Workmen's Compensation Bulletin, No. 1 (November 1923), p. 20.
[158] Wiebe, op. cit., p. 197. See also Bonnett, op. cit., p. 309.
[159] Cited in A. G. Taylor, Labor Policies of the National Association of Manufacturers, University of Illinois Studies in the Social Sciences, Vol. VI, No. 1. The main campaign for health insurance was carried on between 1915 and 1920. The opposition sought to discredit compulsory health insurance as a "German idea." See Lubove, op. cit., Chapter IV.
[160] Taylor, op. cit., p. 150.   [161] Bonnett, op. cit., p. 422.

when we have fought for the freedom of American citizens?"[162] In a grand show of unity of business and labor minds, the *National Civic Federation Review* published an article violently denouncing the "trickery of the group of social reformers who are attempting to foist upon labor a pernicious system of compulsory health insurance."[163] The article contains a long list of dangers inherent in such insurance, including bureaucracy, communism, personal tyranny, and the weakening of individual and family responsibility, in addition to unreasonable cost and unfavorable medical consequences. Its author was not a businessman but a labor leader; he was Grand Chief of the International Brotherhood of Locomotive Engineers and Chairman of the NCF Social Insurance Department.

A more sober but nevertheless negative position was taken by the National Industrial Conference Board. The board accepted the contention that there was an unnecessary amount of sickness in the United States and that this, in turn, was one of the principal causes of poverty. But it categorically denied that compulsory health insurance was a suitable remedy. It concluded that a program of this kind would reduce neither sickness nor poverty, that it would be unjustifiably costly, and that better results could be achieved by developing existing agencies.[164]

It is quite clear that in the minds of businessmen there was a radical distinction between workmen's compensation and other forms of social insurance. This distinction was spelled out by M. W. Alexander, a representative of the General Electric Company:

> Workmen's compensation is not social insurance. Morally and legally it is based, not upon the duty of society, but upon the duty of industry to the worker. Legally its foundation principle is found in the old common law rule that the employer must furnish his employee a safe place to work, including the selection of careful and competent fellow workmen.[165]

The key to this position is the implicit rejection of the theory that in going from employer liability to workmen's compensation, a social right, derived from a social purpose, had been created where formerly there were only private rights and private interests. "The employer," Alexander explained, "has not discharged a social duty; he has merely done justice as between himself and his employees. By no logic can workmen's compensation be

---

[162] See the proceedings of the 1916 conference on social insurance called by the International Association of Industrial Accident Boards and Commissions in *Bulletin of the United States Bureau of Labor Statistics,* No. 212 (June 1917), p. 532.

[163] Warren S. Stone, "Compulsory Health Insurance Legislation, Its Present Status Surveyed and Labor's Position Outlined," *National Civic Federation Review* (February 15, 1919), pp. 5–8.

[164] National Industrial Conference Board, *Is Compulsory Insurance Desirable?* (Boston: N.I.C.B., 1918), pp. 2 ff.

[165] Proceedings . . ., *Bulletin of the United States Bureau of Labor Statistics,* No. 212, p. 765.

called social insurance, nor can our legislation on that subject in this country be considered an opening wedge demanding the general adoption of a scheme of social insurance." [166] The motivation behind this kind of argument is rather obvious. Alexander's main objection was against noncontributory pensions, which he thought would lead to "reliance upon State guardianship" in a country "founded to secure individual liberty of thought and action with opportunities for working out one's own salvation." [167]

With regard to unemployment insurance, business resistance was even stronger than with respect to the other forms of social insurance, in spite of the efforts of men like Commons who tried to show how such schemes would stabilize employment. A *Wall Street Journal* editorial echoed the ancient but still generally held view that assistance to the able-bodied unemployed is bad in itself. "Payment for the unemployed is a remedy incalculably worse than the disease. . . . It is in effect a premium upon malingering and idleness. It is like the English poor law system which created three irreclaimable paupers for one it regenerated." [168] The editorial, instead, advocated improved labor mobility, on the accepted classical assumption that the jobs were there for those who were genuinely willing to work. The low opinion of the unemployed worker's character implied in this assumption was still very much alive.

Unemployment insurance bills were introduced in a number of states but encountered everywhere stiff employer resistance. Massachusetts is one of the states that had shown historically the strongest interest in the problem of unemployment. An unemployment insurance bill was introduced as early as 1916, but the indifference of organized labor and the hostility of employers assured its demise. Another bill, introduced in 1922, was referred to a special commission, which advised against it. The reasoning of the commission is indicative of the attitude of the business community:

> Like other forms of so-called social insurance, compulsory indemnification during unemployment is not consistent with American principles. . . . Just as health insurance has apparently encouraged malingering, unemployment insurance bids fair to encourage shiftlessness and improvidence . . . to the industrious and independent American worker unemployment insurance apparently makes little appeal. [169]

A subtle praise of the worker's virtues, just as the condemnation of his weaknesses, mingled freely in the antisocial insurance ideology. Although this

[166] Proceedings . . ., *Bulletin of the United States Bureau of Labor Statistics*, No. 212, p. 766.
[167] *Ibid.*, p. 774.
[168] "Some Thought on Unemployment," *Wall Street Journal,* July 11, 1919 (Morning edition).
[169] Massachusetts Special Commission on Unemployment, Unemployment Compensation, and the Minimum Wage, cited in Bryce M. Stewart, *Unemployed Benefits in the United States* (New York: Industrial Relations Counselors, 1930), p. 576.

ideology, perhaps, was strongest among employers, it was shared by many workers.

In spite of this general attitude of opposition, there was a small number of progressive employers who established private unemployment compensation schemes and, in some cases, even favored public programs. These people had a different interpretation of worker motivation and behavior. They were concerned with the effects of unemployment on the worker's efficiency "on account of the deterioration of his physique, the loss of regular habits of work, and most of all, through the 'laying down' on the job caused by fear that by working efficiently he will be merely working himself out of a job."[170] Stewart found 13 companies with formal unemployment compensation plans by 1930, although there were many more with informal arrangements.[171] During the 1920s, the movement for unemployment compensation, at least, the voluntary type, received assistance from an unexpected quarter. The advocates of modern management believed that their techniques were suited for the regularization of business activities, and some of them looked to unemployment compensation legislation as the needed incentive to induce managers to adopt these techniques for the stabilization of employment. The American Management Association was the leading organization that promoted modern management methods. A study published under its auspices warned business of the rising tide of social and political pressures that demanded a solution to the problem of employment security. It emphasized that the only alternative to compulsory unemployment compensation was the widespread adoption of private voluntary plans.[172] In 1928, a speaker at an AMA Production Executives Conference told his listeners: "It is now time for the modern business man to give up thinking of it as a business problem which directly affects his company's net income. . . . Unemployment . . . is not only harmful from a social point of view, it is wasteful from a business point of view."[173]

The opinion that business had a social responsibility toward the unemployed was still held by a minority of American industrial leaders during the 1920s. *Iron Age*, the influential trade journal of the iron and steel industry, commented: "The notion that he [the businessman] has any direct responsibility for unemployment which requires serious consideration on his

[170] N. I. Stone, "Continuity of Production in the Clothing Industry," *American Labor Legislation Review*, Vol. XI, No. 1 (March 1921), pp. 36–37. Stone was labor manager for the Hickey-Freeman Company, a pioneer in production regularization.

[171] Stewart, *op. cit.,* p. 463.

[172] H. Feldman, *The Regularization of Employment* (New York: Harper and Brothers, 1925), pp. 403–404.

[173] Ernest G. Draper, "Properity and Unemployment," *Personnel*, Vol. V, No. 2 (August 1928), p. 127.

part is still novel."[174] Businessmen, like economists, believed that booms and busts were inevitable. However, there was a growing recognition by management of its stake in the economic security of the worker, for economic as well as for political reasons.[175] A consequence of this recognition was the rise of welfare capitalism, as a substitute for compulsory social protection schemes and a prophylactic against the welfare state.

Against those odds, the struggle for the establishment of modern social rights had no chance to succeed unless it had the full support of organized labor. Unfortunately, unlike British trade unions, which paid at least lip service to the idea of social security in the early days, American unions were mostly hostile. In this regard there was a striking parallel between them and the German labor movement, although at opposite ends of the ideological spectrum. The bald fact is that in both countries the labor leaders showed more concern for the welfare of their organizations than for the welfare of the working class. To be sure, as organizers of mass movements anywhere, they completely identified the interests of the labor movement with those of the workers. In both countries the negative attitude of the labor leaders was the result of a fear that social insurance would weaken their control over the working masses. In Germany, of course, there were sound reasons for this fear, since the weakening of Socialist influence was one of Bismarck's prime objectives. But, as we shall describe later, German labor leaders soon learned to use social insurance for their own ends in the struggle for power. Moreover, they were inclined ideologically to support rather than to reject the idea of social protection.

For the leadership of American trade unionism, it was much more difficult to become receptive to social insurance, even though social insurance in this country was hardly promoted for the purpose of undermining the unions.[176] The American Federation of Labor, which emerged in the 1890s as the largest and most powerful labor organization in the country, adopted an ideological position that was inconsistent with the social (state) protection of the individual. The federation, as Professor Perlman pointed out in his *Theory of the Labor Movement*, arrayed itself on the side of private property and individual initiative. It opted for "the political weapon only sparingly and with great circumspection."[177] Samuel Gompers argued that political pressure may be used to increase the union's freedom of action, for instance, by seeking laws against injunctions but that the political method was not

[174]*Iron Age*, Vol. CVII, January 13, 1921, p. 141.
[175] See Morrell Heald, "Business Thought in the Twenties: Social Responsibility," *American Quarterly*, Vol. XIII, pp. 126–139.
[176] American employers looked to private welfare plans to achieve this objective.
[177] Selig Perlman, *A Theory of the Labor Movement* (New York: Augustus M. Kelley, 1949), pp. 201–202.

suited for improving the economic security of the worker.[178] That was the job of the unions. It was the job of the constituent unions of the AF of L to promote the interest of their members through their own efforts and through voluntary cooperation with each other, without assistance from the state.

This ideology of voluntarism was a product of practical experience and of a pragmatic approach to the problem of trade union organization in an individualistic and hostile environment.[179] It was a way of turning the ideological position of dominant interests in the community to the advantage of organized labor. Although voluntarism thus became an effective means to legitimize trade unionism, in the eyes of both friends and enemies, the very success of the formula, even though it was limited, led to a doctrinaire rigidity on the part of top labor leaders, particularly Gompers. In a perceptive article, Michael Robin has called attention to the fact that Gompers defended trade union activities in the very same Social Darwinist terms which he abhorred when they were used to justify business behavior.[180] Gompers declared that the desire to lean on the state for support was an indication of "a sort of moral flabbiness." He considered it as a "repudiation of the characteristics that enable Americans to get results." Americans, he argued, "never feared the hard places but dared to wrestle with a primeval country. They were red-blooded men and women with ruggedness in their wills. . . . This is the spirit that has made the American labor movement the most aggressive labor organization in the world. . . ."[181] This identification of labor aggressiveness with the "American spirit" helped to justify trade union action, but at the price of condemning the political approach.

The American Federation of Labor was painfully slow to recognize the workers' need for social insurance. It did not fully endorse workmen's compensation laws until 1909, at a time when the urgent need for those laws had been almost universally recognized.[182] In later years, especially during the years 1917 to 1923, the federation fought for the extension of workmen's

[178] See, for instance, Gompers' statements at the 1914 AF of L Convention, where political action was under debate, in David J. Saposs, *Readings in Trade Unionism* (New York: George H. Doran Co., 1926), p. 397.

[179] See Perlman, *op. cit.,* Chapter V; Also Louis S. Reed, *The Labor Philosophy of Samuel Gompers* (New York: Colombia University Press, 1930), *passim.*

[180] Michael Robin, "Voluntarism: The Political Functions of an Antipolitical Doctrine," *Industrial and Labor Relations Review,* Vol. XV, No. 4 (July 1962), pp. 526–527.

[181] Samuel Gompers, *The Shorter Workday—Its Philosophy,* American Federation of Labor pamphlet (n.d.), p. 35.

[182] Lewis L. Lorwin, *The American Federation of Labor* (Washington, D.C.: Brookings Institution, 1933), p. 409. The early reluctance of the unions was caused, in part by the narrow scope and meager benefits of workmen's compensation laws. Some believed that workers might gain more from strengthened liability laws. For a discussion of contemporary criticisms of liability laws by both workers and employers, see Charles R. Henderson, *Industrial Insurance in the United States* (second edition, Chicago: University of Chicago Press, 1911), pp. 134–135.

compensation coverage to waterfront employees, seamen, and the District of Columbia, for the inclusion of occupational diseases, and for the improvement of benefits. The 1911 AF or L Convention endorsed mothers' pensions, partly with the expectation that assisted widows would stay home to take care of their children instead of bidding down wages in the labor market.[183] Similar labor market considerations, aiming at the enhancement of union power, were relevant for old-age pensions, which may account for a somewhat flexible attitude in this area also.[184] At the 1902 AF of L Convention resolutions were defeated that urged Congress to provide pensions for all citizens over 60 who earned less than $1000 per year.[185] By 1909 the federation endorsed a bizarre pension scheme under the subterfuge of an Old Age Home Guard of the United States Army, and again in 1911, 1912, and 1913 it supported a national old-age pension program as well as pensions for federal employees.[186] Of course, these programs were aimed at needy aged, not active workers.

The strongest federation objections were raised against sickness and unemployment benefits. It is mainly with regard to these forms of protection, which were for active employees, that the federation sensed a threat to its position. Speaking before a social insurance convention in 1916, Grant Hamilton, a member of the AF of L Legislative Committee, was quite explicit that labor's first concern was whether social insurance would interfere with the worker's freedom, especially freedom to organize.[187] On numerous occasions labor leaders expressed the fear that social insurance institutions would hamper organization by "chaining the workers to their jobs" and by increasing the control of employers and the state over the workers' lives. Hamilton, for instance, maintained that "it is well known that able-bodied, skilled workmen have been dismissed from employment at the recommendation of the company physician who found in them the disease of unionism and diagnosed the cases under convenient professional terms."[188] The possibility of using social insurance agents as spies also made union leaders distrustful. In his testimony before a congressional committee Gompers declared:

[183]American Federation of Labor, *History, Encyclopedia, Reference Book* (Washington, D.C.: AF of L 1919), Vol. I, p. 293.

[184]Although not enthusiastic about old-age pensions, Gompers stated at a National Civic Federation Conference in 1916 that workmen's compensation and old-age pensions "carry with them the conviction of their self-evident necessity and justice." Cited in Reed, *op. cit.*, p. 117.

[185]AF of L *History, Encyclopedia, Reference Book*, Vol. I, p. 303.

[186]*Ibid.*, pp. 303–304; also Lorwin, *op. cit.*, p. 109.

[187]Grant Hamilton, "Proposed Legislation for Health Insurance," *Bulletin of the United States Bureau of Labor Statistics*, No. 212 (June 1917), p. 559.

[188]*Ibid.*, p. 563.

I am apprehensive that the attempts of government under the guise of compulsory social insurance for the workers in cases of unemployment, sickness and disability will result in every government agent going into the homes and the lives of the workers as a spy. We have enough already of spies and detectives coming into the lives and workshops of the toilers.[189]

Similar views were expressed by Hamilton.[190]

Aside from these misgivings, labor leaders looked on social insurance as utopian schemes that would lead the labor movement astray by diverting its energies away from immediate and practical improvement of wages and working conditions. "Social insurance," Gompers argued, "can not even undertake to remove or prevent poverty. It is not fundamental and does not get at the causes of social injustice. *The only agency that does get at the cause of poverty is the organized labor movement.*"[191] This view implied that "outsiders" (social workers, college professors, and other intellectuals) were at best misguided in trying to improve the workers' lot through social insurance. At worst, the trade unionists suspected, outsiders were trying to "use" the labor movement for their own purposes. It must have been this fear of having to share power and influence that led Gompers to the rather startling declaration:

> . . . I would rather help in the inauguration of a revolution against compulsory insurance . . . than submit. As long as there is one spark of life in me . . . I will help in crystallizing the spirit and sentiment of our workers against the attempt to enslave them by the well-meaning siren songs of philosophers, statistiticians and politicians.[192]

It is interesting to observe that in Gompers' mind social insurance increased rather than decreased social inequality. He deplored that:

> . . . the first step in establishing social insurance is to divide people into groups, those eligible for benefits and those considered capable of caring for themselves. . . . This governmental regulation must tend to fix citizens of the country into classes, and a long-established insurance system would tend to make those classes rigid.[193]

This prospect was considered particularly damaging to a labor movement that had turned individualism and egalitarianism into ideological weapons.

[189] From testimony before Congressional Committee on Resolution for a Commission on Social Insurance, April 1916, partly reprinted in Samuel Gompers, *Labor and the Employer* (New York: E. P. Dutton and Co., 1920), p. 149.

[190] *Op. cit.*, p. 567.

[191] Gompers' statement at a 1916 social insurance conference. See *Bulletin of the United States Bureau of Labor Statistics*, No. 212 (June 1917), p. 846. (Italics are the author's.)

[192] Gompers, *Labor and the Employer,* p. 149.

[193] Gompers, *Bulletin of the United States Bureau of Labor Statistics,* No. 212, p. 847.

This may not have been true, but Gompers' concern touched on one of the fundamental problems of the drive toward greater equality through expanded social rights—the fact that, often, while one dimension of in-equality was reduced another one was increased. The choice that Gompers made rested on his own evaluation of which of these dimensions was the more important.

The individualistic trade unionist argument against social insurance was expressed most sharply by Andrew Furuseth of the combative Sailors' Union of the Pacific. Furuseth was convinced that social insurance would have a debilitating effect on labor. For him, a trade union was a fighting organiza-tion whose members had to be tough and courageous. In a crude social Darwinist way he suggested, at the 1926 AF of L Convention, that social insurance is a sentimental gesture that kills independence and courage:

> Sometimes it is better to let the wounded die, sometimes it is better to let the old die than sacrifice the fire of fighting and the ability to win battles. . . . This appeal for old-age pensions . . . for sickness insurance . . . for unemployment insurance —what is it? . . . it is nothing more than sentiment that stands in the way of real fighting.[194]

These expressions, perhaps, were more indicative of a mood than of literal convictions, but they did reflect a sense of self-reliant social egalitarianism that spurned protection from above.

Of course, there were exceptions to the rule, that is, leaders and unions who looked favorably on social insurance and on other forms of economic improvement through legislation. At the annual conventions of the AF of L there were always minority voices objecting to the position taken by the federation, but they had a negligible impact. At the Chicago Social Insurance Conference of 1913, G. W. Perkins, the President of the Cigar Makers' Inter-national Union, Gompers' own union, declared himself in favor of social insurance, including unemployment insurance.[195] However, he believed that unions should administer the programs and should be subsidized for this purpose by the state, an idea that could hardly appeal to Gompers.[196] As Secretary-Treasurer of the United Mine Workers, William Green was able to envisage an insurance system, financed jointly by workers, employers, and the state, that might actually encourage the "spirit of independence and freedom."[197] Even though Green was aware of the values of social insurance, his convictions were not deeply rooted.[198] He did not hasten to promote

[194] Cited in Hyman Weintraub, *Andrew Furuseth* (Berkeley and Los Angeles: University of California Press, 1959), p. 184.
[195] *American Labor Legislation Review,* Vol. III (June 1913) p. 234.
[196] *Bulletin of the United States Bureau of Labor Statistics,* No. 212 (June 1917), p. 478.
[197] *Ibid.,* p. 757.
[198] William Green, *Labor and Democracy* (Princeton: Princeton University Press, 1939), pp. 36–37.

social insurance after he became president of the AF of L. As late as 1932, he had doubts about its political desirability.[199]

At the state level a number of AF of L conventions had approved social insurance measures by 1920, but many of the state organizations were "open-minded," in other words, indifferent.[200] Within the Executive Council of the AF of L there were differences of opinion. After declining to support federal bills for unemployment and health insurance during World War I, the council recommended a special committee in 1918 to study accident compensation and health insurance.[201] The committee was approved by the convention of that year, which voted down a resolution demanding the establishment of a comprehensive social insurance program. After a couple of years' debate and discussion, the committee rejected the idea of compulsory health insurance. In 1921 and 1923 the federation reaffirmed its earlier endorsement of old-age pensions, but the labor leaders were still thinking primarily of pensions for the poor and needy, not for workers in general.[202] The American labor movement did not change its attitude toward social insurance until the 1930s. Instead of leading public opinion with regard to social protection, it barely managed to keep up with the common consensus.

We have dwelt at some length on the American case, because it was in this country that liberal ideals and policies were most persistent in the face of the needs and demands generated by industrial society. The result was a vivid demonstration of the conflict between the old liberalism and the new protectionism. In each of the countries surveyed, there was a similar conflict, and each had its own way of managing the tension thus created. The main difference between industrialized Europe and the United States was that here the tension could be successfully managed, for the time being, without the granting of substantial social rights. This difference has been explored in terms of the strength of the liberal tradition, but this does not mean that this strength is unrelated to other factors, such as a country's social and political structure, its resource base, and the speed of its industrial development. One interesting consequence of the strength of the liberal tradition in America was the attempt to formulate an ideology of protection that was suitable for an individualistic environment. This was an interesting attempt to reconcile old values with new policies and, unfortunately, was only partially

[199]James O. Morris, *Conflict Within the AFL* (Ithaca: Cornell University Press, 1958), pp. 138–39; also Irving Bernstein, *The Lean Years, A History of the American Worker 1920–1933* (Boston: Houghton Mifflin Company, 1960), p. 351.

[200]See, for instance, "Attitudes of Labor Organizations," *American Labor Legislation Review,* Vol. VIII, No. 2 (June 1918), pp. 173–178; also Eugene Staley, *History of the Illinois State Federation of Labor* (Chicago: University of Chicago Press, 1930), pp. 279, 496–500.

[201]Morris, *op. cit.,* p. 39. Green, *op. cit.,* p. 35.

[202]Lorwin *op. cit.,* p. 409.

successful. Nevertheless, although it failed to overcome the vested material and ideal interests of business and labor, it set a pattern for American thinking that became very influential when substantial security rights were finally granted in the 1930s.

Part II

ALTERNATIVE PATHS
TO SOCIAL SECURITY

Modern social security systems have an internal complexity that, at best, is confusing to the expert and baffling to the layman. The reasons for this seemingly pointless complexity must be sought in the way that social security programs have evolved through time—through a process of reform, accretion, and expansion. Reflected in this process are changes in social values, in the conceptions of rights and responsibilities, in political motivations and, of course, also in techniques of protection. Although the diverse coverage rules, the eligibility conditions, the benefit scales, the taxing schemes, and the administrative structures certainly cannot be explained in terms of a simple rationale, the different systems do reveal characteristic patterns in the levels and forms of protection, and in the allocation of the burden of protection, which can be understood in terms of the forces that shaped their path of development.

Out of the liberal tradition, discussed in Part I, came one path of development. This path was shaped in various degrees by the struggle with laissez-faire principles, which had to be destroyed or circumvented. One of the forces that helped to undermine laissez-faire as the chief determinant of social policy was the precedent set by the introduction of social insurance in Germany. However, social insurance in Imperial Germany followed an alternative path, since in Germany liberalism had never succeeded in causing a break with traditional protectionism. In a form appropriate to new circumstances, Bismarck's social insurance continued the patriarchal tradition of the absolutist state. Yet another variant of the survival of the patriarchal tradition is represented by the introduction of social insurance in pre-Soviet Russia. The Soviet system of social security, however, has its roots in the attacks on Tsarist patriarchalism and has its own revolutionary tradition.

87

Our task in Part II is thus to trace the course of three major paths of development: paternalism in Germany, liberalism in the United States, and collectivism in the Soviet Union. We shall discuss Germany first, because it was there that social insurance was pioneered. The discussion is in two parts. Chapter 4 deals with the evolution of social protection that culminated in Bismarckian social insurance. It traces the struggle of liberalism against the persistence of traditional patriarchal values. The emergence of social insurance, although continuing the tradition of protection, was also a novel approach that was directed at the threat of insecurity in a period of rapid change. In Chapter 5 we jump to the present in order to compare German social insurance in the mature industrial state with its beginnings in a context of rapid industrialization. The system that has emerged since World War II has shed the original patriarchal flavor and has developed along bureaucratic lines that substitute modern political considerations for the traditionalist considerations of a Bismarck. Thus, we find in Germany the evolution of the patriarchal tradition into a quasi-liberal system, geared to the needs of an expanding, mature economy in the context of political democracy. To sharpen the focus on the nature of the social security reforms in Germany after World War II, a section of this chapter is devoted to the contrasting reforms of the British system during the same era.

The two remaining chapters of Part II are devoted to the United States and the USSR. The United States represents the path of development that emerged out of the defeat of the liberal tradition in the Great Depression. If the liberal tradition was defeated, it was by no means destroyed or, at least, it died a slow death, leaving behind a legacy of problems yet to be resolved. The Soviet system contrasts with both the German and the American experience in that it represents the adaptation of a system of social protection to a centrally planned economy that is aimed at forced draft industrialization under the rule of a totalitarian party. Although its general role is the same as that of social protection in the West, its specific objectives and provisions necessarily reflect the goals and requirements of the Soviet environment.

CHAPTER 4

Germany: Out of the Patriarchal Tradition

SOME COMPARATIVE HISTORICAL CONSIDERATIONS

In England the Industrial Revolution reversed the trend toward a more extensive and more lenient public protection of those who became victims of economic misfortune. The liberal elements that came to power in the late eighteenth and early nineteenth century championed an industrial society based on individualistic principles. Neither resistance from the traditional ruling groups, who were ideologically committed to protection and dependence for the lower classes, nor the counterattacks from the newly created industrial workers, whose initial reactions were often a righteous demand for their "traditional rights," could prevent the triumph of individualism. The system of laissez-faire which prevailed throughout most of the nineteenth century provided only minimal public protection against economic insecurity, at a time when insecurity had greatly increased for large segments of the population. In France the historical circumstances of the evolution of public protection against economic insecurity differed in many ways, but the outcome was another triumph of liberalism. England and France alike made the transition from agrarian and handicraft to industrial society in the context of an individualistic social order in which the dominant view rejected public protection of the individual. Social insurance in these pioneer industrial countries was a late adjustment to the economic and social problems created by industrialization. It was not established until after the countries had gone through the basic economic, social, and political changes engendered by industrialization.

Germany differed in important respects from England and France. Not only did she enter on the road to industrialization well after these two industrial pioneers but she was much more backward economically on the eve of her industrialization and had a more rapid transformation once her economy had "taken-off." As the first major industrial latecomer, Germany, like present-day latecomers, was destined to shift from an agrarian to an industrial order in a relatively short period of time. At the beginning of the nineteenth century, feudal economic institution$ such as serfdom, feudal dues and services, and craft guilds were still characteristic of most German states. By the end of the century, Germany had become one of the leading industrial countries of the world, having surpassed both France and England as an industrial exporting country[1] and as a producer of steel,[2] the key product of advanced industrialism. During this rapid economic and social transformation, Germany had to liquidate a revised *ancien régime* and had to find a solution to the problem of national unification. In England and France these basic political questions had been settled before the onset of rapid industrialization.

These historical circumstances strongly militated against the possibility of a laissez-faire approach to the problems of industrialization in Germany. The rise of a liberal bourgeoisie, the standard-bearer of laissez-faire, did not occur before industrialization in economically backward Germany. It was more a consequence of industrialization. In the early phases of industrialization, during the second quarter of the nineteenth century, the German bourgeoisie had to suffer all too often "humiliations and defeats."[3] With a much weaker tradition than the corresponding classes in England and France, it had to engage in a difficult struggle against a solidly entrenched and aggressively status-conscious aristocracy, in the midst of a postrevolutionary current of restoration. At the intellectual level, the contemporary development of the conservative *Weltanschauung*, for which the landed aristocracy had a special affinity, provided potent ideological weapons against the liberal forces. "The conservative Weltanschauung stood for freedom and the rule of law vis-à-vis absolutism and for authority vis-à-vis the demands of the bourgeoisie."[4] Its adherents saw in liberalism centrifugal forces of social disorder and disintegration. Against these forces they supported order in the form of a hierarchical, patriarchal society, which has "organic" coherence through the "natural" links of family, occupation, and status. They repudiated the forces of economic and social change, whether these forces moved through bureaucratic reform from above or social revolution from below.

[1] F. Luetge, *Deutsche Sozial- und Wirtschaftsgeschichte* (Berlin: Springer Verlag, 1960), p. 459.
[2] W. Ashworth, *A Short History of the International Economy 1850–1950* (London: Longmans, Green, and Co., 1952), p. 35.
[3] F. Schnabel, *Deutsche Geschichte im Neunzehnten Jahrhundert* (Freiburg: Verlag Herder, 1949), Vol. II, p. 9.   [4] *Ibid.*, p. 18.

No doubt, it was a misfortune for the German advocates of liberalism and industrialism that the English and French precedents had made the country aware of the social problems of industrial development well before they were actually experienced. "The thought had a long lead over the actual condition" observes Schnabel.[5] The dislocations and hardships of industrialization in England and France were far more spectacular and, therefore, more noticeable to German visitors and critics, than the slow improvements in the economic position of the industrial worker. The liberal spokesmen for industrialization were put on the defensive, not only against the conservative opponents of modern industry but soon also against the socialists, the radical opponents of capitalism. The German socialists in the pre-1848 period, like the conservatives, based their arguments heavily on the experience of England and France rather than Germany. In this manner, the German liberals had to pay a price for being industrial latecomers. Before they could triumph over conservatism on the right, they had to defend themselves against radicalism on the left. The socialists shared with the conservatives a profound dislike for economic laissez-faire, however much they disagreed with them on alternatives. Being challenged into an early recognition of the social problems of industrialization, it is not surprising that the liberal forces never pushed laissez-faire in Germany as far as they did in England and France. German liberalism, notes von Laue, "broke down at its very core, individualism. . . ."[6] There is much to support this insight, especially in the first half of the nineteenth century. Even when they stressed individual responsibility and self-help, German liberals had a corporate, and sometimes collectivist, flavor to their argument. After all, individual responsibility was not alien to corporative social ideals, and the potentials of collective self-help were being demonstrated by English workers. The German environment was rather unreceptive to the simple and hopeful message of a Samuel Smiles that the social problems of industrialization could be overcome through individual efforts. It is not that the virtues of hard work, steadfastness, and perseverance that Smiles praised were not appreciated in Germany; on the contrary, they were glorified by conservatives and liberals alike. But the notion that this was the road to abundance for the common man somehow remained unconvincing.

The weakness of liberalism meant that the country was, at least, ideologically predisposed to social protection of the individual, since this was implicit in the patriarchal social ideal, as well as in the Christian social ethic, which conservatives emphasized in opposition to the "materialistic" ethic of liberalism. Another consequence of the weakness of liberalism was

[5] *Ibid.*, Vol. IV, p. 202.
[6] T. von Laue, *The Beginning of Social Insurance in Imperial Germany* (unpublished doctoral dissertation, Princeton University, 1944), p. xxv.

the ascendance of the governmental bureaucracy as a major force of change in economic life. This development had far-reaching political as well as economic consequences. By combining and identifying administration with policy making, the bureaucracy was able to increase its own power as the absolutism of the ruling princes waned.[7] It is noteworthy that the great economic reforms of the nineteenth century were not the work of parliaments and political parties but of public servants like Stein and Bismarck.[8] It is a well-known fact that government officials, many of whom had liberal leanings, were a major driving force of German industrial development in the first half of the century.[9] Private entrepreneurship was still weak at that time, and much of the innovating initiative depended on enlightened government officials. Of course, not all of them were progressive; at times, they were a hindrance to private initiative. This was increasingly resented as industry developed and as its spokesmen failed to gain an adequate voice in the management of public affairs.[10] The advent of popularly elected parliaments and political parties in the second half of the nineteenth century did not dislodge the bureaucracy from its dominant policy-making position.[11] The administrative officialdom adopted the attitude that it represented the interests of the state against the conflicting interests of individuals and groups. In this attitude, which was most fully incorporated in Bismark,[12] the bureaucracy perpetuated an important aspect of the concept of monarchical absolutism, which was that the prince is the supreme arbiter of the national interest over and above the conflicting claims of his subjects. This view clearly had highly significant implications for the resolution of social conflict and the reformulation of the "mutual rights and responsibilities" of various social groups in the emerging industrial society. The state was first confronted with the problem of reformulating the rights

[7] This was especially the case in Prussia. See B. Kehr, "Zur Genesis der preussischen Buerokratie und des Rechtsstaats," *Die Gesellschaft* (1932), Part I, p. 108.

[8] It is ironic that neither Stein nor Bismarck had much sympathy for bureaucrats, since their actions greatly increased the power of the governmental bureaucracy. Bismarck, of course, disliked parliaments even more than bureaucrats.

[9] See U. P. Ritter, *Die Rolle des Staates in den Fruestadien der Industrialisierung*, Volkswirtschaftliche Schriften No. 60 (Berlin: Duncker und Humblot, 1961), *passim*; Schnabel, *op. cit.,* Vol. III, pp. 292 ff; Lutz Graf Schwerin von Krosigk, *Die grosse Zeit des Feuers* (Tuebingen: Rainer Wunderlich Verlag, 1957), Vol. I, Chapter XV.

[10] The lower levels of the bureaucracy were usually the least enlightened. After 1830 there was mounting criticism of the "narrow-minded and ossified" attitude of the officials. A. Sartorius von Waltershausen, *Deutsche Wirtschaftsgeschichte 1815–1914* (Jena: Gustav Fischer, 1923), p. 73.

[11] The public policy of Imperial Germany was a policy of government officials . . . ; it was not influenced by interest groups beyond parliamentary necessities. Karl E. Born, *Staats- und Sozialpolitik seit Bismarks Sturz* (Wiesbaden: Franz Steiner, 1957), p. 113.

[12] See H. Rothfels, "Prinzipienfragen der Bismarckschen Sozialpolitik," *Koenigsberger Historische Forschungen*, Vol. VII (1935), pp. 49–64.

and duties of the lower classes in the abolition of serfdom and the liquidation of the compulsory guild system. In these instances, the peasants and artisans were on the whole passive subjects whose fate was decreed from above. As industrialism advanced, democratic and other radical ideas filtered down to the lower classes. The intensification of social problems made imperative a reinterpretation of the rights and responsibilities of the workingman. Liberals and conservatives became engaged in a lengthy debate on how to resolve this social question, but the policies that finally prevailed owed their initiative and objectives to the state. The most significant of these policies was the introduction of social insurance.

The social insurance legislation of the 1880s made social and economic relations among individuals an object of statecraft. It was a conscious attempt at cementing the social fabric of the industrial order, with the interests of the state instead of the welfare of the worker as the prime objective. The task of this chapter is to analyze the place of Bismarck's path-breaking social experiment in the industrialization of Germany. The stress will be on the forces that led to it, how they influenced its objectives, and how they responded to Bismarck's initiative. As a form of indirect social planning that aims at the social reintegration of the workingman, social insurance is only one of a number of possible approaches. Some of these approaches, including factory legislation and the promotion of worker collective self-help and self-defense, were considered by Bismarck and his predecessors. Appropriately, therefore, we begin with a review of the broad phases of industrialization and explore the environment and the conflicting forces that paved the way to Bismarck's reforms.

THE CONFLICT BETWEEN LAISSEZ–FAIRE AND PATRIARCHAL TRADITIONALISM IN EARLY INDUSTRIALIZATION

Until the 1840s the chief means of dealing directly with the problem of poverty were philanthropy and public poor relief.[13] However, the pre-industrial society had a number of important built-in economic security measures. In agriculture, especially in the East, where the manorial system survived, the *Gutsherr* (lord of the manor) had certain obligations to support his peasants in need; in the handicrafts, the guilds provided protection for disabled members and for dependents of deceased members; in mining and smelting, the guild-like *Knappschaften* performed similar functions.

[13] German poor laws, like those of England and France, experienced the trend toward greater leniency in the last quarter of the eighteenth century and greater strictness in the early nineteenth century. See "Armenwesen" in *Handwoerterbuch der Staatswissenschaften* (fourth edition, Jena: Gustav Fischer, 1923), Vol. I, pp. 950 ff.

The attitude of the Prussian government toward the poor, which is of particular interest in view of the importance of Prussia in Germany and her leading role in the development of social protection of the individual, was expressed in the Prussian *Landrecht* (Civil Code), which came into force in July 1794:

1. It is the duty of the State to provide for the sustenance and support of those of its citizens who cannot . . . procure subsistence themselves.

2. Work adapted to their strength and capacities shall be supplied to those who lack means and opportunity of earning a livelihood for themselves and those dependent upon them.

3. Those who, for laziness, love of idleness, or other irregular proclivities, do not choose to employ the means offered them by earning a livelihood, shall be kept to useful work by compulsion and punishment under proper control.

6. The State is entitled and bound to take such measures as will prevent the destitution of its citizens and check excessive extravagance.

15. The police authority of every place must provide for all poor and destitute persons, whose subsistence cannot be ensured in any other way.[14]

The old patriarchal position of the state is clearly defined in these provisions. The poor did not have a legally enforceable claim to protection, but the state unequivocally proclaimed its duty to protect them—to provide either sustenance or work. Parallel to the protective was the disciplinary hand of the patriarchal state. The lazy and the loafers were threatened with compulsory labor and punishment and, appropriately, the police authorities were given ultimate responsibility for those paupers who were likely to be among the least inclined to work. The state, however, did not undertake directly the management of poor relief. It delegated its responsibilities to the local communities, who had to look after their own poor with local resources, although there were regional poor relief agencies to take care of transients. A concern with the prevention of poverty and the employment of the poor was in evidence also in other parts of Germany. Hamburg, for example, is credited with the introduction of a very advanced system of poor relief, which rested on individualized investigations of needs and resources and sought to provide work for all the able-bodied.[15] Other German cities followed the Hamburg example, which was initially very successful. Before too long, however, many of these local efforts turned into failure, partly on account of their financial weakness, and partly on account of the increasing

[14] Quoted from W. H. Dawson, *Bismarck and State Socialism* (second edition, London: Swan Sonnenschein, 1890), p. 19.
[15] For a brief description of the Hamburg system, see K. de Schweinitz, *England's Road to Social Security* (Philadelphia: University of Pennsylvania Press, 1943), Chapter X.

size of the problem of pauperism in a changing society. Even in Prussia, the intentions of the *Landrecht* were often only feebly executed in practice.

The inroads of liberalism were felt in the early nineteenth century, although not as strongly as in England and France. In August 1807, a Prussian governmental commission came out against large-scale relief, even against the granting of permission to gather wood in the Royal forests, on the ground that measures of this sort would "impair the energy of self-help."[16] This doctrinaire argument was chiefly the inspiration of Theodor von Schoen, a high Prussian official and admirer of Adam Smith.[17] This extreme position did not have many supporters in Germany at that time. Poor relief continued to be carried on in most German states at the local level along traditional lines. When a bill to make poor relief compulsory came up in the Rhenish *Provinziallantag* (Provincial Diet) in 1835, it was rejected with the argument that if poverty were to be allowed to become a basis for legal claims against the authorities, the consequences would be disastrous, since the "bond of philanthropy, which binds religion and the poor would be dissolved, and the poor would no longer be timid in their requests."[18] New efforts were made in Prussia to adapt the poor relief system to changed conditions and increased geographic mobility by a law enacted in 1842.[19] This law, which made it easier for individuals to meet local residence requirements for relief and redefined the responsibilities of regional agencies for transient paupers, was followed in later years by most of the remaining German states.

The liberal current within the governmental bureaucracy was mainly directed at loosening the economic tutelage of the Old Regime. The most far-reaching influence of this liberalism was in the areas of peasant and handicraft reforms. These reforms were closely related to the growth of the poor relief problem in the first half of the nineteenth century. The edict of October 9, 1807, which abolished serfdom in Prussia, signaled the beginning of a fundamental economic and social reordering on the land. It established a free market in land, and thereby made possible a more rational utilization of land resources. But it also opened the road to the creation of a landless peasantry at a time when industrial development was still too slow to absorb the excess rural labor supply. The Old Regime on the land had rested on the principle of mutual personal rights and responsibilities between lords and

[16] For a digest of the commission's report, see J. R. Seeley, *Life and Times of Stein* (Cambridge: University Press, 1878), Vol. I. pp. 424–427.

[17] Schoen had studied at the University of Koenigsberg, where he had come under the influence of Kant and Krause. Krause was the chief exponent of Adam Smith's ideas in Germany. Seeley, *op. cit.*, Vol. I, pp. 374 ff.

[18] Quoted in J. Koester, *Der rheinische Fruehliberalismus und die soziale Frage*, Historische Studien No. 342 (Berlin: Verlag Emil Ebering, 1938), p. 65.

[19] See "Armenwesen," p. 953.

peasants: the peasant owed various dues as well as subordination and loyalty: the lord owed protection and guidance. To be sure, in practice the lord's protection was not always kind or effective, but before the emancipation the peasants were also protected by the state, at least as a class, against the loss of the land they cultivated.[20] Freiherr vom Stein, under whose ministry the 1807 emancipation edict was promulgated, sought to continue the peasant protection in order to prevent a landless proletariat.[21] He stood for the development of a sturdy, independent, landowning peasantry that could provide a stable foundation for a rejuvenated state. He was no admirer of liberal ideas, but he was aware of the necessity for the liquidation of the Old Regime. Stein's ideas, however, did not prevail.[22]

What made matters worse was the fact that in the first half of the nineteenth century Germany was confronted with a problem of rural overpopulation. This forced a reevaluation of traditional populationist ideas, just as in France and England. Between 1800 and 1850 the population of the area that became imperial Germany increased by nearly fifty percent, from 24.5 to 35.4 million.[23] Most of the increase was in the countryside. Industrialization did not yet induce large-scale migration to the cities. The resulting disguised unemployment and economic hardship on the land were relieved to some degree by emigration, although this solution to the misery of the lower classes did not become popular until the 1840s.[24] A troublesome growth in rural pauperism thus followed in the wake of the dissolution of the old agrarian order.

It is noteworthy that in Germany the Malthusian fears of overpopulation and consequent pauperism led to reactions that were exactly op-

[20]The so-called *Bauernschutz* (peasant protection) which the Prussian state had pursued largely for military reasons never protected any particular peasant's tenancy rights. It meant that land used by peasants could not be taken away by the nobility. See G. F. Knapp, *Die Bauern-Befreiung* (Leipzig: Duncker und Humblot, 1887), pp. 51–52. As far as other aspects of economic security were concerned, the peasant was largely at the mercy of his lord, who usually followed local custom. The care of sick peasants, for instance, was a matter of local custom; see J. Silbermann, *Der Gesindezwangsdienst in der Mark Brandenburg* (Dissertation, Greifswald, 1897), p. 20. See also G. F. Knapp, *Die Landarbeiter in Knechtschaft und Freiheit* (Leipzig: Duncker und Humblot, 1909) and J. Ziekursch, *Hundert Jahre Schlesicher Agrargeschichte* (Breslau: Ferdinand Hirt, 1915), *Passim*.

[21]Seeley, *op. cit.*, Vol. I, pp. 428 ff.

[22]On the development of the landless peasantry, see Luetge, *op. cit.*, pp. 386 ff; F. Wunderlich, *Farm Labor in Germany 1810–1945* (Princeton: Princeton University Press, 1961), pp. 8 ff.; also P. H. Seraphim, *Deutsche Wirtschafts- und Sozialgeschichte* (Wiesbaden: Verlag Gabler, 1962), pp. 134–136.

[23]Data from Luetge, *op. cit.*, p. 368.

[24]T. S. Hamerow, *Restoration Revolution Reaction* (Princeton: Princeton University Press, 1958), p. 81. Until the 1840s the state took a negative attitude toward emigration, but during the depression of 1846 to 1847 it encouraged it. See O. J. Hammen, "Economic and Social Factors in the Prussian Rhineland in 1848," *American Historical Review*, Vol. 54 (1949), p. 832.

posite from the ones in England and France in the early nineteenth century. In the latter countries, it will be recalled, the Malthusian ideas were seized on by the liberals, who used them as an argument against social protection and for individual economic responsibility. Such a posture required more self-confidence that the German *vormaerz* (pre-1848) liberals could be expected to muster. In Germany, it was the conservatives who leaned on Malthus in their social policy arguments or, rather, they reinterpreted Malthus in the light of their own preconceptions of human nature. They accepted the Malthusian observation that population was rising faster than subsistence but found the cause of this development in the dissolution of the bonds of traditional society and in libertine modern ideas and attitudes.[25] They did not deny Malthus's argument regarding the lack of individual foresight among the lower classes, especially among those who had broken out of the bonds of the traditional peasant and artisan society. But they drew different conclusions from this argument. Malthus wanted to leave the individual to his own destiny, in the faint hope that fear of misery might inculcate foresight. The German conservatives saw in the lack of foresight the need to restore the old social bonds and to restrict individual freedom. In fact, quite a few states in southern and central Germany, but not Prussia, introduced laws that aimed at restricting marriage. In Wuerttemberg, for instance, an individual contemplating marriage had to prove to the authorities that he could support a family.[26]

Malthus and the fear of overpopulation became ideological weapons against liberalism, specifically against the agrarian reforms and the abolition of compulsory guilds. These liberal measures were denounced as "rabble breeding" (*Poebelerzeugung*).[27] The Silesian nobility complained bitterly about the peasants' alleged deterioration of morality under the influence of freedom: "it is a psychological truth that freedom, whenever it is given to a coarse social class, leads to licentiousness and dissoluteness and may threaten the state itself."[28]

Similar arguments were raised against the abolition of compulsory guilds, which was promulgated in Prussia by an edict of November 2, 1810. Guild members in cities throughout the kingdom complained that the edict would inevitably lead to chaos; that it would destroy the economic position of the artisan class;[29] and that it would undermine society by dissolving the

[25] Schnabel, *op. cit.*, Vol. III, p. 356.

[26] Sartorius von Waltershausen, *op. cit.*, p. 35.   [27] Schnabel, *op. cit.*, Vol. III, p. 356.

[28] Quoted in W. Steffens, *Hardenberg und die Staendige Opposition* (Dissertation, Goettingen, 1907), p. 23.

[29] The guilds not only protected prices: they also provided various kinds of benefits for their members and, under the Prussian Civil Code, were responsible for public relief of artisans. See H. Peters, *Die Geschichte der Sozialversicherung* (Bad Godesburg: Asgard Verlag, 1959), pp. 25–26.

bonds of loyalty and duty between masters and journeymen.[30] Conservative intellectual defenders of the guilds agreed that without the rigorous paternalistic discipline that the old guild system enforces through the master craftsmen, without the controls that a compulsory system gives the masters, the journeymen become immoral and rebellious. "Debauchery and neglect of church attendance become common; they [the journeymen] grow coarse, brutish, and unmannerly. . . . Loyalty, obedience, modesty, and craftsmanship become foreign to them. . . ."[31] It should be pointed out that in Prussia, unlike in France, the guilds were not declared illegal. They were no longer compulsory but continued to exist in many of the traditional trades. It was mainly in the newer industrial branches, such as machine construction, where their rigid rules would have been a serious hindrance to development that they could not be tolerated. There was never quite the same liberal reforming zeal with respect to guilds as with respect to agriculture. Some states actually restored compulsory guilds in the restoration period after 1815. It was not until the 1860s that the laws of the various states, capped by the Trade Law of 1869 of the North German Federation, removed most of the remaining restrictions to the practice of a craft. The reasons for this difference in attitude are not readily apparent, unless, as Luetge suggests, the answer lies in the fact that there was less of a political risk in agrarian than in handicraft reform: poor landless peasants would still tend to be conservative, but impoverished artisans might become revolutionary.[32]

Whether or not calculations of this kind entered into the minds of government officials, they were subjected to pressures from both of the ideological currents, one tending toward the maintenance of the old system of tutelage and protection and the other toward laissez-faire and individual self-help. Official policy, in spite of laissez-faire tendencies, was by no means consistent. Beyond official policy, the sentiments of both the ruling and the lower classes were still solidly traditional.

RESPONSES TO THE THREAT OF REVOLUTION IN THE 1840s

The first half of the nineteenth century saw mainly the weakening of the old system of state tutelage, but little progress was made toward the creation of a new system of social protection that was suitable for the emerging industrialization. By the 1840s the need for new forms of collective economic

[30] See, for instance, K. von Rohrscheidt, *Vom Zunftzwange zur Gewerbefreiheit* (Berlin: Carl Heymanns Verlag, 1898), pp. 302, 463, and *passim*; see also Hamerow, *op. cit.*, pp. 31–33.
[31] From a memorandum submitted to minister von Buelow, March 14, 1822; quoted in Rohrscheidt, *op. cit.*, p. 569.
[32] Luetge, *op. cit.*, pp. 395–396.

security was becoming more pressing, and people began to grope for new solutions. The riots of the Silesian weavers in the summer of 1844 were a major factor in awakening the public conscience to the existence of the social problems of industrial change. The riots and their ruthless repression produced a deep moral impact.[33]

The confrontation with the problems of early industrialism generated a multitude of suggested solutions, from liberals as well as from conservatives. A striking feature of the proposals advanced by liberals was their paternalism toward the workers. Prominent Rhenish businessmen, like David Hanseman and Ludolf Camphausen, proposed schemes for worker self-help —savings banks and mutual assistance societies—under the guidance of the middle classes.[34] Other prominent liberals, like Friedrich Harkort and Gustav Mevissen, put particular stress on education, along with mutual assistance. Both argued strongly that it was the duty of the state to rescue the proletariat from the threat of poverty. "The state must intervene," wrote Harkort, "to prevent further deterioration and to keep the stream of pauperism from growing unchecked. . . . We demand that the state step in not only in a directing but also in a helping manner."[35] The help he wanted from the state was in the form of child labor laws, education, and the restriction of hours of work to allow the worker some leisure.

Harkort's position, although imbued with liberal values, also contained strong statist elements. This strain in German liberalism came out even more strongly in the arguments of Gustav Mevissen, who was the son of a manufacturer and, being born in 1815, a member of a younger generation of Rhenish liberal leaders. He clearly viewed the poverty and insecurity of the lower classes as intimately bound up with industrialization and spoke ominously of the coming historical crisis if adequate remedial measures were not taken.[36] The measures he stressed involved the usual liberal demands of freedom, equality, and education. He wanted the state to help the workers to help themselves but, in the absence of state action, he considered it the responsibility of the middle classes to come to the assistance of the workers in the organization of self-help. After 1845, however, he began to stress more and more the need for direct state aid to the working class and to lean toward state socialism, although he still considered political reform to be the

[33] J. Droz, *Les révolutions allemandes de 1848* (Paris: Presses Universitaires, 1957), p. 106.
[34] See D. Hanseman, "Denkschrift ueber Preussens Lage und Politik" in E. Schraepler (ed.), *Quellen zur Geschichte der sozialen Frage in Deutschland 1800–1870* (second edition, Goettingen: Musterschmidt Verlag, 1960), Vol. I, pp. 77–78; also Koester, *loc. cit.*, pp. 24–26, 64.
[35] From F. Harkort, "Bemerkungen ueber die Hindernisse der Zivilisation und Emancipation der unteren Klassen" (1844), partially reproduced in Schraepler, *op. cit.,* Vol. I, pp. 87–88.
[36] See his "Ueber den allgemeinen Hilf- und Bildungsverein" (1845) in Schraepler, *op. cit.,* Vol. I, pp. 80–84.

first order of business.[37] His attitude was indicative of a strong tendency among the younger liberals to lean either toward the socialist or the conservative position in matters involving the problem of poverty, which makes the label "liberal" a bit misleading. They did not carry laissez-faire to its logical conclusion.

The liberal challenge for leadership and the threat of revolutionary socialism brought forth two conservative responses. One was to restore the old forms of protection, especially compulsory guilds. The other was the more novel, and politically more expedient, idea of the "welfare monarchy."

Bismarck, as a member of the Prussian Diet in 1849, was among those who favored the more reactionary solution—the restoration of the compulsory guild system. "Factories make a few individuals wealthy," he said in a speech in the Diet, "but they generate the mass of proletarians, of ill-fed workers whose insecurity of existence makes them dangerous to the state. . . ."[38] He wanted the state to restore the compulsory guilds in order to save the handicraftsmen, "the core of the middle class," whose survival he considered vital to the safety of the state.[39] If he did not understand at that time the economic forces that were reshaping society and had not given much thought to the social problem of industrialism, he was nevertheless quite prepared to subordinate the economic interests of individuals, in particular of the industrialists, to the interests of the state. This principle he never abandoned.

Other spokesmen for traditionalism wanted the crown to take the initiative in social protection and to turn it into a political weapon against the liberals. "Collaboration between crown and proletariat against the liberal bourgeoisie was widely discussed in conservative circles during the Forties."[40] The conservative publicist, Viktor Aimé Huber, proposed an alternative to revolutionary socialism in the form of a cooperative association sponsored by the crown.[41] A more influential advocate of the new political patriarchalism was General Joseph von Radowitz, a close adviser to Frederick William IV. The Prussian monarch was receptive to romantic and conservative ideologies and had shown an interest in promoting the welfare of the working class.

Radowitz was in the conservative tradition of Adam Mueller and Franz von Baader, and moreover he sympathized with Louis Blanc's ideas on the

[37] Koester, op. cit., p. 38.

[38] Relevant passages of this speech are reprinted in the documentary collection by H. Rothfels, *Bismarck und der Staat* (Kohlhammer Verlag, 1958), p. 303.

[39] *Ibid.*, p. 303; see also T. Steimle, "Bismarck als Sozialpolitiker," *Schmoller's Jahrbuch*, Vol. 64, No. VI (1940), p. 97.

[40] Hamerow, op. cit., p. 72.

[41] *Ibid.*; see also V. A. Huber, "Die oekonomische Assoziation" (1849) in Schraepler, op. cit., pp. 138–143.

socialist organization of work, but his own reform program was rather vague.[42] He was convinced that if the state failed to solve the social problem raised by industrialism, it would stand helpless against the "solidarity of misfortune" and would go under.[43] He therefore appealed to the monarchy to rescue the proletariat and the state from the revolution and the bourgeoisie. "Our princes," he wrote in 1846, "have not yet exhaused the resources with which they may survive the struggle against triumphant mediocrity. Let them have but the courage to turn to the masses. There, among the lower and most numerous classes of the population, are their natural allies. . . ."[44]

A scholarly statement of the need for the king to take the initiative in social reform was formulated by one of the country's leading sociologists, Lorenz Stein,[45] who had written a major work on the social development of France since the 1789 Revolution.

> The king, as the embodiment of the pure state idea, stands above the classes of society and their conflicts. . . . The ruling class, however, rises in opposition and wants itself to lead the state in its own interest. The resulting struggle between this class and the king can continue for a time indecisively or with alternating fortunes. But in this struggle the king is always defeated in the end and is either removed or made an impotent representative of the state. . . . To maintain his independent power to act [Selbsttaetigkeit] and high position, the king has only one sure way out in this struggle, namely, to put himself, with all the deliberation, dignity, and vigor befitting the highest power in the state, at the head of social reform in the name of social welfare [Volkswohlfahrt] and freedom.[46]

There were other outstanding academicians, like the economist Johann Karl Rodbertus and the historian Leopold von Ranke, who saw the key to the future in a welfare monarchy. Ranke, in a memorandum to Frederick William IV, was moved by the danger of giving military training to dissatisfied workers.

> For he who serves the state with his life has also a claim on it for his support. The soundest policy would be to satisfy this claim, since as a matter of fact it is dangerous to train year after year the entire youthful population in the use of arms, and then alienate a large and physically perhaps the most vigorous part, leaving it exposed to the agitation of the enemies of all order. . . . The idea arises that under certain conditions the state ought to organize labor and perhaps recognize the right to work, yet it must also respect private enterprise.[47]

---

[42] See J. Baxa, "Die wirtschaftlichen Ansichten von Joseph Maria v. Radowitz," *Jahrbuecher fuer Nationaloekonomie und Statistik*, Vol. 139 (1933: 2), pp. 188–210.
[43] *Ibid.*, p. 205.   [44] Quoted in Hamerow, *op. cit.*, p. 73.
[45] Received a nobility title in 1868.
[46] From his *Das Koenigtum, die Republik und die Souveraenitaet der franzoesischen Gesellschaft seit der Februarrevolution 1848* (Leipzig, 1850), Schraepler, *op. cit.*, p. 130.
[47] Quoted in Hamerow, *op. cit.*, pp. 211–212.

It is interesting to observe that the mass army, made possible by industrialism, created also pressures to heal the social wounds inflicted by industrialism.

By mid-century the problem of the social protection of the worker in industrial society had been raised. The solutions that were proposed, whether by liberals or conservatives, all assumed that the state, or at least the ruling classes, had a responsibility to protect the lower classes against destitution and insecurity. The differences between the two ideological tendencies lay primarily in the extent and in the manner in which the state was supposed to intervene. Liberalism had succeeded in reducing the survivals of mercantilist tutelage in economic matters but, in social policy, patriarchal traditionalism was still the predominant sentiment. The liberal forces, however, were not yet defeated. The welfare monarchy had only been mentioned. In the third quarter of the century, economic liberalism still made converts and could not be counted out among the forces seeking to shape the social rights of the individual in the emerging industrial society.

SELF-HELP VERSUS STATE HELP DURING THE INDUSTRIAL UPSWING (1850 TO 1870)

The depression of the mid-1840s and the Revolution of 1848 exposed the weakness of the workers' economic position and revealed its inherent dangers to the state. Consequently, it might seem, that any further move along the road to industrialism would inevitably bring with it a substantial expansion in social protection. But this was not the case. In the quarter century that followed the revolution, although Germany experienced an unprecedented industrial expansion, the urgency of social protection seemed to decrease rather than increase. The period 1850 to 1873 contains the German "take-off" into sustained economic growth and marks an era of rapid industrialization.[48] It took only thirty years to double the level of real national income that had been reached in 1850 after centuries of development. Between 1851 to 1855 and 1881 to 1885 the real national income of Germany rose from 10.6 to 21.4 billion marks, and from 1881 to 1885 and 1911 to 1913 it more than doubled again, reaching 48.2 billion marks at the end of the period.[49] Between 1851 to 1855 and 1881 to 1885 real per capita income rose 58 per cent, and in the period between 1881 to 1885 and 1911 to 1913 it rose 56 per cent, which was a slightly smaller percentage but a larger

[48] W. W. Rostow, *The Stages of Economic Growth* (Cambridge: University Press, 1960), p. 38.
[49] W. G. Hoffmann and J. H. Mueller, *Das deutsche Volkseinkommen* (Tuebingen: J. C. B. Mohr, 1959), p. 14. The data are for the territory of Imperial Germany in 1913.

absolute amount.[50] In the second half of the nineteenth century Germany was transformed from a predominantly agricultural country into the leading industrial country of Europe, surpassing Britain in major industrial branches in the last decade of the century. Naturally, the whole period was not one of uninterrupted growth. Germany shared in the trade disruption of 1857 and in the depression that hit Europe in 1873. The latter event had important consequences for the development of social protection, but until then the country was in the throes of a feverish expansion, especially in the heavy industries.

The optimism generated by rapid economic development and the political interests of Prussia in the struggle for national unification conspired to make the years from the end of the 1850s to the mid-1870s the heyday of German liberalism.[51] Laissez-faire and free trade reached their greatest popularity and pulled the country away from economic protection, whether at home or abroad. The German free traders had been trying to mobilize popular sentiment for their cause since the 1850s. Their movement, under the leadership of the Englishborn John Prince-Smith, never attained anywhere near the strength of the Anti-Corn Law League in England but did achieve a measure of success in the late 1850s and during the 1860s.[52]

Meanwhile, of course, the problem of insecurity had not disappeared, although rapid economic growth was bound to influence ideas and attitudes with regard to it. The leading spokesmen for economic liberalism in the 1860s were optimistic and no longer viewed poverty as inevitable, as did liberals like Hanseman and Camphausen in the 1840s. The liberal advice to the workers was stated in classic terms by Prince-Smith in 1864: "Work and save. Let your own need be the stimulus, and the enjoyments of those better-off the incentive that gives you the drive to increase your will power to take at least the first step on the road to salvation from economic distress."[53] Since it was a matter of will power, according to Prince-Smith, the road to abundance was open to anyone willing to put his mind to it. This was the same gospel of hope that Smiles preached in England. Equally remarkable, for his day, was the economic argument advanced by Prince-Smith to show that the interests of employers and workers were not in conflict but, in fact, were identical—that it was in the interests of employers to improve the well-being and the sense of security of the workers. In his view, poverty had no utility and low wages were not economy.

[50] Computed from table 2, *ibid.,* p. 14.
[51] W. Zorn, "Wirtschafts– und sozialgeschichtliche Zusammenhaenge der deutschen Reichsgruendungszeit (1850–1879)," *Historische Zeitschrift,* Vol. 197 (October 1963), pp. 323–324.
[52] W. O. Henderson, "Prince-Smith and Free Trade in Germany," *Economic History Review,* Second Series, Vol. II (1950), p. 300.
[53] Quoted in H. Herkner, *Die Arbeiterfrage* (seventh edition, Berlin: Vereinigung wissentschaftlicher Verleger, 1921), Vol. II, p. 123.

The output of an individual who is weakened and dulled by misery is not cheap at all. Well-fed workers always produce much more in relation to their maintenance cost than poorly fed workers. Bad wages give poor work, which is inevitably expensive work. The more capitalistic industrial development becomes, the more important it becomes for capitalism, with its expensive installations and its great, artistically interlaced institutions, to have workers who are careful and reliable. This is only possible with satisfied individuals, who have an interest in the success of the enterprise from which their welfare derives.[54]

It would be difficult to find a better formulation of the economic rationale for securing the welfare of the worker in industrial society. The complexity and the scale of industry make worker good will and cooperation an economic necessity. Whether employers would be enlightened enough to view the problem in this light, as Prince-Smith assumed they would, and whether they knew how to make the workers satisfied, were again different questions. Nevertheless, Prince-Smith put his finger on a crucial economic factor that Marx and his followers in the immiseration school ignored with durable stubbornness.

Hopeful as Prince-Smith's doctrine may have been in theory, it had painfully little appeal to the workers in practice. Indeed, even the more practical self-help schemes, like the Workers' Educational Societies (*Arbeiterbildungsvereine*) and the cooperative societies, failed to attract the industrial masses.[55] After generations of patriarchal tutelage by the state and social superiors, the German workman was not prepared for the gospel of self-help, whether it was preached by liberals, conservatives, or Christian social reformers.[56] This fact was appreciated by the advocates of the welfare monarchy in the 1840s and 1850s, but the crown, once the storm of revolution had calmed down, refused to act. One way out was to force the state to act in the interest of the working class.

This, in effect, was the position taken by Ferdinand Lassalle, one of the founders of the German socialist labor movement, who looked to universal,

[54] Quoted in H. Herkner, *Die Arbeiterfrage*, p. 125. Prince-Smith rejected the "iron law of wages" and argued in terms of the "golden law," according to which wages were mainly determined by the worker's "habits," which were slowly but surely rising with their cultural level. See his "Die sogenannte Arbeiterfrage" (1864) in Schraepler, *op. cit.*, p. 174.

[55] O. Pflanze, *Bismarck and the Development of Germany* (Princeton: Princeton University Press, 1963), p. 224; see also W. Koellmann, *Sozialgeschichte der Stadt Barmen im 19. Jahrhundert* (Tuebingen: J. C. B. Mohr, 1960), p. 158.

[56] Franz Hermann Schulze-Delitzsch, the leader of the cooperative movement, was hardly realistic when he told the workers in 1863 that the spirit of self-help was the genuine German spirit and that looking to the state for help would be betraying the spirit of their forefathers. See his "Kapitel zu einem deutschen Arbeiterkatechismus" in Schraepler, *op. cit.*, p. 182.

direct, and equal suffrage as the means by which the workers could achieve their goals.[57] "When the legislative bodies of Germany are the outcome of universal and direct suffrage, then and only then," he proclaimed to the workers, "will you be able to influence the state to do its duty...."[58] This duty involved the establishment and financing of cooperative associations for the workers. Lassalle wanted the state to do for the worker what he judged the worker, the victim of the "iron law of wages," incapable of doing for himself. "It is the business and task of the state . . . to take the great cause of the free individual association of the working class into its own hand, to promote and develop it, to make it its most holy duty to give you the means and the possibility for your self-organization and self-association."[59] Thus, Lassalle did not reject the cooperative idea; the essence of his economic program was to make cooperative associations an object of state help instead of self-help.[60]

During the reaction of the 1850s a new, progressive policy of social protection could hardly be expected to develop. Official thinking was still wedded to the traditional corporative concepts, which economic reality was making increasingly obsolescent. An 1849 guild-inspired Prussian law, which allowed the municipal authorities to order workers to join mutual welfare funds, had only limited success. For the country as a whole it resulted in the creation of 230 local welfare funds, of which only 60 required contributions from both employers and workers.[61] To encourage the creation of more welfare funds, Prussia went a step further with a law of 1854 that empowered local authorities to order the establishment of welfare funds.[62] For a country that was rapidly creating national markets, this step, which preserved local option, could have little practical significance, although it did strengthen the principle of compulsory insurance.

The sharpening of the constitutional conflict in the late 1850s and the ascendance of Bismarck (in 1862) seemed to offer new possibilities for remolding the relationship between the state and the individual. The Lassallean thrust in this direction has already been pointed out. The potentialities of using universal suffrage to support an autocratic welfare state were being

---

[57] On Lassalle's position in the constitutional debate, see Pflanze, *op. cit.*, pp. 217–218, 225.
[58] From his "Offenes Antwortschreiben an das Zentralkomitee zur Berufung eines Allgemeinen Deutschen Arbeiterkongresses zu Leipzig" in Schraepler, *op. cit.*, pp. 185–186.
[59] *Ibid.*, p. 185.
[60] In theory Lassalle accepted most of Marx's arguments, but in practice he stood closer to Rodbertus and Louis Blanc. He kept in contact with both Marx and Rodbertus, but neither approved of him. For an evaluation of Lassalle's place in the development of the ideas of state socialism, see C. Gide and C. Rist, *Histoire des doctrines économiques* (seventh edition, Paris: Recueil Sirey, 1947), Vol. II, pp. 476 ff.
[61] Hamerow, *op. cit.*, p. 243.
[62] Peters, *op. cit.*, p. 31.

tried out in France by Napoleon III. Bismarck himself had lost faith in the efficacy of social protection tied to the guild system in the early 1850s.[63] As Prussian ambassador to Paris in 1862, he had a close look at the French emperor's system of state protection *cum* state control of the industrial worker.[64] One of his old acquaintances and now collaborator, Hermann Wagener, also had abandoned the traditional views of conservatism on social protection and had become an ardent convert to the idea of the "social monarchy" as early as 1851.[65] He firmly believed that only a welfare monarchy could mend the workers' growing alienation from the crown and pull them away from dangerous agitators like Lassalle. His objective was to convince Bismarck of the urgent need for his initiative in major social reforms in order to capture and to control the emerging labor movement, which he saw splitting off from the liberal Progress party.[66] The economic and social reforms he urged on the Minister President had three main points: (1) the establishment of a minimum daily wage, (2) the organization of corporative institutions by industries, to replace individual by collective agreements between employers and employees, and (3) the recognition of the principle that continued employment in an enterprise will lead the worker to co-ownership.[67] The mixing of feudal and socialist elements in these proposals reveals Wagener's rather hazy grasp of the nature of industrialism. Although Bismarck was receptive to Wagener's ideas, he was too busy with other affairs of state to launch a major program of social reform during the 1860s. Nevertheless, the idea of using the proletariat as an instrument of the state against the liberal bourgeoisie was sufficiently attractive to lead Bismarck to contemplate an alliance with even a radical like Lassalle.[68] In repeated discussions with Bismarck, Lassalle stressed that the proletariat wanted strong leadership and would willingly accept the social dictatorship of the crown.[69]

Bismarck never seriously attempted to put either Wagener's or Lassalle's proposals for producers' associations into practice. "Only twice, for pro-

---

[63] Hamerow, *op. cit.*, pp. 250–251.

[64] Walter Vogel, *Bismarck's Arbeiterversicherung* (Braunschweig: G. Westerman, 1951), p. 142.

[65] W. Saile, *Hermann Wagener und sein Verhaeltnis zu Bismarck*, Tuebinger Studien zur Geschichte und Politik (Tuebingen: J. C. B. Mohr, 1958), p. 46.

[66] Within a week after Bismarck became Minister President, Wagener handed him a memorandum entitled "What Must Happen Next Internally" in which he argued the urgent need for "lifting the curse which turns the mass of the population into the weakwilled tool of the Progress party." The memorandum is reprinted in Saile, *op. cit.*, pp. 133–135.

[67] *Ibid.*, p. 80.

[68] He had become aware of the possibility of this alliance through Wagener, although the latter did not seem to favor it, since he profoundly disliked and distrusted Lassalle. *Ibid.*, pp. 79 ff.

[69] See W. Richter, *Bismarck* (Frankfurt: S. Fischer Verlag, 1962), p. 111.

pagandistic purposes, did he promote such associations."[70] One of these occasions was a producer's cooperative established and subsidized by the state to help out Silesian weavers who were hard hit by a cotton famine resulting from the American Civil War.[71] It ended in failure and discouraged Bismarck from further promotions. He put little value on an alliance with Lassalle and did not share Wagener's urgency of the need for social reform. The feature from Wagener's program that he was willing to push was the legalization of workers' combinations. As early as May 1863, he ordered Itzenplitz, the Minister of Commerce, to draft a bill legalizing trade unions.[72] This, he hoped, would strengthen the workers' self-help capability in dealing with the bourgeoisie, but his main objective was political advantage rather than worker welfare. He aimed at weakening the liberals and by a friendly gesture hoped to strengthen the workers' loyalty to the state.[73] Although Bismarck did not want to organize cooperatives along with the legalization of workers' combinations, as members of his cabinet urged him to do, he naturally hoped to keep the emerging labor organizations under control. That was one of the central features of the Napoleonic system, promote and control the labor movement. When trade unions were finally legalized in 1869, the state had tacked on measures to restrict their freedom. Bismarck strongly supported the penalties against unions for coercing individuals to participate in strikes. By then he had shifted from being the defender of the freedom of combination to the defender of the individual worker against combinations. "His policy no longer aimed at increasing the workers' freedom of movement, but at making them protégés, clients of the state."[74] The fact he had to reckon with, of course, was that since 1863 the German labor movement had revived, and in 1869 a political party, the Social Democrat Labor party, dedicated to the revolutionary program of Karl Marx, was established. Events were moving rapidly and, with them, the kind of social protection that would retain or regain the workers' loyalty to the state.

During the 1870s the balance of forces shifted decisively from self-help to state help. The social legislation passed during the decade, however, still reflected the liberal influence. This was the case with the Employer Liability Act of June 7, 1871. Under this law, which was applicable to the whole of the empire, the employer was liable in cases of industrial accidents, not only if

[70] K. E. Born, "Sozialpolitische Probleme und Bestrebungen in Deutschland von 1848 bis zur Bismarckschen Sozialgesetzgebung," *Vierteljahrschrift fuer Sozial- und Wirtschaftsgeschichte*, Vol. 47 (March 1959), p. 40.
[71] See Pflanze, *op. cit.*, pp. 280–282. Bismarck looked on this mainly as an experiment to test the feasibility of productive associations. See his letter to the local official in charge in Rothfels (ed.), *Bismarck und der Staat*, pp. 316–317.   [72] *Ibid.*, p. 280.
[73] The liberals also demanded legalization of trade unions, thinking that the consequences would be to their political advantage. See Born, *op. cit.*, p. 36.
[74] *Ibid.*, p. 43.

the accident was his fault but also if it was the fault of the fellow workmen of the injured worker.[75] His liability extended to damages, medical cost, and burial expenses in case of death. Although this law certainly marked an advance over the more extreme liberal position that held the employer liable only when injury was the result of his fault, it still left the whole matter of compensation contingent upon the outcome of a civil suit in which the burden of proof was on the victim or his survivors. The state was not yet willing to step in on the side of the worker, who was usually in a severely disadvantageous legal and financial position vis-à-vis the employer. Even when he had the financial resources to sue the employer, the worker was still without recourse in all cases where it was not possible to prove the guilt of the employer or of fellow workmen, which was the normal situation in all purely accidential injuries. In the area of mutual assistance funds the Empire continued the Prussian principle of compulsory self-help on the basis of local option. Two laws were enacted in 1876 to regulate these funds and to correct certain abuses, but this did not help their progress, which continued to be very slow.[76]

The major factors that contributed to a shift in social policy during the 1870s were closely interrelated. Perhaps the first to be mentioned is the depression that began in 1873 and hit Germany with unprecedented severity. Many of the enterprises that had sprung into existence in the wake of national unification and victory over France suddenly collapsed. One of the hardest hit was the iron and steel industry. In iron smelting, employment fell by forty per cent between 1873 and 1874; in 1876 one half of the German blast furnaces were standing idle.[77] Although the depression was an international phenomenon, speculative excesses during the exuberant years between 1871 and 1873 greatly contributed to the crisis. Spiced by the revelation of promotion swindles, the reaction against the excesses took the form of an attack on the idea of laissez-faire.[78] A series of laws, passed in the laissez-faire spirit during the years 1870 to 1972, had indeed facilitated the promotion scandals by greatly easing the formation of corporations and by failing to provide adequate safeguards for investors and the public. Another factor that put economic liberalism in a vulnerable spot was the coincidence between the crisis of 1873 and the elimination of the duties on iron. The iron and steel industry stood in the forefront of the emerging protectionist movement.[79] Powerful industrial associations, such as the Society

---

[75] Peters, op. cit., p. 38.   [76] Ibid., p. 37; Vogel, op. cit., pp. 21–23.
[77] Clapham, The Economic Development of France and Germany 1815–1914 (4th edition; Cambridge: University Press, 1951), p. 284.
[78] Sartorius von Waltershausen, op. cit., pp. 271 ff.
[79] See Ivo N. Lambi, "The Protectionist Interests of the German Iron and Steel Industry, 1873–1879," Journal of Economic History, Vol. XXII (March 1962), pp. 59–70.

of South German Cotton Manufacturers (1873), the Society of German Iron and Steel Industrialists (1874), the Central Union of German Industrialists for the Promotion and Protection of National Labor (1875 to 1876), sprung to life to help in the protection of domestic industry against foreign competition.[80] But, perhaps, even more important in the swing to protectionism was the change in the attitude of the agrarians. Two important economic developments brought the traditionally free-trade agrarians into the protectionist camp. First, during the 1870s, Germany shifted from a position of net exporter to one of net importer of food.[81] Second, the railroad and the steamship were bringing formidable new competitors to the international market for foodstuffs; the price of German grain was threatened by the influx of Russian and Hungarian supplies. The economic interests of the agrarians thus were no longer on the side of free trade but on the side of a protected home market. By the end of the decade they had joined hands with the industrialists in a common endeavor to protect the home market.[82]

This growing protectionist mood was by no means limited to foreign trade. It was part of a move toward a more planned economy.[83] If the state was going to protect the manufacturer, something had to be done for the worker too, especially since tariffs might lead to higher prices. It is most interesting, and hardly coincidental, that two of the leading protectionist iron and steel magnates, Ludwig Baare and Carl Ferdinand Stumm, were also leading spokesmen for compulsory state social insurance. Stumm, the "king of the Saar," can be considered, along with Krupp, as the archetype of the big industrialist who saw the social relations of modern industry in a feudal patriarchal perspective, which was inconsistent with the idea of worker self-dependence. According to Stumm, "since the worker owes obedience to his employer, the latter is obligated, by God and by law, to care for the worker far beyond the limits of the labor contract. The employer should consider himself as the head of a large family whose individual members are entitled to his care and protection so long as they prove themselves worthy."[84] Stumm had experience with the *Knappschaften* of the mining industry and wanted the state to make this system of protection compulsory in other industries. The *Knappschaften* suited him particularly, as Vogel points out, because they gave the employer a dominant administrative position, which was not the case in the mutual assistance funds, where workers were

---

[80] Zorn, *op. cit.*, p. 334.

[81] Clapham, *op. cit.*, p. 210.

[82] See Ivo N. Lambi, "The Agrarian-Industrial Front in Bismarckian Politics, 1873–1879," *Journal of Central European Affairs*, Vol. XX (January 1961), pp. 378–396.

[83] H. Rothfels, "Bismarck's Social Policy and the Problem of State Socialism in Germany," Part II, *Sociological Review*, Vol. XXX (1938), p. 295.

[84] Quoted in Vogel, *op. cit.*, p. 37.

usually in control. As a member of the *Reichstag,* Stumm was very active in promoting compulsory social insurance, which he considered the most effective means at the state's disposal for increasing "the feeling and the interest in unity among employers and workers."[85] With the full support of like-minded industrialists he submitted a plan to the government in 1878 that contained his ideas for a system of compulsory state old-age and invalidity insurance. Baare, on the other hand, was active in the promotion of compulsory state insurance against industrial accidents in order to remedy the shortcomings of the 1871 Employer Liability Act. The memorandum he submitted to the government in 1880 was influential in guiding official thinking in the development of workmen's compensation.

In general, big business rather than the small employer favored a state system of compulsory insurance. Small employers were more inclined to oppose any kind of compulsory system or, at best, to accept compulsory mutual assistance determined by local option. Nevertheless, it is interesting that at the 1874 meetings of the *Verein Fuer Sozialpolitik,* a factory owner, named Kalle, was the leading spokesman for the elimination of local option and the institution of nationwide compulsory insurance against invalidity and old age.[86] His argument against them, like the publisher Franz Duncker and the economist Lujo Brentano, who advocated voluntarism and self-help on the model of the British friendly societies, was that, on the whole, neither employers nor workers were farsighted enough to take the trouble and to bear the expenses voluntarily. "With regard to the employers," Kalle told his audience, "I have only to recall to your mind the agitation of many mine operators to be freed from contributions to the *Knappschaften,* the small participation in the effort to insure the workers not covered by the employer liability act, and finally the opposition against compulsory evening schools for apprentices."[87] And yet, he stressed, a generalization of insurance was absolutely essential, not only to meet a moral obligation of the employer but to remove a major source of discontent among the workers. As a man with practical experience, he maintained also that "the quality of work performance is adversely affected when the worker must look to the future with anxiety and is unable to allow himself the satisfaction of enjoying the present."[88] The kind of insurance system that Kalle envisaged was based on compulsory membership in mutual assistance societies, organized along lines prescribed by the state, but with individual freedom to choose membership in a particular society, except that the state would create societies where none were established voluntarily. He thus stood midway between those who rejected

[85] Fritz Hellwig, *Carl Ferdinand Freiherr von Stumm-Halberg* (Heidelberg: Westmarck Verlag, 1936), p. 189.
[86] See "Verein Fuer Sozialpolitik," *Schriften,* Verhandlungen von 1874 (Leipzig: Duncker und Humblot, 1875), Vol. IX, pp. 64–76.   [87] *Ibid.,* p. 69.   [88] *Ibid.,* p. 68.

compulsion of any kind and those who, like Stumm, wanted a compulsory system that would be under the patriarchal rule of the employer.[89]

Another possibility, of course, was that neither employers nor workers but the state bureaucracy should be in control of the insurance institutions. This view was implicit in the welfare monarchy argument, since one of its major objectives was the promotion of worker loyalty to the state instead of to the employer or to some labor organization. With the rise of the labor movement, especially since it was largely under the banner of Marxism, the question of worker loyalty became a crucial issue and could not help but become a major influence in the deliberations concerning the nature of the social insurance system.

Even before the repeal of the prohibition of worker combinations, labor organizations were being founded in Germany. By 1868, the General German Workingmen's Union founded by Lassalle in 1863 had, according to one source, more than 125,000 members.[90] In the 1860s and 1870s trade unions were being organized by various political groups, but the socialists were the most successful. To Bismarck, who witnessed the Paris Commune in 1871, this was a dangerous development, especially since many of the socialist unions were affiliated with Marx's International Workingmen's Association and apparently accepted its revolutionary creed. Bismarck pondered the consequences of radical leaders being in command of the masses of German workers who were used to military discipline. In 1875 the socialist forces were strengthened further when the Lassallean groups united with the Bebel–Liebknecht Social Democrats and adopted a common revolutionary program. Under the leadership of August Bebel and Wilhelm Liebknecht the Social Democrats were effectively spreading the Marxist message to the masses during the depression years of the mid-1870s, in spite of harassment by the police. In the election of 1877 the Social Democrats attracted nearly one-half million votes and obtained 12 seats in the *Reichstag*.[91] When two attempts were made on the Kaiser's life, although not by socialists, Bismarck was able to take advantage of the inflamed state of public opinion to secure passage of his antisocialist legislation.

---

[89] Kalle stood for *Kassenzwang*, the obligation to be insured, but Stumm's position amounted to *Zwangskassen*, the obligation to be insured through a specific organization without freedom of choice.

[90] S. Perlman, *A Theory of the Labor Movement* (New York: Augustus M. Kelley, 1949), p. 79. Unfortunately, Perlman does not give the source of his figure, which seems rather high. Mehring credits the Union with 40,000 votes in the 1867 election. Franz Mehring, *Geschichte der deutschen Sozialdemokratie* (reprinted, Berlin: Dietz Verlag, 1960) Vol. II, p. 258. Much lower membership figures are given also in Thomas Niperdey, *Die Organisation der deutschen Parteien vor 1918* (Düsseldorf: Droste Verlag, 1961), pp. 296–297.

[91] Wolfgang Pack, *Das parlamentarische Ringen um das Sozialistengesetz Bismarcks 1878–1890* (Düsseldorf: Droste Verlag, 1961), p. 14.

But also he was well aware that mere repression was not enough to resolve the problem of worker alienation, of which the success of the socialist movement was but a reflection. He had declared as early as November 17, 1871, before the depression but in the aftermath of the Paris Commune, that the state had to plunge into the socialist movement and to achieve "that which seems legitimate in the socialist demands" within the existing social and political framework.[92] Again the following year he assured William I that "with mere police measures the problem cannot be solved."[93] It still took several years, during which plans were drawn up and discussed, before he definitely decided on social insurance as the main tool for his social planning. For this delay, economic liberalism among the higher bureaucracy was largely responsible.

SOCIAL INSURANCE IN DEFENSE OF TRADITIONAL AUTHORITY

If conditions had ripened by the early 1880s for the institution of new social rights, it was mainly because of pressure from below. Bismarck's ideological justification of these rights, however, came from above, from the patriarchal conception of the duties of the state. His central political consideration was not the creation of new rights, consistent with a new interpretation of the rights of citizenship, but the preservation of the traditional relationship of the individual to the state. In a sense, social rights were granted to prevent having to grant enlarged political rights. Of course, Bismarck fully intended to alleviate poverty, and to that extent his social insurance was to reduce economic inequality. But the whole thrust of his measures was to preserve the traditional system of political inequality. Thus conceived, as a political weapon, his program became inevitably embroiled with all the forces that sought a larger share of political power. In tracing the development of his program, we shall study how the interplay of these forces shaped the right to protection.

At the opening of the *Reichstag,* on February 15, 1881, the Kaiser sent a message that sounded the starting gun of Bismarck's drive for social insurance. The healing of social ills, the message stated,

> cannot be achieved exclusively by way of repressing socialistic excesses but must be sought simultaneously through the positive promotion of the worker's welfare. . . . The institutions which until now were to protect the worker who found himself in a helpless state because he had lost his ability to work, either by accident or on account of old age, have proven to be inadequate. This inadequacy

[92] Letter to Itzenplitz, reprinted in Rothfels, *Bismarck und der Staat,* p. 329.
[93] Communication reprinted in *ibid.*, p. 331.

has not been a minor factor in inducing members of this social class to seek the road to relief by supporting Social Democratic aims.[94]

These statements, of course, closely reflected Bismarck's position. He was convinced that it was not only politically necessary but also the duty of the Christian state to extend a protective hand to the individual. He often referred to his program as "practical Christianity,"[95] yet ethical considerations were not a strong motivating force for him. Neither the idea of Christian charity nor a collaboration with religiously inspired social reform movements were of practical importance to him. "The state must take the matter in hand," he declared, "not as a matter of charity, but as a right to support."[96] For him this right, at least what he understood by it, was deeply rooted in the Prussian tradition. He liked to recall that, while still Crown Prince, Frederick the Great once said: "Quand je serai Roi, je serai un vrai roi des gueux !" To the taunts from liberals in the *Reichstag* that he was treading the path of socialism, he answered with sarcasm:

> Socialistic are many of the measures that have been taken, and taken for the greater good of the state, and in our empire the state will have to become used to a little more socialism. . . . If you believe that you can frighten anyone with the word "socialism," you hold a view which I have long overcome.[97]

He accepted the notion that a good dose of socialism was inevitable and desirable for both the individual and the state. From private welfare measures he no longer expected much, if he ever did. "Belief in a harmony of interests has been made bankrupt by history. No doubt the individual can do much good, but the social problem can only be solved by the state."[98]

He had no illusions that the state could quickly or simply dispose of a complex problem that had grown increasingly difficult for more than half a century. The skirmishes he had over his first accident insurance bill in the *Reichstag* in 1881 revealed considerable resistance to his plans, and the *Reichstag* elections in October of that year could be interpreted as a repudiation of his economic and social policies. Undaunted by parliamentary reverses, Bismarck got the Kaiser to promulgate, at the opening session of the new *Reichstag*, on November 17, 1881, the historic message in which plans

---

[94] *Gesammelten Werke,* edited by Wilhelm Schuessler (Berlin: Otto Stollberg Verlag, 1929), Vol. XII, pp. 186–187.
[95] Friedrich Luetge, "Die Grundprinzipien der Bismarckschen Sozialpolitik," *Jahrbuch für Nationaloekonomie und Statistik,* Vol. 134 (1931 : 1), p. 584.
[96] Statement to the writer Moritz Busch, reprinted in Rothfels, *Bismarck und der Staat,* p. 359.
[97] *Gesammelten Werke,* Vol. XII, p. 360.
[98] Quoted in Hans Rothfels, "Bismarck's Social Policy and the Problem of State Socialism in Germany," Part I, *Sociological Review,* Vol. XXX (1938), p. 92.

for a threefold insurance system with a corporative administrative structure were indicated. The message to the *Reichstag* stated in part:

> The cure of social ills must be sought not exclusively in the repression of Social Democratic excesses, but simultaneously in the positive advancement in the welfare of the working classes. We regard it as our imperial duty to urge this task again upon the Reichstag, and we should look back with the greater satisfaction upon all the successes with which God has visibly blessed our government if we are able one day to take with us the consciousness that we left to the fatherland new and lasting sureties for its internal peace, and to those needing help greater security and liberality in the assistance to which they can lay claim. Our efforts in this direction are certain of the approval of all the federal Governments, and we confidently rely on the support of the Reichstag, without distinction of parties. In order to realize these views a Bill for the insurance of workmen against industrial accidents will first be laid before you, after which a supplementary measure will be submitted providing for a general organization of industrial sickness insurance. But likewise those who are disabled in consequence of old age or invalidity possess a well-founded claim to a more ample relief on the part of the State than they have hitherto enjoyed. To find the proper ways and means for making such provision is a difficult task, yet is one of the highest obligations of every community based on the ethical foundations of a Christian national life. The closer union of the practical forces of this national life and their combination in the form of corporate associations, with State patronage and help, will, we hope, render possible the discharge of tasks to which the executive alone might prove unable.[99]

After intensive debates and maneuvers over specific aims and methods, health insurance passed in 1883, accident insurance in 1884, and old-age and invalidity insurance in 1889.

The resistance to Bismarck's plans was mainly to the manner in which he was trying to use social insurance as a tool of social and political control. The idea of state help to protect the worker was widely shared in the empire, even by groups who were committed to radically different political ideologies. In academic economic circles the members of the dominant historical school generally leaned toward state protection although they were not in agreement in detail. Scholars like Gustav Schmoller, Adolf Wagner, and Albert Schaeffle stressed the historical traditions of Prussian social protection. For Schmoller, who believed that only social systems dedicated to the common good could survive, the issue of social justice was in the foreground. Social protection was essential for the realization of the ethical ideal of the state.[100] Wagner, an expert on fiscal policy and a leading spokesman

[99] This translation is from William H. Dawson, *Social Insurance in Germany 1883–1911* (London: Scribner's, 1912), pp. 16–17. For the original, see *Gesammelten Werke*, Vol. XII, pp. 270–273.
[100] His hope for his time was that great statesmen would come forth to "take social reform in hand and carry it through in a strong but peaceful manner." G. Schmoller, *Die soziale Frage* (Muenchen: Duncker und Humblot, 1918), p. 633.

for state socialism, stressed the practical aspects. For him any kind of insurance was by its very nature suitable only for state and not for private enterprise.[101] The socialists, ever since Lassalle, had adopted the position that only the state could solve the social problem but, since the founding of the Social Democratic party, the Marxist orientation won out over the Lassallean one, which meant that cooperation with the existing state was rejected because it was a tool of the ruling classes and could not be expected to act in the interest of the worker. Heavy industry, led by Stumm, also favored state protection of the workingman, especially in a manner which enhanced the employer's paternalistic control.[102] Other business groups often approved of the idea of national compulsory insurance as long as it did not enhance state control. Their interest was more in improving industrial relations and in increasing labor productivity than in social reform. The Eastern agrarians, who traditionally rejected the stress on individualism and self-help, were receptive to state intervention on behalf of the industrial worker. They hoped that this might counteract the influence of the new industrial aristocracy, although they were also apprehensive of any strengthening of the state bureaucracy or the labor movement. The Catholics, who had been welded together politically by the *Kulturkampf,* shared the anti-individualistic tradition; they stressed the individual's moral right to existence and acknowledged the duty of the state to guarantee this existence when private means were failing. Resistance to the idea of a compulsory system of state insurance was found for the most part among extreme liberals and extreme conservatives; for the liberals the solution lay in self-help, and for the conservatives in private charity.

The issue in the enactment of social insurance was not the legitimacy of protection but the power and influence that might devolve upon any of the groups connected with the insurance system. The basic question for the participants in the social insurance debate was how the new arrangement would affect the [political] balance of political forces. Since the planned social insurance was a pioneer undertaking, at least as far as size was concerned, its social, economic, and political consequences were not easily predicted and were typically greatly exaggerated. In the transition to industrial society, the loyalty, good will, and vote of the workingman had become something worth capturing or, at least, to be kept from being captured by rivals. These considerations strongly influenced the position taken by Bismarck and his adversaries on what may seem to be technical insurance questions. Who was to gain or to lose if the system became voluntary instead of compulsory? Should it follow along the line of compulsory membership

[101] A. Wagner, "Der Staat und das Versicherungswesen," *Zeitschrift fuer die gesammte Staatswissenschaft,* Vol. 37, No. 1 (1881), pp. 102–172.
[102] See Hellwig, *op. cit.,* Chapter VIII; also von Laue, *op. cit.,* pp. 125 ff.

in freely selected friendly societies, adopt a pattern of compulsory insurance through private insurance companies, or should it be based on state institutions with no freedom of choice ? If state institutions were created, should they be centralized and controlled by the bureaucracy, or should employers and workers be allowed to participate in their administration ? How should cost be shared among the state, the employer, and the worker ?

The answers that Bismarck gave to these questions were based on his conception of the individual's relationship to the state. A concise formulation of the fundamental principles of his policy has been given by Rothfels:

> In its practical objectives, Bismarck's social policy is determined by neither religious nor by provident care considerations; it has to do with neither the soul nor the welfare of the individual or the sum of individuals; rather, it is conceived in principle as state directed, and it aims at the good of the community unified in the state. (das Wohl der staatlich geeinten Gemeinschaft.)[103]

He viewed every social problem "from the point of view of whether and how it affected or endangered the state." [104] In his means he was quite adaptable, or we might say opportunistic, but to his objective, "a state with a strong central power under a solid monarchical summit," he held with "unshakeable firmness." [105]

Until the 1880s Bismarck had concentrated on the external consolidation of the empire. By then, however, the threat of a socialist capture of the working masses drove him to throw his energy and unbending will into the battle for the internal consolidation of the state. To achieve this aim more was required, in his view, than the mere elimination of worker discontent. That might achieve a benevolent neutrality of the worker toward the state. He wanted the worker as a loyal and obedient ally, and to accomplish this the worker's interests had to be closely tied to the state. The state, therefore, had to become the protector of the workingman. Of the major ways in which this could be achieved—namely, by factory legislation, labor legislation, and social security—Bismarck found great merit only in the latter.[106] Aside from fears about keeping German industry competitive in international markets, his paternalistic conception of the role of the employer, which was colored by his Junker background and his experiences as a small employer, militated against factory legislation that regulated matters such as hours, wages, and working conditions. Labor legislation of the kind that would increase trade union security and would strengthen collective bargaining did not seem suited to his aims. Social insurance, in his

---

[103]"Prinzipienfrage der Bismarckschen Sozialpolitik," p. 53.
[104]Luetge, "Die Grundprinzipien der Bismarckschen Sozialpolitik," p. 582.   [105]*Ibid.*, p. 582.
[106]There were also fiscal measures he considered to assist the lower classes. See, for instance, von Laue, *op. cit.,* pp. 100–101.

belief, offered the best possibilities for the kind of human management that would bind the laboring classes to the state.

The social and political issues at stake were brought out most clearly in connection with industrial accidents insurance, since this was the first insecurity problem that Bismarck attacked. The basic alternative approaches were whether to extend and to improve the employer liability law of 1871 or whether to create a compulsory insurance system. The liability approach, to be effective, has to eliminate the problem of searching for the guilty party in accidents and has to hold employers liable for all work-related accidents. This approach was advocated by Theodor Lohmann, one of Bismarck's more liberally oriented collaborators. Lohmann wanted the employers to meet this burden through private insurance associations and to have the workers pay one third of the insurance premium. Unlike Bismarck, he was motivated by the desire not to increase the workers' dependence on the state and wished to encourage private initiative. Bismarck was dead set against any solution via an extension of employer liability. To him, this was not only unfair to the employer, but more important, it left the injured worker looking to private institutions rather than to the state for help. He was equally unreceptive to the participation of private insurance companies in any kind of compulsory insurance plan, since that would intrude the profit motive, speculation, dividends, and the stock market into an area he considered the responsibility of the state. As an agrarian conservative, he would have found an intrusion of this kind not only incompatible but abhorrent. The fundamental principles he thought necessary to achieve his goals were contained in the first accident insurance bill of 1881: compulsory insurance, centralized control by an imperial insurance office, exclusion of private insurance companies, and subsidization by the state.[107] It was to be an insurance system rather than a state assistance program, but workers with an annual income of less than 750 marks were to pay no contributions, and workers in the 750 to 1200 income range would pay one third and higher income workers one half of the insurance premium.

It may be seriously questioned whether an insurance system based on these principles would have served Bismarck's purposes in the manner that he anticipated, but his intent was clear and crude. By insisting on compulsory insurance he meant to exclude self-insurance, which some advocated. The state was to have an insurance monopoly and a tight administrative control, which was consistent with the view of the state as the arbiter among conflicting interest groups. Such conflicts are inevitable in accident insurance when it comes to the determination of rights to compensation, degrees of injury, and levels of pension. The employers were to bear the

---

[107] Otto Quandt, *Die Anfänge der Bismarckschen Sozialgesetzgebung* (Berlin: Ebering Verlag, 1938), p. 25.

lion's share of the cost, but the states would be asked to help out. The argument advanced officially was that this help would be some sort of equivalence for the lowering of state poor-relief expenses that could be expected from the plan. The main reason for the subsidy, however, was the desire to spare the worker without burdening the employer. "If the worker has to pay for it himself," Bismarck noted in the margin of a report, "the effect on him will be lost." [108] The effect on the worker's attitude, not on his welfare, was uppermost in Bismarck's mind.

That such a transparent attempt at the political exploitation of the need for social protection would bring forth strong reactions from political opponents was a foregone conclusion. [109] Max Hirsch, the founder of the liberal trade unions, denounced the bill as an attempt to "forge iron fetters around the worker's freedom of movement." [110] Another leading liberal, Ludwig Bamberger, brought out the analogy between Bismarck's aims and the politically inspired feeding of the proletariat in the decaying Athenian and Roman republics. [111] The socialist press produced scathing excoriations, such as "garrison socialism," tying the worker to the "state welfare chain," and making him a "state slave." [112] If the left liberal and the socialist press found Bismarck's plan totally unacceptable, the Catholics and the Conservatives were mainly opposed to its centralization of power and its subsidization feature. Within each of the political parties, of course, there were differences of opinion; the socialists in the *Reichstag* found much more merit in the bill than the socialist propagandists. The objections of the Catholics, which were shared in varying degrees by the Conservatives, tended to be stated in moral rather than in political terms. For instance, von Hertling, a leading spokesman for the Center (Catholic) party, argued that the state subsidy would put the honorable and industrious worker in the same category as the loafer! He objected to the deadening impersonality of a centralized bureaucratic system that would stifle the development of organic ties between employers and workers. He wanted an "organic" administrative structure, based on occupational groupings. [113] In such a case the internal insurance regulations and the decisions on compensation levels and other matters would be arrived at jointly by employers and workers in the various trades and industries. In theory this might lead to genuine industrial cooperation but, in practice, it could also mean the domination of employers over workers, unless the latter were well organized and protected against

[108] Quoted in *ibid.*, p. 25.
[109] The best analyses of this reaction are in the cited works by Quandt and by von Laue.
[110] Quandt, *op. cit.*, p. 33.
[111] *Ibid.*, p. 44.
[112] *Ibid.*, p. 39.
[113] *Ibid.*, pp. 48–50.

reprisals. This possibility was probably not ignored by the various groups favoring the cooperative structure, which included generally the Center, the Conservatives, and the *Reichspartei*, of which Stumm was the spokesman.

The majority opinion in all the parties was against the state subsidy, the Conservatives agreeing with the Catholics that the worker ought to pay his share. Oddly enough, Stumm, the big industrialist, and Bebel, the Social Democrat, agreed, but doubtless for different reasons, that the employer could and should bear the full cost of the insurance plan by himself. Agreement between the right and the left was revealed in another seemingly paradoxical situation. Bebel was the sole supporter in the *Reichstag* of Bismarck's symbol of bureaucratic centralism, the Imperial Insurance Office.[114] He preferred that decisions affecting the workers should be in the hands of state bureaucrats instead of in the hands of the employers.

It was clear that only with a majority, consisting of a coalition of Conservatives and Catholics, could Bismarck get an insurance bill through the *Reichstag* and that this majority would not accept bureaucratic centralism and state subsidization. After his failure to get an acceptable bill passed in 1881, he was forced to give way first on the administrative issue and second on the subsidy. Two more bills were debated before accident insurance was enacted into law in 1884. Bismarck was in favor of workers' committees sharing in the practical administrative work, but when the bill was passed into law there was little in it that gave administrative responsibility to the workers. They were represented only in committees that dealt with preventive measures. For all practical purposes the system was under the control of the employers, who usually combined into industrial or regional mutual associations. These associations were under the supervision of state insurance offices that were ultimately responsible to the Imperial Insurance Office. The system was thus highly decentralized and was geared to employer self-administration. Although, in the end, the employers possessed administrative control, they also had to bear the full cost, with the exception of those costs connected with the operations of the Imperial Insurance Office.

The Accident Insurance Law of 1884 fell far short of becoming the instrument of social transformation Bismarck desired. The direct tie of the worker to the state via the central Imperial Insurance Office had to be abandoned after the first skirmish with the elected representatives of the people. Bismarck then placed his hope in an indirect tie via corporative organizations that would be directly under the central office. In fact, he had highly exaggerated expectations of the political potentials of corporative associations. In 1883 he told Lohmann that

> accident insurance as such is a secondary matter to him; the main thing is to
> create through it corporative associations which will gradually be expanded to

[114] Von Laue, *op. cit.*, p. 285.

include all the productive social classes in order to provide the basis for an eventual popular representation which will take the place of, or operate along-side, the *Reichstag* as an important codetermining factor in legislation.[115]

Naturally, the *Reichstag* could not be induced to go along with these plans but the Chancellor was willing to use extraconstitutional means if necessary. Even though events turned out differently, it is interesting to contemplate the temptations that the creation of social insurance can arouse in a strong-willed ruler in a time of rapid economic and social change. With the workers left out of the corporative accident associations, the Law of 1884 was hardly a step in the direction of building a corporate state. The associations did not embody an effective representation of economic interest groups, nor did they leave the state in the position of arbiter among them. To be allowed effective participation, the workers were judged too unreliable by some and socially too inferior by others. Operating in a political environment full of tensions and conflicts, the powerful Chancellor was unable to forge the tools of social control that he believed would best serve his objectives.

The emphasis of this discussion has been on the Accident Insurance Law because most of the ideological conflicts were fought out in the course of its enactment. With regard to health insurance, Bismarck took a different attitude. The major alternative to a centralized state administrative structure was the more convenient expedient of building onto the existing guild, factory, industry, and mutual institutions that were then already providing sickness benefits. Local sickness funds were created for trades that had none and parochial funds were created for all individuals in a locality who would not fit into other insurance categories. The resulting organizational structure was highly decentralized, and extensive local autonomy added to its com-plexity. All funds were governed by their members, except the parochial funds, which were administered by locally elected representatives.[116] In general, workers paid two thirds of the insurance premiums and the employers one third, and their representation on the governing bodies was proportional to the contributions. In this manner, the workers were in effective control of health insurance, although factory funds and the miners' *Knappschaften* had rules of their own. Bismarck never tried to introduce the state into this picture. Aside from not wanting to reshape a system already in operation, and already partly regulated by the Law of 1876, Bismarck apparently had less interest in health insurance because its assistance to the worker was of a short-term nature and would not be effective in creating ties to the state.[117]

In the case of old-age and invalidity insurance, however, the value of

[115] Quandt, *op. cit.*, p. 94.

[116] See Dawson, *Social Insurance in Germany*, Chapter II.

[117] Luetge, "Die Grundprinzipien der Bismarckschen Socialpolitik," p. 592.

pensions as a means of attaching the worker to the state came again to the forefront. Bismarck aimed at the dual objective of lessening worker discontent and of increasing their stake in the stability of the existing order. Speaking for the government's bill in the *Reichstag,* he argued convincingly that most workers who vote socialist do so not out of doctrinal conviction but as an expression of protest. This protest was born out of discontent with their economic situation and, to the extent that the proposed social insurance removed a source of discontent, he reasoned, it weakened the hold of the socialists on the workers.[118] In response to his critics, he clarified that he was not trying to influence the socialist leaders but the masses. His reasoning with regard to increasing the workers' stake in the existing order was a bit less sophisticated. Drawing again on his own observations in France, he contended that the reason most Frenchmen tended to support whatever government happened to be in power, even though it might badly manage the affairs of the state, was that so many of them were drawing some, often very small, annuity from the state. The individual tells himself: " 'if the state goes under I shall lose my annuity'; and even though it may be but 40 francs a year, he does not want to lose it; he has an interest in the state." [119] This was not just a low opinion of the intelligence of the average Frenchman; he thought that the same argument would apply to Germany with old-age and invalidity pensions. "I will consider it a great advantage when we have 700,000 small pensioners drawing their annuities from the state, especially if they belong to those classes who otherwise do not have much to lose by an upheaval and erroneously believe they can actually gain much by it." [120] He thought that, even though the average pensioner would have only 115 to 200 marks to lose, this amount would be enough to keep him loyal to the existing state. The common man, he added, would learn to look on the state as a benevolent institution. The extent to which this reasoning was valid depended heavily on the degree of worker alienation from society and how much they resented things that were denied them, especially, the greater recognition of their trade unionism. It has often been pointed out that Bismarck's mental image of the worker was the craftsman and that he never quite understood the psychology of the industrial worker.

The old-age and invalidity bill, which became law on June 22, 1889, a month after Bismarck's speech, was again only a partial success for him. He had intended to make use of the corporative associations that were carrying the accident insurance, but employer resistance kept this plan from even being introduced.[121] This was a defeat for the extension of corporatism.

[118] Speech of May 18, 1889 in *Gesammelten Werke*, Vol. XIII, p. 396.

[119] *Ibid.*, p. 403.

[120] *Ibid.*, p. 403.

[121] Dawson, *Social Insurance in Germany*, p. 19.

Instead, the law set up a bureacratic administrative apparatus, with employers and workers equally represented on certain auxiliary committees. An interesting compromise was reached with regard to financing. Employers and workers were asked to contribute in equal amounts. The contribution by the workers to a system run by the state was considered morally important by all of Bismarck's opponents except the socialists. The argument was that contributions were necessary to preserve the workers' sense of individual responsibility and to prevent "the feeling of receiving a gift and of becoming dependent on the state."[122] This attitude was not inconsistent with acceptance of the idea of social protection, but it did reveal reservations about patriarchalism, which may have been inspired by cost considerations. But Bismarck still wanted to attach the workers to the state. He succeeded in obtaining a direct state subsidy, in the form of a flat fifty mark base pension paid by the Imperial Treasury. Although this was little more than a gesture, he hoped that it would reveal a concern by the state for the welfare of the worker.

SOCIAL INSURANCE AND SOCIALISM

In an evaluation of the place of social insurance in German industrialization, the position of the Social Democrats deserves special attention for several reasons. They were the main, although not the sole, target against which Bismarck hoped to use social insurance as a political weapon. Although all of the parties engaged in the social insurance debate approached it in the light of their own social and economic preconceptions, only the Social Democrats were armed intellectually with a fully elaborated and integrated theory of history, economy, and society. This, of course, was the marxist theory, which, after the purification of some Lassallean strains, became the fundamental creed of German socialism. To view the social insurance debate through marxist eyes is to view it through contrast-conceptions, which is illuminating for the socialist point of view as well as for the one of their adversaries. A detailed analysis of the marxist system obviously would lead us too far afield, but we can examine some of its central tenets and can explore their influence on social democratic thinking with regard to social insurance.[123] Among these tenets are the following.

1. The impossibility of improving the worker's economic position within the capitalist framework.

[122] Luetge, "Die Grundprinzipien der Bismarckschen Sozialpolitik," p. 592.
[123] A very useful treatment along these lines is in Hertha Wolff, *Die Stellung der Sozialdemokratie zur deutschen Arbeiterversicherungsgesetzgebung von ihrer Entstehung an bis zur Reichsversicherungsordnung* (Doctoral dissertation, University of Freiburg, i.B., 1933). A more detailed discussion

2. The exploitation of the proletariat by the ruling classes and their use of the state as a tool for this purpose.

3. The labor theory of value, with its implications of subsistence wages and profit as a surplus value.

4. The historical tendency toward increasing monopolization of industry, increasing exploitation, and growing immiseration.

We shall explore first the general implications of these tenets and then their relation to specific insurance questions.

An essential assumption of meaningful social insurance policy is that it makes possible a worthwhile improvement in the workers' economic position. This assumption runs counter to the marxist position on the uselessness of social reform short of a complete reorganization of the economy. In the 1880s and 1890s the Social Democrats tended to accept a rigid interpretation of this position. By the turn of the century, the rise of the socialist trade union movement and of revisionist ideas forced them to recognize the possibility of economic improvement within the framework of capitalism. Thus, for ideological as well as for political reasons, the Social Democrats were inclined to take a negative attitude towards Bismarck's social insurance plans. However, it would have been politically hazardous to stick only to theoretical objections against social insurance.[124] Their argument was that what Bismarck offered was completely inadequate to remedy the prevailing economic insecurity and to relieve poverty. Social insurance, they said, was an illusion, nothing but another form of poor relief, except that the workers would have to pay for it. It was a means of lessening the poor relief burden on the communities at the expense of the workers.[125] The sums to be paid to the workers were mere *Bettelgroschen*, pennies thrown to beggars, which amounted to nothing in comparison to the sums spent on armaments.[126] Another form of the negative argument was that as long as the worker was not protected against all forms of insecurity, especially low wages and unemployment, social insurance would not work. "What a ridiculous, yet

---

of the socialist position on specific issues with regard to health insurance is in Heinrich Verhein, *Die Stellung der Sozialdemokratie zur deutschen Krankenversicherungsgesetzgebung und ihr Einfluss auf dieselbe* (Doctoral dissertation, University of Halle-Wittenberg, 1916). For a detailed presentation of specific socialist demands after two decades of experience with social insurance, see Friedrich Kleeis, *Der Aus- und Umbau der Arbeiterversicherung* (Berlin: Buchhandlung Vorwaerts, 1907).

[124]The marxist journal *Die Neue Zeit*, which started in 1883 and became a major Social Democratic organ, had as its first lead article a theoretical critique of social insurance in the form of a polemic against Lujo Brentano. See Heinrich Braun, "Das Problem der Arbeiterversicherung und die Auffassung Lujo Brentano's," *Die Neue Zeit*, Vol. I (1883), pp. 9–20.

[125]Bismarck had used the argument that social insurance would lessen the burden of poor relief to obtain a subsidy from the states.

[126]See Wolff, *op. cit.*, pp. 16–19.

terrible, situation it would be if the state were to guarantee the worker's future against weakness, danger, and sickness, and yet let him starve to death in the present. There can only be one motto: everything or nothing."[127] This motto gives a clue to how the socialists dealt with the political problem of opposing social insurance without their giving the impression of neglecting the interests of the worker. A handbill they handed out in the 1884 election explained that "the social legislation hitherto concocted by the *Reichstag* (sickness and accident insurance) is so wretchedly bad that our representatives were forced to vote against it."[128] The more fundamental argument was formulated by Bebel. He maintained that if his party accepted the view that labor protective legislation could substantially alter the worker's economic position, "it would be giving up one of its fundamental principles and would cease to be Social Democratic."[129] The worker should not look to reform of the present order but to the coming of a radically new order. "He who wants reforms should not expect more from bourgeois society than what it can do without committing suicide. But he who wants more should have faith in the development of things, which proceeds more rapidly today than in any other period in world history."[130]

The tenets that capitalism was based on the exploitation of the proletariat by the ruling classes and that the state was an instrument of this exploitation inevitably had a significant influence on the socialist attitude toward social insurance legislation. This view of the state and society was in sharp contrast with Bismarck's notion of the state as an impartial arbiter that stands above social conflict and acts in the interest of society as a whole. The fact that he had openly declared that social insurance was an essential complement to repression in the fight against socialism was quickly turned against him by the socialist propagandists. He could not eradicate us, they triumphantly proclaimed, now he is trying to corrupt us by tempting our families in their misery with a beggarly handout. Their handbills in 1883 to 1884 read: "His bait we despise, his whip we destroy."[131] The Social Democratic Congress of 1883, which convened in Copenhagen, declared, "unanimously and without debate, that owing to the past conduct of the ruling classes it cannot believe in either their honest intentions or in their competence. Rather, it is convinced that the so-called social reform is

[127]Heinrich Mandl, "Arbeiterversicherung und Arbeitversicherung," *Die Neue Zeit*, Vol. I (1883), p. 381.
[128]Quoted in Mehring, *op. cit.*, Vol. II, p. 600.
[129]"Staatliche Lohnregulirung und die staatsreformerischen Bestrebungen der Gegenwart," *Die Neue Zeit*, Vol. IV (1886), p. 5.
[130]*Ibid.*, p. 7. On the hopelessness of legislative reform under capitalism, see also Karl Kautsky, "Das Recht auf Arbeit," *Die Neue Zeit*, Vol. II (1884), pp. 299–303; also in the same journal, "Rodbertus und die Arbeiterversicherung," Vol. I (1883), pp. 524–527.
[131]Mehring, *op. cit.*, Vol. II, p. 584.

nothing but a tactical means designed to lure the workers away from the correct path."[132] Even if it seemed that there were advantages for the worker in social insurance, the socialists insisted, a correct understanding of social theory revealed that advantages were only clever disguises of disadvantages. Was not social insurance a means of shifting part of the burden of poor relief from the wealthy to the worker? Was it not a way of retarding the development of an independent attitude toward the employer and the state? Bebel explained why, in his view, these arguments made sense to the worker. "The ordinary worker cannot grasp that the very same authorities who have rebuffed or trampled on his natural demands for protection against exploitation and oppression, and for freedom of combination and movement, should also be animated with the warmest benevolence toward him."[133] Once this ideological position is granted it, indeed, should not be difficult to interpret social insurance as anything but another trick of the ruling classes.

The economic manifestations of exploitation were the subsistence wage, long hours, intensification of work, and progressive immiseration. The inevitability of exploitation, in Marx's analysis, is supported by the labor theory of value, the tendency toward a falling rate of profit, the expanding reserve army of the unemployed, and the growing monopolization of industry. The scientific validity of this analysis is not important here. What matters is that the Social Democrats accepted it as valid. This accounts in part for the eschatological attitude that social reform was not only unlikely and impossible but really unnecessary, since events were heading for a radical showdown in any case. The post-Bismarckian reformulation of the party's principles in 1891, the Erfurt Program, fully accepted the increasing immiseration thesis and the other harbingers of the impending collapse of capitalism.[134] The Social Democrats, therefore, were not inclined to cooperate with the state in social reform. The Erfurt Program nevertheless contained a long list of social demands. Its major social security demands were complete free medical care and federal jurisdiction over all social insurance programs, with a determining administrative participation by the workers. These demands were still the kind that the socialists knew would not be seriously considered under existing political circumstances.

By the turn of the century, however, there was a relaxation within the party with regard to a strict insistence on growing immiseration and exploitation. The crisis within the party, caused by the notion that the collapse of capitalism was no longer imminent and that socialism might be

[132] *Ibid.*, p. 585.

[133] "Das Gesetz ueber die Invaliditaets- und Alterversicherung im Deutschen Reich," *Die Neue Zeit*, Vol. VII, p. 387.

[134] The program is reproduced in Herkner, *op. cit.*, Vol. II, pp. 355–358.

achieved peacefully, need not concern us here. The Revisionists accepted the idea that immiseration was only relative to the growth in national wealth, rather than absolute. Furthermore, it was recognized that both trade unions and social insurance had enabled the worker to improve his economic position. The improvement was not thought to be very large but enough to prevent misery. This change in interpretation called for a new tactic with regard to social policy. The completely negative attitude was no longer warranted. It was argued now that social insurance actually helped the cause of socialism by maintaining the worker's strength in the fight against capitalism. And, in any case, the workers approved of it, which made it hard for their leaders to be against it. The Social Democrats in the *Reichstag* began to show an increased willingness to participate constructively in the many amendments that were almost continuously under discussion. Therefore, it is appropriate to explore briefly their position on specific issues.

We must emphasize that the Social Democrats never rejected social insurance as such—Bebel had demanded accident insurance as early as 1879 —but they were always highly critical of its political aims and of its specific provisions. Although in their general criticism they could rely on marxist theory, when it came to specific issues they often had to adjust their views for tactical purposes. A good illustration of this can be found with regard to the question of who should pay for the benefits. Marxist arguments are overwhelmingly against worker contributions and for contributions by the employers and by the wealthy in general. First, the worker is unable to pay because he is getting only a subsistence wage. Second, the worker ought not to pay because his insecurity is not his fault but that of the capitalist system, which is operated for the benefit of the capitalists. Third, if benefits must be financed out of wages, they can never be adequate. Fourth, the more heavily the employers are burdened, the sooner capitalism will collapse. Finally, since labor is the sole source of value, employer contributions are nothing but a small partial repayment of what belongs to the worker in the first place.

Against all these theoretical arguments, however, was the practical consideration that representation on the administrative bodies was proportional to contributions. This administrative participation was of great importance to the socialists, since it could be used in a number of ways to influence worker attitudes. The worker, after all, was to some extent dependent on his representatives to defend his interests. He would look to them for advice and support. The socialists actively sought these administrative posts as a way of achieving leverage on the workers, even if only through the aggressive defense of their interests. This ironic consequence of social insurance had not been foreseen either by Bismarck or the Social Democrats in the early 1880s. The best opportunities for the socialists were in connection with health insurance, where labor had a two thirds majority administrative representation and where issues that involved worker conduct arose. There is little doubt that the Social Democrats used their posts to promote political and trade union objectives.[135] They vociferously denounced proposed health insurance reforms that would have given employers and workers equal representation and equal contributions.[136] They treated proposals of this kind as an attack by the ruling classes on the rights of the worker. In their way of thinking, social insurance administration was a basic right of the worker, which should not be surrendered in exchange for a small financial advantage in the form of lower contributions. Ironically, this put them in a position of defending higher worker contributions. Naturally, they were quite willing, and were demanding in theory, to eliminate worker contributions but not at the expense of administrative control. Were not the workers, according to marxist theory, paying for the whole cost in any case? Why should their administrative rights be tied to specific contributions?[137]

In addition, the socialists did not accept the argument, which had strongly influenced German legislation, that worker contributions were necessary in order to maintain the worker's sense of self-respect and individual responsibility. What was important, they maintained, was not a sense of individual responsibility but a sense of solidarity and of collective responsibility. These socially desirable qualities could best be achieved not by worker contributions but by worker self-government.[138]

The socialist doctrine influenced decisions also in other technical matters, such as coverage, benefit levels, the relation of benefits to contributions, and eligibility conditions. The basic socialist position was that social insurance should cover the entire working class, regardless of industry or occupation. They favored raising the base wage above which individuals were not covered under German social insurance. They rejected the insurance idea that benefit levels should in any way be made dependent on contributions. This idea reflects the concept of equity, which is central in private insurance, but should not enter into social insurance, according to the socialists. Since the workers are the victims of exploitation, they are entitled to benefit levels that represent an adequate compensation. The criterion that is relevant is not equity but social justice.[139] This had important implications for financing. In theory, the Social Democrats insisted that the funds necessary to allow adequate benefit levels should be raised by direct progressive

[135] See, for instance, Schmoller, *op. cit.*, p. 399; for socialist denials of administrative abuses, see Eduard Graef, "Zur Reform des Krankenversicherungsgesetzes," *Die Neue Zeit*, Vol. XVIII: 2 (1899–1900), pp. 497–505 and Emanuel Wurm, "Die Ergebnisse der Krankenversicherungsreform," *Die Neue Zeit*, Vol. XXI: 2 (1902–1903), pp. 245–249.

[136] Wurm, *loc. cit.*; also Varain, *op. cit.*, pp. 53–54.

[137] For a development of this thesis, see Gustav Hoch, "Pflichten und Rechte in der Arbeiterversicherung," *Die Neue Zeit*, Vol. XXIII: 2 (1904–1905), pp. 855–857.

[138] See Wolff, *op. cit.*, p. 65.   [139] *Ibid.*, pp. 67–68.

taxation of the wealthy—the beneficiaries of the prevailing system of exploitation. In any case, in marxist analysis, the idea that equity should be a limiting factor on benefit levels can easily be disposed of. Since, in the end the benefits are paid out of production, which is the result of labor only (live or "congealed" in the form of capital), any return to labor as a whole, whether in the form of wages or benefits, is "equitable." It may be observed, however, that this theoretical approach is not inconsistent with differentiated benefits, which the socialists accepted as long as the minimum levels were sufficient to meet a worker's needs.

A generous attitude on benefits always raises the question of abuse. The Social Democrats, who were inclined to find most virtues among the proletariat and most vices among the ruling classes, usually denied the existence of any problem of abuse. In this matter they reacted exactly opposite from those perennial opponents of social insurance who see nothing but abuse. They denounced provisions such as waiting periods and other rules against malingering as attempts by the ruling classes to keep benefits to a minimum.[140] The idea that workers were simulating illness in order to be able to qualify for disability pensions was ridiculed by socialist writers.[141] The tendency was for workers to retire on disability pensions, because they had to reach age 70 to be eligible for old-age retirement. This advanced age, the socialists complained, was reached by very few workers in capitalist society.[142]

Without attempting an exhaustive survey of the socialist position on social insurance, one more issue deserves brief mention in this attempt to illustrate its ideological implications. This was the question of whether social insurance ought to be expanded to include unemployment insurance. The trade unions had developed a very limited system of their own, which they considered valuable as a means of strengthening worker loyalty. In their annual congresses from the mid-1890s on, the Social Democratic unions repeatedly favored expansion of these benefits and, to do so, they were even willing to cooperate with the employers. But, since private programs inevitably meant low benefits, the union demanded assistance from the state in the form of subsidies to trade union programs. The result would have been government-subsidized private plans, which was a form of unemployment insurance several cities in Europe had tried out on a local basis. However, there was no agreement on this question among the Social Democrats. Although the unions wanted to hang on to their programs, the party

---

[140] See Wolff, op. cit., p. 59.

[141] See, for instance, Ludwig Radloff, "Rentenhysterie und Sozialgesetzgebung," Die Neue Zeit, Vol. XXIV:1, pp. 226–231.

[142] Max Schippel, "Die Alters- und Invalidenversicherung der Arbeiter," Die Neue Zeit, Vol. VI (1888), p. 387; also B. W., "Die Altersversorgung der Arbeiter," Die Neue Zeit, Vol. V (1887), p. 231.

insisted on the creation of a public unemployment insurance system. The unions feared that the replacement of private plans by a public system would tend to weaken the internal discipline and loyalty of their organizations.[143] Such "inevitable" provisions, in a public system in a capitalist society, as a denial of benefits to unemployed workers refusing to act as strike breakers, would weaken the labor movement by undermining worker solidarity. Against the universal insurance views adopted by the party, union spokesmen advanced the idea that it was most important to strengthen the position of the most progressive workers—those who belonged to the unions. Finally, a public program would not educate the workers for socialism as well as a program in the hands of the unions.[144]

Hermann Molkenbuhr, a spokesman for the party's point of view, denied that public unemployment insurance would weaken either the unions or class consciousness.[145] On the contrary, the broader the unemployment protection, the less the pressure on the labor market and the stronger the unions would be in the fight for higher wages. A private system that is dependent on state subsidies would open the door to "corruption" by the authorities. Would they subsidize the funds of aggressive unions, or would they favor unions of which they approved? Molkenbuhr was not unaware of the dangers the unions feared. He insisted that in a public system a worker must not be denied benefits if he quits on his own or if he loses his job for "subjective" reasons such as "laziness, carelessness, incompatibility, and drunkenness."[146] If these reasons were accepted as ones for the loss of benefit eligibility, the employers, indeed, would gain too much power over the workers. Molkenbuhr defended his position at the party's congress in Munich in 1902 and obtained its endorsement of public unemployment insurance.[147] But the issue gave rise to heated controversy, which was by no means settled at the congress. What really matters, in deciding for or against unemployment or any other kind of social insurance, noted Mehring a year after the Munich Congress, is *who will gain the most power*—the worker or the state and the ruling classes. "The ruling principle is none but the interest of the proletarian class struggle."[148]

[143] Some writers made similar arguments with regard to health insurance. See, for instance, Georg Roessing, "Gewerkschaft und Krankenversicherung," *Die Neue Zeit*, Vol. XXI: 1 (1902–1903), pp. 405–415.
[144] For a sample of these views, see Bruno Borchardt, "Zur Frage der Arbeitslosenversicherung," *Die Neue Zeit*, Vol. XX: 2 (1901–1902), pp. 486–493.
[145] "Zur Frage der Arbeitslosenverischerung," *Die Neue Zeit*, Vol. XX: 2 (1901–1902), pp. 723–729.
[146] "Zur Frage der Arbeitslosenversicherung," *Die Neue Zeit*, Vol. XX: 1 (1901–1902), p. 558.
[147] Kleeis, *op. cit.*, pp. 30–31.
[148] F. Mehring, "Arbeiterschutz und Staatsgewalt," *Die Neue Zeit*, Vol. XXII: 2 (1903–1904), p. 779.

He accepted the view, shared by Bismarck and the Liberals, that every form of labor protection tended to give the state more power, but for him that was not the important dimension.

> The working class may strengthen the power of the state, if it thereby promotes the class struggle, but under no circumstances should it strengthen the state if this entails a weakening or a crippling of the class struggle. . . . On the basis of this criterion, it is obvious why the working class supports factory laws and why the ruling classes are so violently against them. . . . The state of today, which is under the control of the ruling classes, gains power from factory laws only in the sense that it becomes stronger to develop into a state ruled by the proletariat. But the power that the state of today would gain from unemployment insurance would be quite different. To the extent that this demand is realizable at all for the state of today . . . the state, or rather the ruling classes, would become the unrestrained ruler of the labor market, the battlefield on which the proletariat carries on its fight for emancipation.[149]

If it can be held against Bismarck that he tried to use social insurance as a political weapon, the same accusation is certainly warranted against his most bitter opponents. Under the existing political circumstances, it perhaps was inevitable that institutions that normally would tend to reduce social tension became themselves instruments of social conflict. Bismarck's social policies did not achieve the political objectives he had hoped for, but it would be erroneous to consider them a failure with regard to the problem of social pacification. Social insurance was without doubt an important factor in the mollification of revolutionary ardor in the early part of this century. It contributed to the rise of revisionism and to the greater cooperation of the Social Democrats with the government. It also taught many labor leaders and employers that cooperation on common problems was not an impossibility.[150]

FROM BISMARCK TO ADENAUER

The social security system instituted by Bismarck was bound to undergo many alterations as the country went through major political and social changes. Until the end of World War I, the old authoritarian framework set the effective limits to the evolution of social rights, in spite of the demands for broader benefits from the labor movement. The ascent to power of democratic forces during the era of the Weimar Republic provided an important opportunity for the reformulation of the rights to protection. After

[149] F. Mehring, "Arbeiterschutz und Staatsgewalt," *Die Neue Zeit*, Vol. XXII: 2 (1903–1904), p. 779.
[150] See Heidegger, *op. cit.*, pp. 60 ff.

much debate there was some progress toward making the system a more effective instrument for greater equality. Under Hitler, social security was once more expected to serve as a tool for social control, but the established system was not fundamentally altered. It was not until after World War II that the original system was thoroughly reshaped in line with new concepts of the state and society. The latter reforms will be discussed at length in the next chapter, after this survey of post-Bismarckian developments.

Amendments to the original laws began shortly after their enactment. The first major revisions came in 1911, when the whole system was consolidated into a uniform national insurance code, the *Reichsversicherungsordnung*. During the same year, survivorship pensions were added, social insurance pensions were extended to salaried employees, and sickness insurance was extended to farm laborers. Reflecting prevailing social attitudes, salaried employees were not combined with the workers into the same general scheme. A separate program was created, with different rights and conditions, deemed appropriate for this socioeconomic group. Salaried employees, generally, were presumed to be more susceptible of self-help than workers and less in need of assistance from the state. Although manual workers were covered by the pension laws regardless of earnings, the compulsory coverage of salaried employees was limited by an earnings ceiling.[151] Furthermore, there was no contribution from the state to the pensions of the salaried employees; in the case of the workers, it will be recalled, the state contributed a flat basic amount for each individual. On the other hand, it was argued that salaried employees needed more favorable survivorship provisions than workers, because it was not socially acceptable or customary for middle-class women to take a job outside the home, although the opposite could be expected of working-class women. A worker's widow had to be disabled to qualify for a survivorship pension but not the widow of a salaried employee. Farm laborers were viewed in a paternalistic relationship to their employers and were deemed even less self-dependent than industrial workers. Unlike the latter, they were not accorded the full rights of self-government in their sickness funds. Employers of farm laborers had the right to claim exemption from health insurance for their workers by taking upon themselves the obligation to care for them in the event of sickness.

The old patriarchal tradition was to be pushed aside by the Weimar Republic to make room for the social egalitarian forces that had long been held back. Article 151 of the 1919 Constitution promised a social order based on human dignity, justice, and individual freedom. It was to be expected that the 1920s would generate some basic rethinking of the role of social insurance and would lead to a system more in keeping with popular

[151] Salaried employees had been covered by the original compulsory health insurance act, but again subject to an earnings ceiling.

demands. The first major problem to be attacked was protection in case of unemployment. Initially, several unemployment assistance measures were enacted to cope with the problem of heavy unemployment after World War I. These efforts were combined with the development of public employment offices which were aimed at reducing unemployment by improving the functioning of the labor market. Finally, in 1927, an unemployment insurance program was established. Its coverage was very broad from the beginning, for it was identical with the one for health insurance. The financing was based on contributions from *both* employers and workers. The unemployment insurance system was combined with a nationwide system of labor exchanges under the Reich Office for Employment Exchange and Unemployment Insurance (*Reichsanstalt für Arbeitsvermittlung und Arbeitslosenversicherung*), in which both employers and workers were represented. Other social security changes which occurred during the 1920s marked a growing recognition of economic protection as a social right of the citizen. This was particularly noticeable in the modernization of the poor laws and the emergence of public assistance programs to take their place. Similarly, the establishment of youth welfare programs contributed toward the equalization of opportunity and constituted an important social advance.

In spite of these advances, the hopes of the founders of the republic were far from realized. Inflation and unemployment severely undermined the existing programs, while the financing of new programs inevitably brought out sharp conflicts of interests. It was ironic that social protection, which had few opponents in principle under the old paternalistic setting, should have become a political irritant and a source of factional divisiveness in the democratic state.[152] And it was tragic that in the midst of a growing economic crisis, the burden of social insurance benefits (financing of unemployment insurance) became the issue that triggered the collapse of the ruling coalition (in 1930) and opened the road to totalitarianism.[153]

During the Hitler era (1933–1945) social security policy had to adapt to the objectives of the totalitarian state. The leading changes must be pointed out here, since they are part of the historical legacy of the postwar social security reform debate. Labor and social policy became part of the general system of Nazi economic and political control. The Reich Office for Employment Exchange and Unemployment Insurance was assigned the function of militarizing the labor force.[154] Its task was to achieve control over the labor supply

[152] See Ludwig Preller, *Sozialpolitik in der Weimar Republik* (Stuttgart: Franz Mittelbach Verlag, 1949), *passim*.
[153] See Helga Timm, *Die Deutsche Sozialpolitik und der Bruch der grossen Koalition in März 1930* (Düsseldorf: Droste Verlag, 1952).
[154] Otto Nathan, *The Nazi Economic System* (Durham, N.C.: Duke University Press, 1944), pp. 192 ff.

and to direct the distribution and allocation of labor. Private employment agencies were abolished, giving the state agencies a monopoly in this area. Reversing the long tradition of self-administration, Hitler abolished effective administrative participation by employers and workers and everywhere introduced the leadership principle. This meant that social insurance decisions were now in the hands of individuals picked by the Nazi party and devoted to their aims. The general tendency was toward centralization of power in the hands of the party or individuals whom the party trusted. As the economy became increasingly geared for war production, unemployment was eliminated, but the manpower control measures became more stringent. They progressively restricted the workers' freedom of movement and choice of occupation. Social insurance institutions were used to help control the wage freeze ordered in 1939. "Controllers of sickness insurance were ordered to find illegal wage increases and report offenders."[155] Also pressure was put on insurance physicians to control absenteeism. The Association of Insurance Practitioners informed its members in 1939: "It is more than ever the duty of the insurance practitioner to note immediately when a patient recovers his earning capacity and not leave the matter to be detected by the controlling physician."[156]

Aside from its labor control tasks, the social insurance system became a tool of demographic policy. Several measures were passed to promote family formation and population growth. An act of December 1937 gave women wage earners the right to claim repayment of one half of their contributions toward pensions in case of marriage. Until then only female salaried employees had been entitled to this benefit. Furthermore, the widows of wage earners no longer had to be invalid to be entitled to widow's pensions, if they had more than three children to care for. Finally, benefits for dependent children and allowances to large families were improved. Some of these measures promoted equality, but the explicit aim of the Nazis was often the opposite.

In general, the Nazi social security policy reflected a strong bias against the weak and the politically "undesirable." It played a role in the racist and nationalistic ambitions of the *Fuehrer*. This attitude was of gravest import in the field of social welfare services, which were supposed to be restricted to the "congenitally sound" and the "potentially useful members of the community." The politically undesirable faced annihilation.

In practice, however, matters were not always as extreme as official policy might indicate. That humane traditions did not vanish overnight is

[155] Frieda Wunderlich, *Farm Labor in Germany* (Princeton: Princeton University Press, 1961), p. 243.
[156] Quoted in *Ibid.*, p. 274.

indicated by Nazi complaints. The head of the Central Office for Health and Protection of the People complained that:

> The antiselection process practiced by doctors, which neglects natural selection and elimination, has had an even worse effect than equalization. A considerable percentage of people—asocial and loafers—use the extensive medical care customary for all comrades without deserving it. Consequently the insurance ideal in social insurance must be replaced by the idea of maintenance, that is everyone who has done his duty toward the people's community will be provided for. The extent of aid is not to be determined by some scheme of equaliza tion but by the extent of the person's achievements.[157]

Having paid for insurance was no longer an adequate justification for receiving benefits. Protection was now legitimized by fulfillment of duty to the state. Since a person's achievements in the fulfillment of his duties would presumably be determined by the Nazi party, social security would become a tool for the cultivation of loyalty to the party. The result would be the destruction of social rights as an attribute of citizenship and the creation of a system of paternalistic favors dependent on the zeal demonstrated in supporting the objectives of the ruling party.

This ideological attack on the traditional system of contribution financed social insurance and its corresponding benefits as a matter of right was never translated into legislation, but a program along the lines of this attack was seriously advanced in 1940 by the head of the German Labor Front.[158] This was the Robert-Ley Plan, which advocated a comprehensive and uniform system of pensions for all disabled and all those reaching age 65 who have done their duty to the community. Ley was opposed to a system in which contributions determined benefits. The state was to consider taking care of the disabled and the aged as its "most primordial duty" (ureigenste Aufgabe)[159] and was to meet the cost out of general revenue. The pension level was intended to be high enough to secure a standard of living "natural for a German" but not so high as to discourage private saving.[160] Those disabled in industrial accidents or in war would be entitled to a special bonus. The "enemies of the state" and the "unsocial minority" (Jews) were to be excluded from the program altogether. This plan was to become an important feature of the postvictory National Socialist society. Although the course of history has interfered with the realization of this scheme, its ghost, the freedom devouring Versorgungstaat (approximately: warden state), has haunted many postwar social security reform discussions.

---

[157] Quoted in Wunderlich, op. cit., p. 275.

[158] The German Labor Front (Deutsche Arbeitsfront) was the official Nazi organization that replaced the former trade unions.

[159] Horst Peters, Die Geschichte der Sozialversicherung (Bad Godesberg: Asgard Verlag, 1959), p. 81.

[160] Wunderlich, op. cit., p. 278.

By no means all of the changes in social security during the Nazi era were unfavorable to the insured population.[161] A new program was established for independent artisans. Important improvements were made in some areas of the existing programs, although significant restrictions were imposed in others. It would be difficult to draw up an accurate balance sheet to evaluate these changes even from a strict benefit point of view. This is not the purpose of our discussion, which has mainly attempted to point out how a totalitarian party can turn social insurance into an instrument of economic and social control. In the end, the German social insurance system retained many of its classic features, but the threats inherent in totalitarian control were not forgotten.

During the war the Nazis introduced many changes in social insurance, simply by issuing ordinances rather than enacting new laws. As a result, the system in existence at the end of the war was highly complex and overloaded with special provisions designed to support wartime manpower policies. A thoroughgoing reform would have been necessary even in the case of a German victory. Germany's defeat and the collapse of her economy made reform all the more essential, as well as more difficult to carry out. In part, the difficulty of the immediate postwar period stemed from the division of the country into occupation zones. When the Allied Control Commission failed to take steps toward a uniform reorganization of the social insurance system, the zone and the local authorities proceeded on their own. The inevitable consequence was an increased tendency toward disarray as far as the country as a whole was concerned. Lack of qualified personnel, many of whom had been removed from office during the Nazi era and replaced by persons who were no longer acceptable, and lack of essential documentation (a consequence of the zonal division) made reconstruction an arduous task.

To these problems were added the tremendous needs of the postwar era. The disrupted economy with its many unemployed was additionally burdened with large numbers of war victims, victims of Nazi persecution, expellees and refugees from Communist occupied territories, and some remaining "displaced persons" who had been brought to Germany as forced laborers. The problem of what to do about the pensions rights of former military and paramilitary personnel also had to be faced. Finally, the entire system of benefits, contributions, and income limits had to be brought in line with prevailing wage and price levels. This problem became particularly important after the currency reform of 1948. The three years

---

[161] For a discussion of social insurance improvements during the war period, see Max Bloch, "Social insurance in Post-War Germany," *International Labor Review*, Vol. LVIII (September 1948), pp. 310–315.

after 1949 witnessed considerable activity which was for the purpose of restoring order in the social security system.[162]

Until the mid-1950s, most of the social security enactments were still concerned with restoration and the removal of hardship. The system remained faulty and incredibly complicated. As an almost inescapable consequence of patchwork legislation, there was much overlapping in benefit provisions, although important gaps in protection also existed. Cumulation of benefits (the simultaneous drawing of benefits from several programs) became a widely criticized symptom of the system's shortcomings. The real task of rationalizing social security on the basis of principles that were consistent and consonant with the existing economic and social order still lay ahead. In a declaration to the *Bundestag*, on October 20, 1953, Chancellor Adenauer announced that a comprehensive social reform would be undertaken.[163] It took several years of vigorous debate before fundamental reforms were enacted, but even so the system had already come a long way from its original patriarchalism.

[162] "Social Security Developments in the Federal Republic of Germany since 1949," *International Labor Review*, Vol. LXVI (November–December 1952), p. 485. See also Peter Quante, "Die neuere Entwicklung der deutschen Sozialversicherung und ihre Reform," *Schmoller's Jahrbuch*, Vol. LXXIV (1954), pp. 681–716.

[163] The declaration is reproduced in the extensive collection of documents concerning the German social reforms by Max Richter, *Die Sozialreform Dokumente und Stellungnahmen* (Bad Godesberg: Asgard Verlag, 1955–1968, Section B/III/1, p. 1.

CHAPTER 5

Social Security Reforms in Postwar Germany: Comparisons with Great Britain

After World War II all the European social security systems were in need of fundamental reform. The war had caused many economic and political changes and had erased many landmarks of prewar society. The general feeling was that a completely new start had to be made; society and the economy had to be restructured to assure peace, justice, and security in the future. Underlying the pressure for reform were deep currents of social egalitarianism that had sprung from the common sharing of hardships during the incredibly long war. Egalitarianism, of course, did not mean the same thing in all countries, but everywhere it implied an expanded conception of social rights. Germany represents one variant of the postwar pattern of social policy. Great Britain another. The reformulation of social rights in the two countries was carried out not only against the background of different historical legacies but also in the context of different ideologies. The ideological context of Germany was that of the Social Market Economy and of the "socially conscious state," an attempt to recast some of the traditional welfare concerns of the state in a quasi-liberal mold. The British context was that of an ideological commitment to social planning and to the welfare state. This chapter deals mainly with the German experience and uses British developments chiefly for purposes of contrast, to highlight an alternative. In both countries the claims of the common man on the state were significantly enlarged in different ways, but in neither country was inequality or insecurity fully banished. After the main reforms, demands for further improvements remained alive.

137

THE GERMAN SETTING

The total collapse of Germany at the end of World War II posed fundamental problems of economic and social reconstruction. The Nazi system of
authoritarian control had suddenly disappeared. A new beginning had to be
made, including a restatement of reciprocal social rights and duties and a
formulation of the relationship of individuals to the state. The historical
precedents for this reconstruction were not highly auspicious. After World
War I, Germany experienced the extremes of economic insecurity in the form
of runaway inflation and massive unemployment. These evils, and their
political consequences, now haunted the horizon; they had to be avoided.
But the problems, both material and psychological, facing the battered and
demoralized country were staggering. Chancellor Erhard characterized the
situation as follows:

> Not only were the material foundations of our existence destroyed, but the
> German people had lost their sure sense of an ordering of life suitable for
> them. It was often feared that the chaotic conditions of the early postwar years
> had permanency, that they would last indefinitely. The worst after effects of the
> war were these: the individual was left without an inner compass and without
> any conception of the future; he was overcome by such deep despair, hopeless-
> ness, resignation, and fear that life itself was threatened with extinction.[1]

For the second time within a generation money had little value. Even though
the 1948 monetary reform had an almost magic effect, it could not dissipate
the sense of insecurity left by two major inflations. It underlined the helplessness of the individual, and reinforced the tendency, deeply embedded in
modern German economic history, that the individual must look to the state
for protection.

An important aspect of the unsettled social conditions was the large
number of people that had been uprooted from their native soil. Nazi
settlement policies, the war and, finally, the Communist regime of the
eastern provinces drove many people from their homes and habitual ways of
making a living. Needless to emphasize, when a large part of the population
becomes nomadic the problems of economic and social security multiply,
quite aside from the fact that the war left many families without a breadwinner and destroyed or reduced the earning capacity of a large number of
persons. The partition of Germany and the multitude of refugees naturally
also affected the country's political power structure. Salin points out that
the once powerful Junker class must now be included among the "nomads."[2]

---

[1] Ludwig Erhard, *Deutsche Wirtschaftspolitik* (Düsseldorf: Econ Verlag, 1962), p. 5.
[2] Edgar Salin, "Social Forces in Germany Today," *Foreign Affairs*, Vol. XXVIII (January 1950),
pp. 265–277.

Offsetting these disruptive influences, however, has been the sense of discipline, the industriousness, and the organizational capacity of the German people.[3]

For the restoration of political stability, credit without doubt belongs to the strong leadership of Chancellor Adenauer and to the success of his domestic and foreign policies. He provided the mildly autocratic leadership, within a context of basic freedom, which the German people seem to desire. Karl Jaspers has noted that "there is something in our people which believes in the great leader. . . . The average German . . . trusts authority; the business of authority, he assumes, is to handle politics and relieve him from thinking about it."[4] A historical counterpart of this acceptance of authority has been the expectation of the social protection of the individual. The reformulation of the relationship of the individual to the state must take into account the changed economic and social conditions, as well as the people's aspirations for freedom and security.

The formulation of a new reciprocity of individual and state was cast into the mold of the *sozialer Rechtsstaat*. This is the central concept embodied into the 1949 Constitution of the Federal Republic. It is an attempt to achieve a synthesis, or at least a balance, of two rather opposite constitutional principles, those of the *Rechtsstaat* and the *Sozialstaat*. The *Rechtsstaat*, or state based on the rule of law, stresses the egality of all individuals and recognizes no social or economic distinctions that might undermine formal equality before the law. This is the principle of the Enlightenment's individualism and of the nineteenth century's liberalism; its objective is a maximum of individual liberty and a minimum of state intervention. The *Sozialstaat*, on the other hand, whether its inspiration has been conservative or socialist, has always recognized the social and economic groupings of individuals, rather than just the individual. This recognition of intermediary power constellations has always disposed the *Sozialstaat* towards economic and social intervention. Both of these constitutional principles have deep roots in Germany history.[5] The attempt to reconcile or to balance them was not new, but there was the additional recognition in postwar Germany that previous attempts had ended in failure.

The practical problem, of course, was to define the proper balance of individual and state responsibility in terms of economic and social policy.

[3] For a discussion of the economic significance of these qualities, see Henry C. Wallich, *Mainsprings of the German Revival* (New Haven: Yale University Press, 1955), Chapter XII, "Economic Consequences of German Mentality."

[4] Karl Jaspers, "The Political Vacuum in Germany," *Foreign Affairs,* Vol. XXXII (July 1954), p. 599.

[5] See Karl E. Born, "Idee und Gestalt des Sozialstaats in der deutschen Geschichte" in *Sozialer Rechtsstaat—Weg oder Irrweg?*, Schriftenreihe des deutschen Beamtenbundes Heft 31 (Bad Godesberg: deutscher Beamtenverlag, 1963), pp. 81–105.

Ludwig Erhard, the chief architect of German economic reconstruction, has explained that governmental economic policy was carried out "with a view to overcoming the age-old antithesis of an unbridled liberalism and a soulless state control, to finding a sound middle way between out and out freedom and totalitarianism."[6] The political debate in postwar West Germany indicates that there are different conceptions of this "middle way." One of these is strongly influenced by the revival of economic liberalism in the wake of the Nazi regimentation. The neoliberal tendencies are represented in the concept of the Social Market Economy, which was officially embraced by the governing Christian Democratic party in 1949.[7] The Social Democratic opposition leaned toward a different notion of the middle way. Its economic program has been labeled Socialist Market Economy.[8]

There is considerable overlapping in the economic policies supported by the two major political parties, but the convergence at the policy level hides a significant underlying divergence in economic thinking, which makes for different economic arguments, even when similar policies are adopted. Widely accepted economic assumptions and arguments have their own impact on the long-run trend of policy. Appropriately, therefore, we include in our analysis of the setting of governmental policy a brief excursion into its ideological basis—into the central ideas of the Social and Socialist Market economies.

SOCIAL VERSUS SOCIALIST MARKET ECONOMIES[9]

The ideas of the Social Market Economy have sprouted from the neoliberal movement, which had its main intellectual center at the University of Freiburg. The leading economist of this movement, the late Freiburg Professor, Walter Eucken, argued that "A new type of human being is coming into existence: he is submerged in the masses [vermasst] and dependent on the state. All aspects of life are gradually taken over by the state."[10] For Eucken

[6] L. Erhard, *Prosperity Through Competition* (London: Thames and Hudson, 1958), p. x.
[7] In the *Düsseldorfer Leitsätze*; see Carlo Motteli, *Licht und Schatten der sozialen Marktwirtschaft* (Erlenbach–Zürich: Eugen Rentsch Verlag, 1961), p. 189.
[8] Although this label is very convenient, it does not seem to have common currency in Germany. Apparently Alfred Weber has introduced it into the literature; see Kurt Nemitz, *Sozialistische Marktwirtschaft* (Frankfurt Main: Europäische Verlagsanstalt, 1960), p. 62.
[9] A juxtaposition of this kind can be clear-cut only with reference to the ideas involved. When the labels are applied to political parties and to economic organizations, the dichotomy tends to lose some of its clarity, since the ideas are usually accepted only in part, and there are always internal divisions within such groups.
[10] W. Eucken, *Grundsätze der Wirtschaftspolitik* (Hamburg: Rowohlt Taschenbuch Verlag, 1959), p. 128.

the fundamental social question of the day was no longer greater economic equality or security but preservation of individual freedom.[11] The neoliberals are thus chary of welfare measures. They reject central planning and dirigism of any kind and give monetary stability priority over full employment. Even though it is not appropriate here to explore neoliberal ideas in depth,[12] their implications for social policy are fairly obvious.

The Social Market Economy, however, represents an attempt to reconcile the liberal position with a positive social program. In a slim volume, published shortly after World War II, Professor Alfred Müller-Armack first presented the basic ideas of the Social Market Economy.[13] He addressed himself to the problem of economic and social reconstruction at a time when the country was still in the economic doldrums, shackled by the maze of controls left over from the wartime Nazi system. Any policy of reconstruction, he argued, must be based on a careful reexamination of the alternative merits of the market coordinated and centrally directed economies.[14] Germany was in the position of having experienced both forms of economic organization. Her experience with laissez-faire capitalism, if one may thus designate the pre-Nazi era, was marked by economic instability and social conflict. Nazi dirigism was a reaction to these excesses. As a system of central control, it destroyed individual freedom and undermined rational economic calculation and efficiency. For Müller-Armack and the neoliberals, this is an inevitable outcome of dirigism. It can never remain partial they claim; controls and regulations inevitably multiply and eventually stifle incentive, initiative, and economic progress.[15]

Thus, neither the laissez-faire nor the controlled economy are acceptable alternatives. The appropriate middle-way is the Social Market Economy, which relies on the "free" market but does not exclude social intervention. To justify this intervention, Müller-Armack stresses the importance of the distinction between the allocation and the distribution functions of the market mechanism. He points out that the great economic achievement of nineteenth-century liberalism was to recognize the efficiency of the free market mechanism with regard to the production and to the allocation of resources. Its great failure was to insist that the market also was the best

[11]*Ibid.*, p. 130.
[12]A useful summary of neoliberal economics can be found in Henry M. Oliver, "German Neoliberalism," *Quarterly Journal of Economics*, Vol. LXXIV (February 1960), pp. 117–149; see also Wallich, *op. cit.*, Chapter V.
[13]*Wirtschaftslenkung und Marktwirtschaft* (Hamburg: Verlag für Wirtschaft und Sozialpolitik, 1947).
[14]Müller-Armack deals here with an issue—economic organization—that was dominant in Walter Eucken's economic thought.
[15]This viewpoint is more fully developed in Friedrich von Hayek, *The Road to Serfdom* (Chicago: University of Chicago Press, 1944).

arbiter of income distribution. "It was a mistake with weighty consequences that economic liberalism simply accepted market distribution as being socially and politically adequate, thereby lumping together the problem of the technically appropriate form of exchange with the problem of what is socially and politically desirable."[16] Useful and essential as the free market is, it must never be looked on as an end in itself or as having some natural justification of its own. "It is only an extremely suitable organizational tool, but no more, and it would be a fateful mistake to leave to automatic market operations the task of determining the ultimate social order and of providing on their own for the necessities of political and cultural life."[17]

Because of this historic mistake of liberalism, the failures of the market in the area of distribution became a major cause of the rejection of the market itself. The reaction was not limited to a correction of the distributive process but resulted in the substitution of dirigism for the market mechanism. Müller-Armack emphasizes that the distributive effects of the free market mechanism can be remedied without disposing of the market itself and without losing thereby its incomparable advantages in the preservation of freedom and initiative, and in the allocation of resources. The historical association of the free market with laissez-faire liberalism has led to the unwarranted assumption that these two aspects are inseparable. He argues that the free competitive market is compatible with a variety of social policies. In his view, neither the maintenance of full employment, nor economic growth, nor a socially desirable distribution of income necessitate "disruptive" interventions with the free market.

In Müller-Armack's words, "The essence of the social market economy is the combination of the principle of freedom in the market with that of compensatory social payments [sozialer Ausgleich]."[18] Freedom in the market requires an effective policy of maintenance of competitive conditions, including the elimination of monopolies and cartels. However, the important question is: To what extent does the social market admit government intervention for social purposes? Müller-Armack answers: "The guiding principle of social intervention in the market economy is compatibility with the functioning of market-directed production and its corresponding income formation."[19] In other words, social intervention must not be disruptive, that is, it must not interfere with either incentive or resource allocation.

---

[16] Müller-Armack, *op. cit.*, p. 85.

[17] *Ibid.*, p. 85. It is interesting to observe the difference between this view of the competitive process, the natural law, and the social Darwinist conceptions.

[18] "Soziale Marktwirtschaft" in *Handwörterbuch der Staatswissenschaften* (Stuttgart: Gustav Fischer, 1956), Vol IX, p. 390.

[19] *Ibid.*, p. 391.

In this manner the new economic policy endeavors to achieve economic progress through measures that are consistent with the market [marktkonforme Massnahmen]. It understands thereby measures which achieve their social objective without disruptive intervention with the market apparatus.[20]

What these principles mean when translated into actual policy, of course, depends on how the policy makers interpret them. Müller-Armack believes that the Social Market Economy can bear substantial income redistribution for social purposes precisely because its competitive framework makes it highly productive and progressive. Whether the social goals of the modern state can be achieved within the framework of market consistent measures without "disruptive" interventions, is a question too involved to be considered here. There are, however, some important social policy implications of the Social Market Economy which deserve to be pointed out. In the first instance, the aim of achieving social goals through market consistent measures naturally tends to shape the goals themselves. The Social Market Economy is not the kind of doctrine that is likely to inspire an aggressive social program. This is confirmed by Chancellor Erhard's views on social policy. The self-acknowledged father of the Social Market Economy[21] sees the future of his offspring threatened by social welfare measures.

> The social market economy cannot flourish if the spiritual attitude on which it is based—that is, the readiness to assume the responsibility for one's fate and to participate in honest and free competition—is undermined by seemingly social measures in neighbouring fields. . . .
>
> A free economic order can only continue if and so long as the social life of the nation contains a maximum of freedom, of private initiative and of foresight.
>
> If, on the other hand, social policy aims at granting a man complete security from the hour of birth, and protecting him absolutely from the hazards of life, then it cannot be expected that people will develop that full measure of energy, effort, enterprise and other human virtues which are vital to the life and future of the nation, and which, moreover, are the prerequisites of a social market economy based on individual initiative. The close link between economic and social policy must be stressed; in fact, the more successful economic policy can be made the fewer measures of social policy will be necessary.[22]

Another important implication of the Social Market Economy doctrine is a certain ambiguity with regard to specific policy measures. Erhard calls the welfare state the "modern delusion" and declares himself in favor of limiting instead of expanding the area of collective security. Yet, he admits

---

[20]*Ibid.*, p. 391.
[21]"I am generally called the father of the social market economy . . .," L. Erhard, "Germany's Economic Goals," *Foreign Affairs*, Vol. XXXVI (July 1958), p. 611.
[22]*Prosperity Through Competition*, pp. 185–186.

at the same time that "social security is certainly a good thing and desirable to a high degree."[23] It is difficult to establish in actual practice how faithfully the canons of the Social Market Economy are being observed or how lightly they are being transgressed. Even if they are not inclined toward more social welfare, those who have accepted the doctrine have seemingly little difficulty in reconciling the country's extensive welfare program and the measures that aim at the maintenance of full employment with their views. Critics, on the other hand, are inclined to see a contradiction here and link the country's economic success with the extent to which the doctrine has been disregarded in practice.[24] The more bitter critics, if they cannot deny the success of the Social Market Economy, argue that actual public policy is a direct negation of it.[25]

Of course, ambiguity may well increase the ideological appeal of the Social Market Economy and, hence, its importance as an influence on social policy. There can be little doubt about its success on the ideological plane. A doctrine that champions freedom from state control and individual initiative and responsibility is well-nigh irresistible to anyone who favors unhindered free enterprise. Private enterprise in postwar Germany was badly in need of an effective ideological defense. Governmental economic planning had gathered many ardent supporters. The reputation of private enterprise had been tarnished by the association of some of its top leaders with the rise of Hitler. It is not surprising, therefore, that the Social Market Economy received vigorous endorsements from the country's employer associations.[26] The explicit goal of a social order which offers security, freedom, and social justice not only broadens the appeal of the Social Market Economy but also makes it more effective as an ideological weapon in the hands of those who have adopted it.

Just as the Social Market Economy is a reinterpretation of economic liberalism in the light of recent economic history, the Socialist Market

[23] *Ibid.*, pp. 192, 196.

[24] For some critical observations, see E. Liefmann-Keil, *Einführung in die Politische Oekonomie* (Freiburg: Herder Bucherei, 1964), p. 61.

[25] "How can one speak of a market economy when 80 percent of our needs depend on price regulation in one way or another . . .? It is an effrontery to hold forth with moral indignation against dirigism and at the same time practice it in inumerable areas to the point of destroying individual freedom." From a paper delivered at the 1959 trade union congress by Ludwig Rosenberg; quoted in Karl O. Hondrich, *Die Ideologien von Interessenverbänden* (Berlin: Duncker und Humblot, 1963), p. 87.

[26] The endorsement by the Federal Union of German Employer Associations (Bundesvereinigung der deutschen Arbeitgeberverbände) has been more straightforward than that of the Federal Association of German Industry (Bundesverband der deutschen Industry). The latter, which represents only industrial interests, has been a bit wary of the anticartel implications of the emphasis on free competition. For an analysis of the position of these organizations, see Hondrich, *op. cit.*, pp. 74–80.

Economy is a reinterpretation of socialist thinking to fit the new economic and social environment. Fundamentally, the aims of the two alternative systems are the same. The neoliberals have certainly no quarrel with the goals of "social justice, greater welfare, individual freedom, and world peace," which were adopted by the Socialist International in 1951.[27] The main difference between liberals and socialists lies in the meaning of these goals and in the means suitable to achieve them.

The Socialist Market Economy can be considered the most recent step in the evolution of the revisionist movement which began during the last decade of the nineteenth century. The old slogans and mental constructs, however, were slow to die, even after social revolution had become an anachronism. At their congress in 1921, the Social Democrats were still echoing the radical spirit of the Erfurt Program of 1891.[28] Immediately after World War II, extensive nationalization and central planning were still considered essential for the realization of the party's economic and social goals. Nevertheless, at the party's 1946 congress in Hannover, there were signs that the Nazi experience with bureaucratic control had dimmed the ardor for economic dirigism. The need to protect individual freedom and the desirability of a pluralistic society were specifically recognized. "For socialism there is no sameness and no servitude, no prescribed garrison socialism, no uniformity."[29] The "economic emancipation of the human personality" was made the chief economic policy objective. In addition to the "rediscovery of the meaning of freedom," two other important changes gradually became apparent in the thinking of the German Social Democrats. One of these reflects the abandonment of the central marxist concept of the class struggle; the SPD began to broaden its appeal to the "people" as a whole, rather than to just manual workers. The introduction to its 1954 "Action Program," adopted at Dortmund, declares that the party has changed from being the party of the working class to the party of the people.[30] The aim of the party, the program states, is to help "the workers, the salaried employees, those excercizing intellectual or free professions, the farmers and the handicraftsmen, the merchants and the tradesmen, as well as the invalids and pensioners."[31]

[27] See Nemitz, *op. cit.*, pp. 37–38.
[28] See the 1921 Görlitz Program of the SPD, which is partially reprinted in Nemitz, *op. cit.*, pp. 183–184. The appendix of this book reproduces the main economic policy demands of the socialist programs from the Communist Manifesto of 1848 to the SPD Bad Godesberg Program of 1959.
[29] *Ibid.*, p. 188.
[30] *Ibid.*, p. 37. On the efforts to broaden the appeal of the party and other objectives, see D. A. Chalmers, *The Social Democratic Party of Germany* (New Haven: Yale University Press, 1964) Chapter IV.
[31] Nemitz, *op. cit.*, p. 192.

Another significant change in the party's outlook has been its increasing acceptance of the competitive market as a regulator of economic life and the consequent deemphasis of central planning. In contrast to the 1946 demands for extensive nationalization and planning, the 1954 Action Program contains the striking formula: "Competition as far as possible, planning as far as necessary." The old dogmatic approach of simply listing major industries as self-evident candidates for nationalization was dropped. The nationalization guideline of the Bad Godesberg Program (1959) states rather modestly: "Where a healthy order of economic relationships cannot be achieved by other means, collective ownership is appropriate and necessary." [32]

Even this cursory survey makes it sufficiently clear that there has been a far-reaching reconciliation of economic and social views among the leading political parties in Germany. There has been a major movement toward a central common ground of ideas and policies, with all but the most dogmatic among the neoliberals advocating social modifications of the dictates of the market and with the socialists accepting a central role for the market. The remaining differences between the policies of the two groups are reflections of the biases with which the common ground has been approached. The "social market" advocates have the stronger faith in the efficacy of the free market as a means for the promotion of social welfare and, hence, find less need for correcting its operations. They are always wary that those corrections may in one way or another hurt initiative, incentive, or productivity, and they are less anxious than the advocates of the "socialist market" to combat unemployment and to reduce income inequalities.

Although the socialists may appreciate the value of freedom of choice and the importance of initiative and entrepreneurship, they are less sensitive in this respect than with regard to social welfare problems. They have always had more faith in direct governmental measures than in the indirect effects of the market mechanisms. Their concept of the economic and social order is that of the modern welfare state. Their objectives are well-defined, but their means of achieving them are less so. They insist that some planning, not of prices and products, but of macro-economic magnitudes, is necessary, in order to allow the state to influence the relationships between aggregate consumption and aggregate investment in a manner that will assure continued full employment and stable economic growth. In their view the maintenance of full employment has a very high priority. The handbook on social democratic policy declares that it is "the duty of society . . .

---

[32] Nemitz, *op. cit.*, p. 34. The political opponents of the socialists claim that this is not a genuine conversion but is only a tactical maneuver to get votes. See Erhard's speech at the 1961 CDU convention in his *Deutsche Wirtschaftspolitik*, pp. 567 ff. Within the SPD these changes have aroused lively debates and by no means unanimity of opinion. In general, the younger generation of socialists tend to be the modern revisionists. See Chalmers, *op. cit.*, pp. 60 ff.

to provide to all its ablebodied members the opportunity of constant active participation in economic life."[33] This does not mean that the Social Democrats are not concerned with the problems of monetary stability; no German political party can make light of the threat of inflation. Yet, they naturally do not go along with Erhard, for whom "the social market economy is unthinkable without a parallel stability of the currency."[34] In their 1957 "Social Plan for Germany" they stress the overriding importance of full employment for social rights.

> Full employment, in the sense of an optimal level of employment, is in multiple respects a precondition for an effective system of social security. Only through systematic exploitation of all possibilities can the national product be increased correspondingly. In an economy which tolerates substantial unemployment in branches of industry or in agricultural areas, *the freedom of choice of occupation and the freedom of choice of a place to work* are restricted. . . . Full employment is one of the preconditions of a comprehensive realization of these fundamental rights of the citizen in our industrial age.[35]

Earlier we observed that the Social Market Economy has found a highly favorable response among the country's employers. Similarly, the trade unions have been inclined toward the ideas and policies of the Socialist Market Economy. Labor is an important element of the left wing of both major political parties, but trade unions, especially the large industrial unions, have always been more strongly represented in the Socialist than in the Christian Social camp. In its 1949 *Grundforderungen* (basic demands), the Federation of German Trade Unions (*Deutscher Gewerkschaftsbund*) included nationalization of all major industries, governmental planning, maintenance of full employment, codetermination, and an adequate welfare program. In the following decade, the federation mollified its attitude on nationalization and planning in favor of the free market, but it remained a critic of governmental economic policy and of the Social Market Economy. The federation leaders see the Social Market Economy as the ideal of property, not as the ideal of social justice.[36]

The purpose of this brief comparison of the ideas, values, and policies of the Social and the Socialist Market economies has been to present the most salient features of the postwar ideological setting within which the German social security reforms have been carried out. No explicit attempt has been made to account for the forces that shaped this framework.

---

[33] *Handbuch sozialdemokratischer Politik*, quoted in Nemitz, *op. cit.*, p. 70.

[34] Prosperity through Competition, p. 7.

[35] *Sozialplan für Deutschland*, prepared at the request of the Social Democratic Party (Berlin: J. H. W. Dietz Verlag, 1957), p. 24; original emphasis.

[36] Rosenberg, *op. cit.*, p. 19.

Developments within the country as well as experiences abroad have exercised strong influences on the German reformulation of social rights after the war. Among the foreign influences, special mention must be made of the Scandinavian, Dutch, and British welfare states. The presence of a rival economic system in East Germany also has exercised a subtle influence on the aims of governmental policy. Great Britain is a country that undertook a basic reform of its social security system after World War II, following the principles laid down in 1942 by Sir William Beveridge in his report on Social Insurance and Allied Services. The principles of this report were widely hailed as a fundamental restatement of the social rights of the citizen in the modern state. They have influenced social security thinking throughout the world. Although their impact on German social security reform was at best indirect, and sometimes negative, a short digression on the British system may nevertheless be instructive as an exploration of a contrasting approach.

CONTRASTING CONCEPTIONS: THE BRITISH WELFARE STATE

The nature of a complex set of interrelated economic and social policies is often best understood by way of contrast with an alternative policy approach designed to serve similar purposes. In many respects, postwar Britain faced problems of economic and social reconstruction that were similar to the ones of Germany, although by no means as hopeless. The country had sustained heavy human losses and had suffered tremendous material destruction. This experience, the economic difficulties of the interwar era, and a long history of agitation and reform had conditioned the British people for a break with the past through a new ordering of life. The Labor party, which held the greatest promise for effectuating extensive economic and social change, won a sweeping victory in the first postwar general election in 1945.

Basic structural changes in the economy were deemed necessary to secure new social rights. Maintenance of full employment and the elimination of "wasteful competition" were considered essential. It had always been a fundamental socialist dogma that this could not be achieved without giving the state control over at least the "commanding heights" of the economy. The nationalization of key industries and the central bank were, therefore, the first item on the agenda of structural reform. Aside from any ideological bias, the recollection of the economic hardships of the 1920s and 1930s was a factor in the prevailing lack of faith in the free market and in the attraction to governmental planning. Other important features of the British welfare state program were a highly progressive tax structure and far-reaching reforms in social insurance, social services, and health care.

It is this latter category of reforms that usually come to mind when reference is made to the welfare state. Although it is obviously impossible to review the details of these reforms, an examination of their guiding principles, particularly as they apply to social insurance, is in order. Fortunately the principles underlying the postwar British social insurance reforms were eloquently formulated in a wartime governmental study under the chairmanship of Sir William Beveridge. The ensuing Beveridge Report[37] of 1942 became a landmark in the development of social security thought; its influence has extended to every major country in the world. It set the pattern for systematic social planning rather than piecemeal attacks on separate needs.

The Beveridge Report is a comprehensive statement of the citizen's social right to freedom from want and of the means to implement this right. It is remarkable for what it contains as well as for what it leaves out. Although offering a blueprint of "cradle to grave" protection, Beveridge did not find it necessary to also develop ideological arguments in order to justify its adoption. Nothing could be more indicative of the nearly unanimous acceptance in Britain of the basic concepts of social rights. Beveridge defines his social insurance and related programs as "an attack upon want" and considers them part of a "comprehensive policy of social progress."[38] There is never any question about the desirability or legitimacy of the kind of social plan offered, only about its feasibility and about the best ways to achieve it. Without being doctrinaire in his views, Beveridge was convinced of the feasibility and essential correctness of his plan. "It is clear," he wrote, "that abolition of want . . . is within our means."[39] And he further expressed his conviction that this cannot be done automatically through economic growth: "Abolition of want requires a double redistribution of income, through social insurance and by family needs."[40]

The central idea of the Beveridge Report is the concept of the national minimum benefit. "Social insurance should aim at guaranteeing the minimum income needed for subsistence."[41] This is the basic dimension of the social right to freedom from want. Social provision should be sufficient in amount and duration, not in excess, for what is needed to maintain the national minimum.[42] His approach differed from the one that

---

[37] *Social Insurance and Allied Services.* Report by Sir William Beveridge (American edition, New York: MacMillan, 1942).
[38] *Ibid.,* p. 6.
[39] *Ibid.,* p. 167.
[40] *Ibid.,* p. 7.
[41] *Ibid.,* p. 14.
[42] Beveridge wanted this minimum to be based on empirical investigation of actual needs. He did mention, however, that in the case of national assistance a somewhat lower minimum should be applicable than in social insurance.

prevailed in most countries in that the level of benefits was governed exclusively by the social purpose of the benefit rather than by past contributions or by the past earnings of the beneficiary. We recall that this principle of benefit determination had been demanded by the German Social Democrats nearly half a century earlier. Its basic appeal to socialists is its egalitarian character, since the same minimum applies to all individuals with similar responsibilities. Any system that ties benefits directly or indirectly to past earnings necessarily perpetuates the income inequalities derived from different earning capacities. Beveridge recommended a social insurance system with flat subsistence benefits as well as flat contributions, irrespective of earnings. His reasoning was: "All insured persons, rich or poor, will pay the same contributions for the same security; those with larger means will pay more only to the extent that as tax-payers they will pay more to the National Exchequer and so to the State share of the Social Insurance Fund."[43]

In other words, where the protection relationship between the individual and the state is transparent, in the payment of contributions and in the receipt of benefits, it is strictly egalitarian. The heavier contributions of higher income receivers via direct taxation and government contribution makes it less obvious that rich and poor do not in fact pay the same amount for the same security. The flat benefit and flat contribution approach, Beveridge argues, "has been found to accord best with the sentiments of the British people," and he adds that "There is growing support for the principle . . . that in compulsory insurance all men should stand together on equal terms, that no individual should be allowed to claim better terms because he is healthier or in more regular employment."[44] Taking note of the fact that "the war is abolishing landmarks of every kind," his report aimed at a postwar social order that was to be not only more egalitarian but also was to reflect a greater national solidarity of all citizens. The social insurance system thus becomes an important instrument of social unification by helping to overcome lingering class antagonisms. The income redistribution function of social insurance in the Beveridge program is carried out mainly on the contribution side, with the country's progressive tax structure assuring that the state's contribution would result in a vertical redistribution, from higher to lower income receivers. In combination with the state subsidy, the flat contributions from the insured and their employers, provided that their contributions remain relatively low, tend to minimize the horizontal redistribution which is inherent in most contributory social insurance schemes.[45] Horizontal redistribution, by making the poor pay for

[43]*Social Insurance and Allied Services.* Report by Sir William Beveridge, p. 121.
[44]*Ibid.*, p. 30.
[45]On this problem, see Alan T. Peacock and P. R. Browning, "The Social Services in Great

the poor, tends to create new forms of inequality alongside the social rights created by social insurance.

Any social insurance system that involves vertical income redistribution is suspect for its effects on incentive and individual initiative. Beveridge was well aware of this problem; he observed that "the State in organizing security should not stifle incentive, opportunity, responsibility; in establishing a national minimum, it should leave room and encouragement for voluntary action by each individual to provide more than that minimum for himself and his family."[46] The determination of what is necessary for the maintenance of individual initiative and responsibility is a difficult task, and the answer varies from country to country and over time. For postwar Britain, Beveridge believed that minimum benefit levels and the contributory principle were adequate safeguards. He had no intention of using the benefit structure for incentive purposes which, of course, is not feasible in a system based on a flat national minimum. He hoped, nevertheless, that such a system would act as an incentive by inducing individuals to supplement the floor of protection provided by the state. The history of social insurance in many countries tends to support this assumption. Moreover, this attitude toward the incentive question is reasonably consistent with the ideal stated by Beveridge that "Management of one's income is an essential element of a citizen's freedom."[47] He did not want to limit this freedom more than was necessary for purposes of assuring the universal freedom from want.

In the Beveridge scheme the link between contributions and benefits is not intended to serve incentive purposes but to maintain the individual's as well as the government's sense of responsibility. Beveridge noted that "insured persons should not feel that income for idleness, however caused, can come from a bottomless purse."[48] He insisted that some relationship be maintained between costs and contributions, since this would put pressure on the individual as well as on the government to reduce the extent of dependency. "The Government should not feel that by paying doles it can avoid the major responsibility of seeing that unemployment and disease are reduced to a minimum."[49]

Another fundamental feature of the Beveridge plan is its comprehensiveness with regard to the coverage of risks and its universality with

---

Britain and the Redistribution of Income" in Alan T. Peacock, *Income Redistribution and Social Policy* (London: Jonathan Cape, 1954), pp. 156 ff.

[46] Beveridge, *op. cit.*, pp. 6–7.

[47] *Ibid.*, p. 12.

[48] *Ibid.*, p. 12.

[49] *Ibid.*, p. 12.

regard to the coverage of persons. This again is a reflection of the citizen's social right to freedom from want. "The plan covers all citizens without upper income limit . . . it is a plan all-embracing in scope of persons and of needs. . . ." [50] As in all social insurance programs, however, the social right granted the citizen in the Beveridge plan is primarily the right to be covered, not an absolute right to benefits. Eligibility for benefits is always contingent on the meeting of specified conditions by the insured persons. In the Beveridge plan eligibility for various benefits is dependent on the previous payment of specified numbers of contributions. The payment of contributions is a duty of the citizen that corresponds to his right to draw benefits, rather than a payment in exchange for benefits. Beveridge provided for exemptions and excusals from the duty to pay contributions in the case of very low income receivers, without thereby endangering their right to social insurance benefits. For those people who failed to qualify for benefits, even under these liberal provisions, he recommended the modernization of the public assistance program, in which benefits are contingent on a needs test. In addition, his plan assumed two major forms of protection completely outside the contributory social insurance system: one was allowances for children, to be paid by the exchequer to all families with more than one child *regardless of their income,* and the other was a comprehensive program of health care "without contribution conditions." Beveridge flatly asserted the duty of the state to share in the economic burden of raising children and of restoring health. Without these additional programs, it is difficult to make a social security system based on a national minimum workable. A final assumption on which his comprehensive program rested was that the state would use every means at its disposal to maintain full employment. He seemed much less concerned with the problem of price stability, which might become very difficult in an economy constantly striving to maintain full employment.

The last basic feature of the Beveridge plan that must be noted has to do with organization. Here again the ideas of national solidarity and of protection as a right of the citizen played an important role. It was no longer a matter of protecting the poor or the worker, but the citizen. The idea of "citizens standing by each other" had acquired a special meaning during the war and was now a dominant theme. It had superseded the individualistic theme of self-help as well as the class-oriented theme of dependence and protection. For Beveridge, national solidarity logically led to a national pooling of social insurance risks and rewards, which meant one central fund and uniform benefits as opposed to the pattern of many separate funds, with diverse rules and benefits, which had developed historically as a result of the

[50] Beveridge, *op. cit.,* p. 9.

inclusion of friendly societies into the social insurance system. He considered the "unification of administrative responsibilities" as one of his basic social insurance principles. It meant that there would be only one contribution from each insured person to cover all social insurance risks, paid into one central fund, and one income maintenance payment. Benefit overlapping, which becomes a problem in any comprehensive social security program, would be eliminated, although a person still might combine an income maintenance benefit with a benefit designed to compensate for industrial injuries and with grants for special purposes.

The fundamental features and principles of the Beveridge proposals were enacted into law shortly after the war. The basic act was the National Insurance Act of 1946; during the same year the National Health Service Act was passed, although the health program did not become operative until 1948; other important laws were the Family Allowances Act of 1945, the Industrial Injuries Act of 1946, and the National Assistance Act of 1948. This legislation gave Britain one of the most advanced social security programs in the world. It established statutory guarantees for the social rights of British citizens that became a model for other countries faced with the problem of postwar economic and social reconstruction.

Before the new system was a decade old, however, much dissatisfaction developed with the "subsistence principle." Although it promoted equality, and perhaps a sense of solidarity, among benefit recipients, it generated economic inequality between them and those who still were actively employed. In an economy experiencing rising costs of living and increasing real wages, with benefits always lagging behind, there was a widening economic gap between those still at work and those living on social security. This situation led to a lively political debate of the need to reform the reforms during the 1950s.[51] The most significant outcome of the debate was the abandonment of exclusive reliance on minimum flat benefits. The National Insurance Act of 1959 introduced a second layer of wage-related pensions to supplement the national minimum. This benefit differentiation, which was superimposed on an egalitarian base was a compromise solution combining various ideological positions. It was a solution reflecting the persistence of certain liberal notions as well as of the idea of the national minimum. The insurance principle introduced by the New Liberalism of Lloyd-George and Churchill was given a new role, without discarding the egalitarianism of the break with the old poor law. A completely egalitarian

---

[51] For an analysis of the debate, see Gabriele Bremme, *Freiheit und Soziale Sicherheit* (Stuttgart: Enke Verlag, 1961), pp. 81 ff.

system had been found impractical, mainly because it almost necessarily tied benefits to a level below the lowest common wages.[52]

THE REFORM DEBATE IN GERMANY

The 1949 Bonn Constitution, usually referred to as the Basic Law, states that "The Federal Republic of Germany is a democratic and social federal state" (Article 20) and that the individual member states "must conform to the principles of republican, democratic, and social government based on the rule of law" (Article 28). In addition, it declares that "Everyone has the right to the free development of his personality . . ." (Article 2) and that "All Germans have the right freely to choose their trade or profession, their place of work and their place of training" (Article 12). Aside from references to special provisions for former public servants (Article 131) and to the determination of jurisdiction and administration (Articles 74, 87, 120), this is about the extent to which the Basic Law offers guidance for the development of social rights.[53] In comparison with the social rights provided for in most constitutions of newly created states, the framers of the Basic Law acted with great restraint. They left it to public opinion and the legislators to interpret the meaning of broad terms such as "social state" and "free development of personality." The debate that has been going on almost since the founding of the Federal Republic has significantly contributed to this interpretation. By no means has it been restricted to academic or legislative halls. The political parties have taken positions and issued plans at their conventions and through the press. Employer organizations and trade unions as well as professional associations have stated their views and demands. It is not possible to cover all aspects of this debate, nor is it necessary, since it contains an enormous amount of repetition and much technical detail that are not relevant for our purposes. Therefore, we shall restrict ourselves to the more significant themes and proposals, illustrating the positions of diverse groups and reflecting the various forces at work.

The first aspect of the reform debate that we shall consider deals with the approaches to reform. The issue here is whether reforms will be carried out in a piecemeal, pragmatic fashion, or whether they shall follow a set of well-defined principles, or possibly even a well-worked-out plan. Modern

[52] It is worth noting that in 1959 Sweden also abandoned her traditional egalitarian system in favor of wage-related pension and cash-sickness benefits. See Albert H. Rosenthal, *The Social Programs of Sweden* (Minneapolis: University of Minnesota Press, 1967), Chapters II and III.

[53] For a discussion of constitutional aspects, see Arnold Köttgen, "Der Soziale Bundesstaat" and W. Bogs, "Zum verfassungsrechtlichen Begriff der Sozialversicherung" in H. Achinger (ed.), *Neue Wege der Fürsorge* (Köln: Carl Heymanns Verlag, 1960), pp. 19–55.

social security legislation has shown a tendency toward the achievement of broad goals, as opposed to a more narrow concern of the older legislation with simply providing individual and family protection. This has been described as a shift from the "protectionist" to the "social economic" phase of social security development.[54] Characteristic of the latter phase is the idea of economic and social planning. The function of a social plan is to define the ends and the means of social intervention and to integrate them with other aspects of national policy, particularly in the economic and social spheres. This, in effect, is what the Beveridge Report did for England: it was a comprehensive social plan.

An early advocate of social planning in postwar Germany was the late Professor Gerhard Mackenroth. At a meeting of the *Verein für Sozialpolitik* in 1952, he presented a paper that has had considerable influence on German thinking about the place of social security in the economy.[55] His principle objective in the paper was to demonstrate the necessity for an overall social plan, rather than offer a detailed blueprint. According to Mackenroth, "A social policy which is economically neutral no longer exists today. All-around harmonization and dovetailing of social policy with the economic circular flow and with the social structure is therefore urgently needed."[56] He attacks the problem of protection not from the viewpoint of individual need but from the one of the aggregate amount of resources a society is willing and able to allocate to social security and social services. He can see no upper limit to the socially *desirable* amount of these expenditures: "An absolute too much in social services does not exist."[57] It will be recalled that Beveridge was concerned about the individual's freedom to spend his own income. Mackenroth, on the other hand, stresses economic factors as the practical limit on social spending. He argues that the social plan has to establish the priorities according to which the available resources are to be allocated among risks, services, and individuals. Although he does not elaborate on priorities, he does stress the fundamental importance of a social equalization of the economic burden of raising children, the generation of tomorrow's producers.

With regard to the resources available for social security, Mackenroth makes two important points. First, no matter how social expenditures are financed, whether through general taxation or earmarked contributions, with or without the accumulation of funds, the amounts allocated to social

---

[54] D. Zöllner, "Entwicklungsphasen der Sozialpolitik" in K. Jantz (ed.), *Sozialreform und Sozialrecht,* Festschrift für Walter Bogs (Berlin: Duncker und Humblot, 1959), pp. 402 ff.

[55] "Die Reform der Sozialpolitik durch einen deutschen Sozialplan," *Schriften des Vereins für Sozialpolitik,* New Series, Vol. IV, pp. 39–76.

[56] *Ibid.,* p. 41.

[57] *Ibid.,* p. 44.

security in the real sense must come out of current gross national product.[58] This argument, which has often been overlooked by advocates of the insurance principle, underlines the social character of welfare expenditures by linking them to the circular flow of economic activity. Second, there are three ways in which the amounts allocated to social security can be increased: (1) through the redistribution of the aggregate amounts available for consumption; (2) through the reduction of aggregate investment; or (3) through an increase in the national product. He rightly does not believe that much can be gained by a redistribution of income allocated to consumption and considers a reduction in the rate of investment undesirable. The only remaining degree of freedom, therefore, is to increase the national product.

This line of argument, which ties the development of social rights directly to economic growth, has had an important influence in shaping the structure and growth of social security benefits in postwar Germany.[59] Mackenroth stresses that there must be no provisions "that conflict with the productivity of the economy or the growth of the national product."[60] He criticizes existing programs for their tendency to "sterilize" and misallocate labor. For incentive purposes he favors a sharply differentiated benefit structure, related to previous contributions, on top of a basic minimum financed through general tax revenue. He insists that benefits must be enough below wages to maintain an effective work incentive whenever this is applicable. In other words, there should be an incentive spread between productive and nonproductive income. On the other hand, his approach is compatible with a steady expansion in social services and a gradual rise in benefit levels as productivity and national per capita income go up. As national income rises, more resources can be devoted to welfare purposes

[58] This statement is correct insofar as it recognizes the distinction between the financial and the real aspects of social insurance, but it ignores the fact that the current level of production may be affected by past methods of financing; the accumulation of funds in the past may have restricted consumption in favor of capital accumulation, which may be a factor in greater productive capacity today.

[59] Many of the issues raised in Mackenroth's oft-cited article have been discussed at length in the postwar period. The most comprehensive and suggestive treatment of the economic issues involved in the formulation and execution of social policy is in E. Liefmann-Keil, *Oekonomische Theorie der Sozialpolitik* (Berlin: Springer Verlag, 1961). An interesting analysis of the place of social security in the circular flow of economic activity was carried out by one of Mackenroth's students; see H. Hensen, *Die Finanzen der sozialen Sicherung im Kreislauf der Wirtschaft*, Kieler Studien No. 36 (Kiel, 1955). Other economic issues are discussed in R. J. Willeke, *Die Arbeitslosenversicherung als Mittel der Konjunkturpolitik und Vollbeschäftigung*, Neue Soziale Praxis No. 9 (München: Richard Pflaum Verlag, 1951), and in H. Jecht, *Oekonomische Probleme der Produktivitätsrente*, Schriftenreihe des Bundesarbeitsministeriums No. 4 (Stuttgart: Kohlhammer Verlag, 1956).

[60] *Loc. cit.*, p. 47.

and, as wages rise, benefit levels can be raised without destroying the incentive spread.

In spite of his emphasis on the need for a global plan, Mackenroth does not favor centralized administration. He makes a distinction between central planning and central management, a distinction which is becoming increasingly important today even in socialist economies.[61] He argues that his plan would rationalize social security and would not endanger the traditional system of decentralized administration with participation by the insured, which he considers an important feature of the democratic, social state.

The kind of systematic planning Mackenroth proposes almost inevitably engenders resistance. Existing programs have a built-in resistance to change, which comes with long established rights and anticipations. Furthermore systematic social planning arouses ideological resistance. The acceptance of a rationalized social plan implies an acknowledgment of a very transparent governmental role in shaping the welfare of the individual. It usually means the acceptance of some kind of reform of the market system instead of mere reinforcement against its weaknesses. Political resistance is aroused because once a plan is adopted—and to be meaningful it has to be a long-range plan —its execution is mainly a job for administrators. This leaves less room for parliamentary maneuvering by vote-gathering politicians. Whether social or economic, governmental planning always produces objections on ideological grounds from those who wish to maximize the area of individual choice. Thus, systematic social planning is not likely to appeal strongly to the neoliberals.

These considerations help to explain why the widely accepted arguments for rationalizing the social security system have, nevertheless, not resulted in reform based on a central social plan. The government has had the benefit of thoughtful studies by able scholars who have outlined consistent principles for social reform,[62] but the influence of these studies on official policy is judged to be very weak by competent observers. Within the government there has been no unanimity of opinion, although differences have been greater with regard to emphasis rather than on basic principles.[63]

---

[61] See, for instance, Oskar Lange, "Economic Planning and Management in the Socialist Economy of Poland" in Indian Statistical Institute, *Planning and Statistics in Socialist Countries* (New York: Asia Publishing House, 1963), pp. 157–164.

[62] See, for instance, the study prepared for the former Chancellor, Konrad Adenauer, by H. Achinger, J. Höffner, H. Muthesius, and L. Neundörfer, *Neuordnung der sozialen Leistungen* (Köln: Greven Verlag, 1955). For the Ministry of Labor and Social Affairs a study of fundamental principles and objectives was prepared by Professor Walter Bogs, *Grundfragen des Rechts der sozialen Sicherheit und seiner Reform*, Sozialwissenschaftliche Abhandlungen No. 3 (Berlin: Duncker und Humblot, 1955).

[63] See, for instance, the proposals on fundamental reform principles submitted by the Minister of Labor to the Cabinet on March 22, 1955 and the comments on them by the

It is interesting to observe the difference between the two leading parties on the question of social planning. The Christian Democrats have spoken out on principles of social policy but have never adopted a social plan. The "Hamburg Program" adopted by the party at its 1953 congress noted that "Our *Sozialpolitik* is not an appendage to the Social Market Economy but its goal." [64] However, none of the spokesmen for the Social Market Economy has ever worked out a program of social action consistent with its principles. [65] This leaves the CDU's ideas on the subject in a state of confusion, a reflection of conflicting tendencies within its ranks. The Social Democrats, on the other hand, have offered a comprehensive social plan, representing a concensus of their party's views on the ends and means of social protection. [66]

The *Sozialplan* of the SPD is a comprehensive blueprint for social policy. It deals with social security in its widest sense. Its aim is to provide the foundations for a social policy geared to the economic potentials as well as the economic hazards of what is viewed as a new industrial age—the age of the second industrial revolution, which is characterized by automation and the harnessing of nuclear energy.

> The emerging consequences of the first phase of this new industrial revolution compel immediate action directed at: a constant anticipation of developments, an overall economic and social view, a basic plan, and a systematic, continuous expansion of the foundations of our entire economy. [67]

As is often the case with social plans, the socialist *Sozialplan* aims at more than mere rationalization of existing programs. It is conceived as an instrument of social reform, a vehicle of the creation of a new social order.

> The conditions of life of the working person must therefore be given a new foundation. Only a comprehensive social reform can achieve this. Society has to assure the *basic chances* of life in health, work capacity, and human dignity. Only then does the individual have the *possibility* of responsibly shaping on his own a life for himself and his family. . . . The existing social order, with

Minister for Economy and the Minister of Finance; Bundesminister fuer Arbeit, "Grundgedanken zur Gesamtreform der sozialen Leistungen" in Max Richter, *Die Sozialreform Dokumente und Stellungnahmen* (Bad Godesberg: Asgard Verlag, 1955–1968), Section B/III/1, pp. 1–17; Bundesminister für Wirtschaft, "Stellungnahme zu den 'Grundgedanken' des Bundesminister für Arbeit" in Richter, *op. cit.*, Section B/IV/1, pp. 1–5; Bundesminister der Finanzen, "Stellungnahme zu den 'Grundgedanken' des Bundesministers für Arbeit" in Richter, *op. cit.*, Section B/V1, pp. 1–12.
[64] "Das 'Hamburger Programm' der CDU" in Richter, *op. cit.*, Section G/I/1, p. 3.
[65] See W. Schreiber, "Sozialpolitik in der Sozialen Marktwirtschaft" in *Wirtschaft Gesellschaft und Kultur*, Festgabe für Alfred Müller-Armack (Berlin: Duncker und Humblot, 1961), pp. 596 ff.
[66] Sozialdemokratischen Partei Deutschlands, *Sozialplan für Deutschland* (Berlin: Dietz Verlag, 1957).   [67] *Ibid.*, p. 12.

its continuing unjust distribution of development and life time chances, sets a limit to the restructuring of social benefits. Socialist policy has taken upon itself the task of bursting these constraining limits asunder. These are partly built into the social order, and to that extent any fundamental restructuring of social benefits implies a global reform of social conditions. Our time is in accord with an *intermingling of social measures and personal initiative*. Social circumstances must be arranged such that the vital power of the individual can develop freely. Only then does the individual obtain the freedom to fit into society with a *personality of his own* and to assert himself.[68]

Both parties stress freedom and equality of opportunity. This merely may reflect their realization that these values are very popular. But the parties differ in their views on what the state has to do to assure genuine freedom and equality of opportunity for the individual. The Social Democrats show the greater readiness toward government intervention in order to prevent not only need but conditions that may be conducive to need. "A comprehensive social reform cannot be limited to help in times of need. It calls forth the resources of the community and of the individual to *prevent need from arising*. It creates the *precondition for the citizen's right to self-responsibile existence*."[69] This is a clear rejection of the nineteenth-century liberal view that laissez-faire and equality before the law are the means to achieve self-responsible citizenship. To be sure, the Christian Democrats do not lean toward that kind of unchecked liberalism. They cannot be accused of ignoring the need for establishing conditions conducive to effective self-help. But it is symptomatic of their individualistic leanings that they put great emphasis on measures to encourage individual saving and acquisition of property as a means to achieve greater individual economic security.

The social programs of both parties, however, strongly favor prevention of illness and the rehabilitation of the disabled, the retraining of workers displaced by technological change, and the upgrading of the labor force in general. By helping the worker help himself, these aspects of the social economic phase of social security policy support the ideal of equal opportunity, which is central in the modern concept of social justice. Also these measures are economically valuable as instruments of an effective manpower policy. The differences between the parties lies in their conception of these measures, whether they are instruments of change or of stability.

Our discussion of the social reform debate thus far has dealt with attitudes toward social planning. Differences in attitudes on this modern approach to social security parallel the attitudes toward planning in general. Adherents to the ideal of a free market ecnomy, even when it is prefixed with the word "social," find it difficult to accept systematic central planning of

[68] *Ibid.*, p. 9, original italics.
[69] *Ibid.*, p. 10, original italics.

the individual's economic security. They are always more at ease with a piecemeal approach, which is oriented toward patching up the weaknesses of the market system. Planning tends to introduce a rival conception of economic organization.

We shall now examine the debate with respect to the more traditional issues of social insurance legislation. They are concerned with (1) the universality and comprehensiveness of protection, (2) the level and structure of benefits, (3) the conditions governing the receipt of benefits, (4) financing, specifically the sharing of costs between beneficiaries, employers, and the state and, finally, (5) organization and administration. Our purpose is to indicate the range of alternative approaches and their implications in terms of human welfare.

The question of universality and comprehensiveness deals with the problem of who should be protected and against what kinds of risk. It is closely related to the issue of social planning, since one reason for an overall plan is to assure complete protection in the most efficient manner possible. In the case of the Beveridge plan, it will be recalled, the objective was universal coverage against all major risks. This is consistent with the egalitarian idea that protection is a social right of all citizens, regardless of individual economic circumstances. The German tradition, however, has its roots in the more paternalistic notion that protection is mainly for the "economically weak." Thus, discussions on coverage must deal with the question of whether this is still a valid concept in a modern industrial society. Involved here is the old issue of the appropriate limits of individual and state responsibility for economic welfare. Is compulsory social insurance appropriate in a highly developed economy, and if so, to what extent?

One theme that runs through the social reform debate is the rejection of the fundamental notion of "classical" social insurance, that workers are the "economically weak" element and, therefore, are in special need of protection. This view of the worker is consistent with the social stratification of an industrializing society. Under mature industrialism, however, workers are no longer an economically weak social stratum. Economic growth, wars, and political upheavals bring about a restratification of social groups. A central feature of this restratification in Germany has been the ascent of the worker and the descent of middle class and white collar elements on the ladder of economic security.[70] Mackenroth, for instance, notes that "while the workers have secured their position, other social strata, that formerly seemed to be secure, are today in need ..."[71] Family property was once a seem-

[70] This view of society is analyzed in Leopold von Wiese, "Social Security and Social Ascent as Problems of our Time" (trans. by G. Rimlinger and R. Bendix) in R. Bendix and S. M. Lipset (eds.), *Class, Status, and Power* (Glencoe, Ill.: The Free Press, 1953), pp. 588–595.
[71] *Op. cit.*, p. 40.

ingly safe foundation of economic security, but in an age of total wars, massive inflations, and monetary revaluations, this is no longer the case. The conclusion is therefore inescapable that, in an industrial society, economic protection should not be limited to wage workers. The dynamics of this society expose all its members to the danger of economic insecurity. Social security coverage should, therefore, be universal, or nearly so.

Changes in conceptions of the role of social security also have implications for the degree of protection to be provided. There seems to be general agreement that counteracting the alienation of the working class, which strongly motivated the introduction of social insurance, is no longer an important goal of present German social policy. The reason is, of course, the alienation of labor is no longer a major social problem. The aim of postwar social policy, according to Professor Weddigen, a seasoned expert in this area, is more in the nature of the "contended productive cooperation," the "harmonious interaction," and the "unhindered development of the productive capacity" of *all* members of society.[72] This implies that protection should not be restricted to any particular group, but at the same time it need not be universal. Weddigen defines the optimum degree of intervention as that which provides "maximum economic productivity and social harmony."[73] The exact dosage of individual freedom and social constraint needed to achieve this dual objective varies with time and place. It depends on attitudes toward individual initiative and responsibility, on economic opportunities, on a society's values regarding solidarity and discipline, and on its authority structure.

A general acceptance of the role of social security, as Weddigen defines it, therefore, would not necessarily result in a common agreement regarding who should be protected and to what extent. Weddigen observes with disapproval the trend toward ever more universal social insurance coverage. He believes that there is an adverse effect on productivity when high-income persons are included under compulsory coverage. Since there is usually an upper income limit for contributions, all persons earning above the limit are on a flat contribution and flat pension scheme. In the case of unemployment insurance, the inclusion of highly paid individuals, whose risk of unemployment is normally very low, amounts to a compulsory subsidization of those in less stable jobs, whose incomes are usually lower too.[74] In a more general way, Weddigen argues that the higher an individual's income, the

---

[72] W. Weddigen, "Gegenwartsfragen der Sozialpolitik," *Jahrbücher für Nationalökonomie und Statistik*, Vol. 168 (1956), pp. 427–428.

[73] *Ibid.*, pp. 429–30.

[74] It must be kept in mind here that the employees are required to contribute under the German unemployment insurance system and that the rates are not set according to the unemployment experience of different industries, as is the case in the United States.

lower the potential productivity gains from social insurance, the reason being that the marginal gain in security is not important enough to offset the adverse effects of compulsory coverage.

In spite of the reservations of intellectuals and policy makers, German public opinion leans strongly to "cradle to grave" social insurance. In a 1963 survey, more than 70 percent of the respondents approved of statements like "The Government has to guarantee everyone adequate housing, income, and recreation," and "old-age pensions should be high enough that one no longer has to provide for oneself." [75] Interestingly enough, most people who held these views were also distrustful of the state bureaucracy.

The arguments against extensive dependence on the state are well known. Their meaning should be obvious in a country that remembers Nazi regimentation and confronts Soviet-type collectivism on its borders. Beyond a certain point, economic protection by the state almost necessarily comes into conflict with individual freedom. The experiences of totalitarian countries indicate that the system of protection can become an instrument for the political manipulation of the masses. Even in democratic countries, politicians are not unaware of the vote-getting potentials of social security improvements. The more extensive the system, the more vulnerable the position of beneficiaries. Another old argument against complete protection is ethical in character. This is the view that the individual should not be relieved of the duty to provide, to the limit of his ability, for himself and his family. The state should act only in a subsidiary capacity, helping the individual to help himself. [76] Finally, there are the economic arguments against complete protection. These center on the adverse effects on the incentive and initiative of both the beneficiaries and those who bear the economic burden of the welfare payments.

The positions taken by the political parties and economic interest groups on the question of universality and comprehensiveness, of course, depends on their affinity for one side or the other of the opposing arguments. It is no surprise that the father of the Social Market Economy leans toward limited protection. In a January 1956 article, Ludwig Erhard stresses the close link between economic and social policy in the modern state and argues for a social policy that is in harmony with the principles of the Social Market Economy.

> It contradicts a logic of the market economy, according to which production and consumption decisions are left to the individual, to eliminate private initiative in the provision against the vicissitudes and exigencies of life even in cases where

---

[75] Deutsche Forschungsgemeinschaft, *Soziale Umverteilung*, Mitteilung I der Kommission für dringliche sozialpolitische Fragen (Wiesbaden: Franz Steiner Verlag, 1964), p. 40.
[76] For a statement of this argument, see Achinger *et al., op. cit.*, pp. 22 ff.

the individual is willing and able to act responsibly on his own. Economic freedom and universal compulsory insurance are incompatible.[77]

A defender of the principle of universality might well insist that Erhard overstates his case for polemical reasons. However, Erhard is concerned not only with the economic but also with the psychological effects of too much protection. In a speech to the 1957 CDU congress on the theme of "prosperity for all," he declared:

> We reject the welfare state of the socialist variety and the general collectivist maintenance of the citizen not only because this seemingly well-meant tutelage of the citizen creates dependence, which in the end breeds only submissiveness and kills the spirit of free citizenship, but also because this kind of self-negation, that is, the surrender of human responsibility, cripples the individual's will to work and must lead to the deterioration of economic performance in general.[78]

When the functions of the market are taken over by a dirigist bureaucracy, he goes on to say, economic progress comes to an end and with it, economic well-being. The drive to increased protection leads to inflation and lessens capital formation. The result can only be lower general welfare in the future.

Similar views have been expressed by other leading spokesmen of the Christian Democrats. Two major themes of the guidelines prepared in 1955 by the Social Insurance Reform Committee of the CDU (*Reformausschuss Sozialversicherung der CDU*) are "individual responsibility" and the "need to limit the role of the state."[79] The committee attacked the idea of *allgemeine Staatsbürgerversorgung* (general maintenance of the citizen by the state) as a threat to the valuable forces of self-help, self-responsibility, and individual initiative. More specifically, this means that the committee wanted to limit compulsory coverage to wage-workers and to salaried employees, but with an income ceiling for the latter. It argued that the fact that some self-employed persons occasionally become an economic burden on the state does not justify an invasion of their freedom through compulsory insurance. They must be left to look out for themselves.

However, the resolutions adopted at the 1956 party congress no longer mention the income limit on coverage that was specified by the Social Insurance Reform Committe the year before. Instead, the resolutions declare simply that "Compulsory coverage is to be extended to all working for hire."[80] They even recommend the creation of a separate system of insurance for the self-employed, rather than leaving them to their own devices. The tenor of the party resolutions is in sharp contrast to that

---

[77] L. Erhard, "Selbstverantwortliche Vorsorge für die sozialen Lebensrisiken," reprinted in L. Erhard, *Deutsche Wirtschaftspolitik*, p. 303.   [78] *Deutsche Wirtschaftspolitik*, p. 341.
[79] "Leitsätze zur Rentenversicherung" in Richter, *op. cit.*, Section G/I/3, pp. 9–12.
[80] "Der CDU-Parteitag 1956 und die Sozialreform" in Richter, *op. cit.*, Section G/I/6, p. 19.

of the guidelines worked out the year before by the special committee. The 1956 recommendations point to the need for the following:

> ... fundamental reforms which involve practically all areas of life, namely, securing equal life chances and equal occupational opportunities for young people, protection of the family, especially the family with many children, care of invalids, especially those who have to leave the work force in their most productive years, and care of the growing group of older persons.[81]

If we overlooked the fact that the CDU has a laborite, as well as a neoliberal wing, recommendations of this kind might sound strange coming from a party committed to the ideals of the Social Market Economy.

There were, indeed, prominent party spokesmen who felt impelled to give the warning sound that the acceptable limits of the welfare state had been reached. At the 1957 CDU congress, the President of the *Bundestag, Dr.* Eugen Gerstenmaier, tried to throw cold water on the ardor for more social reform. "In many areas of social legislation and social benefits," he declared, "we stand, in my opinion, at the outer boundary which separates the *Sozialstaat* [socially conscious state] from the *Wohlfahrtstaat* [welfare state], from the floundering *Gefälligkeitstaat* [give-away state], yes, from the highly socialistic *Versorgungstaat* [citizen maintenance state]."[82]

The following year, at the eighth CDU congress (September 19 to 21, 1958) in Kiel, Gerstenmaier returned to the same theme in a major social speech.[83] "Along with the entire CDU of Germany, I belong to those who want to make Germany a *sozialer Rechtsstaat* [socially responsible state based on the rule of law] ... But we observe with apprehension that in many segments of our population these vast social benefits result not in satisfaction but in increased demands."[84] The question must be answered, he told his audience, whether the state has to relieve the individual of the very last economic and social risk of his existence and guarantee social security for everyone regardless of his deserts. He expressed doubts as to whether this is compatible with continued economic prosperity and a free economy. "I tell you once more ...," he went on, "that in all essentials we have reached the outer limits of the *sozialen Rechtsstaats.* We have not much room for action left. If we go beyond it, we run the risk of falling head over heels into the social pattern of modern socialism."[85] His comments raised the troubling issue that the more protection is provided the stronger will be the claims

---

[81] "Entschliessung des Bundesparteitages 1956" in Richter, *op. cit.,* Section G/I/5, p. 17.
[82] "Die Sozialreform auf dem CDU-Parteitag 1957" in Richter, *op. cit.,* Section G/I/7, p. 27.
[83] "Referat Gerstenmaier 'Staatsordnung und Gesellschaftsbild'" in Richter, *op. cit.,* Section G/I/8, pp. 31–38.
[84] *Ibid.,* p. 31.
[85] *Ibid.,* p. 34.

for even more. This issue has been discussed in academic circles, but it seems to be of less concern to practical politicians.

The pronouncements by the President of the *Bundestag* occasioned a vigorous reaction, both within and without the CDU. They exposed the party to the attack of advocating a moratorium on further social reform. Many party members were clearly not of the same opinion as Dr. Gerstenmaier. In fact, at the same congress the CDU endorsed further significant extensions of social benefits, including the expansion of public housing and the improvement of hospital facilities, especially for welfare patients. And again in the "Cologne Manifesto" of 1961 there is little evidence of the idea that the limits of the social state had been reached.[86] The "Cologne Manifesto" calls specifically for the continuation of social reform and lists among its other demands, the further spreading of property, aid to education, aid to the family, assistance in the aquisition of home ownership, the development of recreational facilities, and urban and rural renewal.

Partly, no doubt, in response to pressure from the opposition, a spokesman for the CDU, Hans Katzer, member of the Bundestag from Königswinter, offered a new interpretation of the party's position on social policy in 1961.[87] According to him, Gerstenmaier's pronouncements on the limits of social reform were meant only to be provocative and to highlight the nature of the problems involved, and that neither Gerstenmaier nor the party take the position that social reform has to stop. What the party intends to stress is the need to advance along lines that promote individual instead of governmental responsibility. An important aspect of this promotion of individual responsibility is the spreading of property ownership.

This alternative approach to the problem of economic security has been suggested time and again since the early days of the Industrial Revolution. In recent years, however, it has received increasing attention in Germany as a means to check the spreading of the welfare state and as a method of promoting individual thrift and aggregate capital accumulation. Katzer makes the interesting point that it is not the extent but the methods of economic security that separate the views of the two major parties.

> The social policy alternatives today, if one disregards the special electoral campaign arguments, are differentiated less in terms of their material extent than in terms of the concepts of the socio-economic order from which they derive. The controversies will be decided on the issue of whether our *sozialer Rechtsstaat* will be realized in the form of a *Wohlfahrtstaat* or of a *Versorgungstaat*.[88]

Katzer concludes that the proper limits of social protection cannot be calculated in quantitative terms, such as a given percentage of national

[86] "Soziale Forderungen im 'Kölner Manifest' 1961" in Richter, *op. cit.*, Section G/I/10, p. 43.
[87] "Die CDU zur Sozialpolitik" in Richter, *op. cit.*, Section G/I/10, pp. 43–44.   [88] *Ibid.*, p. 44.

income. The limits depend on the system's impact on individual freedom and economic incentive. A similar defense of the welfare state was presented by Theodor Blank, the Minister of Labor and Social Affairs, in a 1958 Speech. Blank underlined also the spreading of property ownership, through "market consistent" means, as one of the chief methods of enhancing both freedom and security.[89] In his view, a free man must own property. Through property ownership a man acquires a sense of independence, which will counteract the collectivist tendencies inherent in the welfare state.

Thus, in spite of the neoliberal leanings of some of its leading spokesmen, the CDU has found it advisable, in part no doubt as a matter of practical politics, to push toward a more extensive and more comprehensive system of economic security. Almost every year the federal congress of the party recommends some further extension to fill the gaps of complete coverage.[90] This does not mean that the party is renouncing the Social Market Economy, but it does represent a rejection of the neoliberal view that the welfare state must inevitably lead to the destruction of the market economy. On the other hand, one also must observe that the emphasis by CDU spokesmen on "market-consistent" methods of protection has within it definite limits to the extension of the welfare state.

We now consider the position of the socialist party on the question of universality and comprehensiveness of protection. Although the specific demands of the SPD have not differed radically from the ones of the CDU, the long-run objectives of the socialists and their social ideals are different. The socialists do not view welfare measures as a means of strengthening and sustaining the free market economy. They have been accused of seeking to establish socialism through the novel means of comprehensive and universal social security and social services. Indeed, the official pronouncements of the Social Democratic Party can reasonably be interpreted as aiming at something like liberal socialism through the welfare state. For them, social security is not merely a necessary corrective of the market economy but is an instrument of social and economic reform. Their goal is something like the Beveridge version of the social service state, although with less emphasis on centralization, unification and egalitarianism.

The leanings of a political party can be judged by its pronouncements as well as by the zeal with which it has pushed certain types of legislation. The record shows that the Social Democrats have been tireless in pressing for more extensive social rights. They have been a major driving force behind

[89] T. Blank, "Die Freiheit im Wohlfahrtsstaat" in Richter, *op. cit.,* Section N/XVII, pp. 1–15.
[90] See, for instance, the 1964 resolutions, "Parteitag 1964—Entschliessung zur Wirtschafts- und Sozialpolitik" in Richter, *op. cit.,* Section G/I/13, pp. 59–62.

the movement for social security reform. They have constantly set new ideas and proposals before the government and have raised questions in Parliament about the progress of reform. In 1952, when adjustment and repair of the old system, rather than reform, was still the order of the day, the SPD announced its social security reform principles in a document entitled *Grundlagen eines Sozialplanes der SPD.*[91] This was a forerunner of the more extensive social plan published in 1957. There can be no doubt about where the Social Democrats stand on the desirability of comprehensive protection. The preamble to the 1952 document specifies that "Social security must be a foundation of socialist economic policy."[92] Social security is treated as a "precondition of human freedom and dignity."[93] It is to be secured through an overall approach that includes the maintenance of full employment, the maintenance of health, guarantees of individual economic security, and the improvement of the individual capacity to work. Universality of protection is specifically endorsed: "Benefits for the insurance of good health, with maintenance of freedom of choice of physician, are to be provided *for all* in equal measure. . . . *Every aged* and *every permanently disabled person* is entitled to a basic pension paid out of general revenue."[94] Notice that the Social Democrats are no less concerned with individual freedom than the advocates of the Social Market Economy, but their ranking of different dimensions of freedom is not the same. The Social Democrats place a very high value on economic security as an essential precondition of individual freedom, but their opponents stress the dangers to freedom inherent in the governmental measures needed to assure economic security.

The issue of the dangers and limits of social protection is discussed in the Social Democratic *Sozialplan für Deutschland* (pp. 18–27). As one would expect, the tenor of this discussion is in sharp contrast with Erhard's views. The authors of the *Sozialplan* recognize that "Social benefits can be misused for the purpose of controling human beings" (p. 21). They point out that such misuses of social welfare programs have existed in many states, including Nazi Germany, Fascist Italy, Peronist Argentina, and in the countries under communist dictatorship. However, they believe that in an alert democracy these abuses can be avoided through proper organization and administrative safeguards. They argue that those who use the "welfare state" as a bogy to combat the extension of social rights fail to understand the necessity of a sense of individual material security as a precondition for freedom. The *Sozialplan* reveals no fear that protection will hurt incentive and initiative. On the contrary, the point is made specifically that insufficient

---

[91] Richter, *op. cit.,* Section g/II/1, pp. 1–5.

[92] *Ibid.,* p. 1.

[93] *Ibid.,* p. 2.

[94] *Ibid.,* pp. 2, 3. (The author's italics.)

protection will hurt initiative and incentive because it lessens the individual's capacity to look after himself.

Such different evaluations of the implications of welfare programs imply different conceptions of human behavior and motivations. The socialist plan is tailored to group behavior and environmental conditions. It views individuals as conditioned by their environment. The environment, therefore, must be made conducive to incentive. The neoliberals have in mind an individual with a strong internalized drive to get ahead, with an inclination toward self-help, and with a will to overcome economic difficulties, to some extent regardless of environmental factors. They tend to impute to the ordinary man the motivations of the individual who has tested achievement and success and is hungry for more.

Even though the Social Democrats have given up the emphasis on economic planning, they have continued to advocate social planning for universal and comprehensive protection. The *Grundsatzprogramm* (statement of principles) adopted at a special party congress in 1959, which advocates "Competition as far as possible—planning as far as needed," also repeats the demand that the state guarantee a minimum level of security to every citizen. It declares that "every citizen is entitled to a minimum pension from the state in old age, in case of occupational or other disability, and in case of the loss of the family breadwinner."[95] This pension is intended as a basic right of the citizen, as an attribute of citizenship. Regular social security and private benefits would be added to the basic pension provided by the state. The state pension, unlike the other benefits, would not be tied to contributions and, therefore, would be universal.

The resolutions of the SPD congress of 1960 attacked the governing party for statements made by its leaders that the limits of social welfare reforms had been reached.[96] The Social Democrats have taken the position that with the growth of the economy the welfare programs can and must constantly expand. They point out that, ever since the beginning of social insurance, the argument has been advanced that there is a definite limit to possible expansion and that this limit, in fact, has been reached. They have countered Erhard's theme of "Prosperity for All," with limited welfare programs, with their own theme *"Just* Prosperity for All," based on a steady expansion of the welfare state.[97]

Space does not allow us to examine the positions of all political and

[95] "SPD—Grundsatzprogramm von 1959" in Richter, *op. cit.*, Section G/II/6, p. 86.

[96] The Social Democrats also took credit for the fact that the CDU was forced to continue the expansion of the welfare programs. See "Entschliessung zur Sozialpolitik 1960" in Richter, *op. cit.*, Section G/II/8, pp. 91–99.

[97] See the resolutions of the 1962 party congress "Gerechter Wohlstand für Alle" in Richter, *op. cit.*, Section G/II/13, pp. 125–126. (The Author's italics.)

interest groups. The conservatively oriented Free Democrats (*Freie Demokratische Partie,* FDP) want to limit social security to those for whom it was intended originally, namely the "economically weak." They have called for a reduction of welfare expenditures and for more emphasis on individual responsibility and on the spreading of "inheritable property" as a means to greater economic security.[98] Employer organizations are generally sympathetic to the idea of restraining the expansion of benefits.

Many of the considerations that have influenced the various positions on universality and comprehensiveness are relevant also for the bundle of issues relating to the level and structure of benefits. We shall now explore this aspect of the social security debate, after a brief discussion of the nature of the problems involved.

A basic decision with regard to the level of benefits is whether it should provide only a basic floor of protection, a minimum sufficient to ward off poverty, or whether it should aim at meeting a higher standard of comfort for the beneficiaries. It will be recalled that one of the basic principles of the Beveridge plan was the idea of a national minimum. Flat benefits at a low level are consistent with the ideal that the state should interfere as little as possible with the citizen's freedom to spend his income. On the other hand, they are not suitable for incentive purposes. This creates a problem for those who wish to protect incentive through a differentiated benefit structure but also seek to limit welfare expenditures. The desire to keep expenditures low often leads people who profess individualistic ideals to advocate uniformly low benefit levels, which necessarily results in an egalitarian benefit structure.

The idea of a flat national minimum for everybody has found few supporters in postwar Germany. The general tendency has been toward the notion that a person who is no longer able to earn his living should be able to count on more than a mere escape from poverty.[99] It has become widely accepted that benefit levels should enable a man to maintain the standard of living he achieved during his working life. For a worker on an old-age pension this means that retirement income should equal approximately 75 percent of his wage before retirement. This income, it is argued, would maintain the individual's economic and social status. It would provide a guarantee that disability and old age will not become a cause of economic and social *déclassement.* To remain effective over time, such a guarantee requires periodic adjustments of the pension level to current wages. Without these adjustments there would be inevitably a growing gap, in a progressive economy, between the economic status of the retired and the active population.

[98] See Richter, *op. cit.,* Section G/III.
[99] See Deutsche Forschungsgemeinschaft, *op. cit.,* p. 40.

Even though there is a considerable concensus of opinion favoring the maintenance of the pensioner's economic status, there is no unanimity regarding the best means of how to achieve this objective. One argument is that not social security alone, but private pensions and individual savings ought to provide the desired level of income. This is the position taken by Professor Achinger and his colleagues in the study prepared for Chancellor Adenauer. They hold that pensioners should have an income sufficient to maintain their standard of living, but that social security should provide only two thirds of this retirement income. Hence, they propose social security pensions equal to 50 percent of the wage before retirement.[100]

The main arguments against high levels of old-age pensions are infringement on economic freedom and the tendency toward redistribution of income. These arguments are advanced by Professor Weddigen. He takes note of the fact that pensions have risen from about 13 percent of the average wage in 1891, to 20.5 percent in 1937, to 34.5 percent in 1956, and concedes that a further increase is necessary.[101] Nevertheless, he has serious reservations about old-age pensions of 60 to 75 percent of previous wages and about automatic productivity increases. His view is that to increase the pensions of a compulsory system to a level comparable to the pensions of state functionaries means "a quite substantial redistributive levelling of income from work and a mighty step of economic and social policy toward universal state maintenance of the citizen [allgemeine Staatsbürgerversorgung], in other words, toward the establishment of the collectivist principle in our economic order." [102] He calls attention to the danger of "an overloading of the ethics of contribution [Abgabenmoral] and the will to make sacrifices," which "will bring harm to all through a paralysis of private initiative." [103]

Within the government and the CDU the dangers of high benefit levels repeatedly have been stressed, but there also have been champions of benefits high enough to maintain the beneficiary's economic status. The case for pensions at this level was made by the Minister of Labor in 1955.

> Originally pensions had the objective of providing merely a supplement toward subsistence, not even an existence minimum, and much less a guarantee for a standard of living. All those concerned, the Government, the insured, the pensioners, and their families were thinking only in terms of such a supplement. In part this was related to the prevailing conditions under which the pensioner was more closely tied to his family; the family provided

---

[100] H. Achinger et al., op. cit., p. 103.

[101] For a discussion of the rise in pensions in relation to wages, see H. Jecht, Oekonomische Probleme der Produktivitätsrente, Schriftenreihe des Bundesarbeitsministeriums No. 4 (Stuttgart: Kohlhammer, 1956), pp. 10 ff.

[102] Weddigen, "Gegenwartsfragen der Sozialpolitik," p. 435.

[103] Ibid., p. 436.

for the subsistence of its aged members. It was simply seen as desirable and necessary not to let the family bear the whole burden of the aged and to offer it a supplement from another source to lighten its load. This conception of the old-age pension has undergone substantial change, not only here but in the entire world. Today the task of old-age pensions is to safeguard for those no longer at work, and under their special conditions, the standard of living they had earned through a lifetime of labor.[104]

Presumably the "special conditions" of the aged would take into account the extent to which they have been able to provide for themselves through their own efforts. In this connection, the efforts by the government and of the CDU to encourage the spreading of property takes on special significance.

As one would expect, the Social Democrats have come out unequivocally in support of old-age pensions at a level of 75 percent of wages before retirement for those who have worked all their life. Professor Ernst Schellenberg, an SPD member of the *Bundestag,* declared at the 1956 party congress in Cologne:

> The central issue in the new regulation of old-age pensions is the proper relationship between the pension level and the preceding level of earning. Germany has a good model that is relevant for the social security of workers and employees: the pensions of functionaries . . ., which in the case of old-age are normally 75 percent of the last, that is the highest salary obtained.[105]

This attempt to equate the position of the worker with that of higher state officials has far-reaching implications, especially in a country where officialdom enjoys a high prestige and social status.

Professor Schellenberg is not alone in insisting on the 75 percent pension level. His position is endorsed by the trade unions and in the 1957 *Sozialplan* of the SPD.[106] The *Sozialplan* argues against the suggestion by Achinger and his colleagues that a 50 percent old-age pension would enable workers and employees to maintain their standard of living. The Social Democrats maintain that the majority of workers and employees are unable to save enough to provide the additional income needed to achieve a retirement income equal to 75 percent of previous wages. They further point out that industrial pensions cannot be counted on to fill the gap (because only a minority of the workers are entitled to them) and that it would be unfair to hold down on that account the general level of old-age pensions. In their

---

[104]"Grundgedanken zur Gesamtreform der sozialen Leistungen—Kabinettsvorlage des Bundesminister für Arbeit" in Richter, *op. cit.,* Section B/III/1, p. 14.

[105] E. Schellenberg, "Unser Weg zur Sozialreform" in Richter, *op. cit.*, Section G/II/2, p. 8.

[106] *Sozialplan für Deutschland,* pp. 88 ff. The trade unions demanded a pension of 30 percent of wages after 10 years of work, plus an additional 1.5 percent of each additional year of employment, up to a maximum of 75 percent. See "Der DGB zur Sozialreform" in Richter, *op. cit.*, Section H/I/1e, p. 25.

view, pensions must provide a guarantee not merely against "objective need" (subsistence minimum), but against the "subjective need" caused by a reduced standard of living. In the case of sickness insurance, they have strongly supported the equalization of workers' benefits with those of salaried employees. The latter have been entitled to their full salary during the first six weeks of disability since the early 1930s.[107]

The adjustment of pensions to rises in wages has been one of the hottest issues of the social reform debate.[108] Those, like the neoliberals, who stress the individual's freedom to spend his income as he pleases are generally opposed to this kind of built-in increase in welfare expenditure. But there are advocates of the free market who have championed the idea of "dynamic pensions." Professor Wilfrid Schreiber, for instance, has been one of the most ardent advocates of the principle of "dynamic pensions." The principle, as he clearly demonstrates, can be made to meet the requirement of consistency with the market, that is, of equivalence between contribution and benefit. Schreiber makes the ingenious suggestion that a worker's contribution as well as his pension should be calculated in terms of labor (hours-of-work) instead of in monetary units.[109] As labor productivity and the value of the labor unit rise over time, the pension, based on a certain number of labor units, rises along with them. Of course, the principle can be refined to adjust labor units for differences in the quality of labor, so that the length of the work record is not the sole determinant of the pension level.

There is fundamental agreement between the two major parties on the need for periodic adjustments of pensions not only to keep up with rising costs of living but also to allow pensioners to reap some benefit from rising labor productivity. The main difference between the parties is in the method of implementing the adjustments. The Christian Democrats tend toward the position that adjustments must not be automatic, that there must be no rigid coupling of wage and pension levels, that adjustments should be made only after the analysis and evaluation of prevailing economic conditions and trends.[110] The opponents of automatic adjustments generally stress the

[107] The principles of equal benefits for workers and salaried employees and of full pay during the first six weeks of disability are generally accepted in Germany, even by the employers. See, for instance, Bundesvereinigung der deuschen Arbeitgeberverbände, *Memorandum zur Frage der Wirtschaftlichen Sicherung der Arbeiter im Krankheitsfalle,* Köln (March 1963); and *Lohnfortzahlungsgesetz—Stellungnahme zum Entwurf eines Gesetzes uber die Fortzahlung des Arbeitsentgelts im Krankheitsfalle,* Köln (March 1963).

[108] See, for instance, A. Müller (ed.), *Produktivitätsrenten sichern den Lebensabend* (Bad Godesberg: Asgard Verlag, 1956); also H. Jecht, *Oekonomische Probleme der Produktivitätsrente,* Schriftenreihe des Bundesarbeitsministeriums No. 4 (Stuttgart: Kohlhammer, 1956).

[109] W. Schreiber, "Existenzsicherheit in der industriellen Gesellschaft" in E. Böttcher (ed.), *Sozialpolitik und Sozialreform* (Tuebingen: J. C. B. Mohr, 1957), pp. 75 ff.

[110] See, for instance, "Der CDU-Parteitag 1956 und die Sozialreform" in Richter, *op. cit.,* Section G/I/6, p. 21.

inflationary threats of this kind of procedure. Many have also opposed the idea of "dynamic pensions" with the argument that they reduce the individual's capacity to provide for his own future. Furthermore, such systematic increases in pensions are viewed as factors that act to lower the average propensity to save and to lessen capital accumulation and, hence, the economic growth on which the future welfare levels depend.

These arguments have had little effect on the general attitude of the Social Democrats. "The SPD demands that pensions be automatically adjusted to the growth of wages and salaries. For this the benefits of functionaries again may serve as a model." [111] These were Schellenberg's words at the 1956 party congress. He rejected the argument advanced by political opponents, that through automatic pension coupling the SPD is trying to move the army of pensioners into the trade unions' camp. "For us Social Democrats," he declared,

> the coupling of wages and pensions involves a moral principle which goes far beyond any consideration of political tactics, namely the solidarity of young and old in our social order. Every young man should know that whenever he struggles for his own higher share of the national product, he simultaneously intervenes for those no longer able to provide for themselves through their own labor. And he should know that, after decades, when he can no longer work, the succeeding generation will assure him a share of the goods of this world proportionate to his work performance today. Through this reconstitution of the social order a genuine solidarity between young and old will be forged, as well as a stronger interest aroused on the part of the young in the security of the old. [112]

This is certainly an interesting application of the concept of social security. It extends the traditional bond between parents and children to a bond between generations. The Social Democrats have argued also that automatic adjustments are necessary in order to establish a genuine legal claim to improvement. [113] The absence of such a claim, they point out, makes the periodic adjustments dependent on political considerations.

We now come to the question of benefit structure. The preceding discussion has indicated that sentiments in Germany run against flat national minimum benefits and that differential benefits are almost universally accepted. The issue is therefore how benefits should be differentiated, and how closely they should be tied to previous earnings or contributions. Those concerned with incentive effects usually insist on some equivalence between contributions and benefits. They emphasize the so-called insurance principle. On the other hand, the more people are concerned with social planning, the

[111] Schellenberg, "Unser Weg zur Sozialreform" in Richter, *op. cit.,* Section G/II/2, p. 9.
[112] *Ibid.,* p. 10.
[113] *Sozialplan für Deutschland,* p. 100.

more they are inclined to accept substantial deviations from the contribution-benefit equivalence. Social planners tend to stress social solidarity and income redistribution over the individualistic insurance principle, which avoids, when strictly applied, redistribution among individuals.

The CDU has come out much more strongly in favor of benefit differentiation than the SPD. The 1955 social insurance reform committee of the CDU recommended a transparent relationship between benefits and contributions to preserve work incentives. It declared that "The principle, 'the larger the contribution, the higher the benefit,' must be strikingly in evidence."[114] The Christian Democrats and the government recognize, of course, that departures from a rigid proportional relationship between benefits and contributions are necessary to achieve some of the fundamental objectives of social security. But in a system that is financed largely through payroll taxes these departures imply a tendency toward a horizontal redistribution of income, that is, a tendency to have some people help maintain others who may be no worse off than they are. The accusation is that this kind of system forces the poor to pay for the poor and that benefits related to previous earnings tend to perpetuate in retirement the unfortunate position of the lowest income receivers.

It is for these reasons that socialists have generally favored flat benefits financed at least in part through public revenue. The German Social Democrats, however, have accepted the idea of differentiated benefits. They recognize that it is deeply embedded in the country's social insurance traditions. The working population for decades has paid wage-related contributions and expects wage-related benefits. The spokesmen for the SPD like to point out the weaknesses of the insurance principle with regard to providing genuine social security, but the spokesmen for the CDU like to call attention to the virtues of this principle with respect to the maintenance of incentives. The "duty" of the Social Democrats, according to Professor Schellenberg, is to "put into effect more than hitherto the social principle, alongside the insurance principle."[115] The trade unions, as indicated earlier, also have expressed their support for the continuation of the system of differentiated benefits related to previous wages.

One particular deviation from the strict insurance principle has received very wide support and must be pointed out. German pensions take into account the number of years of contributions. This procedure raises obvious difficulties with regard to those years in an individual's working life when he was not gainfully employed for some reason other than unwillingness to take a job. According to spokesmen for the SPD, the workers who retired by 1969 lost on the average almost one third of their earning and contribu-

[114]"Leitsätze zur Rentenversicherung" in Richter, op. cit., Section G/I/3, p. 12.
[115]"Unser Weg zur Sozialreform" in Richter, op. cit., Section G/II/2, p. 8.

tion years on account of years of mass unemployment, World Wars I and II, illness, and other factors.[116] The SPD has been particularly vocal in its demands that these contribution gaps be closed by giving individuals credit for periods of involuntary unemployment and the years spent in obtaining higher education. The government has accepted the principle, as we shall learn below.

In the area of social security financing there is general acceptance among all groups of the continuation of the traditional system of tripartite contributions by employers, employees, and the state. Differences of opinion exist mainly with respect to the share of the cost that ought to be borne by each. However, one particular attack on the existing system must be noted briefly. This is an argument for making social security more consistent with the free market economy by abolishing contributions from the employers.

In all countries, employers have been called on to pay a share of the cost of social security, usually in some proportion to payroll. Although social reformers often assume that employers bear the burden of this tax, its incidence cannot be readily assessed. A strong case can be made that, in most instances, it is shifted back to the workers or forward to the consumers. The view that it, in fact, is shifted back to the workers is the basis for the argument, advanced by Professor Schreiber, that contributions by employers should be abolished.

According to Schreiber, "It is clear to economists today . . . that employer contributions to social welfare programs are nothing but duly earned portions of wages which the market, in accordance with the laws of a free economy, has allocated to workers." [117] He believes that in the absence of legally imposed social charges the trade unions would be able to obtain an equivalent amount from the employers in the form of wages. This belief is based on the notion that trade unions act essentially as a countervailing power in the labor market, and that they bring about results that would obtain if the market were completely free on both the demand and the supply sides. He, therefore, argues that employer contributions be abolished and that workers pay the whole amount directly. As he views it, this action would only bring out into the open what is already a fact. Initially, wages would be raised by the full amount of the contributions that employers no longer have to pay, so that there would be no reduction in take-home pay when the workers take over full financing. The main advantage of this method of financing, according to Schreiber, would be a clarification of the economic burden of social charges and the elimination of the false notion that in social security the worker gets something for nothing.

Schreiber believes that once the worker realizes that it is he who bears

[116]*Sozialplan für Deutschland,* p. 96.
[117]"Sozialpolitik in der sozialen Marktwirtschaft," p. 593.

the full cost of benefits, he will be in a better position to make a rational choice between the amount of his earnings he wants in the form of wages and the amount he wants in the form of benefits. He should be given ample opportunity to share in the decision-making process regarding social security.[118] This area should not remain a hunting ground for vote-seeking politicians who offer "social benefits" to the worker for which he has to pay out of his own pocket.

No political party or major interest group has yet come out in support of Professor Schreiber's views. In general, the CDU and officials of the Adenauer and Erhard governments have leaned more strongly toward contributions by the potential beneficiaries and the reduction of state subsidies than the SPD. One area where this has been especially marked is health insurance. The government has repeatedly tried to introduce various methods of cost participation by insured patients in order to cut the rapidly mounting costs of the system. These methods are usually opposed by the SPD and the trade unions. Whereas the government views this as a method of checking the abuse of health services, the opposition views it as an access barrier to medical care and a hindrance to preventive medicine. With regard to old-age pensions, Professor Schellenberg argued at the 1956 congress that 60 percent of the cost ought to be borne through insurance contributions and that 40 percent should be paid for through public revenue.[119] In his opinion, this allocation is consistent with individual performance on the one hand and broader social goals on the other. Within the government, there have been strong pressures to eliminate the old Bismarckian state subsidy to old-age insurance altogether and to reserve state aid only for assistance programs. These sentiments played an important role in the 1957 pension reform.

In the area of organization and administration there is almost unanimous agreement in Germany that the traditional system of decentralization and participation by the insured must be maintained. The trend, noticable in most countries, toward unification and amalgamation of programs and towards larger administrative units has had little support in Germany. Individual writers have suggested the establishment of a national health service in place of the present health insurance funds, but this suggestion to follow the English model has not been widely accepted. Both parties favor the maintenance of separate programs for groups like manual workers, salaried employees, miners, and farmers, over the creation of larger units of risk sharing. There seems to be a feeling that more homogeneous groups provide a more suitable basis for the reciprocal rights and

[118] For some observations along these lines, see W. Schreiber, "Schein und Wirklichkeit in der Sozialversicherung," *Soziale Sicherheit,* Vol. XI (December 1962), pp. 353–356.
[119] "Unser Weg zur Sozialreform" in Richter, *op. cit.,* Section G/II/2, pp. 14–15.

responsibilities involved in social insurance. The socialists have been eager to defend themselves against accusations that they seek a unified and centralized system of social insurance, which is depicted as a step toward the undifferentiated mass society. They have always argued that participation in administration, rather than contributions, is what maintains the citizen's sense of responsibility. "Through self-administration the awareness is kept alive of the relationship between cost and extent of benefits and of the nature of self-responsible collective self-help."[120] Of course, it is very doubtful, given the character of participation in administration, that these results are actually achieved, but the idea that the representation of the insured on the administrative bodies increases their sense of responsibility and independence from the state is widely accepted and often staunchly defended.

THE MAJOR REFORMS

In spite of the divergence in points of view brought out in the preceding discussion, there is a more-or-less general agreement on most basic issues. The areas of substantial agreement can be summarized as follows:

1. The need for social income protection in an industrialized society is nearly universal; this is related to several factors: (a) work has replaced land holding or property ownership as the source of income for the vast majority of individuals, (b) the modern family is not in a position to guarantee an acceptable level of protection to its members, (c) the dynamics of modern economies expose nearly all members of society to loss of earning capacity or opportunity, and protection, therefore, should not be restricted to a group currently considered "economically weak."

2. Protection should aim at maintaining the economic status of the individual; this is viewed as being consistent with the economic possibilities of an affluent society.

3. Protection should be consistent with economic incentive as far as possible; this implies a social security system that interferes as little as possible with the forces of the free market.

4. The system of social protection should stress the maintenance, restoration, and improvement of the capacity of work.

5. All citizens have an equal right to protection, which means that differential levels of protection based on social status (salaried versus worker) are no longer acceptable.

6. The organization and administration must remain decentralized,

[120]*Sozialplan für Deutschland*, p. 22.

which means, in part, that separate organizations for workers, salaried employees, and other groups will be continued.

7. The real economic burden of those unable to work is borne by those currently active, regardless of the method of financing.

8. Finally, unusual economic burdens, for instance, those resulting from the war, or those inherent in raising large families, should be shared by society as a whole.

These views have become incorporated in the postwar social security reform legislation. Although the first *Bundestag* (1949 to 1953) was primarily concerned with mending the old system and dealing with pressing issues concerning war victims, the second *Bundestag* (1953 to 1957) inaugurated important reforms that were extended further by the third *Bundestag* (1957 to 1961) and, to a lesser extent, by the fourth (1961 to 1965). The reforms have been piecemeal rather than part of a unified, comprehensive social plan. By far the most significant has been the pension reform of 1957. As in most countries, pensions are the largest item in the social security budget. In the workers' scheme there were 43 pensioners (including widows) for each 100 compulsorily insured workers in 1963.[121] Appropriately, therefore, we examine the pension reform in detail, since it provides the best illustration of the new social insurance thinking in postwar West Germany.

The 1957 pension reforms are the most far-reaching since the beginnings of the German social insurance system. We examine only the most important features of the new laws. Since the insurance programs of workers, salaried employees, and miners are separate, three pension reform laws had to be enacted. An attempt was made to equalize the material rights of workers and salaried employees, but miners retained special treatment. The pensions discussed here are for old-age, permanent disability, and survivorship, although we focus primarily on old-age and permanent disability pensions.

The most important feature of the new pension laws is the conscious departure from the old principle of subsistence benefits and the adoption of the principle of maintaining the economic status of the pensioner. A second basic feature, which is implied in the first, is the reestablishment of a closer link between an individual's work and earnings record and the level of his pension. It should be observed, however, that it is not the absolute level of previous earnings that counts, but the wage level in relation to the national average.

[121] Bundesministerium für Arbeit und Sozialordnung, *Uebersicht über die soziale Sicherung in der Bundesrepublik Deutschland* (Bonn: Bundesministerium für Abreit und Sozialordnung, 1964), p. 20.

An insured individual's economic status is determined by his lifetime earnings in covered employment relative to the earnings of all covered individuals. If a man worked 40 years and earned 88,000 DM during that period, and the average covered individual earned 80,000 DM during the same period, the economic status of the man in question is 110 percent of the national average. However, to protect his relative status, the wage base to which this percentage is applied must relate to the national wage level at the time of retirement. The 1957 legislation provides that the individual's percentage ranking be applied to the average wage of all insured individuals (general wage base) during the last three years preceding the year of retirement. For example, if the general wage base is 6000 DM/year, the individual wage base, on which the pension for our hypothetical individual is calculated will be 6600 DM. The amount of his old-age pension then will depend on the number of years he is credited with covered employment. For each year of covered employment, he is entitled to an old-age pension equal to 1.5 percent of his wage base. Thus, if he works 50 years, his pension will equal 50 times 1.5, or 75 percent of his wage base; if he works 40 years, his old-age pension will equal 60 percent of his wage base.

An important fact to be noted is that the wage base is not static but, instead, moves with the three-year average wage level. For purposes of pension computation the general wage base is determined annually. Table 5–1 gives the general wage base used in computing pensions granted in each year from 1957 to 1964. It is obvious that this approach has been an important factor in raising the level of pensions granted each year, since the base increased more than 50 percent over the short period since the

Table 5–1

General Wage Base:
1957 to 1964 in DM per Year

Year	Workers and Salaried Employees	Miners
1957	4281	4320
1958	4542	4590
1959	4812	4862
1960	5072	5126
1961	5425	5381
1962	5678	5737
1963	6142	6206
1964	6717	6788

Source. Uebersicht über die Soziale Sicherung in der Bundesrepublik Deutschland (1964), p. 62.

enactment of the reform legislation. We must expect similar raises in the level of pensions granted each year.

A direct corollary of economic status maintenance is the maintenance of income inequalities. For individuals with similar lengths of credited employment, the relative income differentials that exist during the period of active participation in the work force are extended into retirement, although the absolute differentials are reduced. Only those who are credited with 50 years of covered employment are entitled to a pension that is deemed high enough to maintain their economic status. Others can maintain their status only if they have made provisions of their own or are entitled to industrial pensions.

We must point out, however, that the years of credited employment are not identical with the years of work. The law provides that periods of military service, political persecution and, under specified conditions, periods of unemployment, education, vocational training (past age 15), and illness are credited as periods of covered employment. To this extent, there is an intentional deviation from a direct proportional relationship between earnings and pensions and a shift away from self-help toward group solidarity. A similar deviation is the allowance for dependent children, equal to 10 percent of the national average wage for each child. On the other hand, the new law eliminates the minimum benefit level in future pensions, the base pension that had existed since Bismarck. Coupled with the new method of calculating benefits, this tends to strengthen the link between pensions and previous work and earnings. As a result, the new pension law substantially widens the spread between the lowest and highest benefits, although it also raises the average considerably. A preliminary sample study for the North-Rhine district in 1957 shows that the spread, which under the old law had been 1 : 3, was increased to 1 : 10.[122] In actual fact this spread was mitigated by a special provision that raised the minimum level of pensions already in existence.

Even so, the differential benefit structure incorporated in the pension reform clearly points up the contrast with the egalitarian scheme of Britain and the emphasis on incentive and individual responsibility. Instead of trying to wipe out income inequalities, the pension reform consciously seeks to perpetuate them. In this sense the pension reform helps to solidify rather than to alter the economic basis of the social structure. It helps to prevent the sinking of the pensioners to the bottom of the socioeconomic scale, as well as to prevent a leveling of the income structure.

[122]The sample was for 800 pensioners born in 1875. Under the old law the lowest pension received was 59 DM per month and the highest 158.50; under the new law the spread would have been from 37.10 DM to 381.30 DM. However, under a special provision no pensions were reduced. See Willi Albers, "Oekonomische Wirkungen der Rentenreform," *Finanzarchiv*, Vol. XVIII, No. 1 (1957), pp. 61–62.

The new pensions for permanent disability are calculated in a similar fashion, except that a provision has to be made for years of coverage lost because of disablement. To be eligible for a permanent disability pension, an individual must have 60 months of contributions, as opposed to 180 in the case of old-age pensions. The law credits an eligible disabled individual with covered employment as if he had worked until age 55. Thus, an individual who enters the work force at age 15 (or at age 20, if he spent the last five years in occupational training) and becomes disabled after 60 months of contributions will be credited with 40 years of covered employment. If he is unable to exercise any gainful activity (general invalidity case), his pension will be equal to 60 percent ($40 \times 1.5\%$) of his wage base. If he is unable to earn 50 percent of the wage in his normal occupation (occupational invalidity case), his pension will be equal to 40 percent ($40 \times 1\%$) of his wage base. Clearly, as in the case of old-age pensions, disability pensions are highly differentiated, consistent with the ideal of status maintenance and individual responsibility, but pension differentials here depend mainly on wage differentials and less on years of actual work. This holds true also for survivorship pensions, although in this instance the age of a widow and her ability to work are taken into account.[123]

One of the most important features of the pension reform is the attempt to maintain not merely the relative status of the individual but also the collective status of all pension recipients. Much attention has been attracted by the provision to make the pensions "dynamic," that is, increasing in step with the growth of the national economy. We have learned that the method of computing the wage base brings pensions in line with the level of wages at the time of the initial assessment of the pension. But this offers no protection against falling behind once the pension is in force. Only the continued adjustment of pensions to the growth of the national economy protects the status of pensioners as a group relative to the economically active population. The bill initially submitted by the government provided for an automatic annual adjustment of pensions to the wage level. The fears and doubts raised by such an inexorable ratchet effect, however, led to amendments that make the adjustments discretionary. By September 30 of each year the government has to submit a recommendation for pension adjustments to parliament which is based on the financial condition of the pension programs and the capacity, performance, and rise in productivity of the economy. This recommendation obviously has great economic, social, and even political significance. Therefore, it is prepared by a multipartite body, the Social Advisory Council (*Sozialbeirat*), consisting of members who

[123] For a summary statement of the computation of survivorship pensions, see United States Department of Health, Education, and Welfare, *Social Security Programs Throughout the World* (Washington, D.C.: Government Printing Office, 1961), p. 71.

represent insured individuals, employers, the central bank, and the public.[124] The Social Advisory Council seeks to reconcile and to balance the conflicting interests of these groups, which illustrates, incidentally, a method of resolving the problem of the reciprocity of rights and duties in an industrial society. Adjustments must be approved by parliament and must be enacted into law before they become official. Until now, however, both the Social Advisory Council and parliament have been inclined to grant pension increases every year. Table 5–2 indicates the actual adjustments since the first recommendation in 1958 for 1959. The new method of pension computation and the annual adjustments are mainly responsible for the continued rise in the average level of pensions since 1958. Between 1958 and 1963, the average pension under the workers' program (including old-age, invalidity, and survivorship) rose from 144.00 DM to 174.50 DM per month; the corresponding rise in the salaried employees' program was from 228.60 DM to 287.70 DM and in the miners' program was from 210.20 DM to 377.40 DM.[125]

Table 5–2

Pension Adjustments Effective January 1 of Each Year

Year	Percent Increase
1959	6.1
1960	5.94
1961	5.4
1962	5.0
1963	6.6
1964	8.2

Source. Uebersicht über die soziale Sicherung in der Bundesrepublik Deutschland 1964, p. 67.

The periodic adjustment of pensions would seem to lend itself conveniently to anticyclical fiscal policy. However, as in most countries, the insured persons rights to benefits put severe limitations on the extent to which the payment of benefits can be altered for the purposes of promoting economic stability. "The attitude of the Social Advisory Council may be regarded as an interpretation of the legislation, neither the letter nor the

[124] The public is represented by three social scientists, usually economists.
[125] Uebersicht über die soziale Sicherung in der Bundesrepublik Deutschland 1964, p. 59.

spirit of which suggested that pensions should become yet another instrument of government economic policy."[126] This statement by Dr. Kurt Jantz, the General Secretary for Social Reform, should not be interpreted to mean that the pension reform was divorced from economic policy. What he emphasizes is the fact that the Social Advisory Council, in effect, has taken the view that pensioners have a *right to benefit increases*, if productivity and wage increases warrant them, regardless of possible inflationary effects. This, indeed, is a novel dimension to the right of social protection. Jantz refers to it as a "new 'dynamic' legal concept," arising out of the pension reform.[127]

Even though we make no attempt here to account for all the changes introduced by the pension reform, notice should be taken of the increased emphasis on rehabilitation. The maintenance, restoration, and improvement of the insured individuals' capacity to work, which has long been accepted in Germany as an important function of social insurance, has been substantially expanded by the 1957 pension reform laws.[128] This action is based on the sound principle that it is economically and socially more advantageous to maintain an individual's capacity to work than to pay him a disability pension. Whenever the work capacity of an insured individual is threatened, he is entitled not only to medical care and rehabilitation but also to vocational rehabilitation and to cash benefits during the period of retraining. These cash benefits will be at least 50 percent but not more than 80 percent of the beneficiary's wage during the last 12 months of contributions. The evidence of an increased emphasis on prevention and rehabilitation is indicated by the requirement, since 1959, that agencies administering the pension system taken an active part in combating tuberculosis among the insured and their dependents. These agencies previously had been active in this area, but now they are legally bound to provide the necessary services. Perhaps the best indication of the growing importance of maintaining the work capacity of the insured population is the increase in expenditures for this purpose. The expenditures of the pension schemes for health and rehabilitation measures rose from 446 million DM in 1956 to about 1300 million DM in 1963—nearly a threefold expansion.[129]

Rehabilitation measures enable some individuals, who might otherwise become an economic burden, to participate actively in the labor force. Also the German pension system makes it possible for older workers and salaried employees who are unemployed to withdraw from the labor force before the

---

[126] Kurt Jantz, "Pension Reform in the Federal Republic of Germany," *International Labor Review*, Vol. LXXXIII (February 1961), p. 154.

[127] *Ibid.*, p. 153.

[128] For a summary description of German efforts in this area, see D. Zöllner, *Prävention und Rehabilitation*, Sozialpolitik in Deutschland No. 36 (Stuttgart: W. Kohlhammer, 1962).

[129] *Uebersicht über die soziale Sicherung in der Bundesrepublik Deutschland 1964*, p. 56.

normal retirement age, which is 65 for men and 60 for women in the general schemes.[130] Eligible insured individuals who have reached the age of 60 and who have been involuntarily unemployed for one year or more are entitled to their old-age pension as long as they remain unemployed. Once the normal retirement age is reached, a person is entitled to his pension even though he may remain at work.

The nearly universal coverage of employed persons and the relatively high levels of contributions and pensions clearly indicate that in spite of its neoliberal leanings, the Social Market Economy is in reality an advanced welfare state. For all those who are not self-employed, the coverage is compulsory, unless they are salaried employees earning 15,000 DM per annum or more. The reforms have raised this coverage ceiling from the 9000 DM per annum level since 1957. The Minister of Labor and Social Affairs attempted in the summer of 1964 to make this ceiling for compulsory pension insurance dynamic, by letting it move at a level of 3.5 times the average wage, but he ran into considerable resistance.[131] The contributions under the schemes for workers and salaried employees, which were already at the relatively high rate of 11 percent in 1957, have risen to 14 percent of assessed wages by 1964. One half of this tax is paid by the employee and one half by the employer, except that the employer pays the full contribution if the worker's wage is less than one tenth of the assessed wage level.[132]

Since pensions rise with the wage level, it is necessary that contributions rise in a similar fashion. In part, this is assured by means of a dynamic upper limit of assessed earnings. In the workers' and salaried employees' schemes the earnings ceiling for tax purposes is equal to twice the average earnings level of insured individuals (general wage base). For miners the ceiling is 2.5 times the general wage base. Thus both pensions and contributions are affected by the Social Advisory Council's annual determination of the general wage base. The contribution ceiling for workers and salaried employees rose from 600 DM per month in 1949 to 1100 DM per month in 1964; for miners it rose from 700 DM per month to 1400 DM per month during the same period. This doubling of the level of taxed earnings, along with the rise in rates, indicates a substantial welfare state extension into the realm of the individual's freedom to spend his income.

We pointed out earlier that, under the new method of computation, the state no longer guarantees a minimum pension. But this does not mean that it no longer contributes from public revenue to the pension program. In

[130] Miners may retire at age 60 if they meet certain qualifying conditions.

[131] Werner Reichenberger, "Der Streit um die Versicherungspflichtgrenze," *Sozialer Fortschritt,* Vol. XIII, No. 9 (September 1964), pp. 213–214.

[132] In the miner's scheme the contribution rate is 23.5 percent, of which the employee pays 8.5 percent and the employer 15 percent.

fact, the contributions of the federal government are geared to rise with the expenditures of the pension system. From 1957 to 1964 federal contributions to the workers' scheme rose from 2728 million DM to 4434 million DM; contributions to the salaried employees' scheme from 682 million to 998 million; and contributions to the miners' scheme from 520 million to 1755 million.[133] These substantial contributions from public revenue and built-in increases are further evidence of the country's commitment to an expanding welfare state.

Another important aspect of the reforms was the inauguration of a pension program for self-employed farmers. A law to this effect was enacted in 1957 and was amended for benefit improvements in 1961 and 1963.[134] Coverage under this new branch of social security is compulsory in principle for all farmers. In 1963, approximately 784,000 farmers were contributing to the scheme and 328,000 were drawing benefits. Unlike the other pension schemes, this program does not intend to insure the individual's economic status but simply intends to supplement whatever provisions he has made for old age. Both contributions and benefits are flat amounts, unrelated to previous earning levels.

Initially the pension was set at 40 DM per month for a single person and 60 DM for a couple; in 1963, these levels were raised to 65 DM and 100 DM, respectively. The qualifying conditions for these benefits are of particular interest. To be entitled to an old-age farmer's pension, the individual must be 65 years old, must have paid 180 monthly contributions, and must have given up his agricultural enterprise after age 50. As usual, for those who could not meet the contribution requirement when the program began, special transitional rules were adopted. The important point is that, in order to be eligible for benefits, a farmer must not only withdraw from active agricultural work but must transfer his enterprise through inheritance, sale, or long-term lease. The purpose of this requirement is to induce a shift of agricultural operations to younger, more efficient hands and thereby to raise the country's agricultural productivity. It had become evident that low agricultural incomes were often the result of inefficient operations by older farmers who lacked both the capital and the energy for modernization. By helping those farmers to withdraw from agriculture, the new program achieves important economic as well as social goals. This striking instance of a successful integration of economic and social policy is of particular

[133] *Uebersicht über die soziale Sicherung in der Bundesrepublik Deutschland 1964*, p. 72.

[134] For a more detailed description of this program, see *ibid.*, pp. 80–84; also Richter, *op. cit.*, Sections F/XVI and F/XL; Kurt Noell, "The Federal Agricultural Old-Age Assistance in the Federal Republic of Germany" and "Old-Age Insurance Scheme for Farmers in the Federal Republic of Germany," *Bulletin of the International Social Security Association*, Vol. XIII (January–February) Nos. 1 and 2 (1960), pp. 11–18, Vol XV, No. 9 (September 1962), pp. 190–201.

significance when account is taken of the fact that the Common Market makes the increased productivity of German agriculture a matter of considerable urgency.

After the farmers, the next largest group of self-employed persons are the artisans. The special pension scheme introduced for them in 1938 also underwent postwar reform. In 1963, it was amalgamated with the general worker's pension program, but with special provision that reflected a greater expectation of self-help on the part of artisans. The compulsory participation by artisans aims at providing only a basic pension level, as evidenced by the fact that compulsory contribution is limited to 18 years. Clearly, this is a compromise solution between the demands for complete self-dependence and the demands for full incorporation into the workers' scheme. It avoids the danger of the artisan's failing to provide for himself and becoming a public charge, and it also leaves him more freedom than is left to the worker to use his capital to make provisions for his old-age.

The liberal professions have thus far not been included in the drive toward universal coverage by federal programs. However, they are covered by the statutes of most *Länder*. In 1961 the federal government introduced a bill for an old-age pension program for lawyers. Although it failed to pass, further developments in this direction can be expected.

When we direct our attention away from pensions toward other areas of the social insurance system, we find that the reform movement has had much less of an impact. In spite of a lengthy debate over health insurance, no fundamental changes had been effected by the end of 1964. In October 1958, the Ministry of Labor and Social Affairs made public the main points of a proposed reform, including more stress on preventive care, improved protection for long-time illness, improved benefits for family members, and the sharing of the direct cost of medical care and medication by the insured persons, graded according to family circumstances.[135] The benefit improvements have been carried out, but the Government's attempts, first, to introduce direct cost participation and, later, to introduce a system of rebates that rewarded a low use of medical services have provoked much resistance and have been unsuccessful.[136]

A specific aspect of German health insurance that should be observed is its integration with other aspects of social insurance. Unemployed and retired workers do not lose their benefits; their contributions are paid by

---

[135] See "Official Basis of the Reform of Social Sickness Insurance" and Oscar Umrath, "Sickness Insurance Schemes in the Federal Republic of Germany," *Bulletin of the International Social Security Association,* Vol. XII (March 1959), pp. 117–121 and Vol. XIV (March 1961), pp. 117–130.

[136] On the issues in the controversies surrounding these attempts, see "Das Sozialpaket im Meinungsstreit," *Sozialer Fortschritt,* Vol. XII (March 1963), pp. 58–66.

unemployment insurance or by a pension fund, as the case may be. The state makes no direct financial contributions to the health insurance program. It is supported by equal employer and employee contributions, except in the case of lowest paid workers, where the employer pays the entire contribution.

Although health insurance has not been fundamentally altered, a far-reaching change has occurred with respect to the income security of workers who are stricken by illness. Since 1961, workers are fully protected against income loss during the first six weeks of disablement. In addition to the cash sickness benefit, which ranges from 65 to 75 percent of wages depending on the number of dependents, they are entitled to a wage supplement paid by the employer. The amount of this supplement, which is paid for six weeks, is equal to the amount required to bring the worker's cash income up to 100 percent of his net wages. The position taken by some leading participants in the postwar social reform debate was that the maintenance of the worker during illness was the employer's responsibility. Aside from this argument, however, the main drive behind this legislation came from the pressure to equalize the social security status of workers and of salaried employees. The latter have been entitled by law to their full salary during the first six weeks of illness for more than a quarter of a century. In the more egalitarian postwar era, it is strongly believed that differential treatment of this kind is no longer warranted. The supplementary cash benefits do not yet fully equalize the protective status of workers and salaried employees, since the sick-leave salary of the latter is paid entirely by the employer, whereas the workers pay themselves for part of their cash sickness benefits. There has been a continued pressure by labor spokesmen to remove this distinction. The employers have resisted it vigorously, using as part of their argument the rise of "illness" absenteeism in recent years.[137] The worker, they point out, loses the incentive to work even under the existing system, which reportedly, in some instances, enables him to secure a higher net income by being sick than by working.

In the area of workmen's compensation (industrial injuries) the government succeeded in 1963 in enacting reform legislation, after three bills had failed to pass between 1957 and 1961. The most important change is the adoption of the principle of dynamic pensions for industrial accidents.[138] These pensions now are adjusted periodically (with appropriate modifications) like those for old-age, invalidity, and survivorship. In addition, other benefit improvements have been made. Also it is now easier for victims of

[137] Officials of the Federated Employers' Association have computed, on the basis of government data, that sickness incidence among workers almost doubled between 1951 and 1963.
[138] For a discussion of the 1963 law, see "Recent Developments in Social Security Legislation in the Federal Republic of Germany," *International Labor Review,* Vol. LXXXVIII, No. 6 (December 1963), pp. 630–634.

industrial injuries to draw their benefit in the form of a capital sum instead of a pension. This is partly a concession to those who seek to promote the spreading of individual property. Aside from the improvements in benefits, the new legislation puts primary stress on prevention and rehabilitation. It introduces a whole series of measures to strengthen these aspects of the program.

It is worthwhile mentioning here that German employers are required by law to hire severely disabled persons whose disability is war-connected, the result of an industrial injury, or caused by political persecution. Originally a law imposing this kind of requirement was passed in 1923, but the responsibilities imposed on the employers were widened in 1953 and 1961.[139] Each employer with a staff of nine persons must hire at least one disabled person. Those with more than fifteen workers must hire a number equal to six percent of their total staff, although in public employment the required quota is often larger. Employers who fail to fill their quota may be required to pay 50 DM per month for each unfilled vacancy.[140]

Another important development in postwar Germany has been the introduction of family allowances. By a law enacted in 1954 most employed and self-employed persons became eligible for an allowance of 25 DM per month for their third and each subsequent child.[141] The objective of the law was presumably to make part of the burden of raising large families a responsibility of society as a whole. However, under the 1954 law, the employers, combined in industry-wide associations, were required to pay for the system. This method financing was abandoned under a new law, passed in April 1964, that transfers the financing of family allowances to the federal budget.[142] Eligible families now receive 25 DM per month for the second child, 50 for the third, 60 for the fourth, and 70 for each subsequent child. To receive the allowance for the second child (introduced in 1961), family earnings must not exceed 600 DM per month, but this restriction does not apply to allowances for three or more children. These payments are made normally for children up to the age of 18 but are extended to age 25 if the child is an invalid, a student, or an apprentice. For large families this represents a significant contribution to the vocational training or education of

[139] See "New Act on Employment of the Disabled in the Federal Republic of Germany," *International Labor Review*, Vol. LXXXV (March 1962), pp. 284–291.
[140] This kind of social allocation of relief is more fully developed in the special programs concerned with compensation for war victims and the equalization of burdens resulting from war damages. However, since these are not social security programs in the usual sense, we shall not discuss them here.
[141] For a discussion of the act, see Herbert Lauterbach, "The German Child Allowances Law," *Bulletin of the International Society Security Association,* Vol. VIII (April 1955), pp. 184–195.
[142] "Federal Republic of Germany: Family Allowances Act," *International Labor Review,* Vol. XC (September 1964), p. 282.

their children, although it also helps to raise the productive efficiency of the labor force. The amounts spent on family allowances have increased significantly since the inception of the program, from 445 million DM in 1955 to an estimated 1562 million DM in 1963.[143] Notice also that, in addition to these allowances, the German families are favored by a system of progressive tax exemptions for children.

In the area of unemployment insurance the reforms consist mainly of a series of improvements in the level and kinds of benefit, and in the extension of coverage and comprehensiveness. The most important changes have been aptly summarized by Dr. Friedrich Schmidt, the Vice-President of the Federal Office for Labor Placement and Unemployment Insurance:

> ... the flourishing economy has made it possible for the federal system of unemployment insurance to be steadily improved. This is particularly evident in the extension of insurance protection to other classes of the population (since 1952), the extension and improvement of benefits, especially the shortening of the waiting period from 14 days (1929) to three days (1957), the lengthening of the duration of benefit to 52 weeks (1953), the increase in benefit rates (repeatedly since 1953), the introduction of accident insurance for unemployed persons (1957) and of a bad-weather allowance for building workers (1959), the development of legal protection by the three level system of social courts (1954), and the improvement of safeguards against benefit abuses (1957).[144]

The coverage of the unemployment system is approximately the same as the one for sickness insurance. It is financed by equal contributions from employers and employees, and both groups are represented on the administrative bodies. The number of contributors has increased steadily from 9.5 million in 1951 to 15.8 million in 1963, although the number drawing unemployment-insurance benefits declined from about one half a million in 1950 to approximately 105,000 in 1962.[145]

During the recent years of full employment the major activities of the program have shifted from income maintenance to "measures to prevent and terminate unemployment." This important shift in emphasis perhaps best illustrates the new orientation of German unemployment insurance. The program makes payments and grants low-interest loans for a whole variety of purposes, including travel in search of a job, interview expenses, family relocation costs, the maintenance of separate households in the case of jobs away from home, vocational guidance and counseling, physical and mental rehabilitation, retraining, the cost of acquiring tools or special

---

[143]*Uebersicht über die soziale Sicherung in der Bundesrepublik Deutschland 1964,* p. 94.

[144] F. Schmidt, "History and Evolution of Unemployment Insurance in the German Federal Republic," *Bulletin of the International Social Security Association,* Vol. XVI (October–November 1963), pp. 329–330.

[145]*Uebersicht über die soziale Sicherung in der Bundesrepublik Deutschland 1964,* pp. 98, 103.

clothing, the cost of setting up new agricultural enterprises, and subsidies to employers who hire long-term employed persons.[146] Under specified circumstances, unemployment insurance funds may be used to support the construction of youth and worker centers, public works, and public housing. One of the most interesting aspects of the unemployment prevention drive relates to the efforts to maintain year-round activities in the building industry. To enable employers to meet the extra costs of winter construction, they are paid a subsidy for maintaining employment between December 1 and March 31. Construction workers are entitled to payments toward the cost of special winter clothing and extra travel or separate household expenses. In addition, they are entitled to a bad-weather compensation for working days lost from November to March.

Individuals who are not eligible for benefits under unemployment insurance may qualify for similar, but usually lower, benefits under a special program of unemployment assistance.[147] The number of individuals drawing support under this program has decreased from 910,000 in 1950 to only 17,000 in 1962.[148] This huge reduction reflects both the general prosperity of the country and the fact that unemployment insurance now leaves only marginal gaps in coverage.

Attention also should be given to the legislation enacted for the purpose of promoting the spreading of private property and individual ownership. These measures are not social security programs in the usual sense, but in Germany the legislative promotion of thrift and individual ownership has been debated as an alternative approach to social security.[149] Under a law passed in 1959, and amended in 1963, the federal government pays a premium from public funds on savings deposited for a five-year period. The premium starts at 20 percent for a single individual and rises to 30 percent for a family with more than five children. However, there are limits on the total sums on which premiums can be earned. The annual maximum premium paid ranges from 120 DM for a single saver under age 50 to 480 DM for a saver with more than five children. The state also allows life insurance premiums to be deducted from taxable income, up to specified amounts. Other legislation to encourage thrift and the dispersion of property has been designed to facilitate the acquisition of family homes and of capital stock in industrial enterprises. In the recent denationalization of certain public enterprises (Volkswagen, Preussag, Vereinigte Tanklager

[146]Ibid., pp. 99–100.

[147]For a discussion of the present program, which was established in 1956, see F. Schmidt, "New Measure to Assist the Unemployed in the Federal Republic of Germany," Bulletin of the International Social Security Association, Vol. IX (July 1956), pp. 284–287.

[148]Uebersicht über die soziale Sicherung in der Bundesrepublik Deutschland 1964, p. 103.

[149]For a recent discussion along these lines, see Gerhard Zweig, "Soziale Sicherung und Eigentumsbildung," Sozialer Fortschritt, Vol. XII, No. 7/8 (July–August 1963), pp. 162–164.

und Transportmittel) measures were taken to favor low- and middle-income groups in the acquisition of stock. Under a law enacted in 1961 (Gesetz zur Förderung der Vermögensbildung der Arbeitnehmer) income payments to employees in the form of profit shares and similar premiums are exempted from payroll and social security taxes, on condition that the recipient retains these earnings in the form of savings for a period of five years. This involves considerable advantages for both employers and employees. The apparent objective is to encourage not only thrift but also profit-related income payments to employees, with the ultimate goal of strengthening their stake in the existing economic and social order.[150]

The reforms gave Germany a social security system geared to the potentialities of an advanced industrial economy and attuned to the country's conception of social justice. The relatively high, and almost automatically rising, benefit levels naturally entail substantial burdens, but in a growing economy this need be no problem, provided that the structure of the benefits and that the nature of the burden are socially acceptable. The reforms broadened the equality implied by citizenship—through more universal and more comprehensive coverage and through more equal provisions for various groups—but the increased benefit differentiation reduced equality. The German reforms were not designed to obliterate the inequalities generated by the market system. We learned how the British approach, which had pronounced egalitarian objectives, unintentionally produced new forms of inequality.

The two countries illustrate some of the dilemmas encountered in social security policy that aims at realizing the ideals of individual freedom and of equality among citizens. Every social security system both limits and enlarges freedom. The limits are on the freedom to dispose of one's income as one pleases; the enlargements are on the freedom inherent in a more secure existence. Similar issues arise with regard to equality. If equality means that all pay the same contribution and receive the same flat benefit, the system may not only fail to provide adequate protection but will have no substantial impact on existing inequality. If differential income taxes are levied to pay for equal universal benefits, income equality is increased, but citizens are treated unequally on the contribution side, which also may have adverse incentive effects and, therefore, inherent limits. If benefit levels are tied to contribution levels, all citizens may be treated equally, but existing inequalities are once more perpetuated, and protection may be deficient

---

[150] For a brief discussion of the legislation enacted in this area, see Günter Halbach, *Vermögensbildung der Arbeitnehmer*, Sozialpolitik in Deutschland No. 46 (Stuttgart: Kohlhammer, 1961); also Helmut Arntz (ed.), *Deutschland Heute, Soziale Lage, Soziale Sicherung* (Bonn: Presse- under Informationsdienst der Bundesregierung, 1963), pp. 80 ff; and Richter, *op. cit.*, Section F/XXXIV.

where it is most needed. These problems are ones that are inherent in social policy. Even in countries where social security is not merely a tool of political or economic policy, it still must be decided which dimensions of freedom and equality are most consistent with the prevailing ideals of citizenship. These considerations were not uppermost for Bismarck, but they are of primary importance to the Federal Republic of Germany.

CHAPTER 6

America: Out of the Liberal Mold

The European precedents had demonstrated the strengths as well as the weaknesses of social security, but until the 1930s America remained unconvinced. It could not follow in the footsteps of the patriarchal German tradition, nor could it accept the leveling kind of egalitarianism that inspired the origins of the British welfare state. At home the attacks on the liberal tradition, the attempts to formulate an indigenous ideology of protection, had been only partially successful. The enactment of workmen's compensation and limited assistance programs had not committed the country to the concept of mass protection through a compulsory system. There was still a strong, widespread belief that America was sufficiently different from Europe that this kind of curtailment of individual freedom was unnecessary and even harmful. The rather prosperous decade of the 1920s, although giving occasional cause for concern, had dampened the spirit of reform in America and had renewed faith in the free market system. It was only when the Great Depression revealed in a shocking manner the utter defenselessness of the citizen in the American industrial state that the still potent individualistic tradition could be overcome. The momentous change came when it became accepted that it was the task of the national government, rather than the job of merely state and local authorities, to provide economic security for the citizen. This chapter examines how the liberal tradition was finally overcome and, also, how its influence persisted in the shaping of the right to protection.

THE IMPACT OF THE GREAT DEPRESSION

The 1930s was an important turning point in American economic history. The whole system of capitalist free enterprise was suddenly on the defensive on a scale never before witnessed in America. The shock of the depression was all the greater because it came so shortly after the champions of free enterprise had proclaimed that this system had achieved a new age of un-interrupted prosperity. In the 1930s the system built on individualistic foundations faltered and was failing, in a world in which collectivist methods were mastering for the first time in history the operation of industrial economies. The challenge to the American system was both internal and external, and at the heart of the challenge was the right of the individual to basic security of existence. The time had come for a redefinition of rights and for a restatement of public policy that would assure to the individual at least the elementary safeguards of economic survival.

The depression of the 1930s found the United States woefully un-prepared to deal with the hazards of economic insecurity that are inherent in an industrial society. Aside from workmen's compensation, the American worker was left practically unprotected, in spite of the efforts of a small but dedicated group of social insurance enthusiasts. The almshouse was still the basic public form of protection for those who became dependent and had no relatives to support them. And the almshouse still bore all the stigmas of degradation, disgrace, and defeat. This humiliating method of protection could remain acceptable for as long as only a small fraction of society—marginal social groups—ran the risk of public relief. In a mature industrial society, where millions of wage-dependent workers were exposed to the risk of total loss of income, almshouses were not only inadequate, but the attitudes associated with them added insult to injury. The business com-munity and labor organizations had long argued in favor of private instead of public protection. After half a century of industrialization, however, the achievements of these groups were still pitifully meagre.

A quick survey of the extent of the protection against the major income risks is appropriate at this point. By 1930 the United States had a total population of approximately 123 million and a working population of 49 million. There were about 6.5 million persons over 65 years of age in the country. Unfortunately, we have only rough estimates of the number of aged persons who had any kind of formal income protection. At most, 10 percent of the aged were receiving either a public or private pension. The greatest majority of these pensioners, about 80 percent, were drawing pensions for military service.[1] After three decades of discussion and a decade of agitation, there were nine states with old-age pension (old-age assistance) laws in operation. These programs, which were usually optional with the counties, cared for hardly more than 10,000 aged persons in 1930.[2] Voluntary

[1] Bureau of Labor Statistics, *Care of Aged Persons in the United States*, published as Bulletin No. 491 (Washington, D.C.: Government Printing Office, 1929), p. 3.
[2] Bureau of Labor Statistics, *Handbook of Labor Statistics*, 1931, published as Bulletin No. 541 (Washington, D.C.: Government Printing Office, 1931), p. 479.

industrial pensions had begun as far back as 1875. After the 1920s, a decade of welfare capitalism, their significance was still nominal. Approximately 420 industrial pension plans had about 100,000 superannuated workers on their rolls in 1930.[3] A high percentage of the workers covered under these plans never became eligible for benefits on account of very long service requirements. Old-age benefits paid by trade unions were even less significant. An estimated 15,000 union members drew such benefits in 1930.[4] On the number of persons drawing pensions under civil service, there are no accurate data for 1930. A great many jurisdictions had pension plans for government employees, teachers, policemen, and firemen. An incomplete survey for 1928 shows that there were about 70,000 persons drawing retirement income under these various plans. Nor are there any counts of the number of aged inmates of almshouses. A report for 1924 indicates that there were approximately 86,000 residents, living under generally wretched conditions.[5] By 1930 this number must have risen to at least 100,000, which gave the almshouses the same numerical significance as the combined total of the industrial pension plans.

In the area of protection against loss of income due to unemployment, no social insurance plan had ever been adopted in the United States. There were some private plans in existence, but these covered less than 0.5 percent of the employees in nonfarm enterprises. Of the estimated 107,000 American workers covered by formal unemployment insurance plans in 1930, about 33,500 were under trade union plans, 65,000 under joint employer–union plans, and only 8500 were under unilateral employer plans.[6] The attempts by a few progressive employers to stir up interest in this kind of protection during the 1920s had produced negligible results.

Protection against loss of income due to disability was widespread only with regard to industrial accidents. By 1930 all the states of the Union with the exception of four (Arkansas, Florida, Mississippi, and South Carolina) had workmen's compensation laws. However, this meant by no means that coverage of employees was complete. In 12 states the laws applied only to "hazardous occupations," and almost all states excluded certain industries, for example agriculture and domestic service, and exempted small enterprises. Perhaps an even greater weakness of the system was the many restrictions built into the laws of the various states. The 1931 *Handbook of Labor*

[3] Social Security Board, *Social Security in America* (Washington, D.C.: Government Printing Office, 1937), pp. 172, 176–177.
[4] *Handbook of Labor Statistics*, 1931, p. 510.
[5] Bureau of Labor Statistics, *Care of Aged Persons in the United States*, published as Bulletin No. 489 (Washington, D.C.: Government Printing Office, 1929), p. 6. Not all inmates were aged persons.
[6] Bryce M. Stewart, *Unemployment Benefits in the United States* (New York: Industrial Relations Counselors, 1930), Vol. I, pp. 201–202.

Statistics (p. 904) notes the seriousness of this shortcoming. "The result of the various restrictions has been computed as placing upon the injured worker about 50 per cent of the burden of industrial accidents in the most favorable states and from 65 to 80 per cent in those less favorable."

The extent of private disability and death benefit plans is difficult to establish, but there is no doubt that only a small fraction of the labor force was covered. A study of the Bureau of Labor Statistics discovered 214 companies that participated in mutual benefit associations paying general sickness and death benefits. There were 758,067 employees enrolled under these plans.[7] In addition, there was a handful of trade unions that paid sickness and death benefits, but most of these union programs were on precarious actuarial foundations. Finally, there were, perhaps, a million workers enrolled in industrial group insurance plans, which typically paid death, sickness, and permanent disability benefits. All in all, less than one in ten of the 26 million employees in nonfarm enterprises was covered by any kind of private death or disability plan at the place of employment. And even those who were covered often had but a nominal and uncertain level of protection.

The story of how the depression plunged millions of Americans into misery has been told many times and need not be repeated here. Some aggregative figures may give a useful indication of the magnitude of the problem of insecurity. Real gross national product dropped almost one third, from 181.8 billion dollars in 1929 (measured in 1954 prices) to 126.6 billion in 1933.[8] It was not until 1939 that the 1929 level of real GNP was reached again but, in the meantime, the population had increased by nine million people. The impact on individual security was through both loss of income and loss of assets. For wage workers, unemployment is the most obvious index of income loss. A conservative estimate puts the peak level of unemployment in March 1933, at nearly 15 million, roughly 29 percent of the work force.[9] For the decade of the 1930s, unemployment averaged 18 percent of the work force; it exceeded 10 million annually in 1932, 1933, 1934, and 1938. Even these figures understate the mass phenomenon of unemployment. On account of the turnover among the unemployed, much larger numbers of individuals were unemployed over the span of one year. Moreover, the data do not reveal the large number of individuals who were underemployed or working only part time.

The impact on individuals is impossible to convey through aggregative figures, especially since different groups were affected unevenly. For instance,

[7] *Handbook of Labor Statistics, 1929*, p. 443.
[8] *Economic Report of the President* (Washington, D.C.: Government Printing Office, 1965), p. 192.
[9] National Resources Planning Board, *Security, Work, and Relief Politics* (Washington, D.C.: Government Printing Office, 1942), p. 19. The unemployment data used here are those of the National Industrial Conference Board.

farmers, although not counted among the unemployed, were hit extremely hard. Their share in the shrinking national income decreased from 10.4 percent in 1929 to 7.5 percent in 1932.[10] The price index of farm products dropped from 146 to 65, by more than half, between 1929 and 1932. The ratio of prices received to prices paid by farmers fell from 95 to 61. Although the farmers' real income did not drop as much as their money income, the strictly monetary decline cannot be dismissed because farmers were saddled with more than 9.5 billion dollars in mortgage debt in 1930. Among wage earners, the young, the old, and the Negroes suffered the heaviest unemployment rates. For the country as a whole, annual per capita disposable personal income, measured in current prices, fell from $682 in 1929 to $364 in 1933. In real terms, measured in 1964 prices, the drop was from $1273 to $938; the 1929 real per capita income was not reached again until 1940.[11] The ability of the population to meet such income losses must take into account debts and savings. Unfortunately, we have no data on the distribution of individual liquid assets and liabilities, and national averages are not very meaningful. We know that there was a total of 6.4 billion dollars in consumer debt outstanding in 1929, reflecting the spread of installment buying during the preceding prosperous years.[12] Much of this debt was probably owed by worker families. The majority of them had only negligible liquid savings.[13] The analysis made by Seager 20 years earlier on the spending and saving habits in the industrial society was fully corroborated by a Brookings Institution study.[14] Even some of those individuals who had savings deposits lost them in the avalanche of bank failures, and many others lost their homes and farms through foreclosure.

America had weathered economic storms before the 1930s, but none had been as massive, none had lasted as long, and never had such large numbers been in so vulnerable a position. It was the duration of the depression that forced on the country new ways of thinking about economic insecurity. A report to the National Resources Planning Board in 1942 observes that "had the general decline in economic activity been short-lived, it is probable that the emergency might have been met by methods which had been used in the past—namely, greater reliance on private

[10]Ibid., p. 17.

[11]Economic Report of the President (1965), p. 209.   [12]Ibid., p. 254.

[13]A. Epstein, Insecurity A Challenge to America (third edition, New York: Harrison Smith and Hass, 1936), pp. 108 ff.

[14]A Brookings Institution study shows that savings by farm families with incomes from $2500 to $6000 were typically four to five times as great as the average of nonfarm families at the same income level. The same study concludes that in nonfarm families with under $3000 in annual income, which made up 59 percent of the nation's families in 1929, there were no appreciable savings. See Maurice Leven, Harold G. Moulton, and Clark Warburton, America's Capacity to Consume (Washington, D.C.: Brookings Institution, 1934), pp. 71, 78.

charity . . . the expansion of local public relief and occasional special emergency appropriations of public funds. . . ." [15] However, the severity of the depression vividly demonstrated the inadequacies of these traditional methods. It brought to light the extent of economic risk linkage in a highly interdependent industrial society. One economic misfortune breeds another; declining income leads to declining spending, which forces declining employment; unemployment increases unemployment as additional family members enter the work force in search of earnings, however small. The chain reaction of bank failures and the collapse of the credit structure undermined the sources as well as the spirit of private charity. In early 1933, Professor Slichter of Harvard reported that "the proportion of the unemployed who have exhausted their resources and the resources of their friends and relatives is rapidly rising." [16] Since the beginning of the depression the burden on public relief had doubled every year. Even when the number of unemployed began to decrease, after 1933, the relief burden kept rising because the proportion of those who had exhausted all private resources increased. In the meantime the ability of the local communities to bear the relief burden decreased, as a result of a shrinking tax base and of mounting tax delinquencies. There could be no more convincing argument for discarding the time-honored reliance on the local community. Nor were the individual states capable of meeting the financial crisis. The resources of the national collectivity had to be mobilized.

An important development like the introduction of a complex system of protection on a nationwide scale, perhaps, can be accomplished only in response to a major crisis. In a sense this was true in Germany in the 1880s. The crisis then was perceived mainly by the ruling bureaucracy, which believed that there was an imminent threat to the established order that stemmed from the discontent of an insecure working class led by socialist revolutionaries. The social and political nature of the American crisis in the 1930s was somewhat different. A brief examination of the aspects that relate to social protection is in order.

Probably the most shocking feature of the crisis, the aspect which greatly heightened the sense of deprivation, was the paradox of want in the midst of potential abundance. [17] This applied to all industrialized capitalist countries but was most pronounced in America, the richest country with the greatest economic distress. Comparing the depression of the 1930s

---

[15] National Resources Planning Board, *Security, Work, and Relief Policies* (Washington, D.C.: Government Printing Office, 1942), p. 24.

[16] Sumner H. Slichter, "The Immediate Unemployment Problem," *Annals of the American Academy of Political and Social Science*, Vol. 163 (January 1933), p. 1.

[17] There is whole literature on this paradox. For a thoughtful sample, see J. A. Hobson, *Poverty in Plenty* (London: George Allen and Unwin, 1931).

with the ones of earlier periods, Walter Lippmann, a shrewd interpreter of the contemporary scene, told the National Conference of Social Work in 1932: "This is the first time when it is altogether evident that man's power to produce wealth has reached a point where it is clearly unnecessary that millions in a country like the United States should be in want." [18] This realization was one of the novel and highly disturbing elements of the depression situation. The United States had become an advanced industrial country and thereby had conquered mass poverty. But it had failed to eliminate economic insecurity, because it did not make the institutional adjustments necessary to control the flow of wealth and to protect the sources of income. Having escaped the necessity of poverty, America had become a victim of insecurity. Admittedly, views of this kind were still limited to a fraction of the total population.

Nevertheless, there was a conscious awareness on the part of nearly all thinking people in the 1930s that insecurity on the scale that confronted them was unnecessary and preventable. Very few still adhered to the old doctrine that slumps were economically invigorating . Those who insisted on the self-liquidation of depressions and predicted a quick and automatic return to prosperity were silenced or, at least, discredited. This marked a profound change in American attitudes. It called for a restatement of the economic functions of government. For many people it was no longer simply a matter of correcting abuses and of instituting specific reforms, as had been the case during the Progressive Era. The expectation now was that the government somehow had to take charge of the economy; it had to become responsible for the general performance of the system. There were widespread demands and innumerable schemes for "social planning." The general purpose of all of these schemes was the "management of plenty" by the state for the benefit of society. [19] Again, Lippmann, in the 1934 Godkin lectures delivered at Harvard, took note of the new development in the responsibilities of the state. "The task of insuring the continuity of the standard of life for its people," he told his listeners, "is now as much the fundamental duty of the state as the preservation of national independence." [20] From a quite different source came essentially the same message. The Very Reverend Monsignor Robert F. Keegan stated in his 1936 presidential address to the National Conference of Social Work: "Governmental programs protecting large social groups are imperative. They shall not

[18] Walter Lippmann, "Poverty and Plenty," *Proceedings of the National Conference of Social Work*, Vol. 59 (1932), p. 235.

[19] Most of the planners recognized that some planning was necessary even in normal times. A Brookings Institution study showed that even in 1929, American industry was producing only at about 80 percent of capacity. Edwin G. Nourse *et al., America's Capacity to Produce* (Washington, D.C.: Brookings Institution, 1934), p. 415.

[20] Walter Lippmann, *The Method of Freedom* (London: George Allen and Unwin, 1934), p. 35.

restrict our inherited personal liberty, but they shall surround it with a self-respecting security."[21] The ability of the United States to postpone social protection on a large scale until advanced industrialism was a consequence of its individualistic heritage, which in turn was buttressed by political democracy, social mobility, and economic opportunity. These interacting forces had supported self-help. However, democracy works also in the opposite direction. "The more the political state was democratized," Lippmann argued, "the more imperative it was for private capitalism to give off continued prosperity."[22]

REFORM SCHEMES

We cannot review in detail here the many forms in which popular discontent expressed itself and the many remedies that were offered by all kinds of social healers, who ranged from outright demagogues like Huey Long to the serious social reformers, brought by the New Deal to positions of power and authority.[23] The schemes that attracted large popular followings were those with roots in traditional American protest movements. At first glance it is surprising that there was so little revolutionary sentiment among the populace.[24] A rather small number of individuals, mainly intellectuals, were converted to the doctrines of communism and fascism. Although there was not much proletarian class consciousness in America, there was still a good deal of populist sentiment. There was a strong element of populism in Huey Long's Share-Our-Wealth dream as well as in Father Coughlin's Union for Social Justice. Generally, the target of popular discontent was big business rather than the capitalist system. The recurrent themes of the protest movements were the overwhelming control by big business of the economy, excessive speculation and profits, and an income distribution that did not enable the masses to consume what industry could produce. Many sober thinkers shared these views. The study of the modern corporation by Berle and Means furnished ample evidence on the high degree of concentration of economic power in the United States.[25] In Monsignor Keegan's

[21] Robert F. Keegan, "Democracy at the Crossroads," *Proceedings of the National Conference of Social Work*, Vol. 63 (1936), p. 25.

[22] *The Method of Freedom*, p. 14.

[23] For a convenient survey, see Arthur M. Schlesinger, Jr., *The Politics of Upheaval* (Vol. III of *The Age of Roosevelt*) (Cambridge, Mass.: Riverside Press, 1960), Part I.

[24] W. G. Runciman has observed that in England also there was a surprising lack of militancy during the 1930s, which he ascribes to a sense of helplessness. See his *Relative Deprivation and Social Justice* (London: Routledge and Kegan Paul, 1966), pp. 61 ff.

[25] Adolf A. Berle and Gardner C. Means, *The Modern Corporation and Private Property* (New York: MacMillan, 1933).

view, "continued control of property in the hands of a few can only mean one thing—interrupted social circulation, the feudalization of American Wealth."[26]

An interesting feature of popular discontent was a tendency toward self-help, in contrast to the emphasis on assistance as a matter of social justice. Even the veterans of the Bonus Army marching on Washington did not ask for a handout. They wanted the government to make a payment, albeit premature, on service related certificates awarded to veterans by Congress in 1924. Representative Wright Patman of Texas helped to set the march in motion by introducing a bill in early 1932 that provided for immediate payment of the maturity value of the certificates. Most veterans undoubtedly would have accepted a discounted payment. Around the country the unemployed started many self-help organizations in the early 1930s. The Seattle Unemployed Citizen's League, the Los Angeles Unemployed Cooperative Relief Association, and the Salt Lake City Natural Development Association were outstanding examples.[27] Consistent with American political practice, these organizations typically developed into political pressure groups.

In the context of the development of social protection, surely the most interesting phenomenon of the 1930s was the emergence of the Townsend movement. The first public statement of the Townsend plan for old-age pensions appeared in a letter to the Long Beach Press-Telegram, on September 30, 1933.[28] The lively response to the letter, entitled "Cure for Depressions," surprised even its author, Dr. Francis E. Townsend. Within a few weeks, letters debating the merits of the plan daily filled an entire page of the paper. The good doctor was soon besieged with requests for guidance on how to apply the marvelous cure that he had invented. Barely a month after he had published the outline of his plan, he found it practical to devote full time to the leadership of the movement that he had launched in an astonishingly brief period and with very little effort. By December 1933, petitions calling for the enactment of the pension plan in the United States Congress were gathering a large number of signatures in California. Thereafter the movement continued to gather momentum, and Townsend clubs were organized all over the country. By the time of the 1936 elections, the leaders of the movement claimed to have from 10 to 30 million followers. There were no accurate membership records, and the claim was undoubtedly a wild exaggeration. Holtzman estimates that in 1936 there were probably 2.2 million active club members, about two-thirds of whom were past the

---

[26] "Democracy at the Crossroads," p. 12.
[27] See Irwing Bernstein, *The Lean Years* (Boston: Houghton Mifflin, 1960), pp. 416 ff.
[28] Abraham Holtzman, *The Townsend Movement* (New York: Bookman Associates, 1963), p. 35. The present discussion is much indebted to Holtzman's excellent study.

age of 60.[29] In the absence of an accurate count, this number was large enough in any case to give the appearance that the Townsendites and their sympathizers held the balance of power in many elections. After 1936 the movement weakened; it briefly gathered strength again in 1939 but continuously lost ground thereafter. In 1939, when discontent with the original old-age provisions of the Social Security Act of 1935 had become acute, the paid-up club membership stood at 761,624; by 1953 it had dropped to 22,101.[30]

The plan that attracted such a following was amazingly simple. The original letter suggested that the United States Government pay a pension of $150 a month to every citizen who had reached the age of 60, on condition that he quit working and spend the money immediately. The funds to finance this proposal were to be raised through a sales tax. The whole scheme rested on the idea that spending by the pensioners would pump money into the economy, reactivate consumer purchasing power, revive economic activity, and move the entire country from depression to prosperity. The petition circulating in December mentioned a figure of $200 a month to be paid to every citizen having reached 60 and "whose record is free of habitual criminality."[31] It also substituted a transactions tax for a sales tax. The higher pension was justified primarily on the ground that this amount was necessary in order to have the desired effect on the economy.[32] The first two bills embodying the Townsend plan were introduced in the United States House of Representatives in 1935. Many bills of this kind followed in subsequent years, but the legislative process robbed the original plan of its seductive simplicity.

Although highly attractive in the context of the early 1930s, the basic idea of the plan was not original. As Holtzman points out, monetary radicalism, consisting in naive manipulations of the money supply, had strong historical roots in America and was present in a number of the economic salvation plans advanced during the depression. At least, in a superficial way, there was a resemblance between the monetary panaceas and the ideas of leading economists such as J. M. Keynes and Irwing Fisher. Townsend was able to build up a mass following overnight mainly because, in a hopeless situation, he came forth with a formula for an instant welfare state.

From the point of reference of this book, the most interesting aspects of the Townsend movement are the ones that reveal it as a product of the

[29]Abraham Holtzman, *op. cit.*, p. 49.

[30]*Ibid.*, p. 49.

[31]A copy of the petition is contained in *The Townsend Crusade* (New York: Committee on Old Age Security of the Twentieth Century Fund, 1936), p. 63.

[32]No one seemed to wonder why $400 might not be twice as good as $200. Perhaps Dr. Townsend felt instinctively that medicine which cures when taken in small dosage often kills when taken in large quantities.

American environment. Holtzman stresses the fact that only in America did a mass political movement of the aged develop. Other industrial countries introduced old-age income protection long before the demographic changes that accompany industrial maturity had made the aged such a sizeable minority. Cultural differences made the aged in America a much more isolated group than in other countries. In other industrial countries the aged were not left to fight their own battles; European labor movements did not abandon the aged as did American trade unions. In America there was not a strong enough political left capable of either enacting protective legislation or of forcing the conservative right into passing it out of fear of losing control.[33] Another point brought out by Holtzman is the radical-conservative nature of the Townsend plan, which has something typically American about it. It was a radical nostrum, but it did not seek radical changes in institutions. It had an evangelistic, conservative approach to American institutions. Although it pursued a radical goal, it proceeded strictly along the time-honored legislative path. Behind the ideas of the scheme was an innocent confidence in the productiveness of the American economy and in the adaptability of the profit system. Another strikingly American characteristic was the straightforward "practical" nature of the plan, without elaborate ideological justification. In a sense it was another form of self-help. After all, its basic emphasis was not what society owed the aged, but on what the aged, through their spending of pensions, would do for society. The scheme was not designed to make the rich support the poor; actually, the probable incidence of the transactions tax and the lack of income qualification for pensioners would have made the poor help support the rich.

Even though none of the Townsend bills ever came close to passage, the movement had a major impact on the development of social protection in America. For the first time there was a mass movement that made social protection its principal goal. It dramatized, as nothing else had done before, the need for social income protection. It forced the government to take action, not by threatening the social order, but by mobilizing enough votes to make legislators responsive to its wishes. The Townsend movement was one of the major factors making for inclusion of old-age protection in the Social Security bill. After hesitating on an old-age pension program, Roosevelt told his Committee on Economic Security: "We have to have it. . . . The Congress can't stand the pressure of the Townsend Plan unless we have a real old-age insurance system. . . ."[34] Again in 1939 the Town-

---

[33] Paul H. Douglas, *Social Security in the United States* (New York: Whittlesey House, 1936), p. 4.
[34] Frances Perkins, *The Roosevelt I Knew*, quoted in Holtzman, *op. cit.*, p. 88. Roosevelt's hesitation was not the result of a lack of interest in old-age pensions but of a desire to give unemployment insurance top priority. See Arthur J. Altmeyer, *The Formative Years of Social Security* (Madison: University of Wisconsin Press, 1966), p. 13.

sendites played a crucial role in bringing about amendments that liberalized the Society Security Act of 1935. Their activities illustrate how, in America, pressure groups instead of a class-conscious proletariat were instrumental in the development of social protection.

However, it would be erroneous to conclude that there were no class-conscious activities and proposals in the drive for social security. There was, in fact, a rival to the Townsend scheme that was radical not only in the economic but also in the social and political sense. This was the so-called Workers' Bill for Unemployment and Social Insurance, which was sponsored chiefly by Ernest Lundeen, a farmer-laborite from Minnesota. From 1934 on this bill was introduced for a number of years and gathered substantial support. Its initial introduction, however, was mainly at the instance of the Unemployment Councils, which were under the control of the Communist party.[35] It was reported later, by highly placed Communists, that Lundeen was actually a paid undercover Communist agent and that the original bill had been drafted by the Communist party.[36] Whether this was the case is less important than the fact that the Lundeen bills became the focal point of the social security demands of the radical left.

A common characteristic of the Townsend and Lundeen bills was that they disposed of tremendously complex issues in a very simple manner. The historic neglect of social protection in the United States was bound to breed this kind of approach in a crisis situation. In less than 400 words the first Lundeen bill offered a comprehensive social security system, which included protection against unemployment, disability, maternity, and old age for all workers and farmers who were unemployed "through no fault of their own."[37] It did not specify who was a worker or a farmer, but the intention was clearly to have universal coverage of all who earn an income from work, whether manual or mental. Benefits were to be the same for all and "equal to average local wages." But in no case were unemployment benefits to be less than $10 a week plus $3 for each dependent. Individuals became eligible for benefits as soon as their income stopped, without any waiting period and regardless of the previous employment record. This meant that all those unemployed at the time the bill passed could immediately start drawing benefits. The bill did not contain a revenue clause. It stated simply that "such

[35] A. J. Muste, "The Lundeen Bill," *The Survey*, Vol. LXX, No. 12 (December 1934), p. 376.
[36] Arthur M. Schlesinger, Jr., *The Coming of the New Deal* (Vol. II of *The Age of Roosevelt*) (Cambridge: Riverside Press, 1959), p. 296. The very knowledgeable late Professor Witte refers to Mary Van Kleeck as the "reputed author of the Lundeen bill." Edwin E. Witte, *The Development of the Social Security Act* (Madison: University of Wisconsin Press, 1962), p. 86.
[37] The bill is reproduced in two thirds of a page in *American Labor Legislation Review*, Vol. XXIV, No. 2 (June 1934), p. 68. For critical evaluation of the bill, see I. M. Rubinow, "The Lundeen Bill," *The Survey*, Vol. LXX, No. 12 (December 1934), pp. 377–378; Paul H. Douglas, *Social Security in the United States* (New York: Whittlesey House, 1936), pp. 74–83.

insurance shall be provided at the expense of the government and of the employers," and "no tax or contribution in any form shall be levied on workers." Furthermore, it declared that "it is the sense of Congress that funds to be raised by the government shall be secured by taxing inheritance and gifts and by taxing individual and corporation incomes of $5000 per year and over." The administration of the system, on the other hand, was to be in the hands of elected commissions composed of "rank-and-file members of workers' and farmers' organizations."

The radical parentage of these provisions is obvious. They bear a striking resemblance to the proposals advanced by German socialists around the turn of the century and to ideas that were popular in Soviet Russia during the 1920s. The Lundeen bill was essentially a crude and unworkable scheme for redistributing income from the rich to the less well off. Guaranteed benefits at average local wages, of course, were preposterous, since that was a direct incentive not to work for all those whose earnings were below the average. Professor Eveline Burns observed correctly that "such a guarantee is incompatible with the present economic system."[38] As the lowest paid workers quit their jobs, the average local wage and, consequently, benefit levels would have to keep moving up. Similarly, control of the system in the hands of the beneficiaries, without an effective check from those responsible for financing it, was another invitation to widespread abuse. The cost of the program and its adverse economic effects would almost necessarily have led to serious economic consequences. I. M. Rubinow, the veteran social insurance statistician, estimated in 1934 that "a complete confiscation today of the total surplus of individual and corporate incomes over $5000, applied to this purpose alone, would not be enough to foot the Lundeen bill for unemployment."[39]

Popular support for the Lundeen plan was not nearly as extensive as that of the Townsend Plan. The initial supporters were mainly radical groups, such as the National Unemployed League, the National Unemployment Councils, the Communist party, and the Conference for Progressive Labor Action.[40] Before very long, however, many nonpolitical groups came out in favor of the Lundeen plan, including labor organizations, "a surprisingly large number of social workers," and some economists.[41] Officially, the American Federation of Labor rejected the plan, but in 1935 the Lundeen bill was endorsed by six state federations and 2500 locals.[42]

The motivations of these various groups no doubt differed considerably.

[38] Eveline M. Burns, *Toward Social Security* (New York: Whittlesey House, 1936), p. 136.
[39] Rubinow, "The Lundeen Bill," p. 378.
[40] Muste, *loc. cit.*, p. 376.
[41] Douglas, *Social Security in the United States,* p. 77.
[42] Maxwell S. Stewart, *Social Security* (revised edition, New York: W. W. Norton, 1939), p. 280.

The rank-and-file were probably unaware of the far-reaching implications of the plan. Most of them readily accepted the naive economic argument that underconsumption was the cardinal weakness of the economy and that income redistribution was a matter of both social justice and economic necessity. Workers who had been exposed to radical propaganda were attuned to the social significance of the Lundeen bill's emphasis on income redistribution. Perhaps they were aware also that politically this was something quite different from the Townsend plan. A fundamental difference between the Townsend and Lundeen campaigns lay in the objectives of the initiators and intellectual backers. For Townsend, the pensions themselves were the chief objective. For most of the thinkers behind the Lundeen plan, the ultimate objective was broad social and economic reform. It did not matter much, therefore, that the plan itself was demonstrably unworkable. The Communists seized on it as a useful propaganda prop. Herbert Benjamin, a prominent Communist, said at a Congressional hearing: "Our purpose is to organize the workers in unions, lodges, and neighbourhoods, and build them up in such a formidable force that they will compel Congress, willingly or unwillingly, to meet such a measure."[43] In 1936 the Lundeen plan was included in the Communist and Socialist election platforms.[44] It would have served the purpose of most radicals if the bill had been enacted and, as a result of ensuing economic difficulties, had led to extensive government economic intervention. Paul Douglas, who was very active at the time in the unemployment insurance movement, observed, that in the minds of some advocates there was an "unquestionable desire to use the Lundeen plan as an initial wedge to obtain the socialization of industry."[45]

Some looked on the plan as the formulation of a new conception of individual rights. They hoped that the adoption of this conception would open up a new era of reform. This was the position of Mary Van Kleeck, a well-known and highly respected social worker. Her endorsement of the plan raised many an eyebrow. She was too well informed not to recognize its technical defects, but she defended its basic principles. She wrote:

> Its significance rests upon this different concept of social insurance. . . . Mass provision by government and industry to provide for mass insecurity is the new definition of social insurance. The demand is put forward that compensation shall be sufficient to prevent the lowering of standards of living. There should be no contributions from workers, since such contributions are essentially a

---

[43] "A Social Insurance Spree," *American Labor Legislation Review*, Vol. XXIV, No. 2 (June 1934), p. 68.

[44] Kirk H. Porter and Donald B. Johnson (eds.), *National Party Platforms* (Urbana: University of Illinois Press, 1956), pp. 357, 372.

[45] Douglas, *Social Security in the United States*, p. 81.

deduction from workers' income for living standards and compel workers to share in compensating themselves and other workers for losses that are beyond their control.[46]

Miss Van Kleeck accepted the argument that workers are not paid sufficiently to buy the goods they produce and, hence, she had no difficulty in accepting the financing and administrative arrangement of the Lundeen plan. "Unemployment insurance is a kind of deferred wage bill. As such, it is to be administered by workers for the same reason that they control their own wages after they are paid,"[47] She believed that the country could afford the plan but did not expect it to achieve economic security: "Economic security is probably unattainable except in a planned economy."[48] She noted that the Lundeen plan did not call for a "change in the economic system, but it certainly sets up a challenge to its power to protect the general welfare against the hazards of insecurity."[49] Presumably, if the system failed to pass this test it was due for a change, which was but another way of using insurance as the road to social reform.

REVIVAL OF THE OLD-AGE PENSION MOVEMENT

The Townsend and Lundeen plans were really outside the mainstream of the American social security movement. This movement, we recall, had a very promising beginning during the second decade of the century when its enthusiastic advocates fully expected that health insurance would promptly follow the introduction of workmen's compensation. The sharp depression of 1921 temporarily aroused strong interest in unemployment insurance. In Wisconsin, which led the country, an unemployment bill came within one vote of pasing in 1921. During the remainder of the 1920s it was reintroduced in every legislative session but with little chance of enactment. Bills of this type were introduced also in Massachusetts, New York, Connecticutt, and Minnesota, but no law was passed.[50] The social insurance movement was dormant but by no means dead. Discussion continued concerning workmen's compensation, and pressures began to build up for the enactment of pensions for needy aged by the states. Along with the American Association for Labor Legislation, the American Association for Old Age Security, led by

[46] Mary Van Kleeck, "Security for Americans," *The New Republic,* Vol. LXXXI (December 12, 1934), p. 123.
[47] *Ibid.,* p. 123.
[48] *Ibid.,* p. 123.
[49] *Ibid.,* p. 124.
[50] Edwin E. Witte, "An Historical Account of Unemployment Insurance in the Social Security Act," *Law and Contemporary Problems,* Vol. III, No. 1 (January 1936), p. 157.

Abraham Epstein, and the Fraternal Order of Eagles were leading the struggle for protection for the aged.

It is noteworthy that the renewed demand for old-age protection was gathering strength well before the onset of the depression. During the 1920s eight states enacted old-age pension programs, four of them taking this action in 1929. The depression heightened the legislative interest in old-age pensions more than in any other form of social security. By April 20, 1930, old-age pension plans had been proposed to seven of the eight legislatures meeting that year, with some states introducing as many as three and four bills. There was also a significant change in the nature of the bills. Earlier old-age assistance laws usually had been optional with individual counties within a state. The new trend was toward statewide, compulsory systems, with the state bearing part of the cost. With forty-four state legislatures having regular sessions in 1931 and active campaigns being carried on by labor, religious, fraternal, and welfare organizations, the year inevitably produced an avalanche of old-age bills. The nearly 100 bills that were introduced give an indication of the strength of the prevailing sentiment.[51] Five additional states established noncontributory plans for the needy aged in 1931, which brought the total up to 17.

For several years, welfare organizations, especially the American Association for Old Age Security, had been advocating federal grants-in-aid to state pension plans in lieu of the old demand for federal pensions. In 1930, hearings were held before the House Committee on Labor on bills providing for a countrywide pension program with federal participation. This plan became associated with Senator Clarence C. Dill and Representative William P. Connery, who were its chief sponsors from 1932 to 1934. Committees of both houses reported favorably on the Dill–Connery bill, but it never came to a vote on the floor. President Roosevelt never gave it his full support. In the meantime, the pension movement remained strong at the state level. In 1933 a record number of ten states enacted new pension plans. By the end of 1934, an off-year for regular legislative sessions, twenty-eight states and two territories (Alaska and Hawaii) had old-age pensions. The remaining states joined in subsequent years. In a number of instances the delay was caused by the need to alter state constitutions. In March 1938, Virginia was the last of the forty-eight states to adopt a pension program for its needy aged.

Of course, the chief impetus on the laggard states was the enactment of the Social Security Act of 1935. Under this act, the federal government paid one half of the state pensions up to $30 a month, provided that certain minimum standards were met. Thus, after several decades of a growing need

[51] Edwin M. Fitch, "Legislative Gains for Old Age Pensions," *American Labor Legislation Review*, Vol. XXI, No. 2 (June 1931), pp. 258–260.

and sporadic campaigning, the needy aged were finally given protection rather quickly, considering the number of legislative bodies that had to take action.[52]

The depression brought to the surface and intensified the movement for old-age protection. An unmistakable sign of the shifting tide of public opinion, even before the depression, was the changing attitude of the American Federation of Labor. The Federation had endorsed the "principle" of protection for the needy aged for many years, and in 1923 it even urged its Ohio affiliates to support the state's pension referendum. But not until 1928 did the top labor leadership in the country give any indication that it might work for the enactment of pension laws in all states. After several years of debate and study, the Executive Council of the Federation went as far as to recommend that year that Congress be petitioned "to authorize a commission on old age incomes to study the problem and make a report."[53] By 1929 the organization had grown bolder. With only one dissenting vote, the AF of L Convention adopted an executive council report that recommended the inauguration of "an active campaign for the inauguration of such laws in every state."[54]

There were several basic factors that accounted for the mounting pressure for old-age pensions before the depression. One of them was the demographic fact that America's population was aging. The percentage of the population aged 65 and over had risen from 2.7 in 1860 to 4.1 in 1900, 4.7 in 1920, and 5.4 in 1930.[55] In absolute terms, the number of aged persons more than doubled between 1900 and 1930, increasing from 3,089,000 to 6,634,000. Another important trend was the increase in dependency among the aged. There are no adequate statistics to document this trend, but it is a direct consequence of the increasing number of aged, the advance of urbanization and, perhaps, also a growing difficulty of accommodating older workers to mass production organization. Experienced observers like Henry Seager thought that industry was increasingly unwilling to hire and keep old workers.[56] This view is supported in reports on official investigations in California, New York, and Maryland.[57] Other studies showed that dependency

[52] For a description of the main provisions of the early state laws, see Marietta Stevenson, "Old-Age Assistance," *Law and Contemporary Problems*, Vol. III, No. 2 (April 1936), pp. 236–245.

[53] "Old Age Pensions Finally Favored by AF of L," *American Labor Legislation Review*, Vol. XIX, No. 4 (December 1929), p. 355.

[54] *Ibid.*, p. 354; also William Green, *Labor and Democracy* (Princeton: Princeton University Press, 1939), pp. 55–56.

[55] Committee on Economic Security, *Social Security in America* (Washington, D.C.: Government Printing Office, 1937), Table 26, p. 141.

[56] Henry R. Seager, "Need of Provision for the Aged in New York," *American Labor Legislation Review*, Vol. XX, No. 1 (March 1930), p. 68.

[57] *Social Security in America*, p. 144.

rates were substantially higher in urban than in rural areas. Some of the highest rates were found in New York City, where 74.5 percent of individuals and 48.4 percent of households were dependent in 1930.[58] As a rough approximation, we can guess that there must have been at least 2,000,000 dependent persons in the country in 1930, most of whom depended on relatives for support. The depression often cut off the sources of support the aged had had until then. In 1932 the New York Commissioner of Public Welfare reported that 35 percent of those receiving old-age pensions in New York City had applied for assistance as a direct result of unemployment.[59]

There is a certain historical irony in the fact that it was the high cost of relief in poorhouses that became, perhaps, the most powerful force favoring old-age pensions. Nineteenth century liberals believed that restrictions of relief to poorhouses would reduce the burden on society, mainly because they believed that this would keep down the number of relief claimants. That expectation, of course, was based largely on the assumption that poverty was the result of personal failings. This assumption became increasingly erroneous with advanced industrial development. In spite of the stigma attached to the poorhouse, it was the only alternative left open to a growing number of needy aged. As a result, the insistence on relief in the poorhouse increased rather than decreased the burden of the aged on society.

A survey of the United States Bureau of Labor Statistics showed that in 1930 the average cost per old-age pensioner throughout the country was $14.32 per month. A few years earlier the Bureau of Labor Statistics had estimated the average maintenance cost per inmate in an almshouse to be $27.88, not counting the capital cost of the physical facilities.[60] When amortization of the physical facilities was included, the cost differential was even greater. Table 6–1 gives the pension and poorhouse data computed by Epstein for the early 1930s. This table leaves out the administrative costs of pensions and of processing people for admittance to the poorhouse, but this is not likely to alter the picture significantly. Pensions were cheaper mainly because the payments were based on individual need.

Although resistance to state old-age pensions for the needy did not vanish, the economic factor involved was necessarily a powerful influence on ideologies. Business interests could be convinced of the economic

---

[58] Dependency was defined to include all those aged 65 and over with less than $5000 in property and less than $300 in annual income. *Social Security in America,* p. 151.
[59] *American Labor Legislation Review,* Vol. XXII, No. 1 (March 1932), p. 59.
[60] "Old Age Pensions," *American Labor Legislation Review,* Vol. XXI, No. 4 (December 1931), p. 407.

Table 6–1

Monthly Cost of Supporting an Aged Person

State	Average Old-Age Pension	Cost per Inmate in Poorhouse
	$	$
California	22.08	44.74
Delaware	9.84	46.24
Massachusetts	25.00	47.70
New Hampshire	17.18	44.19
New Jersey	15.28	42.13
New York	23.80	39.61
Wyoming	13.88	78.84
Minnesota	20.28	56.29
Montana	15.55	55.19
Utah	9.00	45.62
Wisconsin	19.27	35.63

Source. Epstein, *Insecurity . . .,* pp. 534–535.

rationality of pensions only if the pensions were hard to get. In a 1930 pamphlet the National Association of Manufacturers still argued against the cost of pensions and still found them "paternalistic" and "injurious to individual virtues."[61] Actually, the states that passed old-age pensions usually insisted on rigorous eligibility requirements. In America, unlike in other countries with noncontributory pensions, eligibility usually required the absence of a close relative capable of furnishing support. Under these circumstances, even the National Association of Manufacturers was inclined to approve of pensions. A 1932 report of its Committee on Employee Retirement Annuities stated:

> Insofar as state or municipal old age pensions or relief acts make possible the more humane and more efficient care of aged and impoverished citizens, such acts when properly safeguarded by rigid eligibility requirements and restricted to relief of the indigent, serve a valid social purpose and are not detrimental to the interests of American business.[62]

It was fortunate for the needy aged that a more humane treatment was also more economical.

The most important political leader who fully appreciated the

[61] "N.A.M. Raises Smoke-Screen in Fight on Pensions," *American Labor Legislation Review,* Vol. XX, No. 2 (June 1930), p. 214.

[62] Cited in *American Labor Legislation Review,* Vol. XXII, No. 1 (March 1932), p. 59.

implications of the position of the aged was Franklin D. Roosevelt. An attack on the New York State poor law and the substitution of old-age pensions in place of it was one of the themes of his 1928 gubernatorial campaign. He told how oppressive it was for him to visit the county poorhouse. "Somehow it tears my heart to see these old men and women there. . . ."[63] In a speech to the New York Women's Trade Union League (June 8, 1929) he stressed the fact that the poorhouse system "is not even an economical solution to the problem. It is the most wasteful and extravagant system that we could possibly devise. It belongs to that past barbaric age when we chained our insane to the walls of our madhouses."[64] It would be idle speculation to try to disentangle Roosevelt's political and humanitarian motivations. It should be observed that he had entered politics as a Progressive and had long favored social legislation.[65] He steadfastly proclaimed his view that it was the duty of the state to look after the welfare of the citizen, but he was equally steadfast in his opposition to welfare programs that smacked of the dole.

As Governor of New York (1929 to 32), Roosevelt had an opportunity to put his welfare ideas to the practical test. In his first Annual Message to the Legislature he called for the extension of workmen's compensation and the creation of a commission to study the problem of old-age insecurity.[66] In a special message, on February 28, 1929, recommending the creation of this commission, he analyzed the nature of the old-age problem.

> Poverty in old age should not be regarded either as a disgrace or necessarily as a result of lack of thrift or energy. Usually it is a mere by-product of modern industrial life. An alarmingly increasing number of aged persons are becoming dependent on outside help for bare maintenance . . . No greater tragedy exists in modern civilization than the aged, worn-out worker who after a life of ceaseless effort and useful productivity must look forward for his declining years to a poorhouse. A modern social consciousness demands a more humane and more efficient arrangement.[67]

Roosevelt made clear in his message that he was looking not only for old-age assistance for the needy but also for a contributory old-age insurance program. He underlined for the cost-conscious legislators the high cost of the existing poorhouse arrangement and the need to find a more economical means to provide for the increasing number of aged.

[63] Franklin D. Roosevelt, *Public Papers and Addresses* (New York: Random House, 1938), Vol. I, p. 43.

[64] *Ibid.*, p. 213.

[65] Daniel R. Fusfeld, *The Economic Thought of Franklin D. Roosevelt and the Origins of the New Deal* (New York: Columbia University Press, 1956), Chapter III.

[66] *Public Papers and Addresses*, Vol. I, p. 83.

[67] *Ibid.*, pp. 209, 210.

The New York Commission on Old Age Security recommended only a standard noncontributory pension scheme for the needy, which was enacted into law in 1930.[68] The governor was disappointed with the limited scope of the commission's recommendation; he called the proposed old-age pension law an "extension of the existing welfare or poor laws." He argued that the commission had not gone to the "real root of the needs," by which he meant that it did not appreciate the rising economic burden of the aged even under a pension scheme. He now was more direct and positive in stressing the need for old-age insurance in addition to noncontributory old-age assistance. In commenting on the commission's report he noted:

> The most successful systems are based on what might be called a series of classes by which a person who has done nothing in his or her earlier life to save against old age is entitled only to old age care according to a minimum standard. Opportunity is offered, however, under these systems for wage earners to enter other classifications, contributing as the years go by toward increased incomes during their later years. In other words, a definite premium should be placed on savings giving the workers an incentive to save based on the prospect of not only food and shelter but on comfort and higher living standards than the bare minimum.[69]

By inducing wage earners to provide for themselves, the burden on the state, that is on the taxpayer of the higher income groups, would be that much lighter. Roosevelt seemed to feel instinctively that some day social insurance would protect the rich from the demands of the poor. He was aware of the economic advantages of the social insurance provision for old age, as demonstrated by experience abroad, but there is no indication that he was aware that he was advocating a principle of social protection that was entirely new in the American context. This principle was that social protection should be extended to include people who were not necessarily in need and to secure for them a level of living above the bare minimum. By the time of the 1930 gubernatorial campaign he was committed to this idea and was prepared to show that this was fully consistent with American individualism.

> I look forward to the time when every young man and young woman entering industrial or agricultural or business activity will begin to insure himself or herself against the privations of old age. The premiums which that young man or young girl will pay should be supplemented by premiums to be paid by the employers of the state, as well as by the state itself. In that way, when the young man or young girl has grown to old and dependent age, he or

[68] For the recommendations of the commission, see "New York Commission Recommends Old Age Security," *American Labor Legislation Review*, Vol. XX, No. 1 (March 1930), pp. 73–82.
[69] *Public Papers and Addresses*, Vol. I, p. 217.

she will have built up an insurance fund which will maintain them in comfort in their years of reduced activity. In this way their assistance will be a result of their own efforts and foresightedness. They will be receiving not charity, but natural profits of their years of labor and insurance.[70]

Here, Roosevelt expressed a theme that became a central one of American social insurance ideology: the beneficiaries protect themselves through their own efforts and foresight. This may be self-help through compulsory collective effort, but self-help nevertheless. And as such it was suited for American conditions, since it was protection without dependence.

THE DRIVE FOR UNEMPLOYMENT INSURANCE

Governor Roosevelt was also an active promoter of unemployment insurance. He provided the sparks to rekindle interest in this form of protection, which had been lagging during the 1920s. In an address to the Governors' Conference in Salt Lake City in June 1930, he argued for the necessity of unemployment insurance.[71] He told the governors that 90 percent of unemployment is wholly without the fault of the worker. Foreign countries had instituted unemployment insurance, "why should we . . . fear to undertake the task?"[72] The most pressing need in the early 1930s was, of course, for measures offering immediate relief. Many argued that more permanent arrangements like unemployment insurance should not be undertaken until the return of prosperity. Alas, during prosperity, the problem was all too easily ignored. As governor and later as president, Roosevelt campaigned for reform during instead of after the restoration of prosperity.

The country's changing attitude toward unemployment insurance manifested itself in a rapidly growing list of proposals and endorsements. The American Association for Labor Legislation took a leadership role by calling a series of conferences in 1930 in which a model unemployment insurance was drafted. More than 30,000 copies of this bill were distributed.[73]

The American Federation of Labor decided in 1932 to reverse its traditional opposition to unemployment insurance. For the first time in history, it declared itself officially in favor of a compulsory unemployment insurance

---

[70] *Ibid.*, p. 417.

[71] "Unemployment Insurance Urged by Governor of New York," *American Labor Legislation Review*, Vol. XX, No. 3 (September 1930), pp. 254–255.

[72] *Ibid.*, p. 254.

[73] "An American Plan for Unemployment Reserve Funds," *American Labor Legislation Review*, Vol. XX, No. 4 (December 1930), pp. 349–356; in 1933 the association published a revised version of its model bill. See *ibid.*, Vol. XXIII, No. 2 (June 1933), pp. 79–95.

system.[74] The 1932 election platforms of every national political party, with the significant exception of the Republican party, contained demands for unemployed insurance.[75] The business community was still hesitant. The National Industrial Conference Board still argued that private industry should be given an opportunity to find a private solution to the problem. However, a number of prominent business leaders endorsed the idea of compulsory insurance.[76]

The growing momentum of the unemployment insurance movement yielded a plethora of bills. No less than 17 legislatures dealt with the issue in 1931. Wisconsin took the lead again with the organization of a strong campaign, 10 years after the first unemployment insurance bill had been introduced in the state. In 1932, Wisconsin became the first state to enact an unemployment insurance law, over the opposition of the state's manufacturers' association.[77] In 1933, 68 bills were introduced in 25 states, but none was enacted into law. Only in 7 states did a bill pass one house of the legislature. Between 1930 and 1936 at least 35 commissions in 19 states studied the unemployment insurance question, and most of them reported favorably. The most important of these commissions, which incidentally favored unemployment insurance, was the Interstate Commission on Unemployment Insurance. It grew out of an interstate conference called by Governor Roosevelt in 1931 and was composed of the representatives of six leading eastern industrial states.

With so much activity in favor of unemployment benefits, it may seem surprising that no legislative success was scored. A major obstacle blocked the road: interstate competition. Unless all states taxed employers in comparable amounts, the employers in the lagging states would derive a competitive advantage over their more progressive neighbors. The country's governmental structure was one of those peculiarities of the historical setting that constituted a serious hindrance to the development of social protection. In a sense it was ironic that the federal system, which had been created to protect the rights of the individual citizen against the encroachment of a centralized power, became a major obstacle to the creation of an institution designed to enable the individual to enjoy his rights. Only a federal program or concerted action by all the states could overcome the obstacle. It was

[74] Thomas Kennedy, "American Labor and Unemployment Insurance," *American Labor Legislation Review*, Vol. XXIII, No. 3 (September 1933), pp. 142–145.

[75] Porter and Johnson, *op. cit.*, pp. 325 ff.

[76] See *American Labor Legislation Review*, Vol. XXI, No. 4 (December 1931), pp. 209–213, 309–310, 313, 385.

[77] In response to pressure from the association, the law was made "conditional on industry's failure to establish a fair voluntary system within a reasonable period of time." No acceptable voluntary solution was found. See Harry Malisoff, "The Emergence of Unemployment Compensation I," *Political Science Quarterly*, Vol. LIV, No. 2 (June 1939), p. 246.

generally believed that a strictly federal program would be unconstitutional. Most social insurance advocates believed, moreover, that protection against unemployment was a state rather than a federal responsibility. The federal government had the power to tax but not to regulate business within a state. Therefore, the solution was to find a way to use the federal taxing power for inducing the states to act in common. A precedent for this approach had already been set by the Federal Inheritance Tax Act. Actually, this act was the inspiration for the Wagner–Lewis bill of 1934.[78] Senator Robert Wagner had introduced several unemployment insurance bills previously but without success. The 1934 bill, which Representative David J. Lewis introduced in the House, proposed a 5 percent federal tax on the payrolls of all employers with ten or more workers. From this federal tax, however, employers were to be allowed to deduct the taxes they had to pay under a state unemployment insurance law, provided the state law met certain basic standards set by the federal government. A state, therefore, could not afford to be without an unemployment insurance plan. This was a skilful way of overcoming the constitutional handicap to direct federal regulation.

The Wagner–Lewis bill did not become law, mainly because the President did not push it. He was in favor of the bill but wished to postpone action until he could put together a broader program of social protection.[79] The Social Security Act of 1935 represented such a program. It contained the tax-offset provision that allowed employers to deduct their contributions under state unemployment insurance. The effectiveness of this approach in securing state action is confirmed by the fact that within less than two years every state had an unemployment insurance law.

Let us examine for a moment the ideas and attitudes that finally helped to bring about unemployment insurance. The Ohio Unemployment Insurance Commission summed up widely shared sentiments when it declared that:

> . . . the lack of a state-wide system of unemployment insurance is a dangerous menace to the safety of the state, to the solvency of public treasuries, to the integrity of family life for thousands of our citizens, to the physical and moral welfare of the children of these families, and to that spirit of independence, initiative, self-reliance and self-support that the people of this country have rightly regarded as the essence of Americanism.[80]

---

[78] Douglas, *Social Security in the United States,* p. 21. Schlesinger does not mention the Inheritance Tax Act and argues instead that the tax-offset provision was "an ingenious plan invented by Brandeis." See *The Coming of the New Deal,* p. 302.

[79] Some of his critics argued that he did not wish to push a major reform that did not originate with him.

[80] George H. Trafton, "America Moves Toward Compulsory Unemployment Reserves," *American Labor Legislation Review,* Vol. XXII, No. 3 (September 1932), p. 129.

A prominent religious leader noted that "the fear of joblessness is dreadfully demoralizing. It robs a man of that sense of security and stability upon which alone permanent character values can be built."[81] An interesting theme emerges from these statements: the lack of social protection was destroying the foundations of individualism. For years, social income protection had been attacked as destructive of individualistic virtues, but now it seemed that the lack of systematic protection was an even greater menace.

Another important myth that was shattered by the depression had to do with the economic efficiency of systematic protection. One of the standard arguments against social insurance had been its high cost, both in terms of the direct outlays and in terms of the adverse effects on the willingness to work. The depression showed that the alternative to systematic unemployment insurance could not be simply a hands-off policy, as this argument implied, but had to be a policy of improvised relief measures to keep people from starving. It became obvious that these unavoidable measures were far more demoralizing and far more wasteful than unemployment insurance. They were extremely costly in terms of misused national resources. Given the political setting, unemployment insurance was in fact a more rational approach, even from a strictly economic point of view. Frances Perkins, Roosevelt's Secretary of Labor, expressed this idea when she observed that "the tendency to scoff at unemployment insurance is fast disappearing. It has been realized that the British unemployment system is far less costly to the public treasury, and far less demoralizing to the individual, than the system of public relief which we have been forced to adopt."[82] In a similar vein, Professor Witte commented in 1935: "Within the last two years realization has come to this country that what used to be called the British 'dole' is vastly superior to our own actual dole. The pendulum has swung over completely and unemployment insurance is now in high favor."[83]

If there was widespread agreement on the desirability of unemployment insurance, there were still major differences of opinion regarding the most desirable techniques. The disagreements were not merely technical. They involved the crucial question of how the burden of protection should be distributed. We learned earlier that the Lundeen plan followed the socialist tradition of simply putting the burden on the high income receivers. This was never seriously debated among social insurance experts. The main debate was over the so-called Wisconsin and Ohio plans. The debate was

[81] Abba Hillel Silver, "Our National Debt to the Unemployed," *American Labor Legislation Review*, Vol. XXI, No. 3 (September 1931), p. 313.
[82] F. Perkins, "On Our Way," *American Labor Legislation Review*, Vol. XXIV, No. 3 (September 1934), p. 108.
[83] E. E. Witte, "The Government and the Unemployed," *American Labor Legislation Review*, Vol. XXV, No. 1 (March 1935), p. 6.

historically meaningful, for the plans differed in the degree to which they sought to incorporate American individualistic ideals.

The essence of the Wisconsin plan was the direct link between the tax levied on an employer and the amount of unemployment for which he was held responsible. It was the extension to unemployment of the principle applied in workmen's compensation. The employer was required to build up a reserve fund, held by the state in his name, through a tax of 2 percent on payroll. Once the fund reached $55 per employee the tax dropped to 1 percent and, when the reserve rose to $75 per employee, there was no further contribution required. Notice that there was no contribution from employees or the state. The employer's liability was limited by the size of his reserve fund. When there was a danger of running out of funds, benefits were to be reduced accordingly. Normal weekly benefits were equal to 50 percent of the weekly wage, subject to a $10 maximum and a $5 minimum. These benefits were payable for a period depending on the length of previous employment, at the rate of 1 week of benefits for each 4 weeks of employment during the preceding 12 months.

The philosophy behind this plan was explained by Harold M. Groves, a professor of finance at the University of Wisconsin and a member of the state legislature. "We have been disposed," he said "to think of unemployment compensation as one of the conditions of a fair labor contract . . . unemployment should be regarded as one of the costs of doing business and necessary irregularity of production should enter into the price of goods."[84] Of course, to the extent that unemployment was preventable through managerial action, the employer was provided with a financial incentive. This was the aspect that was most appealing to Commons, who had helped to draft a similar plan in the early 1920s.[85] He had been emphasizing the preventive features of social insurance since his early experience with workmen's compensation. The appeal to employer self-interest was the feature that made the Wisconsin plan peculiarly American in his eyes. In European plans," he argued, "an employer furnishing 52 weeks of employment pays 52 premiums, and his premiums are turned into a common fund from which unemployment benefits are paid to the employees of his competitor who, perhaps, furnishes only 26 weeks' employment and pays only 26 premiums."[86] In the Wisconsin plan, by contrast, the employer paid only for *his* employees, and he who maintained employment the best paid the least per worker. Commons was aware of the fact that workers generally pre-

[84] Harold M. Groves, "Unemployment Compensation in Wisconsin," *American Labor Legislation Review*, Vol. XXIII, No. 3 (September 1933), p. 124.

[85] The Huber bills of the 1920s, which Commons had originally drafted, also related to the tax rate to employment stability, but they did not set up individual employer reserve accounts.

[86] John R. Commons, "The Groves Unemployment Reserves Law," *American Labor Legislation Review*, Vol. XXII, No. 1, (March 1932), p. 8.

ferred pooled state funds, because this offered a better guarantee that
benefits would be paid in full. "But the employers are most impressed by the
competitive psychology and do not want to turn over to their inefficient
competitors any funds just because their own efficiency gives longer employment to their own employees." [87] This attitude was certainly at variance
with the idea of social security as a method of mutual assistance and social
solidarity. It must be born in mind that Commons' ideal was to adapt
welfare institutions to what he considered the profit psychology of capitalism in order to simultaneously protect the worker and to improve the
efficiency of the economic system. "The main purpose," he declared, "is
unemployment prevention by offering the employer a profit to the extent
that he succeeds in preventing unemployment. *It is extraordinarily an individualistic and capitalistic scheme.*" [88] Another member of the "Wisconsin School,"
Professor Raushenbush, characterized the plan as "involving the least
change in private business consistent with the government's vital interest in
steadier employment and income for the great mass of its citizens." [89] This
was "individualism but enlightened and modified by social responsibility." [90]
In a real sense it was true conservatism.

It is obvious why this plan appealed to most of the people who
looked for a solution to unemployment insecurity that was "consistent with
American conditions." To the extent that unavoidable unemployment could
be related to the production of specific goods or services, the principle of the
plan represented sound welfare economics. Consumers theoretically should
bear the cost of the unavoidable unemployment. In a highly dynamic and
interdependent economy it was highly doubtful whether the cost of unemployment could be equitably distributed in this fashion. The Wisconsin plan
and the similar "American plan" proposed by the American Association for
Labor Legislation mainly obscured the social incidence of the burden of
unemployment insurance. Whether for this or other reasons, these plans
were recommended by the Interstate Commission on Unemployment Insurance, by the great majority of the individual state commissions, as well as by
the American Federation of Labor.[91] The unions were in favor of a system
that had no worker contribution. Employers generally liked the idea of no
state contribution, since it permitted more employer control.[92]

[87] *Ibid.*, p. 9.   [88] *Ibid.*, p. 9. (The author's italics).

[89] Paul A. Raushenbush, "Wisconsin's Unemployment Compensation Act," *American Labor
Legislation Review*, Vol. XXII, No. 1 (March 1932), p. 18.

[90] *Ibid.*, p. 18.

[91] "Growth of the Job Insurance Program," *American Labor Legislation Review*, Vol. XXIII, No. 3
(September 1933), pp. 153–154.

[92] For an interesting view as to why neither employees nor the state should contribute, see Roger
S. Hoar, "Who Should Bear the Cost of Unemployment Insurance?", *American Labor Legislation
Review*, Vol. XXIV, No. 4 (December 1934) pp. 153–154.

Alongside these widespread endorsements there was vocal opposition to the Wisconsin principle. Among its sharpest critics was the veteran social insurance advocate, Abraham Epstein, who characterized the Wisconsin and American plans as "essentially utopian and meaningless for practical purposes."[93] He thought it "almost incredible that professed friends of social insurance should still insist that the chief aim should be the stabilization of employment rather than security and relief for the unemployed."[94] For him a good social insurance theory demanded that the burden be distributed over all elements of society. His objections were to the low and somewhat uncertain benefit levels as well as to the distribution of the cost. Other prominent critics were Paul H. Douglas and Leo Wolman. Like Epstein, Professor Wolman argued that unemployment insurance "should be charged with providing benefits to the unemployed, and not be burdened with the formidable task of effecting fundamental reforms in our economic system."[95]

In contrast to the Wisconsin plan, which was based on explicit ideological premises, the Ohio plan was essentially pragmatic. Its backers aimed at protection of the worker as the primary objective. In the words of Rubinow, a member of the commission that drafted the Ohio bill, "unemployment insurance . . . has a specific social purpose, to relieve distress resulting from unemployment."[96] Whereas the Wisconsin law excluded state and employee contributions on theoretical and ideological grounds, the Ohio bill excluded state contributions and provided for employee contributions on practical political grounds. A major feature of the Ohio plan was the adoption of pooled funds on a statewide basis, rather than individual or industry reserve accounts. Here the idea of mutual assistance took precedence over the competitive ideology built into the Wisconsin plan. The principal advantage of the pool was the greater safety of benefits than that offered by individual reserve accounts, where benefits depended on solvency of the account. Actually, the Ohio bill also provided for differentiated payroll taxes based on company employment experience. The chief reason for this was not that its authors shared the Wisconsin faith in the possibility of employment stabilization, but the "popularity of the idea."[97]

[93]Abraham Epstein, "Enemies of Unemployment Insurance," *New Republic*, Vol. LXXVI (September 6, 1933), p. 94.

[94]*Ibid.*, p. 95.

[95]Leo Wolman, "Stabilization or Insurance," *Annals of the American Academy of Political and Social Science*, Vol. 165 (January 1933), p. 23.

[96]I. M. Rubinow, "Job Insurance—The Ohio Plan," *American Labor Legislation Review*, Vol. XXIII, No. 3 (September 1933), p. 131.

[97]*Ibid.*, p. 135.

THE ENACTMENT OF SOCIAL SECURITY

Before discussing the nature of the social security system that emerged in 1935, let us examine briefly the course of events leading to the Social Security Act. On entering the White House, Roosevelt was faced with the enormous tasks of immediate relief and recovery. Social insurance, which was not an emergency measure but a long-run reform, could not be given immediate attention. As pointed out previously, Roosevelt did not share the views of those who wanted to postpone reform until after recovery, but he hesitated to take immediate action. Many of the friends of social insurance became critical of him when he failed to give full support to the Dill–Connery and Wagner–Lewis bills. Those who worked with the President, however, have testified to his conviction that a piecemeal approach would be unsatisfactory and that a fairly well-rounded program had to be worked out first.

The first step in this direction was taken on June 8, 1934, when he sent his historic social security message to Congress. For the first time in history an American president declared publicly that the Constitution implied the right to individual economic security. "If, as our Constitution tells us," said Roosevelt, "our Federal Government was established among other things 'to promote the general welfare,' it is our plain duty to provide for that security upon which welfare depends."[98] Much like the Roosevelt who had preceded him in the White House, Franklin D. Roosevelt argued that his novel sounding proposals were not designed to change but to conserve traditional American values and virtues. "Our task of reconstruction does not require the creation of new and strange values. It is rather the finding of the way once more to known, but to some degree forgotten, ideals and values."[99] The message spelled out Roosevelt's basic principles of social insurance. He wanted a program that dealt simultaneously with the major sources of economic insecurity but "especially those which relate to unemployment and old age." No specific mention was made of health insurance. With regard to the distribution of the burden, he clearly favored payment by or on the direct behalf of beneficiaries instead of a reliance on general revenue. As he phrased it: "I believe that the funds necessary to provide this insurance should be raised by contributions rather than by an increase in taxation." He stressed also that the program had to be national in scope and based on federal–state cooperation.

Three weeks after this message went to Congress the President created the Committee on Economic Security and the Advisory Council on Economic Security. The committee, under the chairmanship of the Secretary of Labor, Frances Perkins, was ordered to report not later than December 1934 "its

[98] *Public Papers and Addresses*, Vol. III, p. 291.
[99] *Ibid.*, p. 288.

recommendations concerning proposals which in its judgment will promote greater economic security."[100] Professor Witte was appointed Executive Director of the Committee on Economic Security. On his shoulders fell the chief responsibility for preparing within a rather short period of time the proposals for a very complex piece of legislation.[101] Under Witte's guidance the committee drafted a social security plan that followed closely the principles laid down by the President. The final version of the committee's report was not delivered to the President until January 17, 1935, the day on which he sent it to Congress with a special message on social security.

The President's personal desire, as expressed to Secretary Perkins, was for a "cradle to grave" social insurance system. However, in his January message he stressed the danger of trying to do too much at once, which meant that he considered the proposed legislation merely a beginning toward a more comprehensive program. The legislation that he asked to be passed "with a minimum of delay" dealt with four areas: unemployment, old age, dependent children, and public health. With regard to unemployment insurance, his message deviated from the committee's report in the stress that it put on the need for a system that would induce private industry to stabilize employment. On old-age security the President went along with the committee's proposal for a three-layer system of protection: noncontributory pensions for those too old to build their annuities, a basic system of compulsory annuities, and a supplementary system of voluntary state annuities. Aid to dependent children and public health assistance were to be in the form of federal grants to the states. The President observed that he was not recommending health insurance "at this time" but that the subject was still under study. In general, he strongly stressed again the desirability of a system that was self-supporting through contributions. There was no hint of any desire to use social security as a means of income redistribution from rich to poor. It was to be a means that would enable workers to look out for themselves and their fellow workers, not a vehicle for reducing economic inequality among social classes, or for increasing the responsibility of the rich for the poor.

There is no need here to retrace the sinuous path of these proposals through Congress, since excellent first-hand accounts by participants are available.[102] The Social Security Act, which Roosevelt signed into law on

[100] *Public Papers and Addresses,* Vol. III, p. 321.
[101] For an interesting account of the drafting of the Social Security Act, see Edwin E. Witte, *The Development of the Social Security Act* (Madison: University of Wisconsin Press, 1962); also Arthur J. Altmeyer, *The Formative Years of Social Security* (Madison: University of Wisconsin Press, 1966).
[102] See Witte, *The Development of the Social Security Act*; Altmeyer, *The Formative Years of Social Security*; Douglas, *Social Security in the United States.*

August 14, 1935, followed in its essential provisions the recommendations of his January message. Nevertheless, several significant changes were made during the legislative process. The original proposal for a supplementary voluntary system of social insurance pensions was dropped, mainly on the argument that such a program would compete with private enterprise, even though private companies did not write comparable policies at the time.[103] On the plus side, a new program, aid to the blind through federal grants in aid to the states, was added on. There was a lively controversy within Congress over the desirability of exempting employers from the government old-age system if they were willing to substitute a more liberal private plan for their employees. Organized labor, which had shown little interest initially in the Social Security bill, perceived the danger of a proposal of this kind. The unions finally went to work to defeat the proposal and to help with the passage of the bill. The business community was still divided. The United States Chamber of Commerce favored the bill, but the National Association of Manufacturers and its branches in some of the leading industrial states expressed vociferous opposition.

Let us now examine the Social Security Act in the light of the ideas and attitudes about social protection that it reflected. Although, no doubt, it was a major step forward in the development of American social rights, it revealed also that there were still many hesitations and reservations. Certainly, the country and Congress was not ready for the "cradle to grave" protection, about which Roosevelt spoke, and there were many barriers to such a system in Roosevelt's own thinking. In spite of its multiple program character, the 1935 act fell far short of universality of coverage and comprehensiveness of insured risks. This was only partly due to legislative prudence, which counseled against trying to to do too much at once.

In any country, the principles adopted to include and exclude certain groups from coverage tend to reflect prevailing ideas about social equality. We recall that the original German system was designed to protect the manual working class in industry. Therefore, it excluded white collar workers. The American social security system never recognized this dinstinction of social status. In contrast to the common European concept of working-men's insurance, the guiding American idea was that of insurance for the citizen, regardless of social status or level of income. The major groups excluded from both old-age pensions and unemployment insurance were farm and domestic employees, casual workers, employees of nonprofit organizations, and the self-employed.[104] In addition, unemployment insurance was restricted to individuals employed in establishments with 8 or more

[103] See R. J. Myers, "A Federal Voluntary Old Age Insurance System," *American Labor Legislation Review*, Vol. XXVII, No. 2 (September 1937), pp. 125–127.

[104] Government employees were excluded also, but most of them already had pension programs.

employees during 20 weeks in any given year. The chief reasons for these exclusions were technical, usually administrative, or constitutional complications. However, in the background there were also ideological considerations. When Altmeyer, the Chairman of the Social Security Board, urged the inclusion of farm workers in 1939, the Chairman of the House Ways and Means Committee told him: "Doctor, when the first farmer with manure on his shoes comes to me and asks to be covered, I will be willing to consider it." [105] Similar attitudes prevailed with regard to the self-employed, especially the professional groups.

Although the American Social Security Act never formally recognized a status hierarchy among citizens, it left the door open to many inequalities of protection, especially as between the residents of different states. Until the 1930s social insurance thinking had been mainly in terms of state rather than federal action. The size of the country, differences in standards of living, sectional interests, and a heterogeneous population militated against uniformity in protection. For political, constitutional, and sometimes administrative reasons, considerable discretion had to be left to individual states to determine the social rights of American citizens. Only with regard to old-age contributory pensions did the Social Security Act create a uniform national program. This was dictated by the long-term vested interests of such a program and the high mobility of the population. In the case of unemployment insurance and public assistance programs, Congress refused even the establishment of minimum levels of benefits.

The public assistance programs of the Social Security Act (assistance to aged and blind persons and to dependent children) made the need of the recipient a condition of benefit receipt, but Congress did not define "need." The states consequently varied widely in their definition of need and in the measures taken to establish its existence. There have been wide variations in the extent to which the resources of relatives or fixed assets are taken into consideration in establishing need. In this manner, inequalities in social rights were brought about within as well as between states. It is interesting to observe that the original draft of the act had specified that state old-age pension programs must as a minimum assure "a reasonable subsistence compatible with decency and health." This requirement was virtually eliminated by the House Ways and Means Committee when it specified that the requirement had to be met only as far as practicable under the conditions of a given state. In the Senate Finance Committee all references to minimum standards compatible with health and decency were eliminated. "One reasons for this change," Douglas noted, "was the fear on the part of many Southern Senators and Representatives that the earlier provision might . . . compel the Southern states to pay higher pensions to aged Negroes than

[105] Altmeyer, *The Formative Years of Social Security*, p. 103.

the dominant white groups believed to be desirable."[106] This is a pointed illustration of the manner in which social inequality within a country may be a barrier to equal and sometimes adequate social protection.

In the case of unemployment insurance, inequality and inadequacy of protection were natural consequences of incompatible structural objectives of the program. The Social Security Act did not directly set up an unemployment insurance system. It provided for a federal payroll tax and for related rules and standards that were designed to induce the individual states to establish unemployment insurance programs. The federal tax incorporated the offset provision discussed earlier with reference to the Wagner-Lewis bill. This arrangement was consistent with Roosevelt's desire for a pluralistic federal–state cooperative system. The act accommodated also Roosevelt's wish to use unemployment insurance for stabilization purposes. To do this, the federal law allowed lower taxes to be levied on employers who succeeded in stabilizing employment.[107] The states were left free to take advantage of this feature. All but a few immediately adopted the "merit-rating" system, under which the tax rate was based on the employment record.[108] The handling of reserves varied widely from single-employer accounts to statewide pools, including combinations of these two arrangements.

From the point of view of protecting the social rights of the workers, competing merit rating systems inevitably had unfortunate consequences. The lawmakers failed to appreciate fully the paradoxical situation that they were creating. On the one hand, they tried to prevent interstate competition by passing a federal law but, on the other hand, they restored competition by allowing individual states to determine the effective rates of taxation. It mattered little that this freedom was left to the states for the purpose of creating stabilization incentives. Under the pressure of competition from other states, it became extremely difficult to resist the demands for lower taxes within any given state. The result was a serious weakening of unemployment insurance all over the country because of the lack of adequate resources. Thus, in the end, those who had opposed the individualistic trend in unemployment insurance thinking saw their fears come true. One way of preventing this from happening would have been through a minimum contribution rate imposed on all states. A recommendation to this effect had

[106] Douglas, *Social Security in the United States*, p. 100.

[107] Technically all covered employers had to pay a federal payroll tax of 3 percent. The law gave them credit for contributions paid into state unemployment insurance programs up to 90 percent of the amount they owed the federal government. In order to allow lower taxes for employers who stabilized employment the law had to give credit for contributions that were not paid.

[108] For a description of the early laws, see George Trafton, "State Unemployment Compensation Laws," *American Labor Legislation Review*, Vol. XXVII, No. 2 (June 1937), pp. 53–58.

been made by the President's Committee on Economic Security, but Congress refused to accept it.[109] The tradition of freedom of action once more defeated the purpose of collective protection.

Closely related to equality of protection is the concept of the right to protection. Both are indications of the kind of claim to protection a society acknowledges through its social security system. The limitations of this right can take many subtle forms, including the manipulation of benefits, the eligibility conditions, and the administrative procedures in order to enhance the power of those in authority.

The Social Security Act reflected the dominant American attitude that favored guaranteed individual rights. It is interesting to notice, however, that the strength of this guarantee and the means of legitimizing protection varied between different programs. In old-age insurance the right to benefits was from the beginning conceived to be of a quasi-contractual nature. An individual had title to benefits because he had *earned* them. We shall return later to the implications of this manner of legitimizing protection. Unemployment benefits were on a weaker ideological foundation. They were legitimized as a form of compensation for income losses involuntarily sustained by the worker. The weakness of the economic system, not the effort of the individual, legitimized the benefits. Therefore, there was no need to insist on worker contributions nor to stress the link between contributions and benefits.[110] In fact, this form of legitimization made worker contributions seem to be unwarranted. A worker earned his benefits by being an active member of the work force, which meant that the state laws had to include a test for his attachment to the work force.

Public assistance was still justified, as it had been in the past, on what was essentially the principle of social solidarity, or the common good. Its financing was, therefore, from general revenue. By dramatizing the fact that individuals often became dependent without any fault of their own, the depression had strengthened the country's sense of social solidarity. This change in attitude contributed to a strengthening of the right to public assistance. To induce the development of a nationwide system of old-age assistance, the Social Security Act offered a financial inducement to the states by reimbursing them for one half of their expenditures, subject to a maximum of $15 per person per month. The act established certain minimum standards that state laws had to meet in order to be eligible for federal

[109] Altmeyer, *The Formative Years of Social Security*, p. 86.
[110] A number of the early state unemployment compensation laws provided for employee contributions. However, the Republican presidential campaign of 1936 turned public opinion against worker contribution by insisting that social insurance was a "pay-envelope fraud." Several states repealed worker contributions as a consequence. Very few states later enacted worker contributions.

subsidies. Until then, most state old-age assistance laws were optional with individual counties and often made available only under humiliating circumstances. "The Social Security Act," as Altmeyer rightly stresses, "really represented a radical change in the character of these laws. Not only did it require that they be in effect throughout the state, but it also required that assistance must be in the form of money payments and that individuals whose claims had been denied must be given a fair hearing."[111] These requirements illustrate the contrast between the new conception of the citizen's social rights, as incorporated in the Social Security Act, and the old conception of the right to relief that was implicit in the poor laws.

Although the entrance of the federal government into the welfare field greatly strengthened social rights, it also engendered pressures to limit the scope of federal action. In America the issue of federal control became a screen for the resistance of the business community to the extension of social rights. We learned earlier that this resistance prevented the establishment of minimum benefit standards. It hindered also the establishment of adequate administrative standards in old-age assistance. Congress specifically denied the Social Security Board control over the selection, compensation, and tenure of the personnel of the state assistance agencies. An unfortunate consequence of this restriction was the insinuation of local political considerations in the appointment of personnel and the award of benefits. The Social Security Board made serious efforts to eliminate abuses which lessened administrative efficiency and impaired the social rights of the American citizen. Its most notable battle was against political interests in Ohio, which were the worst offenders.[112]

In unemployment insurance the safeguards of the right to protection depend heavily on the interpretation of certain eligibility conditions. To preserve labor discipline and the willingness to work, benefits must be limited to involuntarily unemployed persons who are available, able, and willing to work. Does willingness to work imply that a man has to accept any job offered regardless of working conditions and rate of pay? Clearly, a rigid interpretation of this requirement could easily eliminate almost any kind of protection.

This was an area where common standards were necessary. Under the standards established by the Social Security Act an otherwise eligible worker did not lose his right to benefits if he refused work under the following conditions: (1) if the position offered was vacant because of an industrial dispute; (2) if wages, hours, and working conditions were substantially less favorable than the ones prevailing in the community for similar work; and

[111] Altmeyer, *The Formative Years of Social Security*, p. 58.
[112] *Ibid.*, pp. 75 ff.

(3) if the job required joining a company union or resigning or refraining from joining a bona fide labor organization.

The social and economic objectives of these standards are evident and significant. Although their purpose was to maintain neutrality in disputes between workers and employers, they also favored independent unions. Nothing was said about protecting a worker from having to join a bona fide trade union as a condition of employment. Logically, the standards were one-sided, but they were consistent with prevailing views on labor policy. Another objective was to prevent unemployment insurance from becoming a means to depress wages and working conditions. In addition to the federal standards, the state laws protected individual rights through definitions of involuntary employment and suitable work. The latter definition was necessary in order to protect individuals from having to accept jobs far below their skills. These standards and their application have varied over time and between states, but their general objectives have been the safeguarding of the individual's rights of protection and of the community's welfare against abuse by individuals. It has never been the policy to use unemployment insurance as an instrument of industrial discipline. This is in sharp contrast to the objectives of Soviet social insurance in the 1930s.

Let us now examine the old-age insurance program. This was the most far-reaching measure of the Social Security Act, but ironically there was little popular demand for it, in contrast to the popularity of noncontributory old-age pensions. "Congress," Witte explained. "acted on its own judgment rather than in response to an overwhelming public demand." [113] In fact, it was mainly at the insistence of President Roosevelt that the old-age insurance provisions were kept in the Social Security bill when opposition developed in the House Ways and Means Committee. [114] Since his days as Governor of New York, Roosevelt had argued that old-age assistance alone would be unsuitable. He considered compulsory old-age insurance the most important part of the entire bill, but this was also the part that encountered the most resistance within the House and Senate Committees. This is not surprising, since it meant imposing a system of compulsory insurance on millions of free citizens, regardless of their individual needs. [115] On the other hand, the studies prepared by the staff of the Committee on Economic Security could not fail but to impress Congress with the growing economic

[113] E. E. Witte, "Are Old Age Pensions Worth their Cost?", *American Labor Legislation Review*, Vol. XXVI, No. 1 (March 1936), p. 9.

[114] Witte, *The Development of the Social Security Act*, pp. 94–95.

[115] It may be relevant to point out here that American workers had been much less inclined than European workers to develop voluntary insurance through friendly societies. The step to social insurance was thus greater in this country than in Europe. See Karl Pribram, "Social Insurance in Europe and Social Security in the United States," *International Labor Review*, Vol. XXXVI, No. 6 (December 1937), pp. 742 ff.

burden of old-age dependency.[116] Realistic alternatives had to include an increasing social responsibility in meeting this burden.

Congress could be expected to have a natural affinity for forms of protection that were reasonably consistent with the dominant values of self-help and of rewards related to individual effort. The proposals worked out by the Committee on Economic Security met these requirements. A staff member of the Committee, Professor J. Douglas Brown, explained: "We wanted our government to provide a mechanism whereby the individual could prevent dependency through his own efforts."[117] This was a shrewd formula, for it covered the inevitable element of social compulsion with a veneer of individualism. The central idea, pointed out earlier, was that the individual would earn his benefits and in this manner establish his rights as a beneficiary on a quasi-contractual basis. Frances Perkins, the Secretary of Labor and and Chairman of the Committee on Economic Security, proclaimed that protection was to be afforded "as a matter of contractual right."[118] The emphasis on contractual rights was of strategic significance: in an individualistic society the individual was not to be left dependent on the benevolence of the ruling powers.

In their testimony before congressional committees the staff members of the Committee on Economic Security observed that they had studied European social insurance models but that the measures they were proposing deviated from European practice where it seemed "appropriate to our background and present situation."[119] In England, contributory old-age pensions had evolved as an outgrowth of noncontributory old-age assistance, which in turn had been a modification of relief under the poor laws. In this evolution the focus had remained on social needs, and they in turn governed the character of the protective measures. The English reliance on flat benefits must be viewed in this light. In America, on the other hand, old-age insurance marked a completely new departure, not an emendation of old-age assistance.[120] Its model was private insurance or, more precisely, the industrial pensions that the more progressive corporations had established for their workers.

[116] See Testimony by Murray Latimer in *Hearings Before the Committee on Ways and Means on H. R. 4120*, United States House of Representatives, 74th Congress, 1st Session, Washington, D.C., 1935.

[117] J. Douglas Brown, "The American Philosophy of Social Insurance," *Social Service Review*, Vol. XXX, No. 1 (March 1956), p. 3.

[118] She actually made this statement with reference to unemployment insurance but it applied with more validity to old-age insurance. See *Security* (pamphlet published by the Committee on Economic Security, Washington, D.C., December 1934), p. 6.

[119] *Hearings before the Committee on Ways and Means on H.R. 4120*, January 21, 1935.

[120] An Analysis along these lines is found in J. D. Brown, "British Precedent and American Old Age Insurance," *American Labor Legislation Review*, Vol. XXVII, No. 1 (March 1937), pp. 18-23.

This orientation was characterized by an undue concern with contractual means, as opposed to an emphasis on social ends, which was a way of putting the cart before the horse. Before the House Ways and Means Committee, Brown argued that worker contributions were desirable because "by contributing the individual worker established an earned contractual right to his annuity through his own thrift."[121] He mentioned also that worker contributions encouraged "the development of an adequate system of retirement annuities independent of employer control."[122] It is interesting to note that justification of employer contributions avoided any reference to the paternalistic duty of the employer to look after the welfare of his workers. It stressed instead that the employer's contribution was an "automatic method of meeting the depreciation charges on the human factor cooperating in production similar to the usual accounting charges for depreciation of plant and equipment."[123] This is strikingly consistent with the proposition that the worker earns his benefits as a *factor of production* and contrasts with the view that the worker deserves protection because he is economically weak and occupies a dependent position in the organization of society. Once again, we notice how social income protection is being shaped by market-oriented values.

The Social Security Act provided for equal employer- and worker-contributions to old-age insurance. The original bill drafted by the Committee on Economic Security had envisaged government contributions, but President Roosevelt insisted that the plan must be self-supporting. There was to be no taxing of wealth for the maintenance of worker incomes. Brown explained to the Ways and Means Committee that government contributions would be appropriate because for many years the plan would pay much larger annuities than would be paid for by the first generation of recipients. This arrangement was necessary to avoid postponing far into the future the date when benefits would begin to be adequate. The shortened maturation of old-age insurance was clearly in the public interest, but Congress was no more inclined than the President to meet any of the expenses involved from public revenue.

The emphasis on "contractual" over "social" rights had mainly ideological instead of legal significance, but this ideological dimension was by no means irrelevant. Beside introducing a bias in favor of contributory financing, it put the accent on equity among beneficiaries, which required that benefits be differentiated according to contributions. But the framers of the plan were well aware that the social purposes of old-age insurance could

---

[121] *Hearings . . . on H.R. 4120,* p. 241.
[122] *Ibid.,* p. 241.
[123] *Ibid.,* p. 241.

not be achieved through strict adherence to contractual equity principles.[124] It was impossible to meet basic social needs without some redistribution of income. Under the adopted method of financing, this redistribution was mainly from one low-income group to another, and the gainers were not necessarily poorer than the losers.

This result becomes obvious in a brief examination of the benefit formula. First, we must observe that an upper limit was imposed on taxable wages. This limit was $3000 a year from a single employee.[125] Benefits were based on aggregate lifetime taxable earnings. Monthly benefits were equal to $\frac{1}{2}$ per cent of the first $3000 of aggregate earnings, plus $\frac{1}{12}$ percent of the next $42,000, plus $\frac{1}{24}$ percent of the next $84,000. The average wage in 1935 in nonfarm employment was about $100 a month.[126] The benefit formula enabled a man earning $100 a month to retire with a pension equal to slightly more than 50 percent of his monthly wage ($51.25 to be exact) when he reached the legal retirement age of 65 and had 40 years in covered employment at the same wage. A pension of 50 percent of wages was the level that had been introduced by the more progressive corporations in their industrial pension plans. Interestingly, it was this standard that influenced the thinking of the staff of the Committee on Economic Security.[127]

The formula was a compromise between the principles of equity and adequacy. It clearly favored the lower income groups and those who retired in the early years of the program. However, with a minimum monthly benefit of $10 and a maximum of $85, there could be no doubt about the planners' desire to maintain an incentive differential. By making benefits dependent on total taxable earnings, the benefit level in part reflected the length of work in covered employment. But diminishing returns were built into longer employment. An individual earning the maximum taxable wage would build up credits for a monthly pension of $15 during his first year of work. During his next 14 years he would add only $2.50 each year to his monthly pension, and during the following 28 years he would add only $1.25 to his monthly pension for each year of work. The depression mentality, which was concerned with clearing the labor market of older workers, seemed to counteract the desire to keep benefits proportional to earnings. The same mentality was also a factor in making actual retirement a condition of benefit receipt.

[124]The classic discussion of the question of equity versus adequacy is in Reinhard A. Hohaus, "Equity, Adequacy, and Related Factors in Old Age Security," *The Record* (June 1938). Reprinted in William Haber and Wilbur J. Cohen (eds.), *Social Security* (Homewood, Ill.: Irwin, 1960).

[125]In 1938, 97.1 percent of all covered workers had earnings below the specified maximum. See Michael Resnick, "Annual Earnings and the Taxable Maximum for OASDHI," *Social Security Bulletin*, Vol. XXIX, No. 11 (November 1966), p. 40.

[126]Stanley Lebergott, *Manpower in Economic Growth* (New York: McGraw-Hill, 1964), p. 524.

[127]Brown, "British Precedent and American Old Age Insurance," p. 21.

It should be pointed out that the minimum monthly benefit was not automatic for covered workers who reached retirement age. Those who had earned less than the $2000 in aggregative wages needed for a $10 monthly pension were entitled to a lump sum equal to 3.5 percent of their taxable wages. The minimum pension was thus a matter of administrative convenience instead of an attempt to establish a minimum level of protection. In the lump sum provision, which was akin to a savings withdrawal, we again are made aware of the individualistic, contractual line of thought. But the weakness of the plan's social concern was most pronounced in its failure to take into account the family responsibilities of the workers. The law provided nothing for a pensioned worker's wife or other dependents. Nor were there any insurance benefits for widows and orphans. These shortcomings can be traced to the values of a society that idealized the cash nexus, but the needs that were thereby left unmet could not be ignored idefinitely, although this meant further compromises of the contractual ideal.

AMERICAN SOCIAL SECURITY DEVELOPMENTS AFTER 1935

One of the central themes of this chapter has been the historical conflict between the need for socially assured income protection and the dominant individualistic values of American society. For a long time the balance of forces in this conflict delayed the enactment of a general social security system. It took an economic crisis that called into question the principles of the existing order to shift this balance enough for a victory of the forces seeking social income assurances. Success was only partial—since it still allowed only an inadequate system of protection—but there is no question but that this partial success was a major achievement. A major shift in public attitude was brought about; a broad public demand for social income protection was created, and those in political control had come to accept the idea of a fundamental federal responsibility in this area. This section reviews the major developments since the passage of the Social Security Act. The most important overall trend has been the improvement of the systems' adequacy through the increase of benefits, the expansion of coverage, and the extension to new risks. These advances have not been spread uniformly. The most important ones came in the late 1930s, the early 1950s, and the mid-1960s.

Its history since 1935 demonstrates that once social security was accepted in principle, the forces favoring improvements and extensions had a decided advantage. Interestingly enough, part of this advantage is derived from the technical nature of social security, which necessitates a professional staff of technicians. The very existence of a staff of technical experts provides a built-in mechanism for the expansion of the system, unless the experts are demonstrably incompetent in doing their job. Otherwise, the experts have a decided advantage over outsiders, first in establishing the country's specific needs for income protection, and second in making the technical calculations that show how these needs can be met. These functions have been carried out very successfully by the technical staff of the Social Security Administration, and over the years the Social Security Board has played a very active role in promoting the development of the system through studies and proposals prepared for the President and Congress.[128] The expansion of the programs has been facilitated also by the periodic creation of Social Security Advisory Councils made up of prominent citizens who represent the public, labor, and employers.[129] These councils have made recommendations on all the major social security changes.

Regarding the dynamics of social security expansion, it can be observed also that the expansion of a system is easier than its initial creation because of the weaker ideological position of the opponents. Ideological opposition usually relies on broad, exaggerated generalities about adverse anticipated consequences. Once a system is successfully in operation, these generalities lose their force, even though their ring may remain familiar. Experience has shown, however, that effective resistance to change can be organized when substantial material interests are involved, especially if they are the interests of a well-organized group. The fierce opposition of organized medicine to public health insurance is a case in point. We shall return to this topic later.

The first improvement of the Social Security Act took place in 1939. The amendments of that year were of major significance, since they set a new and broader pattern for American social security. Faced by the need to make the system more socially adequate, the social security planners seized on the concept of "family protection." They found in this concept a welcome means of stretching the original idea of individually earned benefits by extending it to the members of the earner's family. In this manner, social needs could be met with a minimum of ideological conflict with individualistic principles. The emphasis in this approach was on the solidarity of the family, instead of on the solidarity of the nation, which is implied in the universal system of protection advocated by the Beveridge plan.[130] The original old-age pensions were little more than a compulsory annuity program, paying only personal annuities to former contributors. Under the 1939 amendments, the contributor's aged wife, widow, and parents, and his children under 18 became entitled to monthly benefits. The cost of the new benefits

[128] See Altmeyer, *The Formative Years of Social Security, passim.*
[129] Since 1935, five Advisory Councils have been established, namely in 1938, 1948, 1953, 1957, and 1963. Under current legislation, a council is to be established every fifth year.
[130] In one case a person becomes entitled to benefits as a member of a family and in the other case as a citizen.

was partly financed by the abolition of conceivably large lump-sum death benefits (3.5 percent of covered wages) payable to the estate of a deceased participant under the 1935 act. Although some Congressmen denounced this move as "confiscation," the general sentiment was for paying benefits to dependent survivors, who were presumed to be in need, rather than lump-sums to individual estates for the sake of contractual equity.

Two other important changes introduced in 1939 were in the same spirit. One involved the method of computing benefits and the other concerned eligibility. Originally benefits were calculated on the basis of *accumulated* covered earnings, which then meant accumulated contributions. Now benefits were related to *average* covered earnings, which had the effect of considerably weakening the link between benefits and contributions. A weak gesture toward maintaining the link between work and benefits was a new provision under which benefits were increased by 1 percent for each year in which the individual was credited with at least $200 in wages. The changes in eligibility requirements involved a shift from a formula based on total accumulated wages to one based on quarters of coverage. Under the 1935 formula, eligibility required cumulative wage credits of at least $2000 and some employment in each of five years. Under the new formula, a worker reaching age 65 could be eligible if he had as little as 18 months in covered employment. Actually, the system had not yet begun to make payments and was not scheduled to do so until 1942, a delay that reflected the original philosophy of cumulative credits. The 1939 act, however, moved up the date for beginning payments to January 1, 1940, an arrangement that was facilitated by the new benefit and eligibility formulae.

The broadening of benefits and the relaxing of eligibility conditions inevitably increased the extent of income redistribution among participants under the existing method of strict contributory financing. For instance, individuals without families, in effect, were forced to contribute to the support of dependents of fellow beneficiaries. In this respect, the new benefits represented a significant departure from the individualistic ideal of equivalent benefits for equal contributions. The abstract principle of individual equity simply had to give way to the practical requirements of social adequacy. This pragmatic solution did not mean, however, that the ideal of a contributory contractual system was no longer honored. On the contrary, both the ideal and its "violations" have remained key features, as well as a source of tension, in American social security.[131] In justifying this situation,

---

[131] Perhaps a more desirable compromise might have been to weaken the contributory feature and to maintain stricter equity through partial financing from general revenue. This solution has never been accepted by Congress, even though it has been repeatedly suggested by Advisory Councils, including the 1938 Council. Clearly, Congress is more readily moved by fiscal considerations than by abstract principles.

spokesmen for the system have always argued that the pattern established in 1939 does not violate the principle of individual equity. After pointing out that the introduction of dependents' benefits implied "some reduction in the eventual rates of benefits payable to individuals as single annuitants," the 1938 Advisory Council went on to state:

> Not only does such a readjustment of the benefit structure seem socially desirable but such an adjustment can and should be made without doing violence to the principle of individual equity in the case of widowers, bachelors, and women workers, since such persons should receive in all cases insurance protection at least equal in value to their *individual direct contributions* invested at interest.[132]

The council's argument that individual equity is not violated as long as the individual gets the actuarial value of only his own contributions has serious weaknesses. It flatly assumes that the employer's contribution is not earned by the worker and that the worker has no claim to it. It is very difficult to prove that in the absence of employer contributions wages would be higher, but theoretical considerations lead most economists to conclude that at least part of the employer's contribution is shifted back onto the worker in the form of lower wages. To this extent the workers have earned the contribution by having foregone wages. Moreover, the idea that the worker has a claim to the contribution made by his employer has been one of the major historic arguments justifying these contributions. It will be recalled that Professor J. Douglas Brown argued in 1935 that employer contributions were "an automatic method of meeting the depreciation on the human factor."[133] It would seem that there was a fundamental inconsistency between this view and the position of the 1938 Advisory Council, of which Brown was chairman. Inconsistencies of this kind, however, are the rule instead of the exception whenever theoretical principles are brought to bear on complex phenomena such as social security legislation.

Although the compromise between individual equity and social adequacy established in 1939 has remained the pattern for American social security, there have been repeated attempts to upset it from both the right and the left. A major objective of the compromise was, of course, the safeguarding of the contributory contractual system. Aside from its ideological appeal, this system had the significant advantage of removing the financing of benefits from annual congressional appropriations. Perhaps its chief weakness was that it provided "unearned" benefits for some members of the

---

[132]United States Advisory Council on Social Security, *Final Report, December 10, 1939* (76th Congress, 1st Session, Senate Document No. 4, Washington D.C.: Government Printing Office, 1939). (The Author's italics.)

[133]See above, p. 230.

community, but excluded others who may have been more needy but were not "covered."[134] Such a paradox surely made it inevitable that the contributory contractual approach should periodically come under attack. In 1940, Paul V. McNutt, the recently appointed Federal Security Administrator,[135] indicated his support to congressional leaders who sought to replace the contributory system by flat rate, egalitarian pensions financed from general revenue. Again the following year, a Senate committee suggested equal pensions for all, financed half and half by payroll taxes and general revenue. After World War II these proposals came up time and again, usually inspired by the hope of limiting the total level of expenditure. One of the more radical proposals received the unanimous endorsement of the members of the United States Chamber of Commerce in 1952, just at the time when the first Republican Administration came to power since the enactment of the Social Security Act. The chamber's "blanketing-in" proposal sought to abolish the old-age assistance programs and to bring all the aged under a minimum uniform old-age pension financed through payroll taxes. This plan would have restricted total expenditure and would have lessened the tax burden on property owners and higher income receivers. It represented a substantially different distribution of benefits and burdens from that embedded in the existing system. Understandably, organized labor strongly objected to the plan and is given major credit for preventing its adoption.

Attacks on the system's fundamental principle continued in subsequent years, but in the meantime substantial improvements consolidated the old pattern. After a long period, from 1939 to 1950, during which no significant changes were made, the social security system had fallen far behind the rises in incomes and prices. By the late 1940s the inadequacies of American social security had become all too obvious, which left it vulnerable to attack. An advisory council, appointed in September 1947, stated the major deficiencies of the OASI program as follows:

1. Inadequate coverage—only about three out of every five jobs are covered by the program.

2. Unduly restrictive eligibility requirements for older workers—largely because of these restrictions, only about 20 percent of those aged 65 or over are either insured or receiving benefits under the program.

---

[134]The indigent aged, of course, were eligible for old-age assistance, but this required submitting to a detestable needs test.

[135]Altmeyer, *The Formative Years of Social Security*, pp. 122 ff. The new Federal Security Agency set up in 1939 combined a number of existing agencies, including the Social Security Board, United States Employment Service, United States Public Health Service, Civilian Conservation Corps, National Youth Administration, and the United States Office of Education.

3. Inadequate benefits—retirement benefits at the end of 1947 averaged $25 a month for a single person.[136]

These shortcomings were evidence of the fact that, as yet, the system had not established itself as an effective measure of old-age security. A turning point had been reached where the contributory system would have to become substantially more effective or would have to yield to the attacks of the advocates of universal flat pensions.

The main steps to make old-age and survivors' insurance available to a larger proportion of the country's citizens were taken in 1950 and 1954. Through the amendments of those two years, approximately 20 million additional workers became eligible for coverage. Later amendments added additional groups, but the limits of coverage extension had almost been reached. The percent of covered employed work force rose from 64.5 in 1949 to 89.9 in 1955. The main groups that were added to the system were the self-employed, regularly employed farm and domestic workers, the employees of nonprofit institutions, and some government employees. The largest group remaining uncovered were government employees who, for the most part, were covered under separate public programs. Thus by the mid-1950s, nearly all employed persons had become eligible for old-age and survivorship coverage. In the other major branches of social insurance, unemployment and workmen's compensation, coverage has never reached this nearly universal level.

Significant improvements were also enacted in 1950 to make it easier for individuals to qualify for benefits under OASI. A provision was adopted under which a person qualified for benefits if he was covered at least one half the calendar quarters after 1950, subject to a minimum of six quarters of coverage. This meant that, in effect, the starting date of the system was moved from 1936 to 1950. In computing the average wage for benefit determination, the earnings before 1950 could be disregarded. These provisions were necessary for the new entrants, but they tended to raise also benefits for those already covered because earlier low earning years could be disregarded. The total effect of the 1950 amendments was to raise benefit levels by about 80 percent, which roughly restored the benefits' purchasing power of 1940 but took no account of the substantial rise in real earnings that had occurred. There was no indication that Congress was inclined to let the aged share in the rising real income at that time. Since 1950, however, this attitude has changed. Benefits have been adjusted more frequently, and they have roughly kept up with the increase in the country's per capita

---

[136] United States Advisory Council on Social Security, *A Report to the Senate Committee on Finance* (80th Congress, 2nd Session, Senate Document No. 149; Washington, D.C.: Government Printing Office, 1948), p. 2.

disposable income. Between 1950 and 1966 the average monthly benefit of a retired worker rose from $43.86 to $84.35, although annual per capita disposable income increased from $1364 to $2567.[137] The aged, as is indicated, have roughly maintained their relative income position, but this leaves open the question of the adequacy of benefit levels throughout the period. Indeed, in 1966 the average monthly benefit of a retired worker was still less than 20 percent of the average monthly wage in manufacturing. Similarly, in unemployment insurance, benefit levels were only slightly more than one third of average manufacturing wages. Although it may be difficult to state precisely what percentage of wages is required for adequacy, it is easy to make a strong case that benefits below 50 percent of previous earnings, especially in unemployment insurance, are seriously inadequate.[138]

The discussion of developments since 1935 has concentrated thus far mainly on the major improvements that have taken place in old-age and survivors' insurance. Improvements have taken place also in unemployment and workmen's compensation and in public assistance, but there have been no major policy changes in these areas. The most important developments, besides the ones that have been pointed out thus far, have been the extension of social insurance into the areas of permanent disability and health insurance, which were major advances toward making American social security a comprehensive system. The only common benefit still left out completely today is family allowances. Cash sickness benefits in case of temporary disability are available only in four states and for railroad workers.

Loss of income due to disability has never attracted the broad support that is generated by the needs of the aged. This is no doubt related to the fact that disabled persons are not easily organized into an effective pressure group. But there also has been the inhibiting effect of the actual and the anticipated resistance of organized medicine. The 1938 Advisory Council made an equivocal recommendation in which it expressed the social desirability of disability benefits but hedged on the appropriate timing of their introduction. The Social Security Board took a similar position at that time.[139] In subsequent years the board took a positive view and induced Presidents Roosevelt and Truman to strongly endorse the enactment of both disability and health insurance programs. The 1950 amendments presented an opportunity for those programs, but no action was taken other than the one of providing matching grants to the states for public assistance to the

[137] Social Security Bulletin, Vol. XXX, No. 5 (May 1967), Table M–11, p. 29; Economic Report of the President (90th Congress, 1st Session, House Document No. 28; Washington, D.C.: Government Printing Office, 1967), Table B–16, p. 232.

[138] For an excellent survey of developments in unemployment insurance, see Harry Malisoff, "The Challenge of Unemployment Insurance," Industrial and Labor Relations Review, Vol. XIV, No. 1 (October 1960), pp. 35–51.

[139] Altmeyer, The Formative Years of Social Security, p. 97.

permanently and totally disabled. Altmeyer notes that the chief reason for the exclusion of disability insurance was the opposition from organized medicine, employer organizations, and the casualty companies.[140] A spokesman for the American Medical Association warned that a federal disability program "would represent another step toward wholesale nationalization of medical care and the socialization of the practice of medicine."[141] The AMA even attacked as "socialized medicine" the so-called disability freeze enacted in 1954. This provision paid no benefits but allowed the maintenance of eligibility rights acquired before the onset of a disability.[142] The leaders of organized medicine were apprehensive of any public program that required the professional participation of doctors. By 1956, however, opposition was overcome and permanent disability benefits were provided for persons between the ages of 50 and 65 and for those over 18 who had been permanently disabled before reaching that age. In 1958 the benefits were extended to the dependents of disabled workers, and in 1960 the minimum age (50) for disability benefits was eliminated.

Resistance to state health insurance was far stronger than to disability insurance. This resistance merits a brief discussion because it has been an important factor in the shaping of American social security. We recall that early in the first drive to secure state health insurance in this country, in 1915, spokesmen for organized medicine temporarily supported the idea. Since then, however, the leaders of American medicine, and presumably the majority of doctors, have been in fierce opposition. No doubt their opposition was based on the threat they saw to the material interests of the profession. But material concern alone would be too simple an explanation. Any group in such a situation always tends to identify the interests of the group with the interests of society as a whole. Where this can be done successfully, many members of the group come to look on themselves as sincere defenders of the public interest against irresponsible or uninformed outsiders. To understand the attitude of the doctors we have to keep in mind that social security always involves the state in the relationships between individuals, between employer and employee, husband and wife, and parent and child. The relationship most affected by health insurance is the one between doctor and patient. This particular relationship, however, is one which doctors have traditionally insisted must be kept free from intrusion by third parties. Unfortunately, this idealized social relationship has become incompatible with the economics of modern medical care.

[140] *Ibid.*, p. 185.
[141] Quoted in *ibid.*, pp. 185–186.
[142] It meant also that in calculating the average wage for benefit purposes, the months of disability could be omitted in order to achieve a higher average wage and, consequently, higher benefits.

When the possibility of health insurance was considered in the early 1930s, the American Medical Association initiated a determined campaign against it. It informed its members that the House of Delegates had "instructed the Board of Trustees and the Officers of the American Medical Association to use *The Journal* and all the facilities of the Association in opposing the introduction of state medicine in any form." [143] In editorials the *Journal of the American Medical Association* lined up the physicians for battle, stressing the need for a united front and warning against expressing dissenting views. "Unless the medical profession speaks with one voice, the possibilities of successful opposition are threatened." Specialty societies were notified that "the majority of physicians of the United States prefer to express their views on economic, political and governmental questions through organized medicine," which meant the AMA leaders.[144] Individuals and groups who dissented publicly from these views were sharply rebuked. Although in some countries the class consciousness of the workers was an important factor in the development of social security, in America the professional status consciousness of physicians was used effectively to erect obstacles.

A central tenet of the doctrine advanced by the AMA was that the doctor–patient relationship was an integral part of medical care, which itself was strictly a matter of professional expertise. The role of the state was limited to preventing "quacks" from practicing and to providing public health facilities. The people should trust organized medicine to look after their personal health interests. An AMA policy statement contained the following statements:

> The primary considerations of the physicians constituting the American Medical Association are the welfare of the people, the preservation of their health and their care in sickness, the advancement of medical science, the improvement of medical care, and the provision of adequate medical service to all the people. These physicians are the only body in the United States qualified by experience and training to guide and suitably control plans for the provision of medical care.[145]

The physicians looked upon themselves as the self-appointed, exclusive guardians of the national interest as far as personal health care was concerned. They were incensed at the thought that laymen, especially social workers, were trying to enter this exclusive arena. Although calling on the people to have faith in the wisdom of the AMA the leaders of organized medicine derided state health insurance as "the apotheosis of paternalism."

---

[143] *Journal of the American Medical Association*, Vol. 102, No. 19 (May 12, 1934), p. 1611.

[144] *Ibid.*, Vol. 103, No. 2 (July 14, 1934), p. 112.

[145] *Ibid.*, Vol. 104, No. 8 (February 23, 1935), p. 652.

With an appeal to traditional American self-dependence, they noted that "if the American workman . . . cannot be trusted to provide himself and his family with adequate medical service, he must be a different American from those who brought our nation to its present high place among civilized peoples." [146]

The positive themes of the AMA's doctrine had their negative corollaries. The most consistent stress was on the disastrous effect of state health insurance on the quality of medical care. The lack of this insurance was always linked to the claim that the quality of American medical care was the highest in the world. The AMA produced reports on the negative aspects of the British and European experiences with public health insurance. The argument emphasized frequently was that public health insurance would destroy medicine as a profession and would be only the first step toward the socialization of the whole economy. In response to President Truman's 1949 message on compulsory health insurance, an editorial in the *JAMA* observed: "No doubt the most important objection to medicine socialized by nationalization of its control is the well established fact that the taking over of medicine is but the first step toward nationalization of every interest and activity of the nation." [147]

The arguments advanced during the 1930s were picked up with renewed vigor after World War II, when compulsory health insurance once more became an important policy issue. After the 1948 reelection of President Truman, the AMA took the unusual step of assessing each member $25 in order to build up a war chest for the battle against "socialized medicine." With these funds a public relations firm was hired to carry out a nationwide campaign. The purpose of the campaign, the *JAMA* explained, was a "nationwide plan of education on the progress of American medicine, the importance of the conservation of health and the advantages of the American system in securing a wide distribution of high quality of medical care." This massive effort, which centered on the presumed solicitude of American doctors for the health of the American people, was in itself a novel phenomenon in social security history. With the skilled assistance of advertising experts, the doctors effectively combined traditional appeals to individual freedom with an anxious concern for the health of the people. One of the important new themes stressed was the superiority of voluntary over compulsory insurance. "It has been demonstrated," the AMA leaders

---

[146] *Ibid.*, Vol. 104, No. 5 (February 2, 1935), p. 401. A lengthy discussion by a physician of the evils of social security, and medical insurance in particular, can be found in Edward H. Ochsner, *Social Security* (Chicago: Social Security Press, 1936). According to Dr. Ochsner, "Social Insurance is the hybrid offspring of impractical sentimentalism and political expediency.", p. 10

[147] *Ibid.*, Vol. 140, No. 1 (May 7, 1949), p. 111.

proclaimed, "that the voluntary method provides a better and less costly service and avoids the imposition of enormous taxation." In answer to a government report that claimed that approximately 70 million Americans could not afford the high cost of medical care, the AMA pointed out repeatedly how much people spent on liquor and tobacco. The suggestion was that if people lacked the money, it was because they had spent it foolishly.

A discussion in further detail about the campaign against compulsory health insurance would take us too far afield. We must mention, however, that organized medicine was by no means alone in this opposition. Many business leaders, particularly in the insurance industry, shared its views. Organized labor and the organizations of elderly citizens furnished the bulk of the advocates of state health insurance. Although private health insurance made enormous strides forward after World War II, it became increasingly evident that certain gaps would likely remain in its coverage. The aged were the most important uncovered group. They were also the group that had the highest medical expenses and were least able to afford them. To make matters worse, the cost of medical care, especially hospital care, kept rising at a rapid rate. This growing plight of the elderly could not continue to be ignored.[148]

Throughout the 1950s a number of bills were introduced to provide health care for the aged under social security. In addition, two alternative measures were advanced: one involved the establishment of a federal re-insurance plan to underwrite the activities of private insurance companies that covered high-risk groups like the elderly; the other was the expansion of medical benefits for the needy under public assistance. The common element in both alternatives was the limitation of government involvement and the lessening of the potential tax burden. As plans for health insurance under social security matured, the opponents increasingly stressed that this approach would be ruinously expensive and would lead to grave overburdening and abuse of medical resources. The reinsurance plan was abandoned before it was tried, but under the social security amendments of 1960 the assistance approach was given a test. The so-called Kerr-Mills program provided, for the first time, federal matching grants to the states to finance the medical care of older persons who could not afford medical care but were not otherwise eligible for public assistance. Additional funds also were made available in 1960 for the care of persons who were public assistance recipients.

This was still a highly unsatisfactory solution, since health care financing was not available as a matter of right but only on the basis of demonstrated need. From 1960 onward, health care for the aged as a matter of right, as all

[148] For a discussion of the problem, see Gaston V. Rimlinger, "Health Care for the Aged: Who Pays the Bill?", *Harvard Business Review*, Vol. 38, No. 1 (January–February 1963), pp. 108–116.

social insurance benefits, became a high-priority policy objective of the returned Democratic Administration. John F. Kennedy put considerable stress on this objective in his presidential campaign. After several years of public and congressional debate, and with the energetic support of President Johnson, Congress finally passed the Medicare program in 1965. This key program of the Johnsonian "Great Society" provides fairly comprehensive hospital, surgical, and medical care for virtually all persons aged 65 and over. This was the most significant change in the social security system since 1935, and it occurred almost exactly half a century after the early advocates of compulsory health insurance thought its enactment to be the "inevitable next step." What they had grossly underestimated was the extent to which widely shared individualistic values can delay social legislation if they are used adroitly by a well-organized group.

In some important respects, Medicare reflects the long struggle between individualistic and collective interests. Only the hospital insurance part of the program is compulsory and is prepaid through social insurance. The insurance for physician services is on a voluntary but state-subsidized basis with guarantees of the freedom of choice of physician for the patient. Private insurance companies were given an opportunity to participate in this part of the Medicare program. The Secretary of Health, Education, and Welfare is required by law to make use of private insurance carriers as far as possible for carrying out the major administrative functions of the medical insurance plan. This is an unusual and rather typical American resolution of the conflict between private and public interests. As the initial experience with this approach has revealed, it is not without serious administrative drawbacks.

The advent of state health insurance closed the last major gap in the risks covered by American social security. This advance has occurred at a time when the country has entered a new phase of social concern with poverty and income insecurity. There is more concern with these problems today than there has been at any time since the 1930s. Also, when the basic structure of American social security was erected, the country was in a severe economic crisis—there was mass insecurity in the midst of a general economic breakdown. Paradoxically, today's concern with poverty is more closely related to the overall remarkable success of the economy rather than to its failure. We are facing now the problem of poverty-stricken minorities in the midst of general affluence. It is this very affluence, and its context of a worldwide ideological conflict between rival economic systems, that give new urgency to the search for means to assure economic welfare to each and every individual. The desirability of this objective is no longer a matter of serious debate; it has become one of the rights of modern citizenship. One point, however, must be stressed. Social security, as a means of income protection, developed primarily to replace the income of those who have lost their productive capacity. A major income security problem that we face today, however, is that of developing or of restoring productive capacity. This is a question of untrained, inefficient, and unmotivated individuals in an economy requiring chiefly highly skilled and responsible persons. This is a problem that is related to the lack of opportunities and to the lack of aspiration of deprived minority groups, to rapid technological change and to the automation of production, and to the instability of the family and to the insecurity of the home environment. As America continues to improve its existing social security structure, it also has begun to deal with these much more difficult problems of economic and social insecurity.

By the late 1960s, it became clear that the system created in 1935 needed major reform. We have studied how both England and Germany departed from their own social security traditions in the 1950s and how they reshaped the rights of protection in line with the potentialities and needs of advanced industrialism. It would be surprising, indeed, if the American system, which emerged in the midst of a major depression, were ideally suited for an age of affluence and growth. It has become painfully evident that, in spite of repeated improvements, those living on social security benefits do not share in the country's economic abundance. Projections into the future indicate that the gap between them and those still at work is widening.[149] There is little reason to expect that private pensions will bridge this gap.[150] Aside from the level of protection and many secondary issues, a major problem exists with regard to the distribution of the burden of protection. In spite of the fact that social insurance is designed to redistribute income for the sake of social adequacy, the system has continued to rely exclusively on payroll taxes, which are by nature regressive. In effect, rich and poor bear roughly the same absolute burden. After a careful review of theoretical considerations and available evidence, several fiscal experts recently concluded that the payroll tax is particularly burdensome on the poor. They recognize the ideological advantage that this method of financing has had in helping to legitimize social security but believe that the time has come to find more socially equitable ways of sharing the burden of protection. Most observers, however, agree that in the foreseeable future no major reforms are likely. America has shown its willingness to keep its citizens from falling into destitution but, as yet, is not determined to guarantee the maintenance of their standard of living. The country's liberal heritage is still an important factor, making it difficult to follow the European precedents in this modern interpretation of social rights.

[149] See Special Committee on Aging, 91st Congress, *Economics of Aging* (Washington, D.C.: Government Printing Office, 1969), pp. 17 ff.
[150] Ida Merriam, "Social Security Benefits and Poverty," *Social Security Administration, Research and Statistics Note*, No. 6 (February 24, 1967).

CHAPTER 7

Russia : From Patriarchalism to Collectivism

The traditions of liberalism and individualism that played such an important role in shaping social rights in the West were of little consequence in Russia. There, traditional dependence and protection, whatever its meaning in practice, was never challenged by the liberal ideals of individual freedom and equality. The challenge to patriarchal subordination in Russia came from the egalitarian ideals of the revolutionary socialist movement. The Bolshevik Revolution of 1917 created a new social order that was based on the principle of social equality under the dictatorship of the proletarian state. The Bolshevik state proclaimed the right to economic security one of the most important fruits of the revolution and a fundamental right of the Soviet citizen. Before very long, however, social security programs became a weapon in the hands of the ruling party to strengthen its control over the working population. Benefits, eligibility conditions, and administrative procedures were tailored to suit the objectives of those in power. No other country has ever exploited its system of social protection in such blatant fashion and, at the same time, used it as a propaganda device. Nevertheless, the Soviet Union did not remain outside the postwar social security reform movement, and the system that emerged after Stalin finally offered some of the rewards that had long been promised. The evolution of Soviet policy, set in the context of the country's economic development, will be analyzed after a review of the Tsarist policies and the Bolshevik reaction to them.

PROTECTION OF THE WORKER BEFORE 1917

Although Russia was still overwhelmingly an agricultural country in 1917, it had a good start on the road to industrialization. From 1885 until 1900 the country experienced remarkable economic development. Growth lagged in the early years of the century, but regained new momentum in the period from 1907 to 1914. By 1915 about 75 percent of the country's population was still tied to agriculture and approximately 85 percent lived in rural areas.[1] The number of wage workers was nevertheless considerable. It had grown from about four million in 1860 to nearly 18 million in 1913.[2] Of these, 3.1 million were employed in factories and mines and 4.5 million were agricultural laborers. Industrialization had not yet transformed the country, but it had gone far enough to pose problems of social protection of the wage-dependent worker. The extent of protection remained limited at the outbreak of World War I. It was nevertheless more extensive than that which, at that time, existed in the United States—the leading industrial country in the world. In autocratic Russia, as in autocratic Germany, conditions were more favorable for the protection of the worker than in countries with a strong liberal tradition.

Feudalism was still a vital force at the onset of Russian industrialization. Serfdom was not abolished until 1861, and naturally many of the attitudes that had developed during centuries of serfdom were carried over into the post-reform era. One characteristic of Russian feudalism was its emphasis on the absolute power of the Tsar. Although the peasants were subservient to the landed seigniors, they looked to the Tsar as the supreme authority and protector. Throughout Russian history the peasants appealed to the Tsar to redress their grievances against their masters. Their appeals were rarely successful and frequently led to retributions, but the practice kept alive the image of the Tsar as the father of his people. There was a deep conviction among the long-suffering Russian peasant that if the Tsar knew how badly his subordinates were treating ordinary folk, he would right the wrongs. It was this kind of naive faith that led to the practice of popular petitions to the Tsar. Mixed with this faith was a belief in the righteousness of the defenseless subjects. As Turin points out, these attitudes were characteristic of the outlook of those who marched to the Tsar's Winter Palace in 1905. Their petition opened as follows:

> Your Majesty! We, the workmen and citizens of St. Petersburg, our wives, children and parents, have come to Your Majesty to beg for justice and protection. We are all paupers, we are oppressed and overburdened with work; we are often insulted for no reason, we are not regarded as human beings, but are treated as slaves; we suffer and we have to bear our sufferings silently.[3]

[1]Margaret Miller, *The Economic Development of Russia 1905–1914* (second edition, London: Frank Cass, 1967), pp. 32–33.
[2]A. G. Rashin, *Formirovanie Rabochego Klassa Rossii* (Moscow, 1958), p. 172.
[3]Quoted in S. P. Turin, *From Peter the Great to Lenin* (London: P. S. King, 1935), p. 71.

The petitioners stated that they were ready to obey the command of the Tsar, but that he had to protect them and deliver them from intolerable suffering.

In an agrarian feudal society, protection from arbitrariness and oppression was undoubtedly more important than protection against the loss of income. The Tsars did little to interfere with the serfowner's treatment of his serfs. The latter were completely dependent on their master, and it was in his economic interest to assure them the necessary means of survival.[4] This system sometimes functioned reasonably well, especially when there were enough able-bodied members around to support aged and disabled family members. The head of the extended family, the village elders, and the seignior together formed a system of elementary economic protection for the peasant.[5] On the other hand, as in all societies, there were elements living at the margin of society, people who did not "belong" to anybody and who were incapable or unwilling to support themselves through work. Until the sixteenth century these people were ignored by the state and left to the efforts of private charity. From that time on the state began to take notice of the hordes of beggars who roamed the country.

In the late seventeenth and early eighteenth centuries, Western and homegrown mercantilist ideas regarding the treatment of the poor began to influence the attitude of the government. One of the earliest landmarks of Russian thought on public relief is a memorandum addressed to the Tsar in 1682.[6] Its spirit was completely in harmony with the one that prevailed in Western Europe at that time. It strongly stressed the need to separate the able-bodied from the aged, infirm, and children. The memorandum suggested that Russia follow the example of other countries by locking up able-bodied beggars and by putting them to work. For homeless children, it proposed the establishment of special homes in which they would be taught a trade useful to the prosperity of the state. In true mercantilist fashion, the memorandum argued that by putting the idle to work and by teaching them useful trades, the country could manufacture many things that were being imported. In this way, poor relief could help make the country prosperous and independent of foreigners.

The proposals of the memorandum were not enacted into law. The beginning of public regulation of poor relief, like many other things in

[4] For an excellent analysis, see J. Blum, *Lord and Peasant in Russia from the Ninth to the Nineteenth Century* (Princeton: Princeton University Press, 1961).
[5] For a somewhat romantic description of this system, see F. LePlay, *Les Ouvriers Européens* (second edition, Paris, 1877), Vol. II, Chapters I to V.
[6] E. Maximow, "Étude sur l'évolution et l'état actuel de l'assistance publique en Russie" in Direction Générale de L'Économie Locale du Ministère de L'Intérieur, *L'Assistance Publique et Privée en Russie* (St. Petersburg, 1906), pp. 10–12.

Russia, had to wait until the reign of Peter the Great. Peter's outlook was thoroughly mercantilistic. In a series of decrees he ordered all able-bodied beggars to be beaten with a rod and sent back to their masters. Village elders who were lax in their discipline and anyone who supported able-bodied beggars were to be fined. In case of second offenses, beggars were to be condemned to forced labor. Alongside these repressive measures, Peter defined for the first time officially who was responsible for the support of the poor. In the countryside, it was the obligation of the seigniors and other landowners to furnish work to able-bodied indigents and to furnish bread and clothing to those unable to work. In villages where the inhabitants were free peasants owning their own land, the support obligation was imposed on the community. In towns the municipality was charged with the building and maintenance of hospitals and other charitable institutions. Monasteries were charged with providing relief to indigent former sailors and soldiers. On the whole, Peter's action probably did little more than put the sanction of the state behind what was already the usual practice. This meant that for the first time the state officially acknowledged society's obligation toward the poor without, however, creating public institutions for poor relief.

The general pattern of obligations established by Peter I remained in force until the twentieth century. Toward the end of the eighteenth century, under Catherine II, there was a noticeable decline in the emphasis on repressive measures, comparable to similar developments in Western Europe. At that time and during the early nineteenth century a number of charitable foundations were created under the auspices of the crown, which lasted until the 1917 revolution. With the abolition of serfdom in 1861, a reorganization of public responsibility became necessary. This was facilitated by the creation of the zemstvos (provincial assemblies) in 1864 and by the new regulations concerning municipalities in 1870. The zemstvos were charged with regional administrative responsibility, but their efforts were severely restricted by the lack of funds and by a constant interference from the tsarist bureaucracy. In spite of these difficulties the zemstvos made commendable progress in poor relief, as well as in public health and education.[7] Given the size of the country (a population of approximately 130 million in 1900), the total public assistance effort remained extremely modest. The zemstvos' budgets for 1900 allocated 1.5 million rubles for public assistance, and the municipalities allocated about 3 million.[8] According to one estimate, modestly adequate care of the needy in zemstvo

[7] *Ibid.*, pp. 54–55. See also Donald Mackensie Wallace, *Russia* (London: Cassel and Co., 1912), pp. 569 ff.
[8] Maximow, *loc. cit.*, pp. 56, 61.

provinces in 1912 would have required 300 million rubles; the zemstvos, however, spent only 4.5 million.[9]

When we turn from the study of public relief to an examination of the programs for industrial workers, we find more extensive legislation, although the laws on the books did not always achieve practical significance. The tsarist government was torn between conflicting tendencies regarding special wage-earner protection. Certain conservative elements within the bureaucracy insisted, at least until 1905, that Russia had no industrial labor problem that required special legislation; other factions insisted on the need for detailed legislative regulation and for the administrative supervision of industrial relations.[10] A law of June 3, 1886, established what has been called the "First Russian Labor Code." It was partly a response to the growing reslessness among industrial workers over arbitrary fines and dismissals. The law provided for certain elementary forms of protection for the wage worker, but its enforcement by an understaffed contingent of factory inspectors left much to be desired.[11]

In the area of social insurance the three most noteworthy laws passed before World War I were: (1) the law of 1866, which required all factories to furnish free medical treatment for their workers; (2) the law regarding industrial accidents passed in 1903; and (3) the Health and Accident Act of June 23, 1912. Old-age pension programs existed only for government employees. There was little in the way of private voluntary programs. We must keep in mind, however, the fact that the Russian government had many employees, since it owned many large enterprises, including the railroads.

The 1903 act was passed in the wake of considerable industrial unrest and huge strikes. It was primarily an employer's liability act, administered by the factory and mine inspectors, without compulsory insurance. It applied only to factories, mills, and mines, thus excluding the large portion of the workers employed in small establishments.[12] The lack of insurance provision and the denial of benefits on the grounds of worker negligence

[9] Bernice Madison, "The Organization of Welfare Services" in Cyril E. Black (Ed.), *The Transformation of Russian Society* (Cambridge: Harvard University Press, 1960), p. 518.

[10] For a more extensive discussion, see Gaston V. Rimlinger, "Autocracy and the Factory Order in Early Russian Industrialization," *Journal of Economic History*, Vol. XX, No. 1 (March 1960), pp. 67–92; also J. Walkin, "The Attitude of the Tsarist Government Toward the Labor Problem," *American Slavic and East European Review*, Vol. XIII, (April 1954), pp. 163–184.

[11] See Gaston V. Rimlinger, "The Management of Labor Protest in Tsarist Russia," *International Review of Social History*, Vol. V, Part II, pp. 226–248.

[12] See I. M. Rubinow, *Studies in Workmen's Insurance: Italy, Russia, Spain* (Doctoral dissertation, Columbia University, 1911), pp. 2102 ff. The dissertation was part of the 24th annual report of the United States Commissioner of Labor on "Workmen's Insurance and Compensation Systems in Europe, Vol. III.

contributed to the overall weakness of the program, as did the absence of worker participation in its administration. Actually the 1903 act was not the first employer liability law. Laws of this kind had been on the books since the middle of the nineteenth century, but they were restricted to specific industries, such as mining and the railroads, and they were weakly enforced.

The dissatisfaction with the law of 1903 and the lack of income protection in case of general illness led to a number of reform proposals. They were debated at great length and finally culminated in the law of 1912. This law provided for cash benefits in case of work-connected accidents, general illness, maternity, and death. Unfortunately, its coverage was still restricted to under one fourth of the labor force.[13] The financing of work-connected accident benefits was entirely at the expense of employers, although employers and employees shared the cost of the other benefits. On the whole the Russians followed fairly closely the German pattern. As in Germany, in Russia the workers were entitled to participate in the administration of the program to which they contributed. Another feature copied from the German system was the treatment of work-connected injuries as general illness during the first 13 weeks of disablement, which was a burden on the workers.

Because of its narrow coverage and limited benefits, the 1912 law was rather unpopular among the working masses. After the lengthy debate, a more generous law had been hoped for, especially since the larger employers had long favored more protection. "The real merit of the 1912 law," Madison points out, "was ... that it recognized the right of the workers to participate in the organization and enforcement of measures concerning their welfare."[14] This represented a step forward, but it was far from satisfying the labor movement. While the government's bill was still being debated, the Russian Social Democrats held their sixth All-Russian Conference in Prague. Lenin took the occasion to dissect critically the shortcomings of the proposed law.

He opened his attack with the proposition that the working class received only an insignificant share of the wealth it produced, which left the worker completely unable to provide for himself in case of inability to work or of unemployment. Therefore, it was imperative that the state provide a comprehensive system of insurance. The principles on which this insurance should be based, according to Lenin, were as follows:

1. It should provide assistance in *all* cases of incapacity, including old age, accidents, illness, death of the breadwinner, as well as maternity and birth benefits.

---

[13]Madison, *loc. cit.*, p. 521.   [14]Madison, *loc. cit.*, p. 522.

2. It should cover *all* wage earners and their families.

3. The benefits should equal *full earnings* and all costs should be borne by employers and the state.

4. There should be uniform insurance organizations (rather than organization by risk) of a territorial type and under the full management of the insured workers.[15]

These principles, which resemble the ones advanced earlier by the German Social Democrats, have become a guideline for Soviet social insurance.

Lenin compared these requirements with the government's bill, which had been passed by the Duma but had not yet become law. He inevitably found the bill wanting in every respect and denounced its "beggarly rates of compensation" (which had a maximum of two thirds of earnings in case of total disability). Lenin agreed with most socialists that there was no hope for adequate social security under capitalism, especially in Russia. "An insurance reform really corresponding to the interests of the workers can only be accomplished after the final overthrow of tsarism and the achievement of conditions indispensable for the free class struggle of the proletariat."[16] The Prague Conference, therefore, resolved to urge all of its supporters to agitate vigorously against the bill. In case this agitation failed to achieve its objective, the program was to be exploited for political purposes. The Conference resolved:

> Should the Duma Bill become law in spite of the protest of the class-conscious proletariat, the Conference summons the comrades to make use of the new organizational forms which it provides (workers' sick benefit societies) to carry on energetic propaganda for Social-Democratic ideas in these organizational units and thus turn the new law, devised as a means of putting new chains and a new yoke upon the proletariat, into a means of developing its class-consciousness, strengthening its organization and intensifying its struggle for full political liberty and for socialism.[17]

Social security thus became a live propaganda issue. This did not lead to any new laws under tsarism, but it made social security one of the important issues that the Social Democrats would have to deal with on achieving power.

Another legacy of the tsarist period concerns medical care, which was not even mentioned by Lenin. The oversight may be because of the fact that in Russia medical care had long been considered a proper governmental function. The law of 1866, mentioned earlier, transferred this responsibility

---

[15]V. I. Lenin, *Collected Works* (Moscow: Foreign Languages Publishing House, 1963), Vol. XVII, p. 476.

[16]*Ibid.*, p. 477.

[17]*Ibid.*, pp. 478–479.

from the government to the employer in the case of factories, a common Russian practice. Although the law clearly specified the medical facilities to be provided by the factory, it contained no penalties for noncompliance. It was, therefore, very unevenly enforced. In some cases, medical care was provided, but a deduction was made from the workers' earnings. These deductions were made illegal in 1886, which was indicative of the state's conception of the employer's responsibility. In 1892, the 1866 law was extended to apply to mines and to metallurgical establishments. A survey made in 1908 showed that in 1907 about 84 percent of the workers in establishments under state inspection enjoyed some form of medical care through their place of employment. About 44 percent of the 1.5 million protected workers were in establishments with their own hospitals.[18] In the countryside, medical care had become a responsibility of the zemstvos. Although considerable progress was made in providing medical care for the peasants in the early part of the century, the level of care remained rather low. The significance of these measures, however, lies in the establishment of precedents and in pioneer efforts in group medical care. Mark Field has observed that the Soviet regime did not have to start from scratch. "Rather, it continued and amplified, while at the same time it modified and adapted, a pattern which had existed in Russia for more than half a century...."[19]

SOVIET SOCIAL INSURANCE IDEOLOGY

Since the early days of Bolshevik Revolution, social security has been hailed as one of the fruits of the victory of the workers over capitalism. Soviet writers maintain that only a socialist society, which is dedicated to the welfare of the working class, can provide welfare programs and services that fully meet the needs of the population. They argue:

> Under capitalism the necessity for social security arises as an inevitable result of the shortcomings of the capitalist economic system, the lack of faith of the workers in the days ahead, the excessive intensification of work, the dangers of unemployment and premature old age. Only in a socialist society, whose laws of development are not governed by the profit motive but by the fulfilment of the needs of man, is the realization of guaranteed and adequate social security for those unable to work a natural development, springing from the very essence of socialism.[20]

---

[18] Rubinow, *Studies in Workmen's Insurance*, p. 2213.

[19] Mark G. Field, *Doctor and Patient in Soviet Russia* (Cambridge: Harvard University Press, 1957), p. 4.

[20] M. Lantsev, "Sotial'noe Obespechenie v SSSR i v kapitalisticheskikh stranakh," *Sotsialisticheskii Trud*, September 1958, p. 28.

Not only are the reasons for social security different under capitalism and socialism according to Soviet specialists, but also its objectives.

> A comparison of the system of social security of the USSR with what is done in this regard in capitalist countries convincingly shows that the aims of social security in socialist and capitalist countries are entirely different. The system of social security of the USSR covers the most important aspects of the material and cultural aspects of the life of the working population; it is a factor in the improvement of life and of the material and cultural position of the working class; it is one of the levers for the uplifting of all those who work.[21]

As opposed to the beneficial and positive orientation of socialist social insurance, capitalist social insurance is supposed to be essentially preventive and negative.

> Its substance lies in the use of pacifiers—in the form of assistance—in order to protect capitalist property against encroachment from the poor. What underlies social security in capitalist countries is not the needs of man, nor his right to a secure old age, but the interest in profits, the interest in strengthening the capitalist mode of production by way of partial concessions to the worker.[22]

There is no need to belabor such an obvious caricature of social security in nonsocialist countries, even though it is partially true. In most Western countries modern welfare programs arose mainly in response to pressure from the lower classes. The relevant feature of the comparison is what Soviet authorities think of their own social security system.

An important difference between social security systems is the extent to which the rights to protection are granted as a matter of status—either to all citizens or to specific status groups—and the extent to which the rights have to be earned in a contractual manner. In America, the dominant emphasis was on the contractual aspects of social insurance rights. This preference was consistent with the individualistic character of American society and with the emphasis on market-determined reciprocities. In the Soviet Union, on the other hand, the contractual element does not enter into social insurance. The abolition of private ownership of the means of production (with minor exceptions in agriculture and handicrafts) gives the state the power to control the income of all citizens. The planners can determine how much, and in what manner, personal income is to be tied to work performance or to status. Under these circumstances, it is easy to treat welfare benefits as a gift from the state to the citizen.

Soviet social welfare distinguishes between the right to income main-

---

[21] *Ibid.*, p. 30.
[22] *Ibid.*, p. 30.

tenance and the right to benefits that aim to raise living and cultural levels, such as health and education. As in many other countries, the latter benefits are available to all citizens. Income maintenance benefits, however, have traditionally been available only to those who perform hired work. They are the relevant status group. Until 1964, the whole mass of collective farmers was excluded from the public pension program and were left to their own mutal assistance schemes. Although Soviet social insurance is wage related, Soviet theorists insist that it does not involve the contractual concept of an *exchange* of benefits for premium payments. In the words of one author:

> mutuality and reciprocity . . . are not to be found in the mutual relation of the parties in state social insurance. The obligation here lies not on both parties, but only on one—the agency of state social insurance is under obligation to issue funds and to set and pay pensions or other forms of subsistence . . ., whereas the worker or employee has no reciprocal obligations to the agency of state social insurance.[23]

The main practical significance of this is the fact that the right to benefits is in no way dependent on the payment of contributions into social insurance funds. The obligation to pay contributions rests entirely on enterprises, but unlike the situation in many countries, the failure to pay does not jeopardize the right to benefits. "Section 179 of the Labour Code expressly states that failure to pay the contribution may in no case deprive a worker of insurance benefits."[24]

Soviet ideology stresses that social security benefits are a *gift* from the state—a genuine act of governmental benevolence, a true manifestation of socialist humanism. The head of the trade unions, N. M. Shernik, told a meeting of union activists in 1938: "Take any figure in the state social insurance budget; every one of them breathes the warmth and paternal care which our leader and teacher Comrade Stalin manifests daily and hourly toward all people, great and small."[25] The nature and circumstances of many pronouncements of this kind indicate that welfare programs play an important role in official Soviet propaganda, both at home and abroad. To be sure, in all countries social benefits serve in part to inspire loyalty to the state. In the Soviet Union, however, this aspect is especially prominent, as it tends to be in all totalitarian countries. Hardly an occasion is missed to underline the state's and the party's concern for the welfare of the workers and to remind them of the debt of loyalty they owe the rulers.

The reciprocal rights and obligations of the state and the workers in the

[23] A. S. Krasnopolskii, "On the Nature of Soviet State Social Insurance," *Current Digest of the Soviet Press*, Vol. III, No. 46 (December 29, 1951), p. 6.
[24] "Social Insurance in the U.S.S.R.," *International Labor Review*, Vol. XXXVIII, No. 2 (August 1938), p. 229. Krasnopolskii also stresses this point. See *Osnovye Printsipy*, p. 90.
[25] Quoted in A. S. Krasnopolskii, *loc. cit.*, p. 4.

Soviet Union are spelled out in its constitution. Article 120 of the 1936 constitution states in part: "Citizens of the U.S.S.R. have the right to maintenance in old age and also in case of sickness and disability." An important corollary of this article is Article 12, which states: "Work in the U.S.S.R. is a matter of duty and honor for every able-bodied citizen, in accordance with the principle 'He who does not work, neither shall he eat.'" The Soviet literature emphasizes that social insurance along with the right and duty to work are fundamental principles of socialism.[26] It is certainly not accidental that a constitution that guarantees the worker's maintenance and right to work also imposes on him the duty to work.[27] And conversely, the duty to work implies a right to maintenance that goes beyond any individual merit of support, since the maintenance of the worker becomes akin to the maintenance of capital. The state has an almost proprietary interest in the investment in human capital. Its position does bear a resemblance to the one of the slave owner. "In the society founded on labor," writes Krasnopolskii, "where the exploitation of man by man has been eliminated...where people are treated as the *most valuable capital*... comprehensive care of aged and disabled members is natural and inevitable."[28] The significant difference between this society and slavery, as far as treating humans as capital is concerned, is that in Soviet society there is presumably no conflict of interest between the rulers and the ruled. This may not always be the case, but it is part of the official ideology that shapes the relationships between individuals and the state. Those who deviate from this ideology are called "parasites" and "speculators."[29]

As the foregoing discussion indicates, there appears to be at least five major themes in Soviet social security ideology:

1. Comprehensive social security is an integral part of socialist society and expresses its inner harmony.

2. It is a gift of the state as well as a fundamental right of the citizen.

---

[26] A. S. Krasnopolskii, *Osnovnye Printsipy Sovetskogo Gosudarstvennogo Sotsial'nogo Strakhovaniia* (Moscow, 1951), *passim*.

[27] For a discussion along these lines, see Gaston V. Rimlinger, "Social Security, Incentives, and Controls in the U.S. and U.S.S.R.," *Comparative Studies in Society and History*, Vo. IV, No. 1 (November 1961), pp. 110 ff. For a recent discussion of the right to work, see Robert Conquest, *Industrial Workers in the U.S.S.R.* (New York: Praeger, 1967), Chapter I.

[28] *Osnovnye Printsipy*, p. 54. (The italics are the author's.)

[29] The problem of how to handle "parasites," that is, able-bodied individuals who shirk the duty of regular work, has caused considerable discussion in recent years. See R. Beermann, "A Discussion on the Draft Law Against Parasites, Tramps and Beggars," *Soviet Studies*, Vol. IX, No. 2 (October 1957), pp. 214–222; "Parasites Must be Made to Work," V. Krylov, "The Law Must be Passed," V. Yankovsky, "A Necessary Law" in *Current Digest of the Soviet Press*, August 14, 1957, p. 7 and August 14, 1959, pp. 8–9.

3. It is a corollary of the duty to work and, in a general sense, a reward for loyal performance of this duty but not a payment for work done.

4. Its aim is to maintain income and to uplift the material and cultural level of the working population.

5. It influences the workers' standard of living directly as well as indirectly, through its impact on the capacity and zeal for work.

The argument that social security has a favorable influence on both welfare and productivity is looked on as evidence of the inner harmony of socialist society.

> The workers and employees who benefit from the advantages of Soviet state social insurance respond by working even better, by raising even higher the productivity of their labor. This clear example of combination of individual and social interest under socialism is one of the many graphic illustrations of the undisputed superiority of the Soviet social and political order. . . .[30]

This ideological frame of reference has a number of implications for the development and the structure of Soviet social security. First, it implies a universal and comprehensive protection financed without worker contributions. Second, it is clear also that this must not have a negative impact on work habits but, instead, must serve as a tool for the promotion of higher productivity. The state, in fact, has a great deal of scope to shape the structure and the administration of social insurance programs to suit its objectives. The absence of worker contributions and of any form of contractual commitment leave the government great freedom to manipulate the system in the "common interest." Soviet writers are careful to point out that the socialist principle "to each according to his work" applies only to remuneration for work, not to social insurance benefits. Although the contractual earning of benefits is thus denied, the incentive differentiation of benefits is openly acknowledged. Statements in the Soviet literature indicate that the benefit differentiation has been governed primarily by considerations of labor discipline and productivity.

> In addition to differentiation based on the fact that alongside honest and conscientious workers there are also isolated irresponsible, backward, and dishonest people—loafers, slackers, shirkers, and self-seekers—state insurance . . . also widely uses differentiation based on the importance [of an industry] in the national economy and on the difficulty of the working conditions.[31]

The impact of ideological and other factors on the shaping of Soviet welfare programs can be fully appreciated only through an analysis of their historical development. The remainder of this chapter traces the evolution of

---

[30] Krasnopolskii, *Osnovnye Printsipy,* p. 118.
[31] *Ibid.,* p. 140.

the Soviet social security system through the various stages of the country's economic development.

SOCIAL SECURITY FROM THE REVOLUTION TO 1921

There was a wide gap between what the Bolsheviks had promised and what economic conditions would allow in the years immediately following the revolution. The promises were in Lenin's principles of 1912 and in a bill drafted by the Bolsheviks in 1914. Once in power, they could offer no less.

For this reason it is worthwhile to examine briefly the major provisions of the 1914 bill.[32] Coverage was to be nearly universal; it included all who worked for hire as well as self-employed peasants who did not own land, regardless of sex, age, race, religion, nationality, or citizenship. The major exceptions were capitalists and landlords. The list of insured risks was comprehensive. Cash benefits were provided in cases of sickness, accidents, maternity, unemployment, and death. There were also disability and survivorship pensions, but not separate old-age pensions. At the relatively young age of 50, insured individuals became eligible for a disability pension. Another major benefit was free and complete medical care for all covered individuals. In addition, all aged beneficiaries were entitled to institutionalized care, as well as all children and orphans whose parents or guardians desired it. Finally, the bill stipulated obligatory preventive measures against illness and accidents. The level of benefits and pensions was set equal to earnings, subject to an annual maximum of 2400 rubles, which was roughly nine times the average wage in the country.[33] The financing of these generous benefits was to be at the expense of the rich. The bill specified that the funds were to be obtained through the imposition of a progressive tax on property and inheritance, and on the incomes of enterprises and individuals. Exempted from this tax were small enterprises, properties and inheritances, and individual earnings below 2400 rubles a year. An important feature of the scheme was the self-administration of the insured through elected representatives. The administration was to be in the hands of local, regional, and all-Russian social insurance councils. The bill made all conditions, provisions, and payments subject to regulations by the All-Russian Workers' Insurance Conference. It stated specifically that neither the government nor the employers had a right to be represented or to take part

[32] A copy of the bill is contained in D. Antoshkin (ed.), *VKP (b) i Profsoiuzy o Sotsial'nom Strakhovanii* (Nauchno–Issledovatel'skii Institut Professional'nogo Dvizheniia; Moscow: Profizdat, 1934), pp. 148–151.
[33] The average annual wage for the country as a whole in 1913 was 264 rubles. See S. P. Turin, *From Peter the Great to Lenin* (London: P. S. King, 1935), p. 196.

in any of the administrative organs of social insurance. Furthermore, the bill expressly prohibited any deduction from earnings of employees to finance the program, and it provided stiff penalties for any interference by employers or public officials with the work of social insurance representatives.

This bill clearly followed the Leninist principles. It was quite unacceptable to the tsarist government, but it presented the workers with a concrete model of socialist social insurance. It was actually drafted by the elected worker representatives to the Social Insurance Council established by the law of 1912. They submitted it to the Social Democratic faction of the Duma and called on workers around the country to agitate for its passage. During the months following the February Revolution, the Bolsheviks kept agitating for universal and comprehensive social security. They were highly critical of steps taken by the Provisional Government, which they considered totally inadequate.[34]

Five days after its seizure of power, on November 12, 1917, the Bolshevik Government issued a communiqué announcing a radical new social insurance program. Recognizing past commitments, the communiqué stated: "The Russian proletariat has put on its banners comprehensive social insurance for all wage workers and for the city and village poor."[35] It pointed out that previous governments had failed to satisfy the workers' aspirations and promised that the Workers' and Peasants' Government would immediately prepare social insurance decrees based on the proposals advanced by the workers. It reiterated the five Leninist principles that would govern the program: (1) the coverage of all workers and all city and village poor, (2) the inclusion of all risks of income loss, (3) all the costs to be borne by employers, (4) the unemployment and disability benefits to be at least equal to wages, and (5) the full control of administration to be in the hands of the insured. This was the program the militant workers had been clamoring for since 1914. Its practical realization was a different matter.

In the months following its seizure of power, the Bolshevik Government passed a large number of decrees relating to the economic life of the country. But it had practically no machinery to enforce its economic regulations. The only effective decrees were the ones that recognized the developments that were taking place spontaneously, for instance, the spreading of workers' control and the nationalization of enterprises. Unfortunately, a social security system cannot be created in such a manner. The

[34] See Antoshkin, *op. cit.*, pp. 153–158.
[35] *Ibid.*, p. 158. For an English translation, see James Bunyan and H. H. Fisher, *The Bolsevik Revolution 1917–1918: Documents and Materials* (Stanford: Stanford University Press, 1961), p. 308.

dislocation of the economy and the breakdown of labor discipline would have made the rapid introduction of any new program of social insurance extremely difficult, even if the government had had the required administrative apparatus at its disposal.

The laws passed during the early years of the Bolshevik regime, therefore, had little significance, other than they reflected the aims of the new government. The first law (December 11, 1917) established the first unemployment insurance program in Russia.[36] It applied to all temporarily unemployed wage earners, with the exception of those who earned more than three times the average local wage. Benefits were a flat amount, equal to the average local wage, but not exceeding the previous earnings of the unemployed worker. The law stated that funds would ultimately come from progressive taxation of income and property, but until then employers would have to bear the full cost.

A second law, passed December 29, 1917, provided for a program of cash sickness benefits, birth and burial grants, and free medical care. It covered all who worked for hire; financing was about the same as under the previous law; cash benefits in case of illness were set equal to previous earnings. It is significant that in neither case was there any requirement of a specified length of previous employment. Presumably, it was enough to establish one's status as a worker, which was consistent with traditional socialist thinking. To regulate and supervise the programs, the government decreed the establishment of national and regional social insurance councils. These councils were dominated by representatives of the insured workers, the trade-unions, and the factory committees. This was an attempt to implement the notion of a social insurance system in the hands of the insured population. Within less than a year the councils were abolished (if, indeed, they had ever come to life), and the control of social insurance was taken over by various government departments. Although the workers were still represented in the insurance organs, this was a retreat from the earlier Bolshevik ideal of an autonomous worker-managed system. A more significant shortcoming, however, was the failure to enact the promised protection against invalidity, old-age, and survivorship.[37]

By the summer of 1918, the Bolsheviks had entered the phase of War Communism. The state took complete control of all industrial and commercial activities of any significance. Industries were nationalized on a vast

---

[36] For a summary of Soviet labor laws, see Margaret Dewar, *Labour Policy in the USSR 1917–1928* (London: Royal Institute of International Affairs, 1956), pp. 160 ff; on early social insurance, see also Bureau International du Travail, *Les conditions du Travail dans la Russie des Soviets* (Paris: Berger-Levrault, 1920), Chapter VI.

[37] For the best historical account of Soviet social insurance in English, see Jack Minkoff, *The Soviet Social Insurance System Since 1921* (Ph.D. dissertation, Columbia University, 1959).

scale without compensation. The private ownership of land and buildings in cities was abolished. Land was declared to belong to the toilers, and all natural resources were declared to be national property. The first Bolshevik constitution, adopted in July 1918, announced that the Soviets aimed at "abolishing all exploitation of man by man . . ., eliminating completely the division of society into classes, and ruthlessly crushing exploiters. . . ." As the civil war progressed, labor became increasingly militarized. The constitution had proclaimed the universal obligation to work. Strikes were declared illegal, industrial discipline was tightened, and men and women were conscripted for labor in designated industries.

It was in this context of national crisis that a completely new social security program was enacted. By a decree of October 31, 1918, social insurance, or, as it was now called, social security (*sotsial'noe obespechenie* instead of *sotsial'noe strakhovanie*), was extended to cover all those who were gainfully employed, as long as they were not employing hired labor. This included wage and salary earners as well as self-employed peasants, artisans, and others, and the members of their families. The covered risks included all the major contingencies of life. There was protection in cash and kind in case of illness, permanent disability, unemployment, old age, and the loss of breadwinner. There were also maternity benefits and burial grants. Cash benefits and pensions were egalitarian; they were geared to the average wage in a locality instead of to the previous earnings of the beneficiary. The main source of financing was employer contributions. This program of universal and comprehensive protection was consistent with the universal duty to work that had been decreed in 1918 and that became embodied in the Bolshevik Labor Code of 1919. An individual was either working or incapable of work and, therefore, was entitled to support. Unfortunately, very little information is available on the application of this program. In all likelihood it remained a dead letter, especially in view of the fact that most income payments soon had to be made in kind because of hyperinflation. During 1920 and 1921 the government repeatedly ordered that confiscated property be turned over to the local social insurance agencies to enable them to make payments in kind. It was not until after the country pulled out of the economic morass of War Communism that realistic social insurance programs could be established.

SOCIAL SECURITY DURING THE NEP (1921 TO 1928)

The Tenth Congress of the Communist Party, meeting in March 1921, officially adopted the New Economic Policy. This policy, proposed by Lenin, inaugurated a new economic system for the country. The abandonment of

War Communism, an unsuccessful experiment with instant socialism, was dictated by the threat of economic disintegration just after the threat of destruction by force of arms had been overcome. The elimination of the market under War Communism had brought about a system of direct supply allocations that rested ultimately on a confiscatory requisition of food from the peasants. A couple of years of drought added to the woes of the peasantry. By 1920, an epidemic of peasant riots spread through the countryside, especially in the South and the East. In the cities, which were already beset by shortages, strikes were becoming a frequent occurrence and absenteeism was rapidly increasing. In addition to the collapse of labor discipline, the chaotic state of an overgrown administrative apparatus had become a factor in the economic disruption. The revolt of the Kronstadt sailors, a bastion of the revolution, left no doubt in Lenin's mind that a radical shift in policy was in order.[38]

The New Economic Policy created a system of state capitalism in industry and left agriculture, handicrafts, and retail trade to private enterprise. It was an acknowledged retreat from socialism. The state retained ownership of the means of production, including the land tilled by the peasants. However, they were free to operate their holdings as they pleased and to sell their surplus in the market. A tax that was based on this surplus replaced the earlier method of compulsory requisitions. All but the largest industrial establishments were freed from exclusive state control. Some establishments were organized into decentralized trusts, others were given even more extensive administrative and financial independence. Small enterprises were taken over by private businessmen or cooperatives. Although the nature of state control and participation changed during the 1920s, the emphasis during the whole period remained on the application of commercial principles. Private and public managers of industry sought to operate their enterprises at a profit.

From the point of view of the workers and the trade unions, the New Economic Policy created a new and rather ambiguous situation. The state still owned the means of production and exercised various degrees of control, but the introduction of commercial principles, coupled with various degrees of enterprise autonomy, left the door open to genuine conflicts of interest between management and labor. The breakdown of discipline at the end of War Communism had produced dissension among the trade-union leaders and grave misgivings within the party. Lenin and his associates were prepared to carry out reforms, but they would not tolerate indiscipline and dissension. Therefore, it was necessary to subjugate the trade unions, but

[38]The best description of the state of the economy at this time is found in Maurice Dobb, *Soviet Economic Development Since 1917* (New York: International Publishers, 1948), Chapters V and VI.

also to allow them enough scope of action to enable them to function as effective intermediaries between the party leadership and the working class. This ambiguous role of the unions, and hence of the position of the worker vis-à-vis the state, was spelled out in the resolutions adopted by the party's Central Committee in January 1922.

Lenin, who is credited with authorship of the resolutions, began by explaining that the New Economic Policy was a phase of transition from capitalism to socialism that contained features of both systems.[39] It was socialism in the sense that ownership of the means of production remained in the hands of the proletarian state. On the other hand, there were free markets, and socialized establishments were operated on the basis of commercial principles. According to Lenin:

> ... this situation inevitably produces, as far as working conditions are concerned, a certain amount of class conflict between the laboring masses and the directors of state enterprises and their superiors. This is especially the case when account is taken of the need to raise labor productivity and to operate each state enterprise without loss, at a profit, and also in view of the inevitable divisional administrative interests and exaggerated administrative zeal. With regard to socialized enterprises the trade unions therefore absolutely have the duty to protect the interests of the workers and insofar as possible contribute to the raising of their living standard by continuously correcting the mistakes and exaggerations of economic units to the extent that such bureaucratic excesses stem from the state apparatus.[40]

Although the party recognized the basis of economic conflict, it was careful to limit the workers' freedom to protect their interests. Lenin stressed that the prevailing situation was fundamentally different from the one under capitalism. The ultimate aim of strikes under capitalism, he argued, is to destroy the state and to overthrow the ruling class, but under existing conditions the final aim of all mass worker actions can be only the strengthening of the proletarian state by combating bureaucratic excesses and capitalistic vestiges. In defending the interests of the workers, the unions were enjoined not to harm the interests of other groups. Strikes were clearly not to be tolerated:

> The only correct, healthy, and appropriate method for eliminating frictions and conflicts between individual parts of the working class and the organs of the workers' state is a mediatory participation of the trade unions. Through their relevant organizations they may either engage in negotiations with the interested economic units on the basis of carefully formulated demands and proposals, or they may appeal to higher state offices.[41]

[39] The text of the resolutions can be found in W. I. Lenin, *Ueber die Arbeitsgesetzgebung* (Berlin: Deutscher Zentralverlag, 1962), pp. 584–596.
[40] *Ibid.*, p. 586.   [41] *Ibid.*, p. 587.

The rights and duties of the workers under the New Economic Policy were clarified by the RSFSR Labor Code, adopted in November 1922, which became a model for the rest of the country.[42] With the introduction of NEP the compulsory labor service was abolished, and conscripted workers were demobilized. The Labor Code recognized this restoration of a free labor market; it was silent on the right to work and restricted the duty to work to emergency situations. The return to the free labor market was accompanied by increasing unemployment and mounting inflation, which undermined the workers' standard of living. The code specified that hiring had to be done through the local offices of the Commissariat of Labor and that no terms of engagement could be worse than the ones contained in the Labor Code, in collective agreements, and in the rules of the internal order of the enterprise. Wages were to be determined through collective and individual agreements, but they could not be lower than the state-established minimum for a particular occupation. "In return for a guaranteed wage, the Code demanded a guaranteed output."[43] Output quotas were established by the mutual agreement of the trade unions and management. Under Article 57 of the Code: "An employee who fails to achieve the established norm, through his own fault and under normal working conditions, will be paid proportionately to the amount of work done; however, he will not receive less than two-thirds of the standard rate."

Along with other regulations of the employment relationship, the code contained the provisions of social insurance applicable under the new economic system. To some extent, this was simply a restatement of laws that had been enacted the previous year. As indicated earlier, the all-inclusive program enacted during War Communism never acquired practical significance. During the transition to the New Economic Policy, more realistic laws were enacted. They marked the effective beginning of the functioning of Soviet social insurance. Consistent with the reestablishment of the free labor market, the idea of universal protection (excluding capitalists) was abandoned. The new laws applied only to those who sold their labor, thus excluding the whole mass of self-employed peasants, artisans, and professionals. Although the number of covered persons was thus restricted, the new system, as specified in the Labor Code, was very comprehensive as far as the coverage of risks was concerned. It provided for free medical care, temporary disability benefits (payable also in cases where the care of a sick family member prevented a person from working), unemployment benefits, invalidity pensions, survivorship pensions (applicable also in cases where the breadwinner had disappeared), and finally for supplementary assistance, payable to nursing mothers, sick persons, and for burials.

[42] A text of the Code is contained in *ibid.*, pp. 633–660.
[43] Dewar, *op. cit.*, p. 97.

Benefit levels and the duration of benefits varied according to the cause of inability to earn a living. Generally, the conditions were most favorable in the case of temporary physical incapacity. The law on sickness benefits enacted on October 14, 1921, provided for benefits equal to full pay for a period not exceeding four months. The 1922 Labor Code specified that sickness benefits should equal the wage rate for the occupation of the insured at his place of employment and should in no case be less than his earnings before becoming disabled. A separate article of the code, however, states that the central administration of social insurance has the right to reduce benefits temporarily, but not below two thirds of the relevant rate, in cases where there is a lack of funds. This provision strongly reflects the absence of the contractual notion in Soviet social insurance. Amending the earlier law (October 14, 1921), the code made sickness benefits payable from the day of illness until recovery or the beginning of a permanent disability pension. Although a 1924 law introduced a maximum on sickness benefits levels, this was of little importance during the 1920s.[44] No minimum level was introduced until 1955.

The unemployed were treated less generously than the sick. Unemployment benefits were more in the nature of assistance payments to the needy. But the individual's work record was taken into account. Under a law of October 3, 1921, unemployment benefits were payable to persons registered as unemployed with the department of labor who had no other means of subsistence. Skilled persons dismissed from state enterprises were entitled to benefits equal to the local minimum wage; unskilled workers discharged from state enterprises were entitled to benefits ranging from one third to one half of the local minimum if they had three years of service. Benefits for other unemployed workers were left to be determined by the social security bodies.[45] The Labor Code merely added that benefits were dependent on the skill of the worker and on the length of his previous employment, and that they must in no case be less than one sixth of the local average wage. In 1921, unemployment benefits were payable for 15 continuous weeks or for a total of 26 weeks in one year. Under Article 186 of the 1922 Labor Code, the duration of unemployment benefits was left to be determined by the social insurance authorities depending on the worker's skill and previous length of work. The maximum benefit period was set at six months.

With regard to permanent disability and survivorship insurance benefits, the law of December 8, 1921 and the Labor Code were rather vague. In general, these benefits were made to depend on the cause and degree of

[44] Solomon M. Schwarz, *Labor in the Soviet Union* (New York: Praeger, 1951), p. 310; Minkoff, *op. cit.*, p. 199. The 1924 maximum was 5 rubles per day; in 1926 it was raised to 7.5 rubles, L. Ia. Gintsburg, *Trudovoi Stazh Rabochikh i Sluzhashchikh* (Moscow: Akademii Nauk, 1958), p. 76.

[45] Dewar, *op. cit.*, p. 212.

disability and the availability of other resources. As in the case of unemployment benefits, a needs test was involved in the granting of pensions. However, it seems that under the unfavorable economic conditions of the early 1920s these provisions were never implemented. During the following years a system of disability and survivorship pensions was created "that was little influenced by these provisions of the Labor Code; it was supplemented at the end of the decade by a complicated system of old-age insurance."[46] It was not until 1928 that a separate old-age insurance program was introduced, with benefits related to previous earnings. Under a law passed in 1924, pensions for industrial accidents were tied to previous earnings; they ranged from 50 to 100 percent of earnings for the incapacitated and from 33 to 75 percent for dependents.[47] In 1926 the pensions for disability due to general causes also were tied to previous earnings and, thereby, lost some of the public assistance character. According to the estimates of Professor Minkoff, the average monthly pension paid in the years 1924 to 1928 ranged from 31 to 36 percent of the average monthly wage, whereas temporary disability benefits were about 95 percent of the average wage.[48] With the exception of temporary disability benefits, there was a tendency toward an egalitarian benefit structure during the NEP era.

The Labor Code contained especially strong protection for women. Maternity leaves with full pay were granted to working women and were paid as prescribed by the code. Women doing physical labor received a leave of eight weeks before and eight weeks after giving birth, and other working women were entitled to a leave of six weeks before and six weeks after giving birth. Insured working women as well as the wives of insured workers were entitled to "supplementary benefits," which included a layette grant amounting to one month's local average wage and a nursing grant for nine months at a rate of 25 percent of the local wage. This is the kind of benefit that is particularly meaningful for low-income groups. Until 1927 there was no income restriction on eligibility. The income limit that was introduced at that time was well above the average wage, so that the great majority of working class women remained eligible.

Our review of the coverage and of the benefits granted during the NEP era shows that, on the whole, the system was geared to the regular industrial workers, with some preference for those who were skilled and employed in state enterprises. Certainly, this group was of most consequence to the party. The exclusion of the peasants may have violated the spirit of the revolution, but the peasants' attitude, especially toward the end of War Communism, had made amply clear that they could not be relied on for the building of a

[46] Schwarz, op. cit., p. 321.
[47] Dewar, op. cit., p. 245.
[48] Minkoff, op cit., pp. 25, 27.

socialist state. The less favored treatment of the unemployed than the temporarily disabled, no doubt, was related to the greater administrative problems connected with unemployment insurance. This involved the question of eligibility as well as the thorny question of incentive to work.

During the NEP the Soviet leaders never clearly confronted these questions, partly no doubt because their thoughts ran in terms of eligibility as a matter of social class. The tendency was to treat various risks in a different fashion. With respect to cash sickness or industrial accident benefits, there was never any work requirement during the 1920s. This simply meant that if a person became disabled while a hired employee, he was automatically eligible. With respect to maternity leave, the issue was a bit more critical. A pregnant woman had every incentive to take a job and, then, shortly thereafter collect 12 to 16 weeks' leave. It was this kind of consideration that led to a law in 1927 that limited the right to maternity leaves and birth grants to women who had six months of uninterrupted work immediately prior to the time that they became entitled to leave. The objective of this law, explains a Soviet authority, "was to prevent the resources of state social insurance from being spent on people who did not belong to the permanent cadre of the working class."[49] The law, however, never attained practical significance. It was soon discovered that its enforcement was more expensive than the savings that could be realized. In addition, it was declared to be unfair to young women who had entered the work force for the first time.

In the case of unemployment insurance, no specific previous work record was ever required. To be eligible, however, a worker had to be discharged from a covered job and had to register with the labor exchange within a short period after becoming unemployed.[50] The refusal to accept a job offer from the labor exchange usually disqualified a worker for benefits, except in the case of skilled workers who could show that the job would damage their skill. In most countries, unemployed workers are at least temporarily disqualified if they quit voluntarily or are fired for disciplinary reasons. In the Soviet Union this was not taken into account until 1927, at which time persons who had quit voluntarily were denied benefits for one month. At that time the needs test also became more severe. These measures, taken in the mid-1920s, reflected a tightening of labor discipline and a decrease in the industrial labor surplus.

At the beginning of the NEP period there was some feeling that there should be a long period of service as an eligibility condition for general disability pensions. Understandably, if someone is to be supported for the rest of his life, he should have more than a passing membership in the

[49] Gintsburg, *op. cit.*, p. 78.
[50] This account is mainly drawn from Minkoff, *op. cit.*, pp. 150–151.

eligible group. A decree of December 8, 1921 established an eight-year work requirement for permanent disability pensions, which included old-age pensions. The Labor Code of 1922 eliminated this requirement, except in cases where disability was primarily the result of old age. An oldster had to have eight years of continuous service immediately preceding retirement to be eligible for an old-age disability pension. In practice, this distinction between general disability and disability due to old age inevitably led to obvious difficulties. By the middle of the decade there was considerable pressure to tighten up on eligibility conditions. With regard to general disability, a 1925 regulation stipulated that the disability had to occur while the insured individual was employed, or not more than a year after he left work. The following year, it was further specified that the disability had to be reported within two weeks after quitting work. The chief objective was still the prevention of abuse.

> The requirement of a [work] stage, not only for the aged but also for invalids, showed itself to be a realistic means for "keeping insurance funds away from persons who had no right to social insurance." The proposed reform became all the more essential because in the years 1925–27 the resources devoted to invalidity insurance were substantially increased.[51]

The seventh congress of trade unions, meeting in December 1926, recommended the introduction of a work requirement for permanent disability pensions. This was done in March 1928.

In the meantime, there was considerable discussion about the advisability of a separate old-age pension program. Under a 1925 law a person was eligible for a pension if he was 50 years of age, incapable of work, and had worked continuously during the preceding 8 years. Presumably, in such cases the disability requirement was less stringent than in general disability cases. The first separate old-age program in the Soviet Union was introduced in 1928, but initially it was restricted to textile workers. The retirement age was set at 60 for men and 55 for women. In addition to age, a 25-year work record was required for pension eligibility, but there was no longer a disability requirement. Gintsburg notes that this marks the beginning of the use of the work record as a measure of an insured individual's contribution of "useful work" to society.[52] This is highly significant because it represents an important shift in thinking with regard to the right to social security. Previous work requirements mainly were intended to assure that an individual belonged to the status group entitled to protection. Now, apparently, an individual also had to be personally deserving by having contributed to society. The main reason for the shift in thinking, as we shall learn, was the change in economic conditions caused by the onset of rapid industrialization.

[51]Gintsburg, op. cit., p. 63.   [52]Ibid., p. 48.

Before discussing this new phase of Soviet economic development, we must examine at least one more important characteristic of Soviet social insurance, namely, the role of the insured in the administration of the system. We recall that an administration by the insured, without employer participation, was one of the key demands of the Bolsheviks before the revolution. In the early days of the Bolshevik regime, social insurance was in the hands of representative insurance councils. During War Communism it had come under direct control of the state. At the beginning of the NEP, there were trade-union leaders who believed that the unions should manage social insurance, in the place of the former workers' councils. This was contrary to party policy; it was categorically rejected at the Fifth Soviet Trade Union Congress (September 17 to 22, 1922), which resolved that:

> The concentration of social insurance and labor protection matters in a single state organ under unified management and under trade union control is the best means of achieving the designated goals. Therefore, any tendency to turn social insurance into a separate form of the labor movement and to create organizations independent of the state organs is wholly unacceptable.[53]

The nature of the control to be exercised by the trade unions was clarified a month later by the Central Council of Trade Unions.[54] It covered the following aspects:

1. The policing of contribution payments by the employers (who apparently were often in arrears). 2. The reporting of irregularities in contribution payments. 3. The assistance to enterprises in registering with the insurance organs and in explaining to workers that only those in registered enterprises were entitled to benefits. 4. The organization of worker cooperation with the insurance agencies. 5. The lectures on insurance questions to workers. 6. The delegation of experienced trade union members to work with the state insurance organs. 7. The assistance in the improvement of medical services. 8. The assistance in the placement of unemployed workers. 9. The training of staff for labor inspection.

All of these functions were clearly of an ancillary nature and indicate that the unions had little direct authority for making decisions.

Under the 1923 constitution of the USSR the regulation of labor conditions was entrusted to the Commissariat of Labor, which included a department for the central administration of social insurance. At the lower level, the system was organized on a territorial basis, with a social insurance

---

[53]Antoshkin, op. cit., pp. 71–72.
[54]On the role of the trade unions, see Gaston V. Rimlinger, "The Trade Union in Soviet Social Insurance: Historical Development and Present Functions," Industrial and Labor Relations Review, Vol. XIV, No. 3 (April 1961), pp. 397–418.

office serving a particular geographic area. Although these offices were governmental, the executive personnel were selected with the cooperation of the unions and, in theory, were responsible to the unions. The regional office was under the supervision of a committee elected by an intertrade-union conference of the region. The extent to which this arrangement satisfied the traditional socialist demand for worker-administered social insurance is not clear, especially since the unions themselves had to surrender most of their autonomy to the state. Ironically, the reversion to a higher degree of union authority in social insurance matters came about not as a consequence of a resurgence of worker control in industry, but as a result of a more thorough subjugation of the unions to the aims of the party and of the government. This occurred during the forced draft industrialization which began in 1928.

SOCIAL INSURANCE UNDER RAPID INDUSTRIALIZATION (1928 TO 1956)

By the mid-1920s the Soviet economy had recovered enough from the devastation of the war and the chaos of War Communism that serious thought could be given to the next phase of development, the building of an industrial socialist state. There was considerable debate within the top party leadership with regard to the best means of achieving this objective.[55] A major point of disagreement was the speed of industrialization. The party right wing, led by Bukharin, argued for a smooth transition from "restoration" to "reconstruction." Its members believed that the economy could keep on moving forward within the framework of the New Economic Policy. This argument envisaged a gradual industrialization, with capital formation based on the marketed agricultural surplus and the import of foreign capital goods. The left-wing "super-industrializers," among them Trotski, argued that neither socialism nor industrialization could be achieved in this fashion. They insisted that moving forward required much larger amounts of capital than the previous expansion, which was based on the restoration of the economy. They were not willing to depend on the voluntary savings of the agricultural sector and on foreign supplies to provide the needed plant and equipment. Moreover, they stressed that rapid expansion would have to con-centrate on the production of capital rather than consumer goods. This meant, of course, that the income of the peasants and workers would have to be kept low and that they would be called on to work especially hard. After some complicated maneuvers, playing one side against the other, Stalin

[55] For a full account, see A. Erlich, *The Soviet Industrialization Debate* (Cambridge: Harvard University Press, 1960).

decided on the policy of forced draft industrialization. This had far-reaching implications for the development of working conditions and social insurance.

The decision to transform the Soviet Union at a rapid pace from a relatively backward into a modern industrial and socialist state was taken at the Fifteenth Congress of the Communist party, which met in December 1927. It was at this "industrialization congress," as Professor Jasny calls it, that the critical theoretical issues relating to the speed of industrialization were resolved. Stalin emerged as the unchallenged dictator, having used the debate over industrialization "as a device for destroying his enemies and entrenching himself in control of the Party." [56] Through skillful use of this control he managed to take over the secret police, the trade unions, and the army. [57] This tightening of control was essential for carrying out the industrialization program. The fear existed in 1927 that although the country was then enjoying a high growth rate, in the years immediately ahead this rate would drop. Stalin was determined that this drop, foreseen by the Planning Commission, must not be allowed to happen, and that, on the contrary, the rate of growth must be increased. The first five-year plan, adopted formally in April 1929 at the Sixteenth Party Conference, envisaged a very high growth rate for industrial production. [58] Stalin initiated an all-out drive for rapid industrialization, the most ruthless part of which was the forced collectivization of agriculture.

It would take us too far afield to survey here the story of Soviet industrialization. The overall substantial growth of the economy, the radical transformation of the country, and the enormous sacrifices borne by the Soviet people under Stalin are well known. Some facts relating to the growth of the industrial work force should be pointed out, since they have relevance for our discussion.

From 1928 to the 1950s was the period during which the Soviet Union created a skilled and disciplined industrial work force. At the eve of the first five-year plan, the country had 15.5 million persons in its nonagricultural work force, as against 70.6 million engaged in agricultural occupations. [59] By 1959, the nonagricultural work force had grown to 56.2 million, and the agricultural work force had dropped to 52.8 million. Already by 1940 the nonagricultural work force reached 40.8 million, approximately a two-and-one-half-fold increase over 1928. Along with the increased importance of nonagricultural labor, there was the expected shift

[56] R. W. Campbell, *Soviet Economic Power* (Boston: Houghton Mifflin, 1966), p. 21.

[57] D. W. Treadgold, *Twentieth Century Russia* (Chicago: Rand McNally, 1959), p. 263.

[58] For a detailed discussion, see Naum Jasny, *Soviet Industrialization* (Chicago: University of Chicago Press, 1961), Chapter III.

[59] These data are from W. W. Eason, "Labor Force" in A. Bergson and S. Kuznets (eds.), *Economic Trends in the Soviet Union* (Cambridge: Harvard University Press, 1963), p. 77.

of the population from the countryside to the city. In 1928, the urban population constituted 18.4 percent of the total population. By 1940, this percentage had risen to 31.6 and, by 1950, to 38.4. In 1960, a little more than one half of the total population was still classified as rural. In part, the increase in the urban population was due to natural growth, but it was also the result of massive shifts from the country to the city. Eight-and-one-half million peasants entered the urban labor market during the period of the first five-year plan.[60] The greatest influx was in 1931, when the collectivization upheaval contributed approximately 4.1 million peasants to the city.[61] Some of them were fleeing collectivization; some of them had been expelled as uncooperative peasants or as *kulaks* (well-to-do peasants). Industrialization and collectivization thus helped to create a large mass of floating, unskilled labor, which tended to move from job to job, city to city, and sometimes back to the land. The stabilization, training, and disciplining of this raw labor force was one of the major tasks of Soviet labor policy during the 1930s and 1940s.

Although our chief concern is with the role of social insurance, we must study it in the context of the overall labor policy. The measures adopted by the Soviet state after the onset of forced industrialization brought about significant changes in the employer–employee relationship and in the effective rights of the worker. The effort to meet the objectives of the five-year plan in the various sectors of the economy required that a corresponding supply of labor be made available. The government was not prepared to rely on the free labor market to bring about the desired allocation. A number of measures were initiated in the early 1930s that greatly limited the freedom of the worker to choose his place of employment—a freedom stipulated in the Code of 1922. In February of 1930 the labor exchanges were ordered to deal severely with workers who refused a job or retraining.[62] The following summer the Central Committee of the party castigated the Commissariat of Labor for "paying out tens of millions of rubles in relief 'for unemployment' while waging no struggle against self-seeking elements, floaters who refuse to work. . . ."[63] By a decree of October 9, all relief payments to the unemployed were stopped. The labor exchanges were informed by telegraphic wire that "the unemployed are to be given jobs not only within their vocational qualifications but also other work requiring no special skills."[64] Only sickness, attested by a medical certificate, was henceforth to be accepted as a valid reason for refusing work.

[60] Schwarz, *op. cit.*, p. 16.
[61] Eason, *op. cit.*, p. 74.
[62] For a discussion of the transformation of the labor market, see Schwarz, *op. cit.*, pp. 50 ff.
[63] Quoted in Conquest, *op. cit.*, p. 23.
[64] Quoted in Schwarz, *op. cit.*, p. 50.

As indicated earlier, the excessive instability of the work force was the most serious problem faced by the authorities. This involved very high turnover rates, frequent absenteeism, lateness, loafing on the job, and drunkenness. To some extent, these problems were caused by the fact that much of the labor force was as yet unaccustomed to the routine of industrial work, but to a significant degree they were a manifestation of protest against unfavorable working conditions and grossly inadequate housing. These problems were by no means new in Russian industry, but now the government felt that an all-out effort had to be made to combat these threats to productivity. In 1927, the Labor Code was revised to make three days' absence in any month punishable with dismissal without notice. In 1928 to 1929 "comrades' courts" were introduced to take action against negligent workers. These courts acted as a form of public pressure; they also could impose fines on workers guilty of violating industrial discipline. Subsequent decrees introduced stiffer penalties for absenteeism and quitting before the expiration of contracts. From November 1932 forward, "for even one day's non-appearance for work without good reason the worker could be dismissed, deprived of his right to use ration cards issued to him as a worker in a particular factory, and evicted from any housing allotted to him by the enterprise." [65] Evictions had to be carried out immediately, regardless of the worker's lack of housing. Especially severe penalties were prescribed in 1933 against kolkhoz workers who quit their industrial jobs without permission; they were guilty of an economic crime punishable with no less than six months' imprisonment and confiscation of their property.

During the mid-1930s, there was a pause in the enactment of disciplinary labor measures. This was the period during which the great purge spread fear throughout the country. New measures to tighten labor discipline appeared in 1938. The first of them was the requirement that every worker be furnished with a permanent workbook that was to contain a record of jobs held, with reasons for transfers, and the details of promotions and awards. The purpose of the book was to make it easy to identify and to label those with undesirable work habits. Another decree (December 28, 1938) required a month's notice (instead of seven days) for quitting, increased penalties for tardiness and unjustified absenteeism, and altered fringe benefits to reward steady work. Managers who failed to enforce these laws rigorously were subject to severe penalties. Further penalties were established in 1940, including corrective labor at the place of employment, which involved a loss of certain social security benefits and a 25 percent reduction of pay. But the most important development of 1940 was the provision that made it illegal for a worker to quit his job without permission of the management.[66] This complete abolition of the freedom of movement was enacted in

[65] Conquest, op. cit., p. 99.   [66]Ibid., pp. 104–106; Schwarz, op. cit., pp. 106–108.

the shadow of the war. It remained on the statute books until 1956, although by then it was apparently no longer enforced.

We shall now consider the role of social insurance in the context of the new labor relations. Under the circumstances, it was inevitable that social insurance should become one more device to be used by the authorities to carry out their general labor policy. We have already observed the tendency toward stricter eligibility rules in the mid-1920s and, more importantly, the abrupt and unqualified withdrawal of unemployment benefits in 1930. The first formal statement about the new orientation in social insurance was contained in a resolution adopted at a meeting of the party's Central Committee on September 28, 1929, which significantly enough was not made public until two years later. The party rebuked the social insurance agencies for "bureaucratic tendencies," failure to enlighten the masses, and failure to develop strong local groups of insurance activists. This was a clear indication that the insurance offices had failed to anticipate the new line in party policy. They had not adapted themselves to the new requirements of the economy. In the words of the party resolution: "One of the most serious shortcomings of the insurance organs is the lack of necessary attention to the rational distribution of benefits, which takes place without sufficient co-ordination with the aim of industrializing the country and serving industrial workers." [67]

Gintsburg has aptly summarized the role of Soviet social insurance inaugurated by the party in 1929:

> The first five-year plan opens a new era in the history of Soviet social insurance. As early as 1929, the social insurance organs were fully confronted with the task of reorganizing their work to achieve every possible support to the growth of labor productivity and every encouragement to shock work and socialist competition, to heighten the struggle against absenteeism and labor turnover, and to aid in the formation of cadres and in the strengthening of labor discipline. [68]

This theme was elaborated in many party and trade-union statements. Lip service was still paid to the notion that social insurance was a historic right of every Soviet worker—which was won for him by the revolution—but the main argument was that circumstances had changed and that new concepts were applicable. A writer in the labor journal *Voprosy Truda* explained that "during the recovery period, social insurance was an institution for securing the welfare of the working class. Today, in this socialist period, more is required of social insurance than 'security'; social insurance must now serve the purpose of socialist offensive." [69]

---

[67] Antoshkin, *op. cit.*, p. 58.
[68] *Op. cit.*, p. 66.
[69] Quoted in Schwarz, *op. cit.*, p. 309.

The new objectives were translated into changes in benefits, eligibility conditions, and administrative procedures. In 1933 the benefits for temporary disability represented 15.2 percent of the total social security budget, against 11.5 percent for old-age, disability, and survivorship pensions. By 1936, the respective percentages were 20.8 and 11.9, which reflects the tendency toward a relative neglect of those who were no longer able to work.[70] The authorities believed that benefits should now be treated as a work incentive, in line with the new labor policy. In 1929 a previous work requirement was introduced for the first time as a condition of eligibility for temporary disability benefits. We observed earlier that work requirements had been used in connection with old-age pensions and maternity benefits, but the argument then had been that the purpose of the requirement was to define the eligible status group. Now, on the other hand, the clear purpose was to influence the behaviour of the insured workers. The requirement introduced in 1929 was still rather mild, since it applied only to illnesses that lasted less than 15 days. In order to draw benefits equal to full wages in the case of such short-term sickness, a worker had to have a record of, at least, three years of employment in either industry or transportation (rail or water). All others were entitled only to 75 percent of their wage during the first five days of illness, but to 100 percent thereafter.[71]

This was only the beginning. Before long, eligibility conditions were considerably tightened, in the hope that stiffer work requirements would help combat the "fluidity" of the labor force. A decree of June 23, 1931 required that temporary disability benefits equal to full wages be paid only to workers and employees who had at least two years of *unbroken employment* in the present enterprise, at least three years of total previous employment, and who were members of a trade union. Union members with less than one year of unbroken employment at their current job were entitled to only two thirds of their earnings during the entire period of sickness. Other union members, those with more than one year who did not meet full eligibility requirements, were entitled to benefits ranging from two thirds to three fourths of earnings for the first 20 days of sickness and full benefits thereafter. Workers and employees who were not members of a union were entitled to only one half of their pay during the first 30 days and two thirds thereafter. The introduction of the concept of unbroken service at the same establishment clearly was intended to combat not only labor turnover but also absenteeism. Unauthorized absenteeism was treated as an interruption of the unbroken work record.

The concept of unbroken service presented all kinds of administrative difficulties, such as official transfers and discharges which were not the fault

[70]The data are from "Social Insurance in the U.S.S.R., 1933–1937," p. 233.
[71]Schwarz, *op. cit.*, p. 312; Gintsburg, *op. cit.*, p. 80.

of the worker. Also the concept offered many opportunities for enforcing industrial discipline. For instance, a rule introduced in 1932 to 1933 stated that "persons who are discharged from an enterprise or establishment as malicious disorganizers of production cannot count their previous work in that enterprise or establishment as part of their work stage." [72] The developments along these lines reached their climax with the enactment of the important law of December 28, 1938, which was concerned primarily with the strengthening of industrial discipline and with the combating of labor turnover. This new law made unbroken service in the same enterprise the chief determinant of benefits. The new rates for trade-union members were as follows:

Category of Service[73]	Percentage of Wage
Adult workers with unbroken service of:	
More than 6 years	100
3 to 6 years	80
2 to 3 years	60
Less than 2 years	50
Workers under 18 with unbroken service of:	
More than 2 years	80
Less than 2 years	60
Miners and workers in unhealthy occupations with unbroken service of:	
More than 2 years	100
Less than 2 years	60

For workers who were not trade-union members, the benefits were now set at one half the rate paid to union members in the same category.[74] The 1938 law also took into account the kind of work done. Dangerous and unhealthy occupations carried more lenient eligibility rules. The more productive workers were singled out for special rewards. Stakhanovite and the members of "shock brigades" were entitled to benefits equal to full earnings from the first day of illness.

Although the 1938 law greatly increased the work requirements for ordinary workers, it also stiffened the penalties for those guilty of breaches

---

[72] Gintsburg, *op. cit.*, p. 82.
[73] Adapted from Maurice Dobb, *Social Insurance in the Soviet Union* (London: National Council for British Soviet Unity) [*c.* 1943], p. 10.
[74] About 80 to 85 percent of the covered workers were union members. Those who were not were mainly seasonal and part-time workers.

of industrial discipline. Workers and employees who were dismissed for disciplinary reasons or who quit voluntarily were denied benefits altogether until they had been employed for at least six months at a new job. When the penalty of "corrective labor at the place of employment" was introduced in 1940, it was stipulated that the period of corrective labor would not count as part of the service record. The concept of unbroken service was further developed in the postwar years. In 1948 the requirement for full earnings benefits was raised to eight years for ordinary workers; the requirements for lesser rates were scaled up correspondingly. During these years, however, many exceptions were introduced that made the definition of unbroken service less rigorous. For example, a wife could quit without breaking her service if her husband was transferred. To stimulate postwar reconstruction, especially lenient service requirements were established in industries with a high priority. In 1955 these priority rates were again eliminated. The maximum benefit was set at 90 percent of earnings, for which now 12 years of unbroken service was required in all industries.[75]

Thus far we have followed the development of social insurance as a tool of labor control only with reference to temporary disability. In the other branches of social insurance, similar changes were taking place. Work requirements for maternity benefits were made comparable to the requirements for sickness benefits in 1931 and followed the same pattern thereafter. In 1936 the distinction between manual working women and salaried women was removed; all were entitled to a maternity leave of eight weeks before and eight weeks after giving birth. The swing toward a tightening of labor policy in 1938 led to a reduction in the leave to five weeks before and four after giving birth. After World War II, these benefits were again liberalized.

Pensions for disability, old-age, and survivorship were similarly brought in line with the new labor policies.[76] In general, the same principles were applied as in the case of temporary disability pensions. Particular emphasis was put on keeping eligible pensioners in the work force. At first they could draw part and, after 1938, all of their pension, in addition to their regular wage or salary. Enterprises were encouraged to find light jobs for partially disabled or elderly workers. Pension rates were tied to the length of the previous service as well as to the type of employment. In general, workers in underground and hazardous employment could qualify in shorter periods of time, or could retire at a younger age, and also could receive higher benefits. As a percentage of earnings, pensions were as a rule lower than temporary disability benefits. The basic principles introduced into the pension structure during the 1930s are still in force today, as we shall learn below.

[75] Gintsburg, op. cit., pp. 85–87.
[76] For more details, see Schwarz, op. cit., pp. 321 ff and also Gintsburg, op. cit., pp. 37 ff.

Aside from the important changes that the plan era brought about with regard to benefits and eligibility conditions, there were equally as significant changes in the area of administration. Under the system that had evolved during the New Economic Policy, the determination of eligibility and the payment of benefits, were in the hands of governmental agencies organized on a territorial basis. The trade unions exercised an ill-defined role in "controlling" and "influencing" these agencies. With the advent of rapid industrialization, this administrative structure came under severe attack. Ironically, one of the major charges against the agencies was that they treated all insured workers alike. Conducting business in a juridical fashion, which normally is a virtue when practiced by governmental agencies, had become grounds for condemnation. What the party wanted was not an administrative system that was merely competent in adhering to the letter of the law. To help achieve the objectives of the five-year plan, it needed a system that was responsive to the party line and able to make day-to-day decisions in the spirit of party directives. Also these decisions had to be understood and accepted by the workers. The administrative apparatus, therefore, had to be in close touch with the insured workers, as well as to be tuned in on the party line. It is not surprising that the existing administration, which had developed under different circumstances, was unsuited for the new tasks. It was denounced for failing to distinguish between work that was essential to the plan and work that was not, between shock workers and malingerers, and it was especially criticized for acting bureaucratically, in other words, for failing to keep in touch with the masses. None of these objections meant necessarily that the administration had failed to do what the laws had provided for.

The first organizational step in bringing social insurance in closer touch with the masses and in making it a more flexible policy tool was taken in 1931. The decree of June 23 of that year partially abolished the system of regional insurance funds by establishing special occupational funds. Until then, only transportation workers had a separate fund, because they were active in several regions. The objective of the new occupational funds was different: it was to facilitate the special treatment of workers in industries that were considered particularly important in the fulfillment of the five-year plan. The workers in the iron and steel, engineering, mining, chemical, and transportation industries were not to be treated just like ordinary workers. Another important step that was taken in 1931 was the establishment of social-insurance pay centers directly in enterprises employing more than 1000 persons. These establishments were important to the success of the five-year plan. The decree further sought to strengthen contact with the masses by requiring that these centers had to submit all their rules concerning benefits, and their budgets and accounts to the scrutiny of the trade unions. In this manner, approximately 50,000 workers are said to have become involved in insurance work.[77]

This arrangement was only transitory. In the views of the party and the government, the administration of social insurance was still insufficiently adapted to the needs of the five-year plan. The decision, therefore, was made in 1933 to turn over the entire administrative responsibility to the trade unions. This was a very important change. It must be kept in mind that this occurred after the unions had been thoroughly subjugated to the state and had lost the vestiges of independence they still enjoyed under the New Economic Policy. They had become an agency of the state whose primary function was to inculcate labor discipline, to instill a zeal for hard work, and to promote socialist competition. They had lost independent influence over wage determination. To enable them to carry out successfully their task of promoting productivity, it had clearly become necessary to restore to them a basis of influence over the workers. At the Ninth Trade Union Congress (1932), the last to be held until 1949, L. M. Kaganovich stressed that the unions must have something to offer the workers. "The trade union workers must achieve the kind of position that workers will first turn to their union with their needs and demands."[78] This was one of the major reasons for abolishing the Commissariat of Labor in 1933 and for turning over its welfare functions to the trade unions.

In his address to the plenary session of the Central Trade Union Council, Shvernik made it clear that the decision by the government to put the trade unions in charge of social insurance was not accidental. He explained that this function could be given to the unions only after the struggle against the "rightist opportunists" had been won. The latter saw the unions as defenders of the workers against the party and the state. "They forgot that the first obligation of the trade unions is the mobilization of the masses to follow the line drawn by the Party."[79] The task of the unions was to follow the party and lead the masses.

> The experience of the past years brilliantly confirms that only by following the Party line, only under the leadership of the Party, can the trade unions timely manage the turning points of all the stages of the development of the dictatorship of the proletariat, assure their authority over the masses, strengthen their everyday contact with the masses, and march at the head of the masses.[80]

Having made very clear the subordinate authority of the unions, Shvernik stressed that with this authority went nevertheless grave responsibility. "We

[77] R. Abrahamson, "The Reorganization of Social Insurance Institutions in the U.S.S.R.," *International Labor Review*, Vol. XXXI (March 1935), p. 370.
[78] Quoted by N. Shvernik, *O Zadachakh VtsSPS i Professional'nykh Soiuzov v Sviazi im Funktsii Narkomtruda* (Moscow: Profizdat, 1933), p. 8.
[79] *Ibid.*, p. 4.   [80] *Ibid.*, p. 14.

have become complete masters of social insurance, but this also imposes upon us, as I have said, vast obligations and responsibility."[81]

The chief problem facing the unions in the gigantic expansion of the economy, Shvernik continued, was the instability of the work force. This could only be dealt with by eliminating the existing tendency toward egalitarian pay scales and by introducing incentives for improved work. The simultaneous rapid expansion of social insurance funds, he pointed out, gave rise to special opportunities for incentive rewards. He offered the following guidelines:

> Bureaucracy and egalitarianism must be eradicated from social insurance. We must reconstruct the whole social insurance practice in order to give the most privileged treatment to shock workers and to those with long service. The fight against labor turnover must be put into the forefront. We shall handle social insurance as a weapon in the struggle to attach workers to their enterprises and strike hard at loafers, malingerers, and disorganizers of work. . . . At the center of trade-union social insurance work must be care for the worker who has been actively wrestling with the fulfillment of the industrial financial plan and the work norms.[82]

An important aspect of the administrative reorganization was the opportunity to personally involve many trade-union members directly in the day-to-day social insurance work. This was part of the official goal of maintaining contact with the masses, which was essential for the achievement of the productivity goals. Again, Shvernik made this point very clear in his talk.

> We must strengthen the drawing of broad masses of workers and employees into the active work of the trade-union organizations. . . . Only if we draw even more workers into the work of the trade-union organizations, only if we further strengthen the daily contact of trade unions with the workers, can we bring union work to a level commensurate with the huge tasks imposed upon us.[83]

It followed that trade-union members should receive higher disability benefits and favored treatment in the distribution of passes to rest homes and health resorts. Control over social insurance gave the unions leverage in the control of the workers. Not only could the union leaders exercise discretion in making awards, in serious cases they could refuse union membership to an uncooperative worker, which would deprive him of significant benefits.

A number of other significant changes were carried out during the 1930s. After the adoption of the 1936 constitution, which contains broad statements on the rights to social security, free health care, and work,

[81] *Ibid.*, p. 19.
[82] *Ibid.*, p. 31.
[83] *Ibid.*, p. 31.

certain discriminatory features were removed from the Soviet welfare system. In 1937, old-age pensions were extended to salaried employees; they had applied only to manual workers. Also the pension programs were extended to cover for the first time persons who had been deprived of their electoral rights because of their social origin or previous activities. These changes were consistent with the constitution's guarantees to Soviet citizens and with the new emphasis on the individual's economic merit. Certain changes in financial organization reflect a similar orientation. Given the constitutional emphasis on free medical care for all citizens, it was logical that the financing of this care should be under the government budget instead of under social insurance. The trade unions were thus relieved of financing health care. At the same time the financing of old-age, survivorship, and permanent disability pensions and of worker housing was shifted from the social insurance to the state budget.

It is extremely difficult to evaluate the impact of social insurance on the welfare of the Soviet worker during the period of rapid industrialization. There is no doubt about the huge growth of the system, along with the growth of the nonagricultural work force. Between 1929 and 1936 the insured population increased from 10.9 million to 25.6 million.[84] By the outbreak of World War II approximately 30 million people were covered by social insurance.[85] Total social-insurance expenditures increased by comparable amounts, from 0.7 billion rubles in 1927 to 1928, to 7.4 billion in 1940, and to 17.9 billion in 1950.[86] Until the mid-1950s, however, the emphasis remained on care for those still actively in the work force as opposed to benefits for those who had retired. In 1950, the amount spent on pensions was still less than half the total social insurance budget, 8 billion rubles out of a budget of 17.9 billion.[87] Professor Minkoff shows the neglect of pensioners; throughout the period there was a downward trend in the level of pensions in relation to wages. In 1926 to 1927 the average monthly pension was 36 percent of the wage; by 1937 it had dropped to 29 percent, and by 1955 to 23 percent of the wage.[88] Temporary disability benefits were always a much higher percentage of the wage, but they too showed a tendency to fall from more than 95 percent of the wage in the 1920s to 70 to 90 percent in the early 1950s.[89]

[84] "Social Insurance in the U.S.S.R., 1933–1937," p. 228.
[85] Dobb, *Social Insurance in the Soviet Union*, p. 6. Also Minkoff, *op. cit.*, p. 20.
[86] Minkoff, *op. cit.*, pp. 319–310.
[87] Tsentral'noe Statisticheskoe Upravlenie, *Narodnoe Khoziaistvo v 1958 Godu* (Moscow, 1959), p. 906.
[88] Minkoff, *op. cit.*, p. 25.
[89] *Ibid.*, p. 28.

DEVELOPMENTS SINCE STALIN

One of the central themes of this book is the relationship between economic development and social security policy. In no country has the link between economic objectives and social security been more direct than in the Soviet Union. The period we have just reviewed best illustrates this link. In the years following the death of Joseph Stalin (March 5, 1953) we find a new stage of Soviet economic development. We now examine some of the relevant aspects of this stage and determine how social security policy was altered to meet the changing needs.

Although the demise of an individual is normally a precarious basis for marking off a new stage in the economic history of a country, in the case of Stalin there is ample justification for this procedure. The system of highly centralized planning and of the coercive use of power that had guided the country's rapid industrialization after 1928 is properly identified with Stalin. Its successes and failures, its strengths and weaknesses, are closely associated with Stalin's formidable personality. By the time of Stalin's death the country had been transformed into an industrial socialist society, an economic power second only to the United States. But Stalin bequeathed also certain problematic legacies with which his successors had to wrestle. Although he had ruthlessly eliminated all opposition during his lifetime, he could not prevent the development of a certain passive resistance to his policies during the postwar years. The people who had borne the heavy burden of industrialization and the enormous sacrifices of the war were tired of unremitting demands. The time had come for them to partake to a more generous extent in the fruits of their historic labor. The overcentralized and excessively capital goods oriented Stalinist economic machine had to be reorganized to meet their needs more adequately. By far the weakest sector of the economy was agriculture. The drastic collectivization solution imposed by Stalin and inadequate supplies of capital had turned agriculture into the Achilles heel of the Soviet economy.

Our interest lies primarily in the manpower aspects of the post-Stalin era. One of the important changes since the 1930s is the greater scarcity of labor. Professor Eason observes that:

> . . . until recently, manpower resources have been abundant, compared with capital and arable land. The recruitment and allocation of labor for industry, therefore, has not been a serious drain on the agricultural labor force, and Soviet manpower policies, by the standards of the more industrialized countries, have appeared to be wasteful of labor. But the rate of growth of over-all labor supply has now declined and if the pace of industrialization is to continue, this decline must be offset by the more effective utilization of labor.[90]

[90] Eason, *loc. cit.*, p. 41.

There are several reasons for the relative shortage of manpower in the post-war era, including a sharp drop in fertility rates after 1928 and the tremendous manpower losses caused by World War II.

Another important reason is the gradual exhaustion of the substantial manpower surplus that existed in Russian agriculture in 1928. The collective farm system and organized recruitment were effective in eliminating much of the disguised unemployment from the land. But continued less favorable treatment of the agricultural rather than the industrial sector has led to a *Landflucht* of the young. At harvest time there is now an acute shortage in agriculture. Two recent Soviet writers note that the government and the party "are naturally worried by the unwonted mass drift of young people to the towns, the extent of which has been higher than originally foreseen."[91] They point out that in many regions the average age of the agricultural population approaches 50. This is a very serious problem for the future of Soviet agriculture. In spite of long proclaimed goals, the socialist society has not been able to eliminate the economic and cultural backwardness of the village. Past welfare policies neglected the peasant and contributed to this state of affairs, which the authorities are now seeking to remedy.

It will be recalled that during the 1930s the chief labor problem facing the planners was excessive fluidity of the work force. This problem has not disappeared, although it is probably less serious today. One of its chief new manifestations has been a constant flow of labor out of Siberia and the Far North, countering the efforts of the authorities to build up these areas. In the immediate postwar years there was a drift back home of the population that had been moved eastward with the factories during the war. But the movement has persisted, mainly because of inadequate housing and cultural facilities. According to one report, between 1959 and 1963, over a quarter of a million more people left Siberia than moved there.[92] In the older established industrial areas, turnover has remained high and a constant source of serious concern for the authorities. Yet, also, there has been the opposite problem, namely, the hoarding of labor reserves by industrial enterprises. Students familiar with Soviet planning are well aware of the tendencies of Soviet managers to overstate their labor requirements and to conceal labor surpluses.[93] Underutilized labor within a plant provides a safety factor in coping with pressures to fulfill and to overfulfill the plan.

---

[91] M. Sonin and E. Zhiltsov, "Economic Development and Employment in the Soviet Union," *International Labor Review*, Vol. IVC, No. 1 (July 1967), p. 78.

[92] Reported in Conquest, *op. cit.*, p. 107.

[93] See J. Berliner, *Factory and Manager in the USSR* (Cambridge: Harvard University Press, 1957) and D. Granick, *Management of the Industrial Firm in the USSR* (New York: Columbia University Press, 1954).

Reforms introduced in 1965, which stress profit rather than gross output, were designed to combat this kind of waste.

In view of the overall increasing scarcity of labor, the chief emphasis of recent Soviet labor policy has been on more effective utilization of labor resources. Aside from cutting down undesired turnover, this involves primarily the reallocation of labor, the maintenance of its working capacity, and the upgrading of skills. The chief reallocation problems are geographic. Unlike in the 1930s, when there was a rural labor surplus, there is now in some cases a relative urban surplus, especially in small and medium-sized towns. Sonin and Zhiltsov hint that people are able to maintain themselves by working their private plots of land, which is officially looked on as an inefficient allocation of labor. The government naturally wishes to eliminate this "disguised unemployment" and to shift any excess labor to the East and Far North where the shortage is greater. Within industry the reallocation problem concerns primarily workers whose skills have become obsolete or whose jobs have been eliminated by technological advances. As in the West, Soviet Union automation gives rise to the phenomenon of frictional and structural unemployment. The authorities recognize the problem of the technologically redundant worker, and at least one Soviet economist has suggested the reestablishment of some form of unemployment compensation in those cases.[94] However, the emphasis thus far has been on retraining. Under a 1959 government resolution a displaced worker engaged in full-time retraining may draw 100 percent of his former wage for the first month, 70 percent for the second, and 40 percent for the third month.[95] Under another arrangement a displaced skilled worker is guaranteed his former wage for a period of three months when he transfers to a job in another enterprise where his new wage is lower. A number of measures have been taken to facilitate the placement of new entrants into the work force on leaving school. Temporary juvenile unemployment seems to be a fairly widespread problem; it is partly a result of fairly high birth rates in the postwar years.

Among the factors that were likely to influence Soviet social security policy in the post-Stalin era we have pointed out thus far the rising aspirations of the Soviet population and the country's work force requirements. Other elements that should be taken into account are demographic change and urbanization. By 1959 the Soviet Union had 19.7 million people aged 60 and over, as compared with 11.2 million in 1939, and 9.8 million in 1926.[96] The percentage of the aged still in the work force declined from 54.1 in 1926 to 43.2 in 1959, which means that at the latter date there were 11.5 million people over 60 who were no longer working. The drop in work

[94] Reported in Conquest, op. cit., p. 37.

[95] Sonin and Zhiltsov, loc. cit., p. 87.

[96] Eason, loc. cit., p. 54.

force participation by the aged is directly related to the rural-urban shift We recall that by 1960 just slightly under one half of the Soviet population lived in urban areas. They were without the means of self-support that are more readily available in an agricultural environment.

In previous chapters we observed repeatedly that significant changes in social security often did not occur until a crisis situation existed which made imperative a reformulation of the relationship between the state and the individual. A crisis of sorts in the Soviet Union was the Twentieth Congress of the Soviet Communist Party in February 1956. It was at this congress that Krushchev unleashed a ferocious attack against Stalin for the harsh life he had forced on Soviet citizens. Krushchev called for important reforms, including a more adequate social security program. It was in this liberating spirit that shortly thereafter, in May 1956, the draft of a new pension law was published and made available for public discussion. After two months of discussion, in which a wide segment of the population participated, a new pension law was enacted to come into force on October 1, 1956.

The pension system that existed prior to 1956 was very inadequate. The majority of the workers were receiving 150 rubles a month, which was the ceiling established in 1932. In the meantime, wages and prices had risen well above the 1932 levels, but pensions were not adjusted, even though the maximum pension was below the subsistence level. Only specialized workers in key industries were benefiting from more advantageous pension schemes. In the discussions that preceded the enactment of the new law, the question that seemed to have greatest prominence, at least to the extent that the discussions were made public, was the retirement age. Since 1928 the usual retirement age had been 60 for men and 55 for women, after 25 years of covered employment, which did not include most agricultural jobs. There were apparently widespread popular demands for lower retirement ages. Some demands were for a lower retirement age for those who had worked more than the required number of years and for mothers with children; there were also demands for across the board reductions to ages 55 for men and 50 for women. The argument advanced in support of this proposal is highly revealing of the prevailing sentiment: "Our generation has experienced three major wars, has borne on its shoulders all the hardships of the reconstruction of the national economy, and for this has used much of its strength and health."[97]

As enacted, the law left the retirement age at 60 for men and 55 for women, and the covered employment requirement at 25 years. Special provisions, however, were made for occupations involving hard work, for underground, hot, unhealthy occupations, for mothers of large families, and for

[97] Quoted by R. Schlesinger, "The New Pension Law," *Soviet Studies*, Vol. VIII, No. 3 (January 1957), p. 311.

blind persons (see Table 7–1). These special provisions reflect both the desire of the authorities to attract labor into difficult occupations as well as their desire to express society's special concern for particularly deserving individuals. As of January 1968, a new category of workers has been awarded privileged old-age retirement conditions—those employed in the Far North and in similar regions.[98] The current eligibility conditions for other than collective farm workers are given below.

Table 7–1

Age and Service Requirements for Old-Age Pensions in the USSR

Category	Men		Women	
	Age	Years of Service	Age	Years of Service
Ordinary work	60	25	55	20
Difficult work	55	25	50	20
Work in Far North or similar area	55	15 to 20	50	15 to 20
Dangerous work	50	20	45	15
Mother of large family[a]			50	15
Blind worker	50	15	40	10

[a]At least five children, each cared for until each is eight.

Source. Adapted from Robert J. Myers, "Economic Security in the Soviet Union," *Transactions of the Society of Actuaries*, Vol. XI, p. 731.

Under Article 12 of the 1956 law, reduced pensions are provided for those who do not fulfill the service requirement but have at least five years in covered work, three of which were immediately prior to retirement.[99]

With regard to disability and survivorship pensions, the new law followed the principles in force since 1928. There was no length of service requirement for work-connected total disability pensions. Nonwork-connected disability and survivorship pensions had service requirements that varied with the age of the worker and that were higher for men than for women. Under the 1956 law the requirement for men in ordinary work ranged from 2 years of service at ages 20 to 22 to 20 years at ages 61 and older. For women, the corresponding requirements range from 1 to 15 years. Persons doing underground, unhealthy, and dangerous work were given the most lenient service requirements, with only 14 years at ages 61 and older. All such preferential occupational treatment required that at least half the

[98] "Changes in Social Security in the U.S.S.R.," *International Labor Review*, Vol. IIIC, No. 3 (March 1968), p. 311.
[99] For a Russian text of the law, see *Sotsial'noe Obespechenie v SSSR, Sbornik Ofitsial'nykh Materialov* (Moscow: Profizdat, 1962), pp. 7–22.

required length of service was performed in the privileged work category. On the whole, these eligibility requirements reflect both the concept of restricting benefits to a designated group and the idea of an incentive reward for special work.

The notion of incentive is expressed strongly in the pension rates and in special bonuses. The rates for old-age pensions established by the 1956 law are illustrated below (see Table 7–2).

Table 7–2

Old-Age Pension Rates in the USSR

	Monthly Basic Pension as a Percentage of Earnings	
Monthly Earnings	Ordinary Work	Underground, Unhealthy, and Dangerous Work
Under 300r	300r	300r
300 to 350	100 percent	100 percent
350 to 500	85	90
500 to 600	75	80
600 to 800	65	70
800 to 1000	55	60
1000 and over	50	55
Maximum Pension	1200r	

Source. Sotsial'noe Obespechenie v SSSR, p. 25.

The new rates were a vast improvement over the system in existence prior to 1956. The new minimum rate of 300 rubles was set at twice the maximum of the old system, which incidentally testifies to the gross inadequacy of the latter. The de facto flat system was eliminated by the new wage-related scale, itself a compromise between the goals of incentive and adequacy. For the first time in the history of Soviet social insurance, the rate structure was weighted in favor of the lower income receivers. In line with the demands raised during the discussion period, special supplements may be earned on top of the basic pension. Workers and salaried employees who have 15 years of continuous service with their last employer, and those who have 10 years of service above the required minimum, are eligible for a bonus equal to 10 percent of their monthly basic pension. In addition to this incentive bonus there is an adequacy bonus. Pensioners with one dependent are entitled to a 10 percent increase and those with two or more dependents receive a 15 percent increase of their basic pensions. This supplement, which is not granted if the dependent is of working age and able to work, is kept rather low, no doubt, as an encouragement to wives to earn a pension in their own right. It should be noticed also that the supplements cannot bring the pension above the maximum of 1200 rubles per months (or in terms of new rubles—since 1961—120 per month). This maximum is still in effect in 1968, and there is no provision for the automatic adjustment of pensions that have been already awarded, to the growth of national income or to the cost of living. On the other hand, newly awarded pensions tend to rise with the wage level, because they are based on the earnings of either the last 12 months or the best 5 out of the last 10 years.

The benefit formulas for disability pensions have always tended to be complex in the Soviet Union. The system that existed from the late 1930s to 1956 contained many inequities, since benefits varied according to the branch of the economy in which a worker was employed. This kind of discrimination was eliminated, but many other differentiations were retained. The system established in 1956 makes the relationship of pension to earnings depend on the following factors: (a) the cause of disability (whether or not it was work-connected), (b) the type of work (ordinary; underground, unhealthy, or in very hot shops; very difficult), and (c) the degree of disability. Three classes of disability are distinguished: Class I includes the totally disabled in need of constant attendance; Class II includes the totally disabled who do not need constant attendance; and Class III includes those who have a permanent partial disability. Table 7–3 summarizes the wage-benefit relationship of Soviet disability pensions.

Table 7–3

Soviet Disability Pensions (Pre-1961 Rubles)

Type	Percentage of Monthly Earnings		
	Class I	Class II	Class III
Nonwork-Connected Disability			
Ordinary	85% of 500r + 10% of R[a]	65% of 450r + 10% of R	45% of 400r + 10% of R
Very heavy	85% of 500r + 15% of R	65% of 500r + 15% of R	45% of 500r + 15% of R
Underground, etc.	85% of 600r + 20% of R	65% of 600r + 20% of R	45% of 600r + 20% of R
Minimum	300r	230r	160r
Maximum	900r	600r	400r
Work-Connected Disability			
Ordinary	100% of 500r + 10% of R	90% of 450r + 10% of R	65% of 400r + 10% of R
Very heavy	100% of 500r + 15% of R	90% of 500r + 15% of R	65% of 500r + 15% of R
Underground, etc.	100% of 600r + 20% of R	90% of 600r + 20% of R	65% of 600r + 20% of R
Minimum	360r	285r	210r
Maximum	1200r	900r	450r

[a]Remainder.

Source. Myers, op. cit., p. 735.

As this table shows, disability pensions are heavily weighted in favor of the lower income recipients, which indicates a concern for adequacy. This is especially true with regard to work-connected disability, which has always been compensated at a higher rate than nonwork-connected disability. Figure 7–1 brings out an interesting difference between old-age and disability pensions. The latter are much less incentive oriented; disability pensions rise more slowly with higher earning levels and tend to have lower

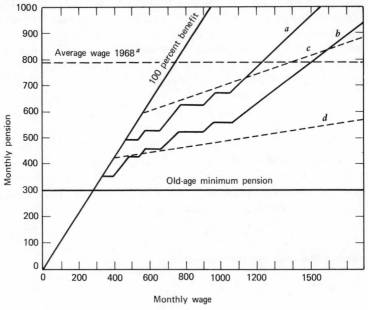

Figure 7–1

Relation of earnings and pension scales (pre-1961 rubles). (a) Old-age pension for underground work with 10 percent service supplement; (b) Old-age pension for ordinary work with no supplement; (c) Class I Disability, underground work, nonwork connected, with 15 percent service supplement; (d) Class I Disability, ordinary work, with no supplement.
[a]Tsentral'noe Statisticheskoe Upravlenie, *op. cit.*, p. 567.

ceilings. This remains true even when the supplements are taken into account. Service supplements are available only for nonwork-connected disabilities, at the rate of 10 percent of the basic pensions for 10 to 14 years of continuous service with the last employer, and 15 percent for 15 or more years of continuous service. In cases of total disability (Classes I and II), there is also a supplement of 10 percent for one dependent and 15 percent for two or more. This reflects once more the concern with adequacy that seems to come to the fore in the disability pension structure. This does not mean that the authorities were reluctant to use disability pensions for incentive purposes. The tendency toward lower disability pensions may indicate a concern with the problem of malingering should these pensions afford too comfortable a living.

The computation of survivorship pensions is quite similar to the one for disability pensions. The pension received by one eligible survivor is the same as a Class III disability pension for the same kind of work and cause of death. For instance, one survivor of an ordinary worker who died from a nonwork-connected cause receives 45 percent of the first 400 rubles of monthly earnings and 10 percent of the remainder. For two survivors, the pension is the same as a Class II disability pension, and for three or more survivors it is the same as a Class I disability pension. Since 1956, some adjustments have been made in the pension structure and the eligibility conditions, but the basic scheme for non-collective farmers has remained unchanged.

One aspect that deserves comment is the relatively low retirement age, especially in view of the country's overall tendency toward a labor shortage. This would seem to be an area where the wishes of the people limit the objectives of the government. Low retirement ages have become part of Soviet social insurance history; it will be recalled that retirement at 50 was one of the Bolshevik demands in 1914. In the meantime, however, life expectancy in the country has dramatically improved, in fact, roughly doubled at birth. At age 60, Soviet life expectancy today (1958 to 1959) is higher than in the United States, 19.3 years as compared to 17.3.[100] To compensate for this loss of manpower, there is increasing pressure in the Soviet Union to keep able-bodied pensioners at work, especially if they are skilled. From 1938 to 1956, although pensions were below subsistence level, a pensioner could draw his full pension while he continued to work. When pensions were raised in 1956, the amount an ordinary working pensioner could draw as a pension remained 150 rubles, the old maximum pension. If he earned more than 1000 rubles a month he received no pension, except if he was in underground or unhealthy work, in which case he was entitled to 50 percent of his pension regardless of earnings.[101] In 1964, the USSR Council of Ministers decided to provide increased incentives for eligible pensioners to remain at work. As of April 1, 1964, working pensioners in certain skilled occupations can get in addition to their wages at least 50 percent of their pension, and in no case less than the minimum pension laid down by law. In regions where the labor shortage is acute, the incentive is increased. For instance, working pensioners in the Urals, the Far East, and Siberia may

[100] Calculated by the chief actuary of the United States Social Security Administration, Robert J. Myers, in "Summarized Translation of 'Tables of Mortality and Average Life Expectancy of the Population of the U.S.S.R., 1958–1959'," mimeographed, p. 6.
[101] For a discussion of this provision, see Minkoff, *op. cit.*, p. 246.

draw 75 percent of their pension.[102] Those who take a job in agriculture may keep their entire pension, regardless of earnings.

The other major social insurance programs also underwent changes in the post-Stalin era. For the first time, in 1955, a minimum was established for cash sickness benefits, but eligibility requirements were tightened. Notice that the latter move against the liberalizing trend occurred before the memorable Twentieth Congress of the Soviet Communist Party. Some minor benefit improvements were made in 1957, such as raising the minimum benefit; it was not until 1967 that a liberalizing of service requirements was carried out. Table 7–4 illustrates the change in service requirements from the law of 1938 until the most recent law, which took effect January 1, 1968. The current law returned to the pattern that existed between 1948 and 1955. In the meantime, improvements had been made by easing the definition of unbroken service. Prior to 1960, cash sickness benefits (for nonwork-connected illness) were not available to a worker who quit his job voluntarily until after six months on a new job. This penalty was dropped in 1960, provided that he took a new job within one month. It was retained, however, for disciplinary discharges.[103]

Table 7–4

General Cash Sickness Benefits: 1938–1968

Benefit as a Percentage of Earnings	Years of Unbroken Service at Last Job			
	1938	1948	1955	1967
100	Over 6	Over 8	Not granted	Over 8
90			Over 12	
80	3 to 6	5 to 8	8 to 12	5 to 8
70			5 to 8	
60	2 to 3	3 to 5	3 to 5	3 to 5
50	2 or less	3 or less	3 or less	3 or less
	Maximum benefit: 10 rubles per day			

Source. Minkoff, *op. cit.*, p. 196; "Changes in Social Security in the USSR," *International Labour Review* (March 1968), p. 311.

The rates indicated in Table 7–4 are payable to adults who are members of trade unions, in the case of nonwork-connected illness. All benefits are

[102] These benefits are not available to ordinary workers who earn 200 (new) rubles a month, but there is no earning limitation on underground and dangerous work. See "Vyplata Pensii po Starosti Rabotaischim Pensioneram," *Sotsial'noe Obespechenie*, No. 6 (1964), pp. 54–58.
[103] *Current Digest of the Soviet Press*, Vol. XII, No. 4 (February 24, 1960), p. 24.

payable from the first day of illness without any waiting period. Workers who are not members of trade unions still receive only one half of the standard rate. In rural areas benefits are 10 percent lower than in the city if the worker has a private plot of land. A similar provision applies to pensions, which are 15 percent lower in the country. Benefits for work-connected temporary disability are equal to 100 percent of earnings, payable during the entire period of incapacity. If the incapacity lasts more than several months, the individual is put into the permanent disability category, which pays lower benefits. There is an interesting ideological twist to the Soviet concept of work-connected disability. It covers not only the regular job but also work performed "for social organizations, saving human life, protecting socialist property, maintaining peace, and so forth."[104] There is no difference between benefits to union and nonunion workers in work-connected disability.

For completeness, mention should be made of maternity benefits and family allowances. We observed earlier that during the 1930s the service requirement for eligibility for maternity leave was increased. During the war this requirement was lowered, and in 1956 it was eliminated altogether. Since then, women have been allowed 112 days of maternity leave regardless of the nature or length of employment. The amount of benefit, however, still depends on previous total and uninterrupted employment. Women with less than one year of unbroken service get two thirds of their recent pay; at the other end of the scale, women with two or more years of unbroken service, and with at least three years of total employment, receive 100 percent of their earnings.[105] In addition, there are lump-sum payments at birth and children's allowances. These payments are intended to "encourage child birth and provide added protection for mothers and children."[106] Very small lump sums, for the purchase of a layette, are granted at each birth; more substantial sums begin only with the third child. These rise from 20 (new) rubles at the birth of the third child to 250 (new) rubles at the birth of the eleventh and subsequent children. Family allowances are quite modest and paid only to families with four or more children. The rate increases from 4 rubles a month for the fourth child to 15 for the eleventh and subsequent children but only over a period of five years for each child. Unwed mothers are under a special program that pays an allowance up to age 12 at the rate of 5 rubles for one child, 7.5 rubles for two, and 10 rubles a month for three or more children. These provisions are mainly based on a law passed in 1944. They have not been substantially altered in the post-Stalin era.

[104] K. Batyguine, "Sickness and Maternity Benefits," *Bulletin of the International Social Security Association,* Vol. XVII, Nos. 8 and 9 (August–September 1964), p. 262.
[105] *Ibid.,* p. 263.
[106] K. Boitsov, "Benefits for Mothers and Children," *Bulletin of the International Social Security Association,* Vol. XVII, Nos. 8 and 9 (August–September 1964), p. 264.

Aside from the pension revision of 1956, the most important social security event of this era has been the extension of state social insurance pensions to collective farmers by a law of July 15, 1964, which went into effect on January 1, 1965. The Russian farmers, other than the ones employed on state farms, collective tractor stations, and similar institutions, had never been covered by state social insurance, although in theory they were included under the programs of War Communism. This represented the most serious gap in the country's welfare system. It was inconsistent with the overall emphasis on social protection and, in recent years, with the agricultural manpower situation. This kind of discrimination against collective farm peasants was hardly an incentive to keep efficient workers on the land, especially after the 1956 pension reform had established the possibility of a reasonable retirement income in most other occupations.

The shortcomings of the collective farmers' protection in cases of old-age and disability had been recognized for many years. The official reason for excluding them had always been that the collective farmers were not part of the socialized economy and, hence, had no claim to the funds set aside for social consumption. In view of the peasants' contribution to the state's income, the weakness of this argument hardly needs comment. In any case, since the early days of the Soviet regime the peasants were expected to provide their own income maintenance through mutual assistance programs.[107] The government tried to promote these programs and to encourage collective farm managements to use them to enforce labor discipline. Thus, the model rules published by the Russian Republic in 1958 contain a paragraph that states: "Aid is refused in the case of members who, without good reason, have failed to complete the minimum number of work units, or systematically infringed labour discipline, or displayed an improper attitude towards work or collective property."[108] In the past the earnings of collective farms have been generally low and highly uneven. Only the farms of the more fertile areas were in a position to give reasonable income guarantees for those of their members no longer able to work. The RSFSR Minister of Social Security noted in 1964 that in spite of the good work done, the old system had serious shortcomings.

> In the determination of pensions for kolkhoz members there was serious lack of coordination with regard to the fixing of retirement age, the length and

---

[107]For a brief survey of the development of these programs, see I. Gushchin, "Razvitie Sotsial'nogo Obespecheniia Kolkhoznikov," *Sotsial'noe Obespechenie,* No. 8 (August 1965), pp. 14–16.

[108]"Model Rules for Collective Farmers' Mutual Aid Societies in the Russian Soviet Federal Socialist Republic," *Bulletin of the International Social Security Association,* Vol. XI, Nos. 10 and 11 (October–November 1958), p. 458.

degree of participation in social production, and the amount of contribution to the pension fund. This situation, naturally, had not only a negative impact on the security of disabled kolkhoz members but also on the development of kolkhoz production.[109]

The old system had the character of an assistance program; it usually paid benefits only in case of need and in the absence of able-bodied family members.

Under the new law, Kolkhoz members are eligible for old-age, disability, and survivorship pensions, and women receive maternity leaves. It establishes a uniform system for all collective farmers in the country in the place of the great diversity that existed formerly. Benefits are financed by a contribution of 4 percent of income from each collective farm, and the remainder comes from the state budget. The 1964 law set the retirement age for men at 65, after 25 years of work, and 60 for women, after 20 years of work. In 1967 the retirement ages were reduced by 5 years and thereby made comparable to the ones of most industrial workers. The amount of the monthly old-age pension is equal to 50 percent of the first 50 rubles of earnings, plus 25 percent of the earnings above 50 rubles, subject to a maximum of 102 rubles per month. The earning period used in the calculation of the pension is the best consecutive 5 years out of the previous 15.[110] In the case of disability and survivorship pensions, the service requirement varies with the age of the beneficiary, but the benefit formula is the same as that for old-age.[111]

In spite of the important post-Stalin changes in favor of welfare objectives. Soviet social insurance remains a tool of the ruling party for the mobilization of the working masses; it is still a means of social control through the involvement of the masses in the activities of the state. For pensioners this is done primarily through social councils. The varied activities of pensioners are described by one Soviet authority as follows:

The social activity of pensioners is notably increasing; they cooperate voluntarily with the standing committees of soviets of workers' delegates, with committees for blocks of flats and quarters, with committees of parents whose children attend schools, with clubs and library councils, with comrades' tribunals attached to the management of blocks of flats and with councils of women. Many pensioners give their time voluntarily to the trade union boards

[109]L. P. Lykova, "Zadacha Gosudarstvennoi Vazhnosti," *Sotsial'noe Obespechenie*, No. 12 (1964), p. 2.
[110]For more details, see P. Machanov, "Old-Age, Invalidity and Survivorship Pensions for Members of Collective Farms," *Bulletin of the International Social Security Association*, Vol. XVII, (August–September 1964), pp. 253–257.
[111]For recent slight modifications, see "Changes in Social Security in the U.S.S.R.," *International Labor Review*, Vol. IIIC (March 1968), p. 312.

of undertakings and their committees. They are members of the committees responsible for fixing pensions and of expertise committees.

Pensioners render voluntary unpaid service in financial establishments. Over 27,000 such voluntary assistants work in district, urban and regional financial establishments in the Russian Federation. They include 21,000 accountants, economists, engineers, and technicians working in undertakings and organizations. They take an active part in the campaign for an economic and rational use of financial resources and state credits, for the development and use of economic reserves guaranteeing an increase in socialist assets, and of budget receipts.[112]

It appears also that most pensioners on collective farms actively participate in field and other work during the busy times of the year.

With regard to benefits for the active labor force, the trade unions still play the role they assumed in 1933. Their basic objective is still the promotion of productivity, although with the changes in the manpower situation since then the emphasis is now somewhat different. Today the maintenance of the workers' productive capacity through the preservation and restoration of health and the prevention of accidents receives more attention than the combating of turnover, which was once the dominant concern. The manner in which Soviet social insurance operates at the factory level and its integration with the drive for increased production can be illustrated in a brief examination of the activities that relate to the incapacity to work.[113] Of primary importance is the fact that adjudication of sickness benefits gives the trade union opportunities and an organization for controlling both voluntary and involuntary absenteeism. First on the list of rights and responsibilities of insurance delegates is the duty to visit the home of a worker or salaried employee of their trade union group who has failed to report for work, either on account of sickness or for any unexplained reason.[114] In one plant this operates as follows: "The shop social insurance commission is given daily the names of those who do not show up for work. Through the leader of the trade union group it informs the social insurance delegate. The sick colleagues are paid a visit on the very same day."[115] What happens if the colleague is merely taking a day off is not clear, but it prob-

[112]M. Derevnine, "The Community's Participation in the Work of the Social Security Services," *Bulletin of the International Social Security Association*, Vol. XVII, Nos. 8 and 9 (August–September 1964), p. 268.

[113]The following description is drawn from Gaston V. Rimlinger, "The Trade Union in Soviet Social Insurance: Historical Development and Present Functions," *Industrial and Labor Relations Review*, Vol. XIV, No. 3 (April 1961), pp. 412–416.

[114]*Spravochnik Prosoiuznogo Rabotnika* (Moscow, 1958), p. 300; see also A. Gorbunov, *Strakhovoi Delegat* (Moscow, 1958), p. 10.

[115]J. Lytschkin, "Die Abteilungskommissionen fuer Sozialversicherung" in *Die Raete fuer Sozialversicherung in den Betrieben* (Berlin: Tribuene Verlag, 1954), p. 72.

ably depends on his relations with his delegate, since the latter has to make a report of his visits.[116]

If he is sick, the delegate, who is likely to be a woman,[117] has a number of responsibilities, which illustrate incidentally how Soviet social insurance combines labor discipline and welfare. She must make sure that the disabled worker receives prompt medical attention. She makes an initial check of the sickness certificate issued by the physician, which is the essential document for the authorization of cash benefits, but which has implications also for the control of absenteeism. For in addition to specifying the nature of the worker's illness, the certificate prescribes the treatment the worker has to follow. And it is a major responsibility of the delegate to check on the patient's faithful adherence to the prescribed treatment. For instance, if he refuses to take prescribed medicines, stay in bed as ordered, or go to the hospital if the doctor finds it advisable, the delegate has to report him to the social insurance commission, which has the authority to deny cash sickness benefits. A certificate is valid only for a few days and has to be renewed by a physician, who also is under pressure to cut absenteeism rates.[118] The insurance delegate will be careful to keep the worker seeking to gain more sick leave from switching doctors, for this is illegal in most cases.

The delegate's contact with the sick worker aims at promoting quick recovery, and it would be unfair to picture her as a mere truant officer. She is expected to do whatever she can to help make the patient feel at ease, whether at home or in the hospital. If necessary, this may include anything from feeding the children and cleaning the home for a sick working mother, to doing errands or reading the newspaper. The idea behind this seems to be that "although this help may consist of little, insignificant services, it is extremely important to the sick person, it supports his strength and contributes to a more speedy restoration of his health and return to work."[119] To the extent that this system works as claimed, it also may contribute significantly to the worker's morale.

If a worker needs to go to the hospital, the delegate's contribution to his welfare and "quick recovery and return to work" includes the performance of additional tasks. Aside from general "control" over the services rendered to sick colleagues, these tasks range from helping the worker get through the apparently involved and delay-prone admission procedure, to

[116] In some instances, the delegates make oral reports at the meeting of their trade union group, in addition to routine written reports. See M. V. Borodina, *Komissiia po Sotsial'nomu Strakhovaniiu Nashego Tsekha* (Moscow, 1956), p. 43.
[117] More than one half of the insurance delegates in the country are women.
[118] The issuance of sickness certificates is heavily regulated. For some of the basic regulations, see "Vydacha Bol'nichnogo Listka," *Okhrana Truda i Sotsial'noe Strakhovanie*, No. 3 (March 1959), pp. 84–87.
[119] Gorbunov, *Strakhovoi Delegat*, pp. 28–29.

assistance in arranging appointments with specialists, where waiting lines may be the obstacle to be overcome. The delegates are urged also to keep a watchful eye on the doctors' safe-keeping and handling of blank sickness certificates.

In the past, severe criticism has been voiced of the trade union's performance in the area of control over medical services. N. M. Shvernik, chairman of the All-Union Central Council of Trade Unions, made the statement to the Eleventh Congress of Soviet Trade Unions in 1954 that "A substantial shortcoming in social insurance work is the deterioration of medical aid and the unsatisfactory hospital facilities ... at a number of enterprises, which has caused an increase in the sickness rate."[120] It appears that the 1957 reorganization of social insurance and the current emphasis on the role of the regional trade-union staff physicians were partly motivated by the need to improve services for the workers.[121]

To those workers who have been recommended by the plant physician for a stay at a rest home or sanatorium, the insurance delegates can render further services of a welfare and quasi-disciplinary character. The number of people recommended is usually larger than the number of passes allocated to the plant. It is the task of the delegates to represent the members of their group before the social insurance commission and to supply information about their situation at work and at home, since both the health needs of the worker and his conduct on the production line will influence the commission's decision.

More pressures against absenteeism and additional levers of labor discipline are brought to bear in the social insurance commission's main decision-making area, the examination of sickness certificates for approval of the payment of disability benefits.[122] Preferably in the presence of the insurance delegate and of the worker concerned, if he has returned to his job, the commission reviews the continuity of the work record of the claimant in order to determine at what percentage of wages the temporary disability benefits ought to be paid. In doing so, it also has an opportunity to review the claimant's sickness record and, perhaps, to ask him questions about his health and hygiene habits. No doubt, practice in this respect varies widely and is related to the extent to which those in charge share the view

[120] *Pravda*, June 8, 1954, *Current Digest of the Soviet Press*, Vol. 6, No. 23 (July 21, 1954), p. 27.
[121] See M. Kaziev, "K Voprosu ob Uluchshenii Meditsinskogo Obsluzhivaniia Trudiashchikhsia," *Okhrana Truda i Sotsial'noe Strakhovanie*, No. 3 (September 1958), pp. 13–17.
[122] For a description of the involved processing of sickness certificates from the doctor, to the shop timekeeper, to the personnel office, to the social insurance commission and, finally, to the chief accountant and the disbursing office, see "Oformlenie Bol'nichnykh Listkov na Predpriiatiiakh ili Uchrezhdeniiakh" and K. Batygin, "Naznachenie i Vyplata Posobii po Vremennoi Netrudosposobnosti," *Okhrana Truda i Sotsial'noe Strakhovanie*, No. 4 (April 1959) pp. 79–81 and No. 10 (October 1959), pp. 67–68.

of one head of a factory social insurance commission who claimed that "Each ruble, each kopek made available by the state for temporary disability payments . . . is spent in the interest of strengthening labor discipline and raising labor productivity."[123]

A good part of the work of the functioning groups working under the direction of the social insurance commission relates to the combating of sickness, accidents, and absenteeism. In the case of the "institutions for children" group, this may be done indirectly by promoting the kind of child care that will lead to a minimum of absenteeism for the working mother.

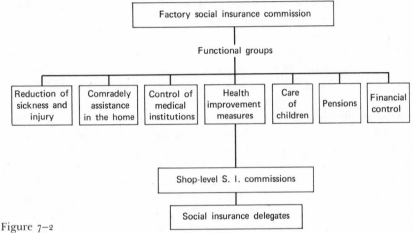

Figure 7–2

Social insurance organization at the factory.

Of more direct concern with disability and with the environmental conditions related to disability is the work of the first four of the seven groups shown in Figure 7–2.

These four groups, incidentally, usually also have the largest staffs. Two of them, the group for "comradely assistance in the home" and the group for "control of medical-care institutions" mainly organize and control the work of the insurance delegates in these areas on behalf of the social insurance commission and give them whatever instruction and assistance they may need in the execution of their duties.

One of the major tasks of the group for "reduction of sickness and injuries" is the compilation and analysis of the statistics on sickness certificates. Its objective is to find out which illnesses have been the most common cause of absenteeism, which illnesses have increased or decreased during specific periods, how current statistics compare with past records,

[123] Lytschkin, *op. cit.*, p. 72. Evidence of cases of lax or practically nonexistent control are not lacking, especially for outlying regions. See, for instance, N. Kazachenko, "Zdes' Nuzhen Profsoiznyi Glaz," *Okrana Truda i Sotsial'noe Strakhovanie*, No. 2 (August 1958), pp. 15–17.

how different departments of the factory compare, and sometimes how the record of its factory compares with the records of other factories. "It must carefully examine sickness certificates with the diagnosis 'grippe,' and find out which doctors excuse from work for longer periods of time and for what reasons."[124] Information gained in this and in other ways is used in putting pressure on physicians and plant directors, in working out sickness prevention programs,[125] and in launching health campaigns. The physician who is too liberal with sickness certificates runs the danger of being accused of undermining the factory's economic plan.[126] On the other hand, an eager factory director also may become the target of criticism if the union should relate unusually high sickness rates to excessive overtime.[127] In factory health campaigns, the group for "health improvement measures" plays an important role. It organizes and coordinates the efforts of the insurance delegates, the plant medical personnel, and the labor protection commission. It makes extensive use of all available information media in the factory to heighten the workers' awareness of sanitation and personal hygiene problems.

It is clear enough that the various measures enumerated, which are carried on as part of the implementation of the social insurance program, are an important aspect of industrial relations in the Soviet Union. The extent to which they contribute to increased productive effort is much more difficult to establish, however. Whatever their contribution to the workers' morale may be, it seems fairly certain that these measures have some success in reducing absenteeism. Unfortunately, no overall statistics to verify this claim are available, and there is no reason to believe that the cases of individual plants reported in the literature are typical.[128] Nevertheless, these

[124] A. Gorbunov, "Kak Proveriat' Pravilnost' Vydachi i Oformleniia Bol'nichnykh Listkov," *Okhrana Truda i Sotsial'noe Strakhovanie*, No. 2 (February 1960), p. 60.

[125] These programs may be concerned simply with temperature control in given shops or with weather stripping, or may involve a broad range of measures and be included in the labor contract with the factory.

[126] The implications of this problem are discussed in M. Field, *Doctor and Patient in Soviet Russia* (Cambridge, Mass.: Harvard University Press, 1957), Chapter IX.

[127] One interesting case is reported in which the union fined the plant director 300 rubles for having ordered massive overtime in disregard of union objections, but at the same time the regional economic council gave the director a premium of 1064 rubles for overfulfillment of the plant. I. Chevtaev, "Blizhe k Liudiam, k Proizvodstvu," *Okhrana Truda i Sotsial'noe Strakhovanie* No. 1, July 1958, p. 28.

[128] In two large steel plants, the number of absenteeism cases dropped in the neighborhood of 26 percent and the number of days lost about 40 percent between 1954 and 1958; see G. Vernikov, "Nash Opyt Trudoustroistva Bol'nykh," *Okhrana Truda i Sotsial'noe Strakhovanie*, No. 6, June 1959, pp. 37–39. For other striking examples, see A. Egorichev, "Po Primeru Azovstale" and P. Kliuev, "Profilaktorii Sverskikh Metallurgov," *Okhrana Truda i Sotsial'noe Strakhovanie* No. 5, November 1958, pp. 52–54 and No. 8, August 1959, pp. 45–47; see also E. Fomina, "Der Rat fuer Sozialversicherung und sein Aktiv" in *Die Raete fuer Soziversicherung in den Betrieben,*

individual cases do show that dramatic success can be achieved under certain circumstances.

This chapter has shown how the Soviet authorities have molded the country's social security system to suit their objectives at various stages of development. It is fair to say that only within the last ten years or so has their system paid serious attention to those who are no longer producers. This is reflected in the growth of the number of pensioners as well as in the growth of expenditure. In 1941 there were 4 million pensioners in the Soviet Union, most of whom were probably at least partially employed. By 1966 the country had close to 27 million pension recipients, not counting approximately 5 million recipients of military pensions.[129] On January 1, 1966, there were 7.9 million kolkhoz members on the pension rolls. Unfortunately, there are no data available to show the level of the average pension or the average cash sickness benefit received. The growth in global expenditures is illustrated in Table 7–5. Total expenditures in the 15 years after 1950 multiplied 5.6 fold. Most remarkable is the shift in expenditures in favor of pensioners. A noteworthy fact is the growth of the percentage of the state budget allocated to social insurance, from 4.4 in 1950 to 10.4 in 1965.

Table 7–5
(Soviet Social Insurance Expenditures 1950 to 1965 (in Millions of Rubles))

	1950	1958	1960	1964	1965
Total expenditures:	1867	5914	7165	9598	10541
1. Grants, including	727	1513	1847	2195	2857
(a) Temporary disability benefits	542	1055	1329	1605	1963
(b) Maternity, birth, nursing	176	450	509	582	616
2. Pensions	814	4946	4946	6957	7407
3. Sanatoria and rest homes	185	226	256	300	364
4. Children's services	96	92	89	112	136
5. Other	45	26	27	34	47
Total expenditures (as a Percent of State Budget):	4.4	8.9	9.6	10.4	10.

Source. Tsentral'noe Statisicheskoe Upravlenie, *Narodnoe Khoziaistvo v 1965 g* (Moscow, 1966) pp. 782,786. (Military Pensions are not included).

p. 41. A sober analysis by a plant physician, indicating much more modest overall results, a drop of 16.7 percent in days lost over a ten-year period, is contained in M. Egorov, "Kogda Rasskryvaiutsia Tsifry," *Okhrana Truda i Sotsial'noe Strakhovanie*, No. 3, September 1958, pp. 48–52. For more recent experiences, see the collection of articles in *Rabota Profsoiuznogo Aktiva Po Sotsial'nomu Strakhovaniia* (Moscow: Profizdat, 1965).

[129] *Narodnoe Khoziaistvo v 1965 Gody*, p. 607. These numbers include dependents.

In 1963, the Soviet Union spent a much higher percentage of gross national product on social security than the United States—10.2 percent versus 6.2 percent. Also, the USSR still lagged behind other major West European countries, such as West Germany (15.3 percent of GNP), France (14.6 percent), Sweden (13.5 percent), Italy (12.8 percent), and the U.K. (11.2 percent).[130]

It is reasonable to expect that in the future the size of the Soviet insurance budget will continue to grow, as it is doing in other countries. The question remains whether the post-Stalin trend toward increased emphasis on welfare goals, as opposed to the older overriding emphasis on production, will become more pronounced. There are indications of conflicting trends in this matter. Recent economic reforms have put renewed stress on the role of incentive payments to workers.[131] On the other hand, officials still pay at least lip service to the idea that as communism advances the country will move toward the application of the principle: "From each according to his ability, to each according to his need." According to the Russian Federation Minister of Social Security:

> . . . in its future planning of social policy the Soviet Union proposes to develop a social consumption fund for the fulfillment of the needs of members of the community, whatever the quantity and quality of the work performed . . . The community will be fully responsible for the support of anyone who is unfit for work. Pensions will rise progressively, and there will be a gradual transition to a uniform pension scheme for incapacitated persons.[132]

In other words, after half a century of Soviet rule, the original goal of an egalitarian society in which all those who are too old, too young, or unable to work are fully sharing, on an equal basis, in the national wealth remains one to be achieved in the future. After many years of highly un-equal benefits for higher production, the early aspirations for a system of equal social protection for all are still alive. Of course, in practise this would mean equal rewards for unequal work, but in Soviet theory this would not constitute unequal treatment, because benefits are a gift and not a payment for work. It is doubtful, especially in view of the past emphasis on differential benefits, whether this ideological tour de force would over-come the incentive problems of a flat benefit system that seeks to main-tain the workers' standard of living. Flat benefits work only if they are geared to minimum needs, not to the maintenance of a living standard. As long as

---

[130]Based on computations by the ILO. See Walter Salenson, "Social Security and Economic Development: A Quantitative Approach," *Industrial and Labor Relations Review*, Vol. XXI, No. 4 (July 1968), p. 569.
[131]See Edmund Nash, "Labor Aspects of the Economic Reform in the Soviet Union," *Monthly Labor Review* (June 1966), pp. 597–602.
[132]Lykova, *loc. cit.*, p. 222.

the Soviet planned economy generates income inequalities, just as market systems do, it is difficult to understand how social security could both eradicate these inequalities and could provide adequate protection without reacting adversely on the economic system. The limits on Soviet social security as a tool for economic and social equality are basically the same as the ones in the West, regardless of ideological and institutional differences.

Part III

POLICY OBJECTIVES AND APPROACHES

Our discussion up to now has had a historical context. We have been concerned with the historical processes of the interacting forces that shaped modern social security. Certainly, this kind of perspective is essential for an understanding of social security and its place in our society. But this is by no means the only way one can make a comparative study of social security. An obvious alternative is to approach the problem in the theoretical context of alternative economic systems. This approach is explored in this section. We shall show how social security techniques can be fully integrated with the principles of either a free market economy, a command economy, or a mixed economy. In spite of the fears of old-time liberals and of the claims of old and new socialists, there is no theoretical incompatibility between genuine social security and capitalism.

CHAPTER 8

Alternative Economic Systems and Social Security

SOCIAL SECURITY AS A SECONDARY DISTRIBUTIVE SYSTEM

The institution of social security programs can be no more neutral in the economic than it is in the social sense. The interrelationships between the objectives and the methods of social security and the ones of governmental economic policy, therefore, must be considered. On the whole, economists have been surprisingly little concerned with this question. This is partly because of the tendency, especially among the American economists, to view social security as strictly an institutional problem that is outside the boundaries of economic analysis. It is also, in part, the result of a failure to appreciate the extent of the potential impact of social security on productive activity. The conventional theory of income distribution has dealt only with the income of factors of production and has ignored the income provided by organized social action.[1] However, the development of the aggregative theory of income and employment and the rapidly increasing importance of social security contributions and payments in the circular flow of the economy recently have begun to attract the attention of economists to the problem of the interrelationships between the social security system and the economic system.[2] The policy problem is primarily one of giving the social security system a structure and objectives that are consistent with, and

[1] For some relevant comments on this point, see V. Carlson, *Economic Security in the United States* (New York: McGraw-Hill, 1962), pp. 203–204.
[2] See, for example, G. V. Rimlinger, "A Theoretical Integration of Wages and Social Insurance," *Quarterly Journal of Economics,* Vol. LXXVII (August 1963), pp. 470–484; M. S. Gordon, *The Economics of Welfare Policies* (New York: Columbia University Press, 1963); E. Liefmann-Keil, *Oekonomische Theorie der Sozialpolitik* (Berlin: Springer Verlag, 1961); H. Hensen, *Die Finanzen der sozialen Sicherung im Kreislauf der Wirtschaft,* Kieler Studien No. 36 (Kiel, 1955).

if possible reinforce, the kind of economic system a country wishes to prevail. Social security programs become part of the economy's institutional framework and can affect its operations in many direct and indirect ways. The intended nature of this impact is the central issue in the coordination of economic and social security policies. The aim of this policy coordination may be simply a social security system that interferes as little as possible with the forces of the free market in the employment and allocation of economic resources. Presumably, this would be the policy objective of a freely competitive market economy. At the other extreme, coordination may mean the complete integration of the social security system with the mechanism and priorities of centralized economic planning. The expected policy of a centrally planned command economy is to make social security an objective as well as an instrument of the economic plan. An intermediary approach would be that of a mixed economy, in which market forces and public regulation and control exist side by side. Social security in this case may be used as a policy instrument, primarily, in dealing with the problems of aggregative income stability, but it also may serve as an important tool in the organization and the development of human resources.

The methods of coordination depend heavily on the nature of the economic system. To focus on the problems of interaction between social security and the economic system, it is useful to consider social security as a system of secondary income distribution that is legislatively superimposed on the country's economy. Social security redistributes income over time and among individuals. The principles of this redistribution are determined by the objectives of social policy and tend to differ from the principles of "functional" income distribution. "Functional" income payments are rewards to factors of production. They perform their economic function in an optimal sense when they attract and allocate these factors in strict accordance with the requirements of economic efficiency. Income payments from social security cannot be evaluated by the same test of optimality; they must be evaluated in terms of the socially determined needs or rights of the beneficiaries. Moreover, social security payments go chiefly to totally or partially unemployed and unemployable persons, in other words, individuals outside the sphere of production. But the fact that these payments are a nonfactor income based on social principles of distribution does not make them economically neutral. They can and do influence both the supply and the demand side of aggregative output. On the supply side, social security programs can have an important impact on the quantity and the quality of human resources that are available for productive purposes. They may influence also the supply and the availability of capital. On the demand side, social security income is an obvious element in the aggregative demand, especially for consumer goods. Depending on the circumstances, this may contribute either to economic stability or to inflationary pressures. Finally, social security programs may be economically significant by contributing to an environment conducive to economic progress through their impact on economic and social stability.

The task of this chapter is to examine the general economic functions of social security. In it, we show how, in theory, this system of secondary distribution can be designed and administered for the purpose of supporting governmental economic policy. The three general cases cited above are considered: the freely competitive market economy, the centrally planned command economy, and the mixed economy. In each case, of course, the social objective of secondary distribution may either reinforce or conflict with the objectives of economic policy. Where conflict arises, it becomes a problem of determining the priorities of objectives.

THE OPTIMUM SOCIAL INSURANCE PLAN IN A FREE MARKET ECONOMY

The policy objective of the free market economy may be taken to be the institution of a social security system that interferes as little as possible with the forces of free competition. It is understood that this is the economic side of social security policy, which may have to be reconciled later with its social objectives. The classical concept of a free, competitive market system presupposes the liberal state. The most important characteristic common to both is the individual's freedom of action. Within his income and his abilities the individual is free to act as he pleases, as long as he does not violate the laws of the state. The basic purpose of these laws is not to limit his freedom but to protect it from infringement by others. The major duty of the liberal state is to safeguard the freedom of the individual. It can be argued that social insurance, which almost always has elements of compulsion in it, is incompatible with this concept of the liberal state. But even some of the most staunch defenders of liberalism have come to recognize that the enjoyment of freedom requires some minimum guarantees of economic security. Professor Hayek, for instance, argues that with regard to genuinely insurable risks, "the case for the state's helping to organize a comprehensive system of social insurance is very strong."[3] He sees "no incompatibility in principle between the state's providing greater security in this way and the preservation of individual freedom."[4] Practical experience supports this argument. Even if for technical or social reasons the

[3] F. Hayek, *The Road to Serfdom* (Chicago: University of Chicago Press, 1944) (Phoenix Books, 1961), p. 121.
[4] *Ibid.*, p. 121.

participation in a given program has to be compulsory, in reality this compulsion has little or no effect on individual freedom. It is true that freedom may be restricted in the sense that the individual's power to act is limited but not in the sense that his desire to act is limited. If we take for granted that the consensus of opinion is in favor of social insurance, the main problem is to arrange the system so that it is consistent with the desires of the largest possible majority. We may assume that the desire of consumers is to maximize their satisfaction and that the aim of entrepreneurs is to maximize their profits. The optimum plan is one that maximizes both the satisfaction of the participants and the profits of their employers and also abides by the basic rules of the market economy.

Such a program is consistent with the optimum allocation of economic resources, and it may even increase the level of output and employment of the economy. How should this optimum program be organized? To answer this question it is necessary to work out a rigorous theoretical model in which economic conditions as well as the attitudes of the program participants are clearly defined. We develop an optimum old-age pension plan. Ideally, the whole social security system should be considered because the existence of multiple programs, each with its own benefits and contributions, affects the optimum rates of contribution and benefit and the optimum eligibility conditions of any particular program. It is very important that social security programs be coordinated not only with economic policy but also with each other. But a completely coordinated optimum system presents tremendous theoretical difficulties, which remain largely unexplored.[5] A resolution of these difficulties is not essential here, since our main purpose is to illustrate the analytical implications of the liberal market approach. The optimum plan is intended to be an analytical bench mark instead of a ready-made policy prescription, since the assumptions on which it is based are not easily realized in practise.

The optimum plan is developed in three basic steps.[6] First, a theoretical model will be developed for the simultaneous determination of optimum labor cost, take-home pay, benefit, and contribution rates in the context of an old-age social insurance plan for which all relevant features, other than benefit and contribution rates, are given. Labor supply and demand and the workers' preference pattern for wages and old-age benefits also are assumed to be given. Second, the role of the plan's conditions of benefit

---

[5] For a discussion of the structuring of unemployment insurance with regard to resource allocation, see P. W. Cartwright. "Unemployment Compensation and the Allocation of Resources" in M. Abramovits *et al., The Allocation of Economic Resources—Essays in Honor of Bernard Francis Haley* (Stanford: Stanford University Press, 1959), pp. 65–81.

[6] The following analysis is drawn from the author's article in the *Quarterly Journal of Economics,* August 1963.

eligibility, of the rate of return on invested funds, and of other basic elements that are initially assigned arbitrary values, are investigated. Third the model is expanded to take into account changes in benefit conditions and in interest rates, since a complete solution of the model requires, along with the optimum rates' mentioned above, an equilibrium return on invested pension funds and an optimum set of eligibility conditions for the receipt of benefits. Finally, the theoretical analysis is followed by a brief exploration of its major implications, one of which is the fact that, theoretically, old-age social insurance plans can be designed to reduce labor costs and to increase employment.

A brief description of the pension plan to be considered and a statement of operating assumptions are necessary at this point. The plan is to be a social insurance old-age pension program that is introduced in an economic system characterized by profit-motivated firms and satisfaction-maximizing workers. The industries in which the plan is introduced are assumed to be not only privately owned but also perfectly competitive in both the factor and the product markets. The state administers the program but does not bear any of its costs; it collects the social insurance contributions from the employers and makes benefit payments to the workers. All contributions are levied in the form of a payroll tax on workers. Workers look on these contributions as coming out of their earnings and employers treat them as part of their labor cost. After deductions for administrative overheads, the funds collected by the state are channeled into loans to private firms at the highest rate of interest obtainable for the given sums to be placed at any particular time. Furthermore, it will be assumed that no other pension plans are available or that workers will always prefer the present plan. Finally, technology is given.

There are clear reasons why workers should prefer the suggested social insurance plan over the alternative of taking all their earnings in current wages and of arranging their own pension plan through an insurance company. A private plan is likely to be more expensive because of selling costs and the higher operating costs that result from its smaller scale. Workers also might prefer the suggested plan because they do not have to choose between complex competing plans and premium payments are automatically deducted from the pay check. Moreover, payments have to be made only when there are earnings and in amounts related to the level of earnings.

Optimum Pay-Pension Package: First Approximation. The labor market conditions of a given industry in which old-age social insurance is to be introduced are described by the demand and supply curves in Figure 8–1. Before the plan is introduced, there is a single-valued equilibrium wage, W_0. The introduction of the program, however, will enable employers to

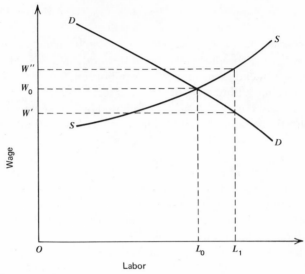

Figure 8–1

substitute future for present income and to offer workers alternative combinations of present take-home pay and future pensions in lieu of the single wage. This does not violate the assumption of perfect competition. In equilibrium, the individual employer must pay the remuneration dictated by the market. The alternatives open to an employer who paid the W_0 wage rate before the plan went into effect are indicated by the line W_0O_0 in Figure 8–2. Each point on this line, which may be called an income offer line, represents a take-home pay-pension packet whose cost equals W_0. If take-home pay, the horizontal distance from the vertical axis to a point on the line equals W_0, the pension equals zero. Otherwise, the difference between W_0 and take-home pay is the amount that is withheld by the employer and that is turned over to the state to pay for the corresponding pension level. The amount of additional pension income that can be obtained for each dollar of wages withheld is given by the slope of the offer line. This ratio is determined by the characteristics of the plan, the workers covered, and the rate of return on invested pension funds.

Of course, it is possible to translate any point on the original labor demand curve into a corresponding income offer line, each corresponding to a different wage rate and quantity of labor demanded. Since all combinations on an offer line have the same total cost to the employer as the wage indicated by the intersection of the offer line with the horizontal axis, they all correspond to the labor demanded at that wage. The labor demanded, given any pay-pension package on W_0O_0 in Figure 8–2, is L_0 in Figure 8–1.

Because of the difference in the timing and the duration of the payments of wages, contributions, and pensions, ambiguity may be encountered in interpreting Figure 8–2. The pensions indicated on the graph are payable monthly for the entire retirement period, assuming that the beneficiary does not violate any rules and become disqualified. For the convenience of graphical illustration, a time dimension is added also to the horizontal axis. The labor cost, take-home pay, the contribution rates indicated there are paid for during a period equal to the average number of years of contribution by all workers in the plan. This period is somewhat arbitrarily chosen, but its effect is merely to change the scale of the horizontal axis and, hence, to change the slope of the curves on the graph. It obviously

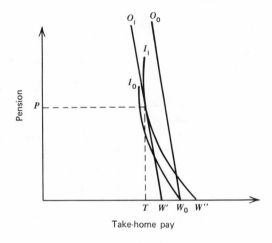

Figure 8–2

does not affect the substance of the analysis. It means that now the slope of the income offer lines represents the monthly pension that is payable per dollar of monthly contribution over the average contribution period.

The introduction of old-age social insurance also gives workers an opportunity to choose between different combinations of present pay and future pension. The workers who supply the amount of labor L_0 for the wage W_0 before the pension scheme is in effect now are willing to supply that same amount of labor in return for alternative combinations of take-home pay and future pension. The indifference curve so constructed indicates their willingness to substitute future for present income by forgoing some of their take-home pay for future pension benefits. For the time being it is assumed that they all have the same preference pattern and that the take-home pay and pension combinations for which they will supply the quantity L_0 of labor is represented by the line W_0I_0 in Figure 8–2. This line is their common income indifference curve. Take-home pay is the horizontal distance from the indifference curve to the vertical axis. The difference between W_0 and take-home pay is the monthly income the workers are willing to forgo for the corresponding future pension.

The slope of the indifference curve depends in part on the pension program and in part on worker attitudes, which are here taken as given but which will be examined further below. The welfare maximizing decision regarding work and leisure is not involved here; it is given and presumably indicated by W_0 and L_0. The income indifference curve reflects a welfare maximizing decision with respect to the allocation of income through time. This holds true for all wage levels, since any point on the labor supply curve can be translated into an income indifference curve.

The basic elements of the model, a set of income offer lines and a set of income indifference curves, have now been introduced. The solution consists in finding take-home pay, pension, and contribution rates that are consistent with profit maximization and worker satisfaction. The standard condition for profit maximization—equality of wage and value of the marginal product—is still valid, but it must be remembered that the "wage" now includes both take-home pay and an amount retained for pension contribution. The maximization of worker satisfaction requires paying them that pay-pension package which gives them the highest level of income and employment consistent with the employers' attempt to maximize profit. As long as there is a difference between the employers' offer and the workers' attitude with regard to the valuation of present and future income, there is a possibility for mutal gain through an intertemporal reallocation of income. Therefore, a necessary condition for achieving the objective of maximizing worker satisfaction is that the workers' marginal rate of substitution of future pension for take-home pay is equal to the pay-pension rate of substitution offered by the employer through the pension plan.

A graphic presentation of the model's solution illustrates the equilibrium determination of pension, take-home pay, and contribution rates consistent with the dual maximization condition. In Figure 8–2 the original equilibrium wage W_0 is translated into the offer line W_0O_0 and the indifference curve W_0I_0. It readily can be observed, however, that, as drawn, W_0O_0 and W_0I_0 fail to meet the equilibrium requirements. The only point they have in common is W_0. If employers were to pay the wage W_0 they would fail to maximize profit because they could hire the corresponding labor supply L_0 for a smaller outlay. Disregarding their common point, all pay-pension combinations on the W_0I_0 indifference curve are less expensive than the combinations on the W_0O_0 offer line.

The opportunity to operate at lower labor cost would induce employers to increase employment. The amount of employment they would offer at each unit labor cost is given by the original labor demand curve. Each lower level of labor cost can be translated into a new offer line located to the left of the previous offer line.

Similarly, as the offer lines move to the left with expanding employment, the indifference curves move to the right. As indicated by the labor supply curve, higher levels of labor remuneration must be offered to attract more labor to the industry. Each higher level of remuneration can be translated into a new indifference curve to the right of the previous one. The indifference curves and the income offer lines indicate the possibility of reducing labor cost (the employers' valuation) and also of increasing labor remuneration (the workers' valuation).

The equilibrium is reached when the offer line and the indifference curve for an identical level of employment become tangent. In the present case this occurs at the tangency of the offer line $W'O_1$ and the indifference curve $W''I_1$. Both W' and W'' correspond to the same level of labor demanded and supplied, namely, the quantity L_1, which is the new equilibrium level of employment. The social insurance program, therefore, has resulted in an increase in the level of employment in the industry from L_0 to L_1.[7] The equilibrium pension is P, take-home pay is T, and the monthly contribution is $W'-T$. These values satisfy the profit maximizing condition that wage, or rather labor cost in this case, equals the value of the marginal product: $T+(W'-T) = W'$. They satisfy also the condition of maximizing worker satisfaction, which requires that the workers' marginal rate of pay-pension substitution equals the substitution rate of the employers' offer:

$$\frac{dp}{d(W''-T)} = \frac{dp}{d(W'-T)}.$$

In addition to increasing employment from L_0 to L_1, the introduction of the social insurance program has resulted in a reduction in unit labor cost from W_0 to W' and in an increase in remuneration for the workers that is equivalent to $W''-W_0$. This follows from the difference in valuation that workers and employers put on labor remuneration, and it would not matter, theoretically, whether the difference is caused by a social insurance pension or by a pension the worker buys on his own.

Of course, these results follow directly from the assumed shapes of the

[7] This takes into account only microeconomic effects. Although the introduction of the pension plan tends to raise the full employment level of income, there is no assurance that it will generate the aggregate demand necessary to attain this level of employment. This will depend on the distribution of the increase in income between consumption and investment and on the effects of this distribution. For a general discussion of the macroeconomic effects of social security, see S. E. Harris, *Economics of Social Security* (New York: McGraw-Hill, 1941).

labor demand and supply curves and from the shape of the offer lines and indifference curves. Circumstances may exist where the slope of the indifference curve is steeper throughout than that of the offer line, which would naturally preclude a tangency solution. Before discussing a further expansion of the model, it is appropriate to examine briefly the factors determining these slopes.

The Shape of the Offer Lines. The slope of the offer lines is the reciprocal of the insurance rate, which can be defined as the monthly contribution required to purchase one dollar of monthly pension income. The factors that determine the value of this rate are the actuarial characteristics of the plan, including the rate of return that is earned on the investment of the pension funds. What must be taken into account from the actuarial point of view, aside from the interest rate, are elements such as (1) the expected average length of time that elapses between earning and receiving a pension, (2) the expected ratio of eligible claimants, weighed by the size of their claims, to the total weighted number of those who have paid contributions, (3) the anticipated weighted average benefit duration, and (4) the cost of benefit administration. Each of these elements can be affected by conditions of benefit receipt that specify the length of the required service period, the retirement age, and other rules for the qualification, as well as the disqualification of prospective beneficiaries. With more stringent conditions, the slope of the offer line tends to increase, whereas the opposite occurs with more liberal provisions.

In a commercial insurance plan the insurance rate would normally vary with the age of the insured worker at the time of his entry into the plan, but in a public or semipublic program this is usually not the case. Nor is it necessary from the incentive point of view if the program is compulsory or has a fairly long service requirement. As long as adverse selectivity can be avoided, a uniform community rate has the advantages of administrative simplicity and political acceptability.

The impact on the insurance rate of the rate of return that is earned on pension funds presents a slightly more complex problem. The funds collected periodically are invested in long-term loans to private firms but, since we are dealing with a very large source of loanable funds, a nationwide insurance program, we cannot assume that the rate of return is independent of the insurance program. It might be more realistic to assume a downward sloping demand curve for insurance funds, reflecting a downward sloping aggregate marginal efficiency of capital schedule of the borrowing firms. Given the demand curve, the equilibrium rate of interest depends on the amount of funds supplied. But under the optimum plan the supply of these social insurance funds is a function of their rate of return. Other things being equal, the higher the rate of interest, the higher the pension payable per dollar of contribution. Hence, within certain limits, the higher the rate of interest the larger the optimum rate of contribution (the smaller take-home pay) and the total amount of insurance funds supplied. The equilibrium rate of interest on these funds, therefore, must be determined simultaneously with the optimum rates of take-home pay, contribution, and pension.

The constant slope of the offer lines implies that the cost of insurance is not affected by the scale of operation. It might be more reasonable to assume that at low-pension levels the unit cost is higher, in which case the offer lines would be flatter in their lower range. This is an empirical matter that does not affect the substance of the analysis, although it might significantly influence its practical consequences.

The Shape of the Indifference Curves. The slope of the indifference curves, as pointed out earlier, is the workers' marginal rate of substitution of future for present income—of pension for current pay. It is evident that a given set of indifference curves can apply only to a group of workers that is homogeneous with respect to pay preferences. From a practical point of view, this means that workers would have to be classified into several pension categories, each grouping individuals with similar preferences.

Workers who are given an opportunity to choose between present and future income would maximize their satisfaction through substitution until the subjective value of any level of pension income would equal the current income foregone to obtain that pension. It is reasonable to assume that, in most instances, the income indifference curves would indicate a decreasing marginal utility of pensions as the pension component of the remuneration rises, and a rising marginal utility of take-home pay as larger amounts are contributed to pay for future pensions. The increasing steepness of the slope of the curves is intended to reflect this diminishing marginal rate of substitution of benefits for wages. It is probable also that the curves become flatter as the level of labor remuneration increases. This would mean that the higher the income, the greater the marginal utility of a given pension. But at all income levels there is likely to be a point where further reductions in take-home pay for the sake of higher pensions become unacceptable. At that point the indifference curve becomes vertical.

Aside from the relative marginal utilities of pension and current income, which account for the curvature of the indifference curves, there are factors that affect the subjective value of a given pension income and, hence, the shape of these curves. The most important of these factors are: (1) the workers' rate of time preference, (2) the time span between the payment of contributions and the receipt of the pension, and (3) the degree of certainty with which workers can anticipate receiving the benefits when they reach retirement age. The concept of time preference is used here in a very broad sense and is meant to include not only the Boehm-Bawerkian elements accounting for "the agio on present goods"[8] but also the expectations of changes in price levels (unless the pension is adjusted to price level changes) and in the availability of goods in the long run. This last element may play a role in newly developing countries which exhort the workers to make sacrifices in the present in exchange for abundance in the future. In the context of pension analysis, time preference may be expected to vary with the present age of covered individuals, their expected retirement age, their level of income and assets, their place of residence (urban rural differential), and their occupation. The contribution pension time span depends mainly on the workers' present age and on the age at which they expect to retire, the earliest retirement age being set by the plan. A later retirement age raises the rate of time preference and lengthens the time span; hence, people like physicians and farmers, who expect to work until an advanced age, would tend to weight current income more heavily than others. The certainty of receiving the pension ties in most closely with the nature of the plan, since it depends on the rules of eligibility and disqualification. To summarise, the higher the rate of time preference, the longer the benefit contribution time span, and the more restrictive the benefit conditions, the lower will be the subjective value of an expected pension and the steeper the individual curves, and vice versa.

Optimum Conditions of Benefit Receipt. In the first approximation to the optimum pay-pension package, the plan's conditions of benefit receipt are taken as given, although, as pointed out above, a change in them can alter the slope of the offer lines and the shape of the indifference curves and, hence, the equilibrium pension and contribution rates. Therefore, these rates are not optimum unless they are based on optimum conditions of benefit receipt. Benefit conditions are considered optimum if they tend to maximize the economic welfare effect of the plan. The nature of this welfare effect calls for a brief examination.

An old-age social insurance plan is an important technological improvement in economic organization. It is not surprising then that it has welfare implications beyond the social advantages directly associated with the maintenance of income. By comparison with the nonpension labor market equilibrium, three possible kinds of economic gain can be related to the operation of a pension plan: (1) an expansion in employment, which is indicated in Figure 8–1 by $L_1 > L_0$, (2) a reduction in average labor cost,

[8] E. von Boehm-Bawerk, *The Positive Theory of Capital* (trans. by W. Smart, New York: Stechert, 1923), Book V, Chapters II and III.

which is shown by $W' < W_0$ (Figures 8–1 and 8–2), and (3) an increase in the subjective value of income paid to the workers, which is reflected by $W'' > W_0$ (Figures 8–1 and 8–2). The sources of these gains are the increase in income over time attributable to the investment return and the increase in the utility of income due to its intertemporal redistribution. The extent and the distribution of these gains among workers, employers, and consumers depend on the shapes of the labor demand and supply curves and on the shapes of the offer lines and the indifference curves.

What concerns us here is solely the effect of changes in benefit conditions. They operate only on the shapes of the offer lines and indifference curves. Their direct effect is on the value of $W'' - W'$, the second and third types of gain combined. Nevertheless, we point out that the shapes of the labor demand and supply curves determine the employment effect as well as the relative importance to each other of the other two kinds of gain. The flatter the labor market curves, the greater the employment effect for any value of $W'' - W'$ and, of course, the employment effect moves in the same direction as the value of $W''-W'$. The steeper the labor supply curve relative to the demand curve, the greater the income effect $(W''-W_0)$ relative to the cost reduction effect (W_0-W').

The nature of the optimum conditions of benefit receipt now can be stated more precisely. Benefit conditions may be considered optimum if their effect on the offer lines and indifference curves maximizes the difference between W'' and W', in other words, the combined income increase and cost reduction effect. Any change in benefit receipt conditions that makes benefits more attractive tends to flatten the indifference curves and, hence, to increase $W''-W'$. This can be verified by the inspection of Figure 8–2. However, to the extent that this same change increases also the cost of pension benefits, it simultaneously flattens the offer lines, which tends to reduce $W'' - W'$. Whether a given change increases the welfare effect depends then on which movement is the greater. For instance, a general lowering of the retirement age from 65 to 60 might be too costly to be advisable, but the introduction of a flexible retirement age, with appropriately higher pensions for those who choose to retire late, might very well increase $W'' - W'$, unless the added attractiveness is offset by a higher administrative cost. Higher administrative expenses would flatten the offer lines.

Equilibrium Rate of Return on Pension Funds. The remaining step in the analysis is the determination of the equilibrium rate of return on pension funds. The rate of return is in equilibrium when it is consistent with the optimum pension and contribution rates and also equates the supply of and demand for pension funds. In other words, the rate used in the determination of the offer line must be the equilibrium rate in the money market in which the funds are invested. The demand schedule in this market is given and represented by *DD* in Figure 8–3. The supply schedule *SS* consists of pension funds and other sources of capital, the amounts of the latter being given and represented by *S'S'*. The *S'S'* curve is not the supply curve that would exist in the absence of the pension plan. It is a supply curve that takes into account the plan's effects on the aggregate level of income and on the level of direct saving by workers and by other income recipients. The supply of pension funds depends on the total number of workers in the plan and on the average level of contribution. The contribution, as was noted earlier, depends in part on the rate of return. The equilibrium rate of return may be found by deriving a pension fund supply schedule that is consistent with the optimum pension and contribution rates and by adding it to the given *S'S'* schedule.

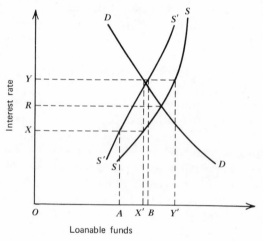

Figure 8–3

The derivation of the pension-fund supply schedule is simplest if we focus attention on one particular group of workers in the plan. The indifference curves and labor-market schedules for the group are given, but to derive the offer lines a particular rate of interest, equal to *OX* in Figure 8–3, is now specified. This rate determines a family of offer lines that intersect the horizontal axis of Figure 8–4 at an angle α. The equilibrium offer line and indifference curve are designated by O_x and I_x. The resulting monthly insurance contribution per worker in this group is *xx'*. When similarly applied to all groups participating in the plan, the *OX* rate of return yields a total contribution fund *AX'* (Figure 8–3). The interest rate *OX* and the corresponding total capital supply *OX'*, consisting of *OA* from other sources and *AX'* from pension funds, determine the first point of the total capital supply schedule *SS* (Figure 8–3).

An OX' supply of capital, however, would yield a return of OY which, obviously, is not an equilibrium rate but may be used to determine a second point on the total capital supply schedule. The OY rate determines a new family of income offer lines, which intersect the horizontal axis (Figure 8–4) at an angle β. The new equilibrium offer line will be O_y, and the new equilibrium indifference curve will be I_y. The new contribution per worker is yy' (Figure 8–4) and the total amount contributed BY' (Figure 8–3). The interest rate OY and the corresponding total capital supply OY' determine the second point on the total capital supply schedule. We can proceed in this manner until we determine the equilibrium rate OR (Figure 8–3) or, for that matter, the entire SS schedule. The shape of this schedule depends

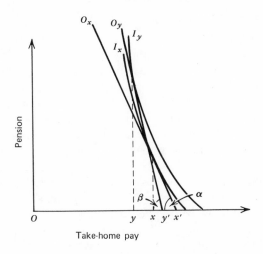

Figure 8–4

on the shapes of the indifference and labor demand and supply curves, and also on how much a given change in interest rate alters the slope of the offer lines.

Some Final Considerations. The model for an optimum pension plan illustrates how, in theory, social insurance can be fully integrated with the mechanism of a market economy. It is a plan that minimizes the element of compulsion and is consistent with the rational allocation of resources. Since it adjusts to the forces of the market, instead of seeking to alter them, it may be suited to a policy of social stability but is clearly not suited to the purposes of social or economic reform. By demonstrating the possibility of economic gains in the form of lower labor cost, higher worker renumeration, and increased employment, the optimum plan provides a theoretical basis for a rationalized policy approach. But, as is usually the case in economics, the theoretical model does not furnish the policy maker with a blueprint for action. It tells him what results are possible under what conditions, and it shows him the interdependence of the variables with which he is dealing and the consequences of changing them. The optimum plan can be useful, even if it is unrealizable in practice, as long as it gives the policy maker an idea of the manner and the extent to which the structure of a given social insurance program deviates from the optimum model. It might help in making policy decisions with regard to changes, for instance, in deciding whether, from a strictly economic point of view, it is preferable to finance an increase in benefit by raising the tax rate or by raising the taxable wage base. A raise in the tax rate affects all participants, whereas a raise in the wage base affects only those whose earnings are above the previous taxable wage base.

As a guide to policy the foregoing analysis nevertheless suffers from significant limitations. It suffers from the usual weaknesses associated with the marginal productivity theory of wages. To the extent that a country's wage structure is itself irrational, it might seem rather fanciful to try to superimpose on it a highly refined incentive benefit structure. This may be an argument against pushing the rationalization of the benefit structure to the point of diminishing returns, but it is not a valid argument against the attempt to approximate an incentive benefit structure. Another problem arises from the fact that the concept of optimum is strictly economic. It might well develop that a plan which is optimum by the rules of the market economy is wholly inadequate from a social point of view. In most countries that have wage-related social insurance benefits, the minimum levels are usually below the amount that could be considered an adequate minimum income. This indicates, at least, some attempt not to counteract the market forces completely, even though in most instances the benefit structure favors the lower-paid workers. But the liberal state need not compromise in this fashion. It need not sacrifice either the economic rationality of social insurance or the minimum income objective of social security as a whole. It can do this by leaving the problem of guaranteeing a minimum income to the sphere of public assistance, rather than using social insurance as an instrument of income redistribution. In this manner, the public assistance programs, which pay benefits based on need, can be an important factor in supporting the overall economic rationality of the social security system.

Another important policy problem relates to the question of information. The institution of an optimum plan requires fairly extensive knowledge about the behavior and preference patterns of individuals. How could the policy makers possibly obtain the necessary data on which to base their decisions, especially since these data are subject to continuous change? This question arises with any differentiated benefit plan that attempts to be more or less rational and implies a strong argument in favor of flat benefits. However, if either arbitrary differentials or flat benefits are rejected, the only alternative is to develop techniques for gathering as much information as possible about the wishes and attitudes of the social insurance participants. Unfortunately, in most countries, there is a woeful lack of knowledge in these respects. Yet, the tendency of benefit levels to rise over time increases the incentive element in them and makes more urgent the rationalization of the benefit structure.

SOCIAL SECURITY IN THE CENTRALLY PLANNED COMMAND ECONOMY

As in the case of the liberal market economy, the economic functions of social security in the centrally planned command economy are determined by the objectives of economic policy and by the structure and mechanism of the economic system. Most basic is the fact that in countries with command economies the state has a monopoly, or nearly so, of the material means of production. The only important exception is found in agriculture, where special ownership conditions often prevail, which helps to account for the fact that agricultural workers are frequently excluded from otherwise nearly universal social insurance systems. Another fundamental feature of the command economy is the absence of the market and the price mechanism as the central coordinators of economic activity. The directing and coordinating functions are taken over by the planning mechanism, which is a decision-making apparatus that is based on a series of partial short-run plans which are more or less integrated with a central long-run plan. The market interplay of supply and demand is replaced by an administrative method of balancing the demand for final and intermediary goods with the available and anticipated resources. In the market economy it is consumer spending, through its influence on price and profit, that ultimately directs the allocation of economic resources. In the command economy the resource allocation is determined directly by the planners. However, there are limits to the extent to which planners can directly allocate resources. Hence, they are always inclined to build into the planning mechanism the incentives to induce the right kind of action at the lower levels of decision making which are beyond their practical influence. This is especially applicable to the area of the labor market and of industrial relations. No matter how powerful the state may be, in a complex economy run on the basis of large-scale organizations, it is impossible to achieve an efficient use of manpower through force. A final feature of the command economy that we must mention is the system of priorities. Consumer demand is not ignored, but its resource allocation function is eliminated. The planners in the totalitarian command economy do not operate on the assumption that an approximation of maximum social welfare can be achieved through consumer sovereignty. Their production directives are based on the priority of the objectives established by the dominant party. As a rule these objectives are inspired by broad political considerations instead of by the immediate consumer welfare. This formulation of objectives is consistent with the role of the ruling party as the interpreter and representative of the interests of the country as a whole. The possibility of a divergence between the party's view of the country's interests and the actual interests of the consumers is usually not recognized.

Intensified industrialization and maximum rates of economic growth have been the overriding objectives of the Soviet-type command economies. For political as well as for economic reasons, the countries involved have sought to achieve the status of world power in as short a time as possible. Consequently, they have given top priorities to the development of heavy industry at the expense of light industry and agriculture, and they have stressed the output of capital equipment over the output of consumer goods. An approach of this kind inevitably puts a heavy strain on the economic system. To meet the demands of superiors and to achieve that which is possible, the impossible is often planned. Aside from being wasteful, this ideology conditioned approach to economic decision making creates a situation of permanent emergency, in which insufficient resources are continuously stretched in the extreme to meet inordinate demands. It follows that all available means must be used to mobilize human resources to their fullest extent. Social security institutions easily can be pressed into the service of human resource mobilization and development, and it would be unreasonable not to expect the command economy to do so. It is an axiom of large-scale enterprise that those in command need the cooperation and good will of those who are commanded in order to be able to operate with any degree of efficiency. To obtain the utmost from those at the bottom of the chain of command requires means to offer rewards, to instill discipline, and to promote a zeal for cooperation. Welfare programs can be better moulded to meet these needs in a totalitarian and command system than in any other.

Before looking at the role of social security in the area of manpower and labor relations, we must point out that a comprehensive social security program also can have important macroeconomic effects. In a centrally planned economy it can be designed to increase the rate of social saving and, hence, of capital accumulation. This may seem surprising, since the rate of saving and of capital accumulation is determined by the planners when they decide on the proportions of total output that are to be allocated to consumer goods and to capital goods over a given period. Maximum capital accumulation implies that the output of consumer goods and, hence, of real wages must be kept to a minimum. The lower the real wage rate, the smaller the purchasing power of the worker, and the lower the amount of national output that must be devoted to consumer goods. There is no need, in a centrally planned system, to be concerned about the problem of maintaining aggregate effective demand through consumer purchasing power; in a market system the measures that reduce consumer spending might have a severely adverse effect on capital accumulation. Social security schemes can be used to depress the wage level and to reduce total labor cost. The argument here is different from the one developed earlier to show the possibility of lower labor cost through wage-related social insurance benefits in a competitive market economy. For the moment, we are discussing the impact on the general level of wage rates instead of on the rate structure, and we are concerned with benefits that are not related to wages. The state planners determine both wages and benefits, and they can combine them in whatever manner best suits their purposes.

Let us determine how they might proceed if they wished to minimize total labor cost. They are aware that labor cost is not simply the amount paid in remuneration, but that it depends on the relation of remuneration to labor output. This means that the wage structure, including wage-related social security benefits, must be differentiated in order to reward skill and effort and to promote the acquisition of skill. Skill differentials in wages are necessary also to reduce the wasteful employment of skilled workers on unskilled jobs. The wage structure is thus largely dictated by the requirements of economic efficiency and, consequently, leaves the planner little room for manipulation. In deciding on wage relations and benefit levels they, in fact, may do best by approximating the results of the perfect market model. On the other hand, it can be argued that the general level of wages has little bearing on efficiency, provided that the minimum rates are high enough to maintain the capacity to work. If low wages tend to affect the willingness to take a job, this can be counteracted by social and political pressure that emphasize the duty to work, as well as by social security eligibility requirements. A low wage level in this kind of a political environment also may be quite effective in pushing all the members of a family into the work force. The task of the wage planners is, therefore, twofold; first, to determine the rate structure that is conducive to maximum efficiency, and second, to anchor the level of wages to the minimum acceptable rates of this structure. These minimum acceptable rates may be thought of as the lowest politically manageable rates that are consistent with the maintenance of physical vigor. In the absence of social security this, presumably, would be sufficient to allow an unskilled worker with an average-size family to maintain his capacity to work and to support his dependents at a level of minimum decency.

The significance of a comprehensive social security system, especially one with many family benefits, is that it makes possible a lower minimum rate and, therefore, a lower general wage level, than would be the case without social security. Since wages are paid on the basis of efficiency, the minimum rate and all other rates are the same for bachelors with no dependents than for heads of family with several dependents. Without social security of any kind and little prospect for private charity, minimum rates must be geared to the needs of heads of families with dependents. But a rate that would enable a worker to support a number of children and to provide a small reserve against the ordinary emergencies of life would leave an independent bachelor with a considerable economic "surplus." The way to eliminate the possibility of such a surplus is to set the lowest rates of the wage structure by the requirements of a person without dependents. The wage should be just enough to allow one person to manage by himself. This can only be done, however, if the state pays direct subsidies to the workers who have dependents that the state feels cannot be expected to earn a living. These subsidies, which are normally unrelated to wages, are paid in the form of family allowances, birth grants, and other kinds of child support. Of course, these forms of family support must be added to total labor cost but, in the aggregate, labor cost will still be lower because no subsidies are paid to persons without eligible dependents. It is conceivable that workers with high enough wages to support their families are in this manner given more income than would be the case in the absence of social security. Should this be the case, it is always possible to impose an income ceiling on the eligibility for family allowances. We should add that this kind of minimum wage planning is especially important in the early stages of industrialization when the need for savings is particularly pressing. Even in countries without central planning, but an abundant supply of unskilled labor, private employers sometimes introduce privately financed family allowances as a means of keeping down the general level of wages. In a centrally planned economy this can be accomplished more systematically and on a universal scale. Even if the objective is not the reduction of wages to a minimum, this kind of support for workers' families still can be regarded as a special kind of income redistribution that alleviates the hardships of forced industrialization without encroaching on savings. For it tends to be a redistribution that takes from the not-so-poor and gives to the poor. By protecting specifically the most vulnerable segments of the population, it tends to lessen resistance and thereby to facilitate a general policy of economic austerity. This can be viewed as an increase in what might be called the economy's elasticity of forced accumulation, which is the relative increase in accumulation for a given relative increase in economic coercion.

The establishment of free or subsidized nurseries for small children and of summer vacation camps for older children is another social service with important implications in an economy where all resources are mobilized to the fullest extent. The most direct effect is that mothers are relieved of daytime care for children and are made available for work in offices and factories. This is a very important addition to the labor supply. Indirectly, these social services may increase the capital available for industrial development by reducing the amount that must be devoted to housing. The argument is as follows. During industrialization, as many workers leave agriculture and migrate to industrial centers, there is a great need for new housing, which can only be met by vast capital investments. Obviously, if only one person in each household is employed, it takes a lot more housing to provide lodgings for a given number of workers than if both husband and wife are employed. Any measure that helps to put wives and other members of a family into the work force, therefore, will reduce the amount of housing needed and will save the capital as well as the extra amount of labor that the additional construction would have required. There can be little doubt that in a rapidly industrializing society these savings can be extremely significant.

In the areas of labor and manpower policy, social security and social services are an indispensible tool for the social engineering of the command economy. They are used in three major ways: (1) as incentives to increase the supply and efficiency of labor and to facilitate its distribution to points of priority and unattractive areas, (2) as instruments of labor discipline, and (3) as a means to maintain and upgrade the quality of the work force. A fundamental difference between the command economy and the liberal economy is that incentives are designed to achieve the purposes of the planners rather than to maximize the welfare of the beneficiaries. In the choice of risks to be covered, a command economy normally will omit the risk of unemployment. The absence of unemployment benefits can be considered as an aid to labor discipline or, if you will, a negative incentive to encourage willingness to work. To be sure, mass unemployment is not a problem in planned economy, but individual unemployment because of a lack of suitable jobs at a given time and place are unavoidable in a dynamic economy. Only by destroying all freedom of movement and by replacing the labor market by a system of conscription can this kind of unemployment be completely eliminated. The absence of unemployment support, especially in a low-wage economy where all economic opportunities are controlled by the state, tends to force the individual to do whatever work is available instead of remaining idle waiting for a "suitable" job. Similar negative incentives can be built into the structure of survivorship benefits. They can be limited in a manner that assures that all able-bodied survivors of working age will enter the work force. This is particularly relevant for widows with small children. Low survivorship benefits will induce a widow to put her children in the nursery and to take a job. Again the fact that the command economy eliminates the possibility of income from property makes a measure of this kind much more effective than it might be in a system based on private property. The only sources of economic security in the command economy are wages or salaries and social security, and all of them are controlled by the state.

On the positive side, wage-related social security benefits and eligibility conditions can be designed to influence productivity and the supply and allocation of labor. If the planners are interested only in productivity, they may very well wish to design their social insurance programs in a manner similar to the one that was developed above the competitive economy. We must point out, however, that in Soviet-type systems the social security benefits are usually treated as a gift from the state to the individual. But this need not hinder their manipulation for incentive purposes, since there is no absolutely compelling reason why gifts should be equal. In fact, the concept of benefits as a gift, by doing away with insurance and actuarial considerations, tends to give greater freedom to the planners to shape benefits and eligibility conditions for the purposes of achieving specific aims. They may wish to single out for special treatment certain industries or geographic areas with high priorities in the development of the economy. Workers in these sectors may be allowed higher benefits and more liberal eligibility conditions than workers elsewhere. The intention of these special privileges would be to encourage productivity most in the most crucial areas of the economy and to enable them to attract the best workers. In addition to this attempt at influencing the allocation of labor, the planners may wish to increase the labor supply by influencing the length of the working life of the workers. They can do this through the payment of special supplementary benefits based on the length of service and on service after the normal retirement age. To encourage regular work habits and to combat voluntary absenteeism, they may take the length of uninterrupted work into account.

The most important incentive aspect of social security is probably in the area of ideological rather than material incentives. This is where the stress on benefits as a gift from a benevolent state plays an important role. The state, the ruling party, and the man at the head of the party and state are credited with a sense of deep concern for the welfare of the individual. The enormous resources of the state and the party machinery for agitation and propaganda are used to remind the worker constantly of the extensive benefits that are provided for him. Along with these reminders are endless exhortations to harder work, the improvement of skills, and for a general zeal for increasing productivity. The link between the worker's productivity and the state's ability to provide even greater benefits and a better life is emphasized over and over again. In this sense social security benefits are used not only to promote the political loyalty of grateful workers but also to create an atmosphere conducive to good will and cooperation.

Closely related to ideological incentives is the matter of industrial discipline. Discipline is another way of assuring worker cooperation. Social security programs can aid in the strengthening of discipline through the disciplinary features of their benefits and eligibility conditions as well as through their administrative apparatus. Certain types of benefits may be denied to workers who are guilty of breaches of discipline, or in less severe cases the benefits may be paid at a lower rate. More significant is likely to be the element of discipline inherent in the organization of social security administration. The state can increase its control over the behavior of the workers by having the trade unions and large numbers of the most active workers participate in the day-to-day administration and adjudication of social security. Many workers are thereby drawn into the web of rules; they become involved with the system and act as its agents who are in daily contact with the masses. This aspect of social security administration fits in well with Bendix's characterization of the ideologies of managerial control in the communist state.

> The dictatorial party makes every effort to enlist informal leaders and non-cooperating individuals in the drive for productivity and in its campaigns of political agitation. In doing this the party tends to isolate within the ranks of the work force those individuals who are most active and, hence, most capable of turning tacit consensus into solidary action. This separation is justified as cardinal principle of dictatorial rule. Activists are declared to be the vanguard of the working class by their cooperation with the policies of the party they prove their superior understanding of the workers' interests. . . .[9]

Bendix stresses the fact that the organizational commitment of the most active workers direct their energies into channels controlled by the party, toward ends desired by the party, and also helps to prevent potential centers of worker resistance. It must be borne in mind that in the dictatorial state the trade unions are essentially instruments of the state. They are expected to carry out important duties for the state, by assisting in the enforcement of discipline and in the drive for greater productivity, but they do not have the source of authority of trade unions in free countries— namely, the power to influence wages in an effective manner. However, the administration of social security furnishes them with a basis for authority as the representatives of the workers' interests and, hence, helps them to carry

[9] *Work and Authority in Industry*, p. 443.

out their duties. This authority can be strengthened even more by making benefit levels dependent on membership in the trade unions, since in that case expulsion from the trade union has far-reaching economic consequences.

Finally an economic policy objective of social security is the maintenance and upgrading of the work force. The argument can be made that in a command economy where all the uses of the resources are controlled by the state, the maintenance and development of the work force is akin to the expansion and maintenance of the supply of capital equipment. The labor supply represent the stock of "human capital" that is at the disposal of the state. Since the state imposes on everyone the duty to work, it has a direct interest in maintaining the individual's capacity to work. A comprehensive program of medical care, prevention, and rehabilitation is, therefore, an essential component of social services. Even recreation for the workers legitimately becomes a function of the totalitarian state when the "human capital" view is adopted, since its cost can be treated as an expense for the maintenance of human efficiency. Social security in the command economy differs from its counterpart in a private enterprise system not only in terms of its socio political objectives but also in the sense that it combines the public and private welfare measures found in a private enterprise economy into comprehensive and more-or-less universal public programs. In the command economy the interests of the state and those of the employer are one and the same and, therefore, there is no need to distinguish between public and private measures of labor welfare.

SOCIAL SECURITY IN A MIXED ECONOMY

The social security policy of a mixed economy is likely to be somewhere in between the theoretical extremes of the liberal and the command economies discussed thus far. This is inherent in the underlying philosophy of the mixed economy, which Professor Viner has aptly characterized as being torn between two opposite doctrines:

> on the one hand, the doctrine that free competition is the most effective stimulus to improvement, leads to the closest approximation of material rewards to social contribution, and maximizes flexibility and adaptability to changes in tastes, processes, and relative abundance of productive factors, the fundamental proposition of nineteenth-century laissez faire liberalism; on the other hand, the doctrine that free competition leads to duplication of facilities and services, to booms and busts, to the crushing of the weak by the strong, and eventually to private monopoly.[10]

[10]J. Viner, "The United States as a 'Welfare State'" in S. W. Higginbotham (ed.), *Man, Science, Learning and Education*, Semicentennial Lectures at Rice University (published by Rice University, 1963), p. 217.

In the theoretical system of the liberal economy, the state leaves the determination of the structure of social security benefits to the market forces. In the hypothetical command economy, social security is fully integrated with the objectives of the ruling party and with the mechanism of central planning. In the mixed economy, which is sometimes called the welfare state, the state is quite willing to interfere with and to alter the forces of the market but, also, the concern for individual freedom and the rights of property force it to stop far short of central planning and control. Social security programs, therefore, may be adapted to assist in the achievement of the economic objectives of the mixed economy, provided that this adaptation does not restrict individual freedom. The state cannot be allowed to appear to be manipulating social security programs to enhance its power over the individual. This means that only measures of an aggregative or incentive character are acceptable, but disciplinary features are not. The major economic objectives with regard to which social security programs are likely to play a role are the promotion of economic stability and the development and maintenance of the individual's capacity and opportunity to work. The emphasis on the incentive to work and on income redistribution in policy formulation will depend, in part, on the social value placed on a close relationship between individual performance and rewards. More directly, however, it depends on the evaluation of the effects of income security on individual behavior. Two contradictory arguments have been advanced on this issue. One is the old argument that a degree of income insecurity is necessary to maintain the incentive to work. Sometimes this argument is re-stated in terms of the disincentive effects of compulsory social security and of the income redistribution that is likely to be associated with it. In either case, the economic policy implication is the negative one of limiting the extent of social security to its bare minimum. The other argument is that a basic sense of security is conducive to hard work and is essential for the maintenance of the high levels of aggregate spending required by a prosperous economy. This view is conducive to an extensive social security system and to income redistribution in favor of the lowest income receivers, who presumably have the highest marginal propensity to consume.

The concern of the mixed economy with the problem of ironing out booms and busts inevitably directs attention to the place of social security contributions and payments in its arsenal of countercyclical weapons. Being more or less countercyclical in their nature, these contributions and benefit payments function as automatic stabilizers. As such, they fit in well with the kind of indirect planning, through influencing aggregative magnitudes, that is characteristic of the mixed economy. However, it should be borne in mind that this kind of fiscal planning for economic stability can be effective only in a fully developed market system that is preferably also a mass consumption economy. In such a situation the state must recognize that there is a significant interdependence between social security programs and the level of economic activity. Not only do these programs tend to contribute to the maintenance of a high level of activity but, unless a serious and prolonged drop in economic activity can be avoided, the continued operation of many social insurance programs cannot be assured. This is most obvious in the case of unemployment insurance, which can be effective in dealing with partial and temporary unemployment but which is found to falter in a case of prolonged mass unemployment. The financing of other programs is often geared to the current receipts of pay-roll taxes, and a severe drop in these receipts might force a reduction in their benefit payments at a time when these payments are important in the maintenance of aggregative demand. Social security programs are, therefore, an integral part of the overall problem of the maintenance of a high level of economic activity in the mixed economy.

An important question relates to the extent to which a country is willing to structure its social security programs for the express purpose of increasing their countercyclical effectiveness. Unemployment insurance has the most important countercyclical effects and is usually the most adaptable to a compensatory stabilization policy. Theoretically, it is possible to vary both contributions and benefits in relation to the business cycle. In recessions, taxes would be reduced, or suspended, and benefits would be increased and would be paid for a longer duration. The administration of eligibility conditions also can be made countercyclical; in recessions there would be a more liberal interpretation of requirements than in prosperous times. There are also ways in which the countercyclical effectiveness of old-age pension programs might be increased. Often the financial structure of these programs would be undermined if contribution rates were altered countercyclically, but it would seem to be quite feasible to suspend old-age retirement taxes during recessions and to substitute in their place a direct governmental subsidy. In countries where the government already participates in the financing of these programs, it would mean primarily a temporal rearrangement of public and private contributions. On the benefit side it might be impractical to change benefit levels countercyclically, but it still would seem feasible to alter retirement eligibility conditions to achieve that effect. For instance, in recessions the retirement age might be lowered a year or two in order to allow older persons to leave the labor market. Or, this liberalization of retirement conditions might be restricted to persons who actually have become unemployed. The acceptability of these measures depends heavily on a country's conception of social security; it is not easily reconciled with a strict philosophy of earned benefits.

To increase the effectiveness of social security as a tool of economic policy, the programs should be integrated as much as possible with the measures to improve the functioning of the labor market and the economic opportunities of the individual. This is especially relevant in the case of benefits, such as unemployment and temporary disability benefits, which are paid to individuals who are still in the labor force. The administration of unemployment benefits usually is connected with a system of public employment offices, but often the results are not as favorable as one might expect, in part, because the offices lack information on vacancies. An improvement in the flow of this information, therefore, would be a desirable step forward. In countries, for example, the United States, where unemployment taxes are based on the layoff experience of the individual employer, it might be possible to establish a system for obtaining information on vacancies by basing the tax not only on layoffs but also on vacancies created. This would not only supply information but would also increase the employer's incentive to create new jobs. The technical problems of how to evaluate bona fide vacancies may make it difficult to carry out a plan of this kind. Its virtues would have to be tested in actual practise.

Assistance to workers in structurally depressed areas is another method of support (with considerable theoretical promise) that can be combined with unemployment insurance to improve the functioning of the labor market. Willingness to relocate can be made a condition of the eligibility for extended unemployment benefits. By itself, however, relocation assistance would not be effective if available employment opportunities in new areas demanded new skills and training. In this case, relocation assistance would have to be combined with assistance in retraining. Again, the problems connected with these programs are numerous, but this is not the place to analyze them, since the present objective is mainly to illustrate the economic policy potentials of social security in the mixed economy. Notice, however, that there is an important interdependence between measures to improve individual economic security and the measures to improve the quality of the work force. The more industrially advanced the economy is and, hence, the more scarce labor is in relation to capital, the more important it becomes from the economic point of view to maintain and to improve the quality of the work force. Measures such as retraining, health protection, and rehabilitation, therefore, are likely to play a central role in the social security system of the mixed economy.

The fundamental problem of a mixed economy does not lie in finding the techniques to integrate social security and economic policy, but in determining the most appropriate boundaries between the fields of action left to the state, the private employer, and the individual. The extent to which social security can serve as an instrument of general economic policy depends on how this problem is resolved.

CHAPTER 9

Conclusion

Social Security has become as much a part of a modern economy as large-scale industry, mass distribution, mass communication, and a co-ordinated financial system. Its development has been more controversial than the development of these other components of industrial society, but today its suitability and necessity are no longer questioned. We have demonstrated theoretically that social security programs can be integrated with either pure market economies or centralized command economies. We

Table 9–1

Countries Spending More Than 5 Percent of GNP on Social Security in 1963, by Rank of Expenditure

Rank	Country	Percent	Rank	Country	Percent
1	Czechoslovakia	16.9	13	Norway	10.6
2	Austria	15.9	14	Yugoslavia	10.5
3	West Germany	15.3	15	USSR	10.2
4	France	14.6	16	Canada	9.8
5	Belgium	13.8	17	Finland	9.5
6	Luxembourg	13.8	18	Portugal	9.3
7	Sweden	13.5	19	Ireland	9.1
8	Italy	12.8	20	Australia	8.0
9	Netherlands	12.7	21	Switzerland	7.4
10	New Zealand	11.9	22	Iceland	7.2
11	Denmark	11.9	23	The United States	6.2
12	United Kingdom	11.2	24	Japan	5.2

Source. International Labour Organization, *The Cost of Social Security, 1960–1963* (preliminary), reported in Walter Galenson, "Social Security and Economic Development," *Industrial and Labor Relations Review*, Vol. XXI, No. 4 (July 1968), pp. 568–569.

have shown historically that these programs are compatible with either democracy or dictatorial rule and can be adapted to an egalitarian or a hierarchical society. It is clear also that the need for a highly organized form of income protection increases as a society becomes industrialized and urbanized and that this need is independent of the nature of the socio-economic order. Social security is as essential under socialism as it is under capitalism. The countries (for which data are available) that spent more than five percent of gross national product on social security in 1963 are ranked in Table 9–1. This table shows that most of the countries that spend more than five percent of GNP on social security are highly developed countries. With the exception of Portugal, there is no country on the list that might count as underdeveloped (in terms of per capita income), although Iceland, Ireland, and Yugoslavia are usually counted as semi-developed.

The developing countries are in a special situation. They can borrow from a wide range of patterns of social protection that have proved successful in countries that industrialized earlier. The developing countries, unlike the pioneers of industrialization, do not have to demonstrate the practicality of modern social rights; their problem is one of choosing the most suitable pattern. This is a pattern that corresponds to the needs of the country; one that is consistent with its development goals and that is adapted to its social and economic order.

This study analyzes the manner in which the major industrial countries handled these problems in the course of their development. It shows how the problems of want and the means of handling them changed as the countries moved from a traditional agrarian setting to industrialization and then to a mature industrial society. Each stage has a configuration of economic conditions and social forces that has relevance for the development of social protection. The countries analyzed represent three different socioeconomic settings of industrialization. The first is industrialization by private entrepreneurs, under the aegis of the liberal state, with the entrepreneurial class achieving a dominant power position. This situation was achieved in the United States and approximated in England and France. The second context is that of an authoritarian political and social structure; industrialization is still primarily the work of private entrepreneurs, but their interests and ideas do not become dominant; the class interests of the industrialists remain subordinate or must compromise with the interests of the monarchy, the state bureaucracy, and the landed classes (Imperial Germany and Tsarist Russia). The third setting is the one of socialized industrialization directed by a ruling totalitarian party (Soviet Russia).

Social protection in the traditional agrarian society was very limited for economic as well as for social reasons. In the traditional peasant economy the family was the economic unit that employed its members. In terms of the basic essentials of life, such as food, clothing, and shelter, the family achieved a certain degree of self-sufficiency. For the most part, employment was not determined through the labor market. The family took care of its aged and incapacitated members, often by assigning light jobs to them. Although protection from want was thus overwhelmingly an individual and family responsibility, one of the chief characteristics of the traditional setting was the subordinate position of the "lower classes." They did not share in the affairs of government, nor were they expected to have opinions about them. In theory, the reciprocity of traditional society consisted of the duty of work and obedience from those below and the duty of protection and guidance from those above. In this setting, there was very little social conflict over the question of social protection, no doubt because want was both general and customary and because the "lower classes" accepted their subordinate position. Although there was a humane concern about destitution, public relief measures were shaped by the interests of the state in a numerous and industrious work force. Poor laws were intended to relieve destitution, not to eliminate poverty. Relief was to be sufficient to facilitate the maintenance of public order and to be administered in a manner that encouraged regular work habits. The problem of relief in the preindustrial society, therefore, was primarily a police and sanitation problem. It was not a question of social rights.[1]

During industrialization the whole nature of the problem of social protection changes, in part, because of the great social and economic dislocations that accompany the creation of an industrial work force. Bendix writes:

> These dislocations terminate the traditional subordination of the "lower classes" in the preindustrial society. Though this development varies considerably with the relative speed and with the social setting of industrialization, its result is that the "lower classes" are deprived of their recognized, if subordinate, place in society. A major problem facing all societies undergoing industrialization is the civic reintegration of the newly created industrial force.[2]

The development of social rights inevitably plays a crucial role in the handling of the problem of civic reintegration. The establishment of socially guaranteed rights to protection from want is one of the major means by which a new status can be secured for the industrial masses. By helping to

---

[1] In developing countries today it tends to be a question of social rights because of the politization of the lower classes prior to their becoming industrial wage workers.

[2] Reinhard Bendix. *Work and Authority in Industry* (New York: John Wiley, 1956), p. 434.

define a new reciprocity among the members of the industrial society, it helps to establish a new place for the common man—a place that is consistent with a new conception of his rights.

Several alternatives are open to the industrializing society with regard to the question of social protection. It may deny the claim to protection as being inconsistent with the new economic and social order. Or it may accept the claim to protection as a means of reinforcing the traditional authority relationships between the "ruling" and the "lower" classes. Or it may energetically promote the right to protection as a means of strengthening the authority relationships of a new social and economic order. Nevertheless, in any society in which social forces are free to express themselves, there are always conflicting tendencies.

The countries that denied the right to social protection during the period of industrialization were the ones with the strongest liberal and individualistic traditions—the United States, England, and France. Therefore, we must consider how these countries dealt with the problem of civic reintegration. England and the United States differ somewhat from France, insofar as in the latter country industrialization was much slower and, consequently, social dislocation was less acute. Both England and the United States succeeded in overcoming the alienation of the lower classes during industrialization without substantial social guarantees of protection from want. To a large extent, this success can be attributed to the high degree of acceptance by the industrial working classes of the liberal ideologies of the entrepreneurial classes. These ideologies identified the ability to be self-dependent with a readiness for individual freedom. By the same token the claim to protection was associated with an acceptance of the traditional tutelage of the lower classes. Within this ideological context, freedom and protection became mutually exclusive. These views were consistent with the interests of the entrepreneurial class in an unfettered labor market. The ideological emphasis, of course, was not on these private interests but on the national interest. In England the Malthusian theory of population provided the chief economic rationale for demonstrating the harmful consequences of social protection. It absolved, in effect, the new "ruling class" from responsibility for the poor. In the United States a similar function was performed by Social Darwinism. Both of these theories embodied the more general proposition of classical liberalism that achievement of the highest national interest was conditional on the unhindered pursuit of individual interest. Within this framework, protection harmed not only the nation but the protected classes more than anyone else.

These views, of course, were not always fully articulated and were never completely accepted by all members of either the "ruling" or the "ruled" classes. In England and in the United States the workers were more successful than in France in turning the liberal ideologies to their advantage. If the liberal arguments for freedom, equality, and self-help were inconsistent with social protection, they nevertheless could be turned into weapons for self-protection. The trade unions arose in this manner as the workers' means of collective self-protection. They helped to define the place of the worker in the industrial society and to secure substantial rights for him through private instead of public action. The more successful the unions were in fulfilling this function, the more they were opposed to economic protection through governmental action. In retrospect, this opposition was based on mistaken conceptions of trade-union self-interest and of the need for broader social protection.

When modern social security did emerge in the countries that were the home of classical liberalism, economic development was well past the industrialization phase. The basic concepts of liberalism—freedom and equality—had undergone profound changes. In their new context, these concepts were no longer inconsistent with social protection; on the contrary, they required it. At this stage of industrial development, the growing scarcity of labor relative to capital and the higher requirements of skill and cooperation suggested a labor policy aiming at the conservation and improvement of the capacity and willingness to work. Protection of the worker from want and worry thus became an economically rational (profit-oriented) activity even in a free market economy. In addition to concern with the economic aspects of productivity, there arose a broader concern with national efficiency that demanded a policy of protection. This need must be viewed in the perspective of the social changes wrought by industrialization. It was perceived clearly by writers like Croly and by states-men like Theodore Roosevelt, Lloyd-George, and Winston Churchill. They realized that the loyalties that had bound society together in the past had become eroded in the conflict between the economic inequalities of capitalist civilization and the ideologies of freedom and equality which this civilization had nurtured. To be efficient, and in the long-run survive, the industrial state required the solid allegiance of its citizens. "Citizenship," T. H. Marshall has pointed out, "requires a bond of a different kind [from that which existed in the past], a direct sense of community membership based on loyalty to a civilization which is a common possession."[3] But there could be no common possession of a civilization in a society in which wealth accumulated while large segments of the population lived in or near destitution. The bond required by citizenship was further endangered as the deprived segments of the population gained organizational strength and political power. They would no longer tolerate the fact that in dire need they

[3] T. H. Marshall, *Class, Citizenship, and Social Development* (Anchor Books edition, Garden City, N.Y.: Doubleday and Co., 1965), p. 101.

could obtain relief only under conditions that were humiliating and degrading.

By the beginning of the twentieth century the concept of citizenship had evolved to the point where a sense of community participation could no longer survive on patriotic sentiment alone but required substantial participation in the fruits of industrialism. In Marshall's words: "The diminution of inequality strengthened the demand for its abolition, at least with regard to the essentials of social welfare."[4] Social security thus emerged, in the countries mentioned, as part of the array of social rights associated with the status of citizenship in the industrial state. Its principal objective was to guarantee a specified minimum level of income below which no citizen was to be allowed to fall. Subsistence below the national minimum, in effect, was declared inconsistent with the status of citizenship. Of great significance also was the nature of the income guarantee: it had to be free from any stigma that might impair the individual's status of full membership in the national community. In England this guarantee had from the beginning a strong egalitarian flavor, which made it independent of the individual's economic merit. In the United States, where the tradition of individual achievement and reward had remained much stronger, the income guarantees were scaled as closely as possible to the individual's previous performance.

The social right aspect was left in the background in America, and the individually earned contractual element was brought to the forefront. In this manner, social protection could be formulated in the accustomed language of individual self-help. The main deviation from traditional individualism, which was not emphasized, was that now the decision of whether he would provide for himself was no longer left to the individual. The compulsory contributory social insurance system established simultaneously the right and the duty of income protection. This right and duty became an important aspect of the new reciprocity among the citizens of the industrial state. It had important implications for the relationship among classes. To the extent that those who might become poor were forced to protect themselves from want, society as a whole, but particularly the rich, was protected from the poor. In this sense, social insurance has become an important form of protection for the rich.

Germany was the country that chose the second alternative. Instead of denying protection, those in power insisted that it was the duty of the state to protect the industrial worker against the major economic hazards of life. Germany, consequently, introduced social security at a much earlier stage of industrialization than England and the United States. From a sociological point of view, the introduction of social insurance in Germany was quite

---

[4]T. H. Marshall, *Class, Citizenship, and Social Development*, p. 106.

different from the introduction of income maintenance programs in the other two countries. To be sure, in both instances, the advent of modern social protection was a response to pressure from below; in both cases, there was the demand that certain extremes of economic inequality be eliminated by shoring up the lower end of the income scale. But the German response necessarily was the one of an authoritarian society ruled by an autocratic government. The objective of social protection was thus the elimination of the kind of economic inequality and insecurity that was "unjustified" within this social and political setting. The Kaiser said that the state must meet the "justified" demands of the worker for basic security. At stake was not the loyalty of citizens to an egalitarian, democratic system, but the loyalty of the lower classes to hierarchical order. The loyalty of the industrial masses to the monarchy—the summit of the existing order—was Bismarck's avowed goal. Although his chief opponents were the Socialists, he hoped that by creating a direct worker interest in the state he could neutralize the influence of all political parties. For this reason even those who favored the existing order could not follow Bismarck in all details, but they realized that new methods of protection had become necessary in order to uphold the traditional reciprocity of protection from above and loyalty from below. Herein lies the crucial difference: the hierarchical society protected the worker to keep him satisfied with his traditional subordinate place; the democratic society protected him so that he would not feel that he was in a subordinate position. In one case, protection justified inequality; in the other, equality justified protection.

The negative attitude of the German Social Democrats toward the introduction of social insurance is readily understandable. They could not accept the paternalistic Bismarckian conception of social protection. Their goal of social and economic equality was endangered, so they believed, by the Bismarckian social laws. For them the right to social protection was based on a demand for economic restitution to the exploited proletariat. Consequently, they demanded a system of comprehensive income maintenance and health protection paid for entirely by the capitalists—the exploiters. Neither the socialist conception of protection nor its burdensome benefits were acceptable to those who governed Imperial Germany. The degree of protection that was accepted was one that would alleviate hardship but would not undermine the individual's sense of duty to look out for himself. This protection did not define, nor aim at, a national minimum below which no citizen was to be allowed to subsist. It aimed at a level that was thought sufficient to prevent the alienation of the working class. There may be no material difference between the two levels, but the conception was different. At this stage of German industrialization, the mere demonstration of protection through the alleviation of hardship was likely to satisfy the aspiration of the industrial worker. It was during the Weimar era, after the old order had been overthrown, that new conceptions of the citizens' right to social protection became dominant. They were not to be realized until after World War II.

In turning to the Soviet Union, we encounter the third alternative that an industrializing country may adopt with regard to the development of social protection. Since the early days of the 1917 Revolution, the Soviet government has proclaimed social income protection as one of the fundamental rights of the citizen. The Soviet citizen was declared to be entitled to comprehensive protection at the expense of the state. This right was said to be one of the chief fruits of the revolution. The state that was created by the revolution legitimized its existence by the rights and benefits it bestowed on all those who earned their living from work, especially manual work. Social class inequalities were suppressed. Although all citizens were declared equal, a new form of subordination emerged. This was the subordination to a ruling totalitarian party.

In the hands of the party, welfare programs acquired a meaning that they never had in a democratic setting and that was only hinted at by Bismarck. The Soviet conception and use of social security contrast most sharply with American ideas and practices. Behind the American insistence that benefits were an earned individual right was the fear of government control. It was a fear that if benefits had the character of a grant from the state, the independence of the individual would be threatened. Bismarck, on the other hand, wished the state to pay for social insurance precisely for the purpose of increasing its influence over the workers. Bismarck administered an autocratic state, but he still had to contend with a good deal of organized opposition which limited his power. In the Soviet Union all organized opposition was eliminated. Social security became one of the means by which the Communist party increased the dependence of the individual on the state. The peasants, who had their own means of self-dependence, were left out of it. Social security was hailed enthusiastically as a gift from the benevolent state and a demonstration of the party's concern for the "welfare of all, great and small." All were to put their faith in the state and their trust in the leadership of the party.

In the hands of the totalitarian party, social security became a means to enhance the state's control over the labor force. This control was exercised through the benefit structure as well as through the administration of social insurance. The day-to-day administration of social insurance provided an excellent means for increasing the contact between the party and the laboring masses and for involving large numbers of people in a governmental activity. The trade unions offered an almost ideal organizational framework. After they were subjugated by the party, they were put in the position of a subordinate intermediary between the party and the masses. They organized groups of insurance activists which absorbed the energies of potential troublemakers. The party laid out the targets; the unions' task was to use social insurance in a manner calculated to maximize achievement of the targets. Only the Soviet Union managed to turn social insurance into an instrument of labor discipline. In no other country was the right to social protection used in such discriminatory fashion. No other country has exploited to such a high degree the engineered dependence of the individual on the state and turned welfare programs into such blatant instruments of political propaganda.

We have tried to assess the role of social security in the course of the industrialization of several leading countries. At that stage of development the major task of social security in the Western countries was to wipe out the extremes of inequality and insecurity, in order to attenuate alienation and alleviate suffering. In the Soviet Union it played a more active role in the economic and social transformation of the country. As we move now to the stage of the mature industrial economy, we may wish to compare the role of social security then and now. In looking over the historical experience, we find that there are important elements of continuity as well as change. Social security is now, as it was then, a means of integrating the individual into the social whole, a means of enabling him to participate to a greater extent in the common possession of our industrial civilization. What has changed is the nature of the problem of social integration and the aspirations of the average citizen. Originally, social insurance was mainly workingmen's insurance; it was intended for those who were presumed to be "economically weak." Today, it is no longer aimed at the working class but has become a right of all citizens. In all countries there are strong pressures toward making social security universal and comprehensive. This trend is consistent with the changing objectives of social policy, allowing for variations between countries. The reconciliation of mutually hostile social classes is no longer a major concern. The central objective has shifted to a higher plane of social integration: from combating hostility and discontent to building constructive collaboration and productive efficiency.

The basic reason for this shift is, of course, the fact that the social wounds inflicted by industrialization have been healed. In the meantime, however, the growing affluence of industrialized countries is changing the standards of social protection. In societies with a demonstrated productive capacity, it becomes almost daily less tolerable to have anyone living below an adequate national minimum.[5] There is ample evidence for the

---

[5] Professor Burns points out that the concept of a basic minimum has gained nearly universal acceptance. E. M. Burns, "Social Security in Evolution: Towards What?", *Industrial Relations Research Association Proceedings, 1964*, p. 20.

growing intolerance of poverty in the midst of wealth. It is considered unnecessary and unjust, as well as economically wasteful. Students of economic growth have emphasized the role of skills and training as primary factors in raising national productivity. To the extent that poverty may be due to the lack of these factors, or to poor health, it is evidence of a waste of the most valuable of all resources—human beings.

In the United States, where extremes of wealth and poverty are associated with racial discrimination, there has been a remarkable rediscovery of the problem of poverty and inequality. This is a special case of the belated extension of the rights of full citizenship to racial minorities, but it poses acutely one of the problems of social protection in an affluent society. This is the problem of how a democratic society can adequately protect the able-bodied who have not shared in the cultural advantages of the industrial civilization and have not acquired the work ethic and achievement drive of this civilization.[6] The news media refer to this problem under the heading of "welfare crisis." The argument of the critics is that social security, specifically public assistance, is creating most of the problem it was intended to solve. Welfare payments made on the basis of need but without strong deterrent are said to perpetuate the problem of dependency. Often these payments are made to members of the groups with the lowest level of skills, the least education, and the smallest hope for social advancement and economic improvement. The extension of the social right to an adequate national minimum to these groups leaves them only a limited incentive to work. Some of them, especially mothers of dependent children, are better off on public assistance than on the low wages they may be able to earn and be deprived of assistance. In the long run, the only solution of this problem is to develop assistance schemes with built-in work incentives and, more generally, to raise the level of skills, broaden the opportunities, and to heighten the aspirations of the underprivileged groups.[7]

Sweden, which traditionally had adhered to a basic egalitarian benefit, has adopted differentiated benefits related to previous earnings. German old-age pensions go as high as 75 percent of earnings; Soviet old-age pensions range from 50 to 100 percent of earnings. The objective of the benefit structure has been made most explicit in Germany: it is to maintain the standard of living achieved through work, instead of merely preventing poverty. There are strong reasons for believing that this will become the

[6] This problem is not altogether absent in other countries, not even in the Soviet Union, as the debate over social "parasites" indicates.

[7] For a summary discussion of current proposals, see George F. Rohrlich, "Guaranteed-Minimum-Income Proposals and the Unfinished Business of Social Security," *Social Service Review,* Vol. 41 (June 1967), pp. 166–178.

accepted standard for mature industrial societies. In fact, it is part of a double standard that consists of a basic minimum for all and a rate calculated to maintain an established level of living for those whose earnings from work has lifted them above the minimum.

This double standard inevitably perpetuates among those no longer at work most of the income inequalities inherent in the structure of earnings from work. We learned earlier that Soviet officials believe that eventually their country will adopt an egalitarian system of benefits. At present, however, the Soviet Union and most other countries believe that, above a minimum level of protection, differentiated benefits are justified for efficiency. This is a kind of inequality that appears necessary and legitimate. Indeed, an attempt to maintain equal benefits, which necessarily would have to be below the normal earnings of common laborers, might have strongly adverse effects. It would create a situation in which large numbers of people would have to face a substantial drop in their standard of living on withdrawal from the active labor force. Although they may not have to live in poverty, the drop in the standard of living would still tend to cause an acute sense of deprivation. It is only by helping the citizen to maintain the rather high standard of living to which he has become accustomed, that modern social security can prevent what Runciman calls "relative deprivation" and the sense of social injustice it generates.[8] In the mature industrial society, social security, therefore, has the dual task of eliminating unacceptable manifestations of economic and social inequality and of maintaining inequalities that are legitimate and purposeful.

[8] See W. G. Runciman, *Relative Deprivation and Social Justice* (London: Routledge and Kegan Paul, 1966), Chapters II to V.

Name Index

Subject Index

free trade movement, 103
German Labor Front, 134
imperial, 2
Kulturkampf, 115
laissez-faire in, 98, 141
liberal bourgeoisie, 90
liberalism in, 91, 97, 99, 102
Malthusian ideas in, 96
message of the Kaiser, of 1881, 112
Nazi policies, 132
Nazi regimentation, 162
North German Federation, 98
Old-age and Invalidity Law of 1889, 121
pauperism, problem of, 95
pension, reform of 1957, 176
protectionism, 109
Provinziallantag, 95
Reich office for employment exchange and
    unemployment insurance, 132
Reichstag, 110–112, 118–121
Robert-Ley plan, 134
role of bureaucracy, 92
trade law of 1869, 98
trade unions, and social insurance, 128
Weimar Republic, 130
Grant, for birth, 259
for burial, 259, 260
for layette, 265
matching, 238
"Great Society," 243
Guardians of the Poor, 22
Guild, system, 93
Guilds, compulsory, abolition in Prussia, 97
desire to restore, 100

Hamburg, poor relief system, 94
Hardships, God-given, man-made, 8
Harmony of interests, 113
Health insurance, compulsory, campaign
    against, 242
    case for, 68
    compared to compulsory education, 69
    debate over, 186
    delay of, 222
    exemption of farm laborers, 131
    opposition of A.M.A., 240
    opposition to, 239
    and quality of care, 241
    voluntary versus compulsory, 241
Hôspital général, 25

Human behavior, interpretation of, 16

Ideals, individualistic, in unemployment in-
    surance, 218
liberal, persistence of, 12
of protection, traditional, 12
Ideas, neoliberal, 141
Ideology, contractual, 7
of social insurance for America, 66ff.
of Soviet social insurance, 252ff.
Idleness, mother of all vices, 17
Immiseration, 126
Immorality of marrying without capability of
    support, 40
Inadequacy of protection, 225
Incentive, and adequacy, compromise between,
    286
bonus, 286
effects, adverse, 37
to marry, 15
Income, distribution, functional, 306
effect, 317
indifference curve, 312
inequality, perpetuation of ,180
intertemporal reallocation of, 312
minimum, guaranteed, 338
offer line, 310
offer lines, family of, 318
redistribution, 324
security, effect on behavior of, 329
Individualism, rejection of, 115
Industrial injuries compensation, ease of
    introduction, 5
Industrial revolution, 38
Industrial safety, movement for, 67
Industrialization, forced draft, 269
setting of, 334
"Industrialization congress," 270
Inequality, 341
diminution of, 338
of income, 150
as justification of protection, 339
perpetuation of, 174
of protection, 225
social, 1, 8, 13
and social insurance, 112
Insurance, contributory, 212
group, 196
monopoly, state, 117
principle, 156, 173